PRAIRIE HOME COOKING

PRAIRIE HOME COOKING

400 Recipes That Celebrate the Bountiful Harvests,
Creative Cooks, and Comforting Foods
of the American Heartland

JUDITH M. FERTIG

ILLUSTRATIONS BY SARA LOVE

THE HARVARD COMMON PRESS
Boston, Massachusetts

THE HARVARD COMMON PRESS
535 Albany Street
Boston, Massachusetts 02118

Printed in the United States of America
Printed on acid-free paper

Library of Congress Cataloging-in-Publication Data

Fertig, Judith M.
Prairie Home Cooking : 400 recipes that celebrate the bountiful harvests, creative cooks, and comforting
foods of the American heartland / Judith M. Fertig.
p. cm.
Includes bibliographical references and index.
ISBN 1-55832-144-6 (alk. paper).
ISBN 1-55832-145-4 (pbk. alk paper)
1. Cookery, American—Midwestern style. I. Title.
TX715.2.M53F47 1999
99-14392
CIP

Special bulk-order discounts are available on this and other Harvard Common Press books.
Companies and organizations may purchase books for premiums or resale,
or may arrange a custom edition, by contacting the Marketing Director at the address above.

Cover and text illustrations by Sara Love
Cover and text design by Kathleen Herlihy-Paoli, Inkstone Design

10 9 8 7 6 5 4 3 2 1

To my family, who taught me what *home* and *cooking*
are all about —Jack Merkle, Jean Vanderhorst Merkle, and Julie Merkle Fox

And to my children, who are still learning —Sarah and Nick Fertig

CONTENTS

ACKNOWLEDGMENTS

First of all, a big thanks to Bruce Shaw, Publisher of The Harvard Common Press, who had seen a magazine article by me on prairie food and got this rewarding project started. My editor par excellence, Dan Rosenberg, deftly shaped this book with a clear eye, wry sense of humor, and a great amount of patience. Christine Alaimo, Skye Stewart, and everyone else at The Harvard Common Press have really helped give the subject of prairie home cooking the audience it richly deserves.

This project would have been a lot more difficult without the friends who have become family to me: my good friend and agent, Karen Adler; my walking buddy and taste-tester, Ellen McCormick; and all the members, past and present, of the infamous Cookbook Club: Kathy Smith, Mary Langley, Gail Parnow, Dee Barwick, Dianne Hogerty, Rose Kallas, Vicki Johnson, Roxanne Wyss, Jane Guthrie, Carole Cottrill, Bobbi Marks, and Lou Jane Temple. My thanks also to the friends of my formative cheeseburger years, who drove with me through Frisch's many times without ever stopping to eat anything: Rene Jones, Debbie Baird, and Sherry Morgensen. My appreciation, too, for all the meals and memories shared with Linda Kirkwood Smith and Susie Canan Butler and their families.

I thank Jill Silva, food editor of the *Kansas City Star*, and all the culinary stars who have graced my "Come Into My Kitchen" column and who have welcomed me into their homes and their lives. Thanks also to Colman Andrews, Christopher Hirsheimer, and Connie McCabe of *Saveur* magazine for a terrific experience in wheat country. And my deep appreciation for all the Heartlanders who generously gave of their time to talk with me about the place they call home: Jim Stevens of Maytag Dairy Farms, Judith Schad of Capriole, Justin Rashid of American Spoon Foods, John Schumacher of the New Prague Hotel, and many, many others.

INTRODUCTION

When I first moved with my family to Kansas in the early 1980s, I remember driving away from the Kansas City, Missouri, airport and looking out the window at the big sky. For a girl used to the seven hills of Cincinnati, this wide expanse of horizon was something exciting and new. Soon after we were settled in, we all became sky-watchers. In the spring and summer there was the drama of thunderclouds and twisters we could see gathering momentum from miles and miles away. On clear nights there would be a midnight canopy of stars that seemed so close you could touch them. The wide daytime skies would range from clear blues to blizzard grays. In August the summer haze was punctuated by the bright orange flight of monarch butterflies.

Pam Houston, the author of *Cowboys Are My Weakness*, also moved to the prairie as an adult. "It wasn't where I had come from," she writes, "but when I moved there it just took me in and I knew I couldn't ever stop living under that big sky."

For the European immigrants who came here in the nineteenth century, the sea of grass that was the prairie was an alien environment. Many of the new arrivals settled, of course, along the banks of rivers, where trees and brush broke up the monotony of grass. Inland, too, groves of oak and walnut provided more relief, as did wild scrub plants like mulberry, chokecherry, and wild plum, common in low-lying areas.

Today the prairie has changed. Less than one percent of the original four hundred thousand square miles of prairie survives in its natural state. Enclosed by fences and windbreaks, tamed by machinery and the will of man, the prairie is rangeland, dairyland, and breadbasket. The eastern prairie, from Ohio to Iowa, now is the Corn Belt. The first sweet corn of the season is an occasion to celebrate in Ohio, and the October corn harvest in Iowa is as orderly and true as a Grant Wood painting. The lush and rolling pastureland of the Dairy Belt, where America's best cheeses are made, stretches down from Wisconsin to southern Indiana. The Wheat Belt fans north from Kansas through Nebraska into the Dakotas and Canada. Hard red winter wheat, which grows through the winter and is harvested in June, dictates the rhythms of the year in Kansas and much of Nebraska. In the Dakotas, where the winters are harsh, spring wheat, planted in the spring and harvested in the fall, takes over. On the western edge of the prairie, where in most places it is too dry to farm, the wide open spaces provide rangeland for grazing cattle and buffalo.

The richly patterned geographical quilt of "fly-over country"—the great expanse that you see from the plane window as you fly from one coast to another—is home to ethnic communities of all kinds, where festivals celebrating cultures as diverse as Czech, Norse, Russian Mennonite, and Sioux are occasions to remember the past and observe traditions in the present. In the pages of this book, you will meet some of the people who contribute to this region's culinary and cultural melting pot: great home cooks, farmers, specialty food purveyors, experts on regional foods, and even writers of essays and fiction.

The settling of the midwest coincided with the flowering of a literature that was truly American. Prairie writers continue to discover and rediscover their regional identities. Not only do we gain a sense of place from the works of authors as varied as Willa Cather, Susan Power, Louise Erdrich, and Jane Smiley, we also savor the tastes of the region. For these writers, past and present, food is evocative and full of meaning. In the novels of Willa Cather, the changing foods and wares on the dinner table reflect changes in families' fortunes and status, as virgin Nebraska prairie gives way to hardscrabble sodbuster farms and then to lush fields of wheat and corn. In the works of Louise Erdrich, we witness the slow process of Native Americans becoming westernized, leaving their nomadic buffalo-hunting lives and their diet based on parched corn and dried buffalo meat for reservation life, with a new diet of bannock, fry bread, juneberry jelly, and "Indian fruitcake." In Jane Smiley's *A Thousand Acres*, we see how an arrogant disregard for the environment poisons the land, the food, and the family. We marvel with W. P. Kinsella when "moonlight butters the Iowa night." As we read these writers, we sense how the kitchen was a haven, the farm a little world all its own, the root cellar a treasure trove of jewel-colored preserved

and canned goods from the garden.

Midwestern cooking, in its history and in its present forms, goes a long way toward defining what American cooking is all about. Food here is simple and comforting. As *Bon Appétit* magazine recently noted, "The cooking rooted in the middle of America has finally been 'discovered.'. . . Not only is this food delicious, but it offers an edible history of the settling of our country as well." Although Sunday dinner at grandma's is but a memory for many far-flung families, foods that say "comfort," "family," and "farm" are returning to favor. They get a lot of play in food magazines and they are being reinterpreted by well-known chefs in major cities.

Within each Heartland family is a legacy of dishes savored and dinners shared. My mother, sister, and I, for example, treasure the old brown-covered school-style notebook that belonged to my grandmother, Gertrude Willenborg Vanderhorst. The pages are faded and brittle now, and the recipes she gathered therein, written in pale blue fountain pen ink on the lined paper, are sometimes barely legible. A recipe like Spiced Tomato Catsup (see page 43) brings back a rush of memories for my mother, who recalls the delicious spicy smell coming from her neighbor's kitchen and Mrs. Seebohm bringing over a plate of still-warm catsup that they would sample with pieces of homemade bread.

Once each farmstead had its own culinary system, which was based on foods grown or produced at home or gathered nearby. Garden vegetables and orchard fruits went to the table as side dishes, as desserts, or as preserved foods like relishes, pickles, or jellies. Homemade cheese (see Fresh Farmhouse Cheese, page 39) was eaten plain, as a filling for noodles and dumplings, or, perhaps, in a German Cheese Tart (see page 393). I am happy to report that the big-city chefs who are reviving midwestern regional food are also making their own fresh cheeses, preserved foods, and condiments. The further good news is that the typical Heartland meal of generations ago—a variety of garden-fresh dishes, plenty of home-baked bread made from grains you ground yourself, smaller portions of meat, and desserts made with fresh fruit—is also a healthy way to eat today.

The relish tray, a salute to the days when housewives took pride in the homemade pickles and preserves they made, still appears on many tables. Homemade watermelon pickle, sweet-and-sour cucumbers, horseradish beets, pickled vegetables, and corn relish are set out in little glass dishes for everyone to take a spoonful. These are the

earliest prairie appetizers, healthful, refreshing, and delicious.

On the prairie, home-baked bread never went out of style. The earliest farmhouse breads, which required a starter sponge and a long rising, are now back in style in trendy city bakeries and among home cooks. Wheat buns and honey buns and traditional breads like Russian Mennonite zwieback continue to grace midwestern tables. Fragrant cinnamon rolls or kringlor baking in the oven still provide the best reasons for getting up in the morning.

Beef has always been the meat of choice: tender steaks and juicy hamburgers grilled over an open fire, brisket slow-smoked over hickory wood, and savory Sunday pot roast braised to perfection. Nonetheless, a tender pork roast accompanied by braised red cabbage, or pan-fried chicken with seasoned green beans, or baked walleye pike have been and remain worthy competition. Sometimes the main course is a savory pie, a specialty of the midwest. The offerings range from pasties to pierogis of all kinds to the mysterious runza and the French Canadian tourtière.

With the main dish, of course, are the potatoes in any manner, from potato dumplings to blue cheese or horseradish mashed potatoes to simple boiled or baked potatoes. Vegetables from the garden are eaten fresh in the warm months and preserved in rows and rows of glass canning jars for the cold months.

Microbreweries have made a major comeback on the prairie, and their specialties are often wheat beers made from grain harvested nearby. Locally brewed wheat beers are enlivened with a squeeze of lemon, the perfect quaff for a July day when the temperatures soar above a hundred. The mellow flavor of wheat beer also works well in marinades and vinaigrettes, where it can replace some of the oil.

Heartland wines, from Michigan and Missouri in particular, have garnered attention and praise from such prestigious tastemakers as the *Wine Spectator*. Up until Prohibition, Missouri, not California, was the country's leading wine producer. Midwestern varietals, made from European grapes grafted onto native varieties better equipped to withstand the hot summers and cold winters, are making a comeback.

For dessert, variety is the key. For the midwestern cook worth her salt, when company is coming (and sometimes every day), no less than two desserts, one of which is usually a pie and the other of which might be a homemade cake or a gelatin dessert, are called for. Desserts often follow the progression of fresh fruits in the garden or in the wild: strawberries, rhubarb, and gooseberries in spring and early summer; raspberries, blackberries, chokecherries, mulberries, wild plums, and elderberries in July and August; peaches in late summer; and apples and pears in September and October.

Now imagine an old quilt spread out under a big prairie sky. On this quilt an array of sweet and savory dishes from the small towns (and the small towns within big cities), farms, and ranches in America's Heartland beckons you to taste the best of prairie home cooking.

BREAKFAST COMES FIRST

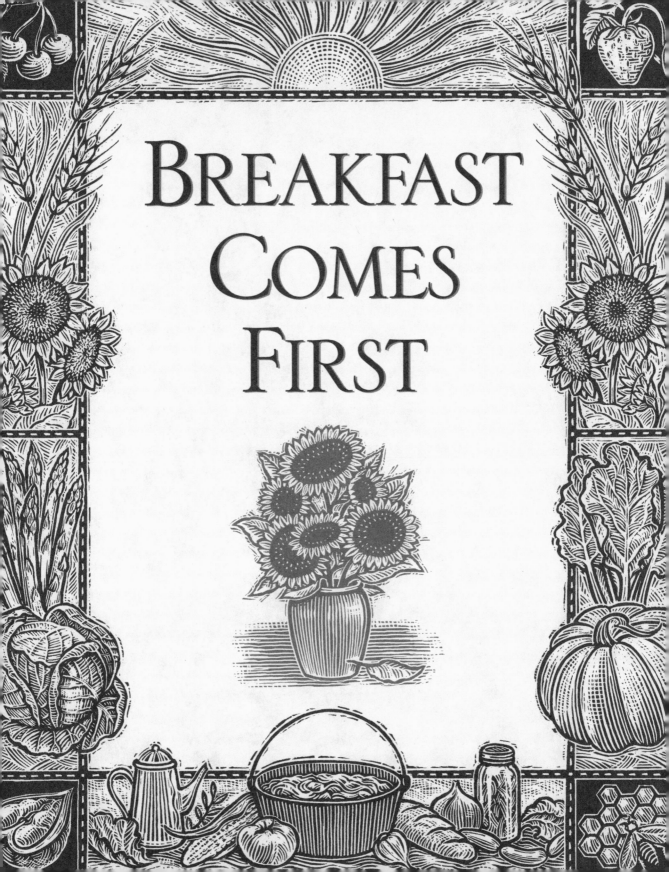

BREAKFAST COMES FIRST

GREAT PLAINS GRANOLA

Amber waves of grain, sweetened with honey and studded with chopped nuts and dried fruit, fill your cereal bowl with the bounty of the prairie. Enjoy this granola for breakfast with warmed or cold milk, or later in the day as a dry snack.

SERVES 8

½ cup finely chopped hickory nuts
    or almonds
½ cup finely chopped pecans
1 cup rolled oats
1 cup cooked wheatberries
    (see Note)
½ cup flaked sweetened coconut
½ pound (2 sticks) unsalted butter
1 cup wildflower or other
    medium-colored honey
1 teaspoon ground cinnamon
½ cup dried cherries or raisins
½ cup dried cranberries

1. Preheat the oven to 325 degrees. In a large bowl, combine the nuts, oats, wheatberries, and coconut. Stir well to blend. Melt the butter in a saucepan over medium heat, add the honey and cinnamon, and stir well to blend. Pour this mixture over the grain mixture and stir again to blend.

2. Lightly oil two baking sheets. Transfer the granola to the sheets, spreading it evenly and patting it down gently. Bake the granola for 30 minutes, or until it is golden brown. Set it aside to cool. When the granola is cool, break it, over a large bowl, by hand or with a knife into small chunks. Stir in the cherries and cranberries. Store the granola in an airtight container.

NOTE: To cook wheatberries, soak them for 1 hour in water to cover. Drain them, add them to a saucepan with new water to cover, and simmer, partially covered, for 45 minutes to 1 hour, stirring occasionally and adding more water if necessary, until the berries are soft but still chewy.

BLUEBERRY COMPOTE

Family farms throughout the prairie have had to diversify to survive. Some farmers now grow organic produce by subscription: People pay one fee up front and receive a fresh bag of produce weekly throughout the growing season. Other growers apportion some or all of their crop to U-Pick, in which people come and pick their own produce. Throughout the Heartland, U-Pick farms offer blueberries, strawberries, gooseberries, black raspberries, and golden raspberries. When fresh blueberries are in season, this compote may be served warm or cold with french toast, waffles, pancakes, or other breakfast and brunch foods. It's delicious with lemon tarts or bars, too, and it's beautiful when served in a glass bowl.

SERVES 4

2 cups sugar
2 tablespoons fresh lemon juice
1/4 cup fresh orange juice
4 cups blueberries

1. Bring the sugar, lemon juice, and orange juice to a boil in a saucepan over medium-high heat. Reduce to a simmer, add 1 cup of the blueberries, and cook, stirring, for 4 minutes. Remove the pan from the heat and set it aside to cool slightly.

2. Transfer the mixture to a food processor or blender and process or blend until smooth. Pour the sauce over the remaining blueberries in a medium bowl and stir gently to blend. Serve warm, or cover and refrigerate to serve cold.

FRENCH CREAM CHEESE WITH HOMEMADE PRESERVES

As a make-ahead focal point to your breakfast or brunch table or to give as a gift from your kitchen, this mold of honeyed cream cheese with layers of homemade preserves almost looks too pretty to eat. Like a small frosted cake topped with edible flowers or slivered almonds, it hides three layers of homemade preserves, ready for the swoop of a butter knife to spread it on toasted bagels, brioche, or bread. I like to serve this on a small glass cake stand, surrounded by fresh herbs and flowers, to show it off a little bit. This recipe also works with lowfat cream cheese. Use your best ruby-colored, golden, and dark purple preserves. Miniature versions, made in small ramekins, would add a delightful touch to each plate at a bridal breakfast.

SERVES 6 TO 8

32 ounces cream cheese, softened
3/4 cup wildflower or other
    medium-colored honey
2/3 cup Old World Red Currant
    Jelly (page 72), raspberry jam,
    or strawberry preserves
2/3 cup Ground Cherry Preserves
    (page 45), Honeyed Carrot-
    Ginger Marmalade (page 78),
    or apricot preserves
2/3 cup blackberry jelly or Wild
    Plum Jelly (page 74)
Toasted slivered almonds or edible
    flowers, for garnish

1. Line the bottom and sides of a 4- to 5-cup bowl or cylindrical mold with plastic wrap, leaving enough extra wrap at the top to completely enclose the mold. In a food processor or blender, combine the cream cheese and honey.

2. Spoon ¼ of the cream cheese mixture into the bottom of the mold. Spread the red preserves over this layer, leaving a ½-inch border around the perimeter. Top with another ¼ of the cream cheese mixture, and follow with the golden preserves, again leaving a ½-inch border. Top with another ¼ of the cream cheese, followed by the purple preserves, again with a border. Smooth on the remaining cream cheese. Cover with plastic wrap and refrigerate until the cream cheese is its original consistency, about 2 hours.

3. To serve, tip the cream cheese out of the mold and onto a serving plate or cake stand. Unwrap it carefully, and garnish the top with the almonds or edible flowers.

RED RIVER CHERRY OR CRANBERRY MUFFINS

When my brother-in-law was growing up in Connecticut, his mother served their large family what he and his siblings called "Red River gravel," a whole-grain cereal not much beloved by the children. This same cereal, made from prairie grains grown in the Red River Valley of Manitoba and processed in Alberta, makes great muffins, however—for adults and kids both. They're a delicious way to add cracked wheat, flaxseed, and rye to your diet. Look for Red River cereal in better grocery stores and health-food stores.

MAKES 2 DOZEN MUFFINS

⅓ cup canola oil or corn oil
1 cup Red River cereal or other cracked-wheat cereal
2½ cups bread flour
½ cup dry milk powder
2½ teaspoons baking powder
1 teaspoon ground cinnamon
3 eggs, beaten
⅔ cup packed brown sugar
¾ cup dried cherries or cranberries
3 tablespoons wildflower or other medium-colored honey

1. Preheat the oven to 400 degrees. Line 24 2⅔-inch muffin cups with paper liners.

2. In a saucepan over medium-high heat, bring the oil and 2 cups water to a boil. Add the cereal, and cook, stirring occasionally, for 2 minutes. Remove the pan from the heat and set it aside until it is cool enough to handle.

3. In a medium bowl, combine the cooked cereal with the flour, milk powder, baking powder, cinnamon, eggs, and brown sugar. Stir by hand to blend. The batter will be lumpy. Fold in the dried fruit and honey. Fill each muffin cup ¾ full, and bake for 20 to 25 minutes, or until the muffins begin to brown and a cake tester inserted into a muffin comes out clean.

FROM BATTLE CREEK

On Christmas Day in 1865, Ellen White, at her home in Battle Creek, Michigan, had a vision. She saw the ailing, dyspeptic members of her husband Elder James White's congregation restored to the bloom of health. She was convinced that a better diet, consisting of more whole grains and fiber, would effect this transformation. Battle Creek was the national headquarters for the Seventh Day Adventists, the Whites' religious affiliation, and Mrs. White set in motion a course of action which, she thought, would bring all Seventh Day Adventists around the country back to better health. She persuaded her husband to offer a scholarship to a young man named John Harvey Kellogg, who set out to study medicine and nutrition in New York City.

As a student who wanted a healthier diet, Kellogg cooked for himself, unusual for a young man of his day. That's how the idea of precooked cereals came to him. Until then, whole or cracked grains—corn, wheat, barley, rye, oats—had to be cooked in water to make a sort of gruel. "It often occurred to me that it should be possible to purchase cereals at groceries already cooked and ready to eat, and I considered different ways in which this might be done," Kellogg wrote. After two years of trial and error he introduced the first ready-made cereal, which he called "Granola," to the patients at the Seventh Day Adventist health sanitarium in Battle Creek.

Soon to follow were corn flakes, developed by Dr. Kellogg and his brother, Will, and grape-nuts, so named because they were sweetened with dextrose or grape sugar and the product had a nutty flavor.

Kellogg and others who developed Mrs. White's vision warned against the "dietetic evils of pastries" and a host of other foods they thought should be taboo. They probably would not applaud the modern midwestern cook's penchant for sprinkling healthy corn flakes on top of casseroles, crushing them as a coating for fried chicken, or making them into holiday cookies.

Tom's Northern Plains Rhubarb Muffins

"On the northern plains, rhubarb is your first spring crop, and it produces good stalks right through the summer," says my friend Tom Isern, a history professor at the University of North Dakota. "So any day from May through September you can cut a stalk or two for these muffins."

Makes 12 muffins

1 cup 1-inch-long slices rhubarb,
    from 1 to 2 stalks
1 cup all-purpose flour
1 cup packed brown sugar
1 teaspoon baking powder
1/2 teaspoon baking soda
1/2 teaspoon salt
1 egg
1 cup milk
1/2 cup canola oil or corn oil
1/2 cup chopped nuts, such as
    pecans or walnuts
1 tablespoon butter, softened
1/4 cup granulated sugar
1 teaspoon ground cinnamon

1. Preheat the oven to 375 degrees. Butter, or line with paper liners, a dozen 2 2/3-inch muffin cups. Microwave or steam the rhubarb until it is soft but not mushy.

2. Combine the flour, brown sugar, baking powder, baking soda, and salt in a large bowl. Stir in the egg, milk, and oil, then fold in gently the rhubarb and nuts. Pour the batter into the muffin cups, leaving them about 3/4 full. Stir together the butter, sugar, and cinnamon in a small bowl, and sprinkle this streusel mixture on top of each muffin. Bake for 35 to 40 minutes, or until the muffins begin to brown and a cake tester inserted into a muffin comes out clean.

Kringlor

Mellow and buttery with just a faint taste of almond, these tender oval pastries are a hit in many midwestern bed-and-breakfast inns, where they are sometimes called "Danish Puffs." Kringlor are easy enough to make for the novice baker, but tasty enough to please everyone.

Makes 2 pastries, to serve 12

1/2 pound (2 sticks) unsalted butter
3 cups all-purpose flour
3 eggs
1/2 teaspoon almond extract

FOR THE GLAZE:
1 cup sifted confectioners' sugar
1 tablespoon butter, softened
1/2 teaspoon almond extract
Light cream

1. Preheat the oven to 375 degrees. In a medium bowl, cut 1 stick of the butter into 2

cups of the flour until the pieces are the size of small peas. Sprinkle 1 tablespoon of cold water over 1/3 of this mixture, and gently toss with a fork. Push this third to the side of the bowl. Repeat with the other two thirds. When all the dough is moistened, shape it into a ball and divide the ball in half. On an ungreased baking sheet, pat or roll each piece of dough into a 12-by-4-inch strip.

2. In a medium saucepan, bring to a boil 1 cup of water and the remaining 1/4 pound of butter. Remove the pan from the heat, and add the remaining 1 cup of flour all at once. Whisk the mixture vigorously until it is smooth. Let the mixture rest and cool for 5 minutes. Add the eggs, one at a time, beating well with a wooden spoon after each addition. Stir in the 1/2 teaspoon almond extract. Spread half of the dough evenly over each pastry strip. Bake for 40 minutes, or until the pastry is golden and puffy. Transfer the kringlor to a wire rack, and let them cool slightly.

3. While the kringlor cool, make the glaze: Combine the confectioners' sugar, 1 tablespoon butter, and 1/2 teaspoon of almond extract with enough light cream to make a drizzling consistency. Drizzle the glaze over the kringlor. Cut the pastry into 1-inch diagonal slices, and serve.

ST. LOUIS GOOEY BUTTER COFFEECAKE

Local legend has it that in St. Louis in the 1930s, a thrifty German baker added the wrong proportions of ingredients when he was making coffeecake. The result was this confection, with its pudding-like filling, that has become a St. Louis tradition. Although many versions, from purveyors like the Lake Forest Bakery in Clayton and the Missouri Baking Company on "The Hill" in St. Louis, have their proponents, the gooey butter cake from the former Heimburger Bakery is the classic one adapted here. After a stressful week, waking up on a Saturday morning to the smell of fresh-brewed coffee and to a piece of gooey butter cake with fresh strawberries on the side is a just reward for the virtuous. If you double this recipe, you'll have a cake to freeze for later.

MAKES 1 COFFEECAKE, TO SERVE 8

FOR THE CRUST:
  1 cup all-purpose flour
  3 tablespoons granulated sugar
  5 tablespoons unsalted butter,
     softened
  1 tablespoon ice water, if needed

FOR THE FILLING:
  1 1/4 cups granulated sugar
  3/4 cup (1 1/2 sticks) unsalted butter,
     softened

1 egg
1 cup all-purpose flour
2/3 cup evaporated milk
1/4 cup light corn syrup
1 teaspoon vanilla extract

Confectioners' sugar, for garnish

1. Preheat the oven to 350 degrees. Lightly oil or butter a 9-inch-square baking pan. In the bowl of a food processor, mix the flour and sugar together. By pulsing on and off, cut in the butter until the mixture resembles coarse crumbs. If necessary to make the dough hold together, add the ice water through the feed tube and blend a few seconds until the

MEET ME IN ST. LOUIS

In 1722, a French clerk named Pierre Laclede traveled up the Mississippi River from New Orleans with his thirteen-year-old clerk, Auguste Chouteau, looking for a good spot for a trading post. They found one at a spot now called Laclede's Landing in St. Louis. The ambitious Laclede dubbed the tiny outpost St. Louis in honor of the patron saint of the French King Louis XV.

The savvy Laclede soon became a wealthy man from the river traffic in furs, and St. Louis grew. A midpoint along the Mississippi halfway between the wilderness to the north and the cosmopolitan city of New Orleans to the south, St. Louis was also a buffer between the settled east and the wild west. Lewis and Clark left this tiny bastion of civilization for their long trek up the Missouri River to the Pacific Northwest in 1804. By 1817, the first steamboats had come to St. Louis, ushering in a new age in transportation. Samuel Clemens, born in nearby Hannibal, immortalized this era, writing under the name Mark Twain. By 1861, St. Louis had grown to a population of 160,000, and that was before the great influx of German immigrants and of freed slaves from the post-Civil War South.

From this diverse history has come a culinary legacy that ranges from angel food cake, first whipped up by African-American cooks in early-nineteenth-century St. Louis households and made famous by Miss Hullings's tea room, to sautéed frog legs, popular in the area for as long as anyone can remember. The 1904 St. Louis World's Fair, which celebrated the hundredth anniversary of the Lewis and Clark Expedition, introduced Americans to the hot dog on a bun, ice cream in a cone, iced tea, and peanut butter. And, in 1931, St. Louis resident Erma Rombauer wrote the cookbook that has remained an American classic, The Joy of Cooking.

mixture holds. Pat the dough into the bottom and up the sides of the baking pan.

2. Make the filling: In a medium bowl, cream together the sugar and butter with an electric mixer until light and fluffy. Beat in the egg until well blended. Alternate mixing in a little of the flour and a little of the evaporated milk until both are incorporated. Add the corn syrup and vanilla extract, and blend one last time.

3. Pour the batter into the prepared crust, and bake for 25 to 35 minutes, or until the cake is nearly set. The top should remain moist; do not overbake. Let the cake cool slightly in the pan, garnish with confectioners' sugar, and serve.

APRICOT KOLACHE

During the long prairie winters, one of life's contentments for Bohemian farm wives was to invite their friends over for coffee and kolache on a cold afternoon. Small yeast cakes filled with homemade preserves would come out of the oven, warm and fragrant. For just a short while, the women could forget the cold, the isolation, and the uncertainty of farm life. For just a short while, there was delicious food, deep and rich coffee, a warm house, and good friends. At the Czech Days festival every June in Tabor, South Dakota, kolache filled with apricots or nuts help celebrate this heritage.

MAKES 4 DOZEN KOLACHE

FOR THE PASTRY:
1¼ cups milk, warmed to 105 to 115 degrees
1 (¼-ounce) package dry yeast
¼ cup plus ½ teaspoon sugar
1 egg plus 1 egg yolk
6 tablespoons canola oil or corn oil
¼ cup heavy cream
3½ to 4 cups all-purpose flour
½ teaspoon salt

FOR THE FILLING:
1 pound dried apricots
¾ cup sugar
1 teaspoon vanilla extract
½ teaspoon ground cinnamon

FOR THE GLAZE:
1 tablespoon sugar

1. Make the pastry: Combine ⅓ cup of the milk, the yeast, and the ½ teaspoon sugar in a medium bowl. Let the mixture stand at room temperature until it is foamy, about 5 minutes. Beat the egg and the yolk together in a separate bowl, then beat in the ¼ cup sugar, the oil, the cream, and the remaining milk. In a separate large bowl, combine 1 cup of the flour and the salt. Add the yeast and egg mixtures to this bowl and beat until smooth. Beat in enough remaining flour, ¼ cup at a time, to make a soft and slightly sticky dough. Turn out the dough onto a work surface and knead it for 5 minutes. Cover the dough with a tea towel and let it rise for 1 hour.

2. Make the filling: Bring the apricots and 1½ cups water to a boil, reduce the heat, and simmer, covered, for 10 minutes. In a blender or food processor, blend to a puree. Stir in the sugar, followed by the vanilla and cinnamon. Set aside.

3. Lightly oil or butter a large baking sheet. Shape the dough into balls 1½ inches in diameter and place them on the sheet about 3 inches apart. Let the dough rise until doubled in size, about 45 minutes.

4. Preheat the oven to 425 degrees. Make an indentation in each dough ball, leaving about a ½-inch rim of dough around the edge. Spoon in a rounded teaspoon of the apricot filling. Let the dough rise for 15 to 20 minutes more.

5. Bake the kolache for 8 minutes. Remove them from the oven and let them cool on wire racks. Meanwhile, make the glaze by heating the 1 tablespoon sugar in 3 tablespoons water until the sugar dissolves. Brush the glaze over the kolache.

VARIATION:

Kolache are also delicious filled with 1 cup Plum Butter (page 67), or other preserves of your choice.

NOTE: The kolache dough can also be made in a bread machine on the dough-only cycle.

BAKED CINNAMON APPLE FRENCH TOAST

If you assemble this dish partially the night before, you can wake up and know that a wonderful breakfast for your family or friends is just minutes away. Grind your beans and brew your coffee, squeeze some fresh orange juice, and savor this treat still warm from the oven. When pears or plums are in season, you can substitute either for the apples.

SERVES 6

6 slices homemade bread or
    1 small loaf French bread,
    sliced
2 eggs
1½ cups milk
2 teaspoons vanilla extract
3 large tart apples, peeled, cored,
    and cut into thin slices
½ cup sugar
1 teaspoon ground cinnamon
1 tablespoon butter, cut into small
    pieces

1. Lightly oil, or spray with cooking spray, a 9-by-13-inch baking pan. Arrange the bread on the bottom of the pan. In a bowl, whisk together the eggs, milk, and vanilla until smooth and well blended. Pour this mixture over the bread. (The dish can be prepared

ahead to this point, covered, and refrigerated for several hours or overnight.)

2. Preheat the oven to 400 degrees. Arrange the apple slices on top of the bread. Combine the sugar and cinnamon and sprinkle this on top of the apple slices. Dot evenly with butter. Bake the toast for 35 minutes, or until the apples are soft and the custard has set. Let cool for 5 to 10 minutes before serving. Serve with maple syrup, Red Currant Syrup (page 58), or Home-Churned Butter (page 40).

1. Stir together all of the ingredients in a bowl. Lightly oil a large griddle, skillet, or crêpe pan.

2. Heat the griddle or pan over medium heat. Using 1/4 cup of batter for each, cook the crêpes 1 at a time, tipping the griddle or pan if needed to spread out the batter thinly and evenly. Fold each crêpe in half then in half again, as you would fold a pocket handkerchief. Keep the crêpes warm in the oven until all are cooked. Serve with maple syrup or a fruit syrup such as Red Currant Syrup (page 58), or with fresh berries and crème fraîche.

LACY HANDKERCHIEF CRÊPES

These delicate Swedish pancakes are served folded like pocket handkerchiefs with lacy trim. As the crêpes cook on the griddle, the edges take on a lacy appearance. They make a festive Sunday breakfast. If you like, you can make the batter the night before.

SERVES 6 TO 8

3 eggs, beaten
2 cups milk
2 heaping teaspoons sugar
1/8 teaspoon salt
3/4 cup all-purpose flour
6 tablespoons butter, melted

OLD COUNTRY SOUR CREAM BREAKFAST CRÊPES

In both Polish and Hungarian households through the midwest, you will find these tender, thin-as-paper sour cream pancakes, stuffed with a sweetened pot cheese filling, for breakfast or dessert.

SERVES 6 TO 8

FOR THE CRÊPES:
2 cups milk
2 eggs, beaten
1 cup sour cream
2 tablespoons granulated sugar
1 1/2 cups all-purpose flour
1/4 teaspoon salt

1 teaspoon vanilla extract
1 tablespoon canola oil or corn oil

FOR THE FILLING:
    1 cup Fresh Farmhouse Cheese
        (page 39), pot cheese, or ricotta
    3 tablespoons granulated sugar
    1 teaspoon grated lemon zest
    ½ teaspoon ground cinnamon

Confectioners' sugar, for garnish

1. Beat the milk and eggs together in a bowl. Add the sour cream and blend well. Gradually mix in the sugar, flour, and salt until you have a thin batter. Stir in the vanilla. In a separate bowl, stir together all of the filling ingredients.

2. Heat the oil in a skillet over medium-high heat. When the skillet is hot, pour in 3 tablespoons of the batter to form a very thin pancake. When bubbles break through the surface of the pancake, flip it and cook the other side. Keep the crêpes warm until all are cooked.

3. Stir together all of the filling ingredients in a bowl. Place about 1 tablespoon of the filling on one end of a crêpe. Fold the ends over and roll into a cigar shape. Place the filled crêpe on a plate or platter, folded side down, and dust with confectioners' sugar. Repeat until all of the crêpes have been filled. Serve warm, at room temperature, or chilled.

FEATHERWEIGHT WHOLE WHEAT PANCAKES

CLOTH OF GOLD

"The wide field of wheat began to wave and rustle and swirl in the winds of July. . . . Level, russet here and there, heavy-headed, wide as a lake, and full of multitudinous whispers and gleams of wealth, it stretched away before the gazers like the fabled field of the cloth of gold."

—HAMLIN GARLAND,
Under the Lion's Paw

Anyone who grew up in a wheat-farming community in the Great Plains remembers the wonderful flavor of breads and pancakes made with freshly ground grain. With the resurgence of interest in homemade breads, grain mills for the home kitchen are once again popular. At the Thistle Hill Bed-and-Breakfast in Wakeeny, Kansas, fresh wheatberries are gathered after the harvest and ground at the farm shortly before making these pancakes.

SERVES 6

2 cups whole wheat flour
1 teaspoon baking soda
3 tablespoons sugar
1/2 teaspoon salt
2 eggs, well beaten
1/4 cup white vinegar
1 3/4 cups milk
1/4 cup canola oil or corn oil

1. Sift together the flour, baking soda, sugar, and salt in a small bowl. In a large bowl, combine the eggs, vinegar, milk, and oil. Whisk the dry ingredients, a little at a time, into the egg mixture until you have a smooth batter.

2. Lightly oil a griddle or skillet and place it over medium-high heat. When it is hot, use a large spoon to transfer the batter onto it. Turn the pancakes when the underside is browned, but before the bubbles break through the upper surface. Remove from the heat when the other side begins to brown, and keep warm until all are done. Serve immediately, with maple syrup or, if you like, with Midsommersdag Elderberry Syrup (page 59) and Home-Churned Butter (page 40).

AMISH FRIENDSHIP PANCAKES

These have become the official "house" pancakes at my home on Sunday mornings. They rise beautifully on the griddle and have a faintly sour and yeasty flavor that makes other pancakes taste dull by comparison. Once you've made the Amish Friendship Starter, these pancakes are as easy to prepare as ones you make with a mix.

MAKES A GENEROUS DOZEN 6-INCH PANCAKES

1 cup Amish Friendship Starter
   (page 347)
1 egg, beaten
1 cup self-rising flour
1 cup milk, or more if needed
Vegetable oil or butter for the
   griddle

1. Stir together the starter, egg, flour, and 1 cup milk in a bowl. You will have a thick batter; add more milk if necessary to make a batter that can be poured.

2. Lightly oil or butter a large griddle or skillet and place it over medium heat. Pour the batter to make pancakes with a diameter of 6 inches. Cook the pancakes, turning when the bubbles reach the surface, until they have begun to brown on both sides. Keep warm until ready to serve. Serve with butter, perhaps Home-Churned Butter (page 40), and

with a fruity syrup, such as Midsommersdag Elderberry Syrup (page 59) or Chokecherry Syrup (see below).

WILD RICE PANCAKES WITH CHOKECHERRY SYRUP

Chokecherries are native to the Great Plains. They grow from Oklahoma up through the Dakotas and into the prairie provinces of Canada. The small scrub trees blossom in spring and produce tiny wild cherries that ripen to a dark burgundy in July. Norwegian immigrants loved chokecherry syrup on cream and bread; the Sioux eat it on fry bread; and almost everyone enjoys it on wild rice pancakes or homemade ice cream.

MAKES AT LEAST 12 6-INCH PANCAKES

> 1 cup all-purpose flour
> 2 tablespoons sugar
> 1/2 teaspoon baking soda
> 1/2 teaspoon salt
> 1 1/4 cups buttermilk
> 2 eggs, beaten
> 1 cup cooked wild rice
> 4 tablespoons butter, melted
> 1 recipe Chokecherry Syrup
>   (recipe follows)

1. Stir together the flour, sugar, baking soda, and salt in a large bowl. Add the buttermilk and eggs and stir to blend. Fold in the wild rice.

2. Heat a griddle or cast-iron skillet until it is hot enough to evaporate a drop of water. Brush the surface with some melted butter and pour out about 1/4 cup of batter for each pancake. Cook the pancakes until bubbles dot the surface, then flip and cook for 30 seconds on the other side. Keep warm until ready to serve. Serve with the Chokecherry Syrup.

CHOKECHERRY SYRUP

MAKES ABOUT 4 CUPS

> 6 cups fresh chokecherries
> 1/4 cup fresh lemon juice
> 4 cups sugar

1. Rinse the chokecherries and place them in a saucepan with water to cover. Bring to a boil, reduce the heat, and simmer for 15 minutes or until the cherries have burst. Strain the mixture through a sieve, pressing on the chokecherries to release as much juice as possible. You should have about 4 cups of juice.

2. For each 4 cups of juice, add 1/4 cup lemon juice and 4 cups sugar. Bring the syrup to a boil and boil it for 1 minute. Let the syrup cool slightly and serve it warm, or pour it into clean jars and store it in the refrigerator, to be reheated later.

Creamed Chicken on Indian Griddle Cakes

Here is a big and savory breakfast dish of long lineage that tastes best when there's an aroma of burning logs in the air and a rime of frost on the cornfields. In the late nineteenth century, breakfasts were large and sometimes elaborate affairs—a practical help for the cook, who could simply put out cheese, sausages, and pickled vegetables for lunch, then gear up again for a large dinner. In the 1877 second edition of *Buckeye Cookery and Practical Housekeeping*, a compilation of recipes from Ohio housewives, the following fare is recommended for Sunday breakfasts in the autumn: quail on toast, fried oysters, Saratoga potatoes, Indian griddle cakes with syrup, corn oysters, stewed peaches, broiled prairie chicken, fried trout, boiled Irish potatoes, nutmeg melons, coffee, and Vienna chocolate. If you serve this dish with Autumn Dried Apple Compote (page 382), you'll be ready to hike, rake leaves, or sit through a chilly football game.

Serves 6

FOR THE CREAMED CHICKEN:
    1 cup chicken stock
    ¾ cup light cream
    ¼ cup diced yellow onion
    ¼ teaspoon fresh-ground black
        pepper
    ¼ teaspoon cayenne pepper
    ¾ teaspoon salt
    ¼ teaspoon dried thyme
    ½ cup all-purpose flour
    3½ cups cooked chicken, diced
    2 tablespoons butter

FOR THE GRIDDLE CAKES:
    ½ teaspoon salt
    ½ teaspoon baking soda
    3 teaspoons sugar
    ½ teaspoon baking powder
    ½ cup flour
    1 cup plus 2 tablespoons cornmeal
    1 egg, beaten
    2 tablespoons canola oil or corn oil
    1 cup buttermilk
    ¼ to ½ cup milk

1. Make the creamed chicken: Pour the stock and cream into a large saucepan over medium heat. Stir in the onion, peppers, salt, and thyme. In a small bowl, whisk together the flour and ¼ cup cold water until the mixture forms a smooth paste. Whisk this paste into the stock mixture and continue whisking until the mixture begins to boil and then thicken. Reduce the heat to low, and stir in the chicken pieces and butter. Heat until the chicken is warmed through, 5 to 10 minutes. Keep the chicken warm over low heat; or, if you are making the creamed chicken the night before, cover and refrigerate it and reheat it the next morning.

2. Make the griddle cakes: Mix together all of the dry ingredients in a large bowl. Add the egg, oil, and buttermilk and stir to make a

smooth batter. Add enough milk to make a thin batter. Heat a griddle until it is very hot and brush it with butter or more oil. Pour 1/4 cup of batter for each pancake. Cook the pancakes until they are bubbly on top and light brown on the bottom, flip them, and cook the other side until it, too, is light brown. Keep the pancakes warm until ready to serve.

3. To serve, place several griddle cakes on each plate and top them with the creamed chicken.

GINGERBREAD WAFFLES WITH PEAR SAUCE

These homey waffles add up to an awfully good reason to get up in the morning. The pear sauce is easy and delicious, but for a quick substitute try applesauce, sautéed apples or pears, maple syrup, or pecans.

MAKES ABOUT 6 LARGE WAFFLES,
TO SERVE 3 TO 6

FOR THE PEAR SAUCE:
4 ripe pears, peeled, cored, and
*   diced*
1/4 cup wildflower or other
*   medium-colored honey*
Juice of 1/2 lemon

FOR THE WAFFLES:
2 cups all-purpose flour
1 tablespoon baking powder
1/2 teaspoon salt
1/2 cup packed brown sugar
1/2 teaspoon ground cinnamon
1/8 teaspoon ground dried ginger
1 cup milk
1/3 cup molasses
1/4 cup canola oil or corn oil
1 egg

1. Make the sauce: Place the pears, honey, and 1/4 cup water in a saucepan and bring to a boil over medium heat. Reduce the heat and simmer, covered, for 10 minutes, or until the fruit is soft. Add the lemon juice and mash with a potato masher. Transfer to a serving bowl.

2. Combine the flour, baking powder, salt, brown sugar, cinnamon, and ginger in a medium bowl. Add the milk, molasses, oil, and egg, and stir until well combined. Cook in a waffle iron, for about 90 seconds. (The cooking time will vary with your waffle iron and with your preference for doneness.) Serve immediately, with the pear sauce.

PRAIRIE SUMMER BRUNCH

The June sky is a brilliant blue, the weather is fine, and life is good. Sit back and relax with a Prairie Kir as your guests enjoy a late-morning meal you have made ahead:

Prairie Kir, see page 113

Cornhusker Corn Casserole, page 308

Scrambled Eggs with Homemade Croutons and Chives, this page

Sausage, Apple, and Cheddar Plait, page 31

Blueberry Compote, page 5

SCRAMBLED EGGS WITH HOMEMADE CROUTONS AND CHIVES

While reading in a 1968 community cookbook from German Village, a section of Columbus, Ohio, settled by German immigrants in the nineteenth century, I came across a recipe whose taste memory was as vivid to me as a color photograph. Savoring the dish in my imagination, I remembered having it for Sunday breakfast after church, and even for dinner on a day when I had stayed home from school with the measles. Homemade bread and onions sautéed in a little butter are the base for these delicious scrambled eggs, a dish with south German roots. This is my version, loosely based on the German Village rendition.

SERVES 2

2 tablespoons butter
1 small yellow onion, chopped
1 cup cubed homemade or
    good-quality bread
4 eggs
2 tablespoons milk
½ teaspoon salt
½ teaspoon ground white pepper
1 tablespoon minced fresh chives

1. Melt the butter in a skillet over medium heat. Sauté the onion and the bread cubes until the onion is translucent and the bread cubes are golden, about 6 to 8 minutes. While the onions cook, whisk the eggs with the milk, salt, and pepper in a bowl.

2. When the onions are done, pour the eggs into the skillet. Stir and scramble the eggs, incorporating the onions and bread cubes, until the eggs are done the way you like them. Serve sprinkled with minced chives.

HUNGARIAN OMELET

Cleveland has one of the largest populations of Hungarians outside of Hungary. This influence shows in a wealth of family bakeries and restaurants, in the savory aroma of *gulyás*, goulash, in home kitchens, and in breakfast dishes like this one. Use sweet Hungarian paprika, not one of the hotter and more bitter varieties.

SERVES 4

5 tablespoons unsalted butter
1 medium yellow onion, chopped
1 cup sliced mushrooms
½ cup sweet Hungarian paprika
6 eggs, beaten
½ teaspoon salt
½ teaspoon fresh-ground black
* pepper*
Sour cream and chopped fresh
* parsley or green onion,*
* for garnish*

1. Heat the butter in a large skillet over medium heat. Add the onion, and sauté it until it is golden brown, 8 to 10 minutes. Add the mushrooms and paprika and cook, stirring occasionally, until the mushrooms begin to wilt, about 5 minutes. Meanwhile, whisk the eggs, salt, and pepper together in a small bowl.

2. Reduce the heat to low. Pour the egg mixture over the mushrooms and onions in the skillet. Cook the omelet slowly for about 10 minutes, or until it is done enough to be flipped over without running. Flip it, and cook it for 3 to 4 minutes on the other side.

3. Cut the omelet into wedges and serve it garnished with a dollop of sour cream and a sprinkling of fresh parsley or green onion.

CAMPFIRE BREAKFAST

A childhood memory I treasure is of an outdoor breakfast with my large extended family at Winton Woods in Cincinnati on Memorial Day. While we cousins ran around and made a nuisance of ourselves, the great aunts arranged the homemade coffeecakes and got the coffee started in large tin pots over an outdoor fire. The men fried bacon and sausage in old cast-iron skillets, and then scrambled the eggs. Then we all sat down at picnic tables to this wonderful breakfast, our appetites sharpened by the cool morning air and the great aroma of food cooked over an open flame.

I did not realize then that our outdoor breakfast was similar to meals that pioneers on the Oregon Trail sat down to a hundred years before. After the wagon trains heading west had stopped to get fresh supplies at a trading post, this "Campfire Breakfast" of today would have been a typical dinner back then. Today, visitors to the Stuhr Museum of the Pioneer in Grand Island, Nebraska,

LITTLE TOWNS ON THE PRAIRIE

The Little House books, beloved of generations of children, narrate the journeys of the Ingalls family throughout the midwestern frontier. The family moved seven times in ten years, sometimes doubling back on their tracks. The following small towns, once outposts of civilization, are now thriving communities and the homes of Laura Ingalls Wilder museums and historic sites. Enter the kitchens and you will be able to imagine Ma frying salt pork and making gravy to go over sourdough biscuits.

❧ PEPIN, WISCONSIN. A recreated log house represents Laura Ingalls Wilder's 1867 birthplace. When Pa could hear the sound of his neighbor's ax, he knew it was time to move on.

❧ INDEPENDENCE, KANSAS. A replica of the Little House on the Prairie, located thirteen miles southwest of town, shows visitors what life was like for sodbusting families. Because Pa had built their homestead, in error, on land they did not own, they had to move.

❧ WALNUT GROVE, MINNESOTA. Now a farm town of 625, Walnut Grove was the Ingalls family's home for three and a half years, until Pa's crops failed. You can see the depression where the family lived in a dugout.

❧ BURR OAK, IOWA. This town, just across the Minnesota border, represents the "lost years" in Laura's account of her family's history. From 1876 to 1878, Ma and Pa helped run the clapboard Masters Hotel, and it was not a good time. Their infant son, Freddie, died on the journey there. The family lived next door to a saloon. And they were so poor that a doctor's family tried to adopt Laura.

❧ DE SMET, SOUTH DAKOTA. Who could forget the terrible blizzard that lasted for months, and the family's joy in opening a barrel of oysters, originally intended for Christmas dinner, when the train finally got through in May?

❧ MANSFIELD, MISSOURI. Laura, her husband Almanzo, and their daughter Rose moved to Mansfield in 1894. All the Little House books were written in their farmhouse here.

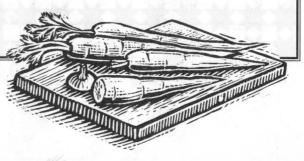

can sample pioneer food like this in special outdoor-cooking classes.

SERVES 4

8 strips hickory-smoked bacon
1 large yellow onion, diced
3 large potatoes, peeled and diced
6 eggs
Salt and black pepper to taste

1. Cut the bacon into 1-inch pieces and fry it in a large cast-iron skillet over medium-high heat. Once it is done the way you like it, remove the bacon from the skillet, drain it on paper towels, and set it aside.

2. Carefully pour off all but about 1/4 cup of the bacon grease from the skillet. Fry the onion and potatoes in the bacon grease over medium heat, stirring occasionally, until the potatoes are browned, 10 to 15 minutes. Beat the eggs together in a small bowl and add them to the skillet. Cook the eggs, stirring, for 3 to 4 minutes. Season with salt and pepper and serve, with the bacon sprinkled on the top.

SCALLOPED HAM AND EGGS

When you read the anonymous compilation *Buckeye Cookery and Practical Housekeeping*, published in 1877, you learn that midwestern housewives used to do vigorous things with eggs. On page after page, eggs are rumbled, scrambled, scalloped, pickled, poached, baked, boiled, curried, and frizzled. For all the rough-and-tumble action, exquisite care was given to all the dishes even as simple a one as scrambled eggs. Sweet milk was heated in an earthenware pie plate with a piece of butter "the size of a walnut." When the milk was nearly boiling, the eggs were cracked into the milk, one by one, then gently cut by a spoon or knife and scraped up from the bottom as they cooked. The result, as the author noted, "should be in large flakes of mingled white and yellow, and as delicate as baked custard." I have updated this breakfast dish of baked or shirred eggs topped with buttered breadcrumbs, but it's still simple and delicious.

SERVES 4

4 thin slices country ham or
    smoked ham
4 eggs
4 tablespoons light cream
Salt and black pepper to taste
1/2 cup fine breadcrumbs
2 tablespoons butter, melted

1. Preheat the oven to 400 degrees. Lightly oil, or spray with cooking spray, 4 ramekins or individual baking dishes.

2. Cut the ham slices into smaller pieces and arrange in the bottom of each ramekin. Carefully crack an egg on top of the ham, then drizzle the yolk with the cream and season with salt and pepper. Mix the breadcrumbs with

the melted butter and sprinkle the buttered crumbs on top of the eggs in each dish.

3. Bake for 8 minutes, or until the yolk is opaque. Serve hot, accompanied, if you like, by fresh sliced melon or other fruit.

FRESH HERB FRITTATA

Somehow, this dish tastes best in the late spring, when fresh herbs first green up in the garden. This traditional-style frittata is light and delicate, delicious served with steamed asparagus, a homemade coffeecake like St. Louis Gooey Butter Coffeecake (page 10), or Honeysuckle Berries (page 171).

SERVES 4

8 eggs
1/2 teaspoon salt
1/2 teaspoon white pepper
1 tablespoon minced fresh
    tarragon
1 tablespoon snipped fresh chives
1 tablespoon minced fresh Italian
    parsley
4 tablespoons olive oil
Parsley sprigs, for garnish

1. Whisk the eggs with the salt, pepper, and herbs in a bowl. Heat the oil in a large non-stick skillet over low heat. Pour in the eggs

and cook for about 4 minutes on one side, or until they are set.

2. Carefully loosen the frittata with a spatula, cover the skillet with a large plate, and invert the skillet so that the frittata falls onto the plate. Place the skillet back over the heat and slide the frittata back into the skillet. Cook the other side for 3 to 4 minutes more, or until the frittata is cooked through and solid enough to be sliced. Remove from the heat, cut in wedges, and serve, with sprigs of parsley.

TOMATO AND ZUCCHINI SCRAMBLED EGGS

In late summer when your garden is in full production, this savory egg dish is terrific for breakfast, or even for a light dinner. Pick smaller zucchini, which are more flavorful and less watery, and the freshest tomato you can find. Fresh peaches or berries, or a cheesy popover, make nice accompaniments.

SERVES 4

6 tablespoons olive oil
3 green onions, white part and
    some green, chopped
1 garlic clove, minced
5 small zucchini, trimmed and
    sliced thin

1 large tomato, peeled, seeded, and
chopped
8 eggs
Salt and black pepper to taste
1 teaspoon minced fresh Italian
parsley

1. Heat the oil in a large skillet over medium heat. Add the green onions, garlic, zucchini, and tomato, and sauté them for 5 minutes, or until the tomato juices begin to evaporate. Beat the eggs in a bowl and stir in the salt, pepper, and parsley.

2. Pour the egg mixture into the skillet and stir the eggs until they are scrambled and set. Serve warm.

HEIRLOOM SEEDS

"The garden looked like a relief-map now, and gave no indication of what it would be in August; such a jungle! Pole beans and potatoes and corn and leeks and kale and red cabbage—there would even be vegetables for which there is no American name. Mrs. Kohler was always getting by mail packages of seeds from Freeport [Illinois] and from the old country."

—WILLA CATHER, Song of the Lark

SAVORY CHEESE SOUFFLÉ

This stylish soufflé, a fine brunch entree or light supper, provides a great platform for showing off the wares of some of the great cheesemakers from the midwest's Dairy Belt.

SERVES 6

5 tablespoons unsalted butter, plus
more to butter the soufflé dish
1/3 cup grated Gruyère cheese,
such as Roth Kase from
Wisconsin
1/2 cup all-purpose flour
1 3/4 cups milk
1 cup crumbled blue cheese, such
as Maytag Blue from Iowa
1 teaspoon salt
1/4 teaspoon fresh-ground black
pepper
4 eggs, separated

1. Preheat the oven to 350 degrees. Lightly butter a 1-quart soufflé dish. Sprinkle the bottom and sides of the dish with the grated Gruyère and set the dish aside.

2. Melt the 5 tablespoons of butter in a saucepan over medium heat. Whisk in the flour. Add the milk and cook, whisking constantly, until the mixture thickens. Stir in the blue cheese, salt, and pepper. In a separate bowl, whisk the egg yolks. Whisk about 1/4 cup of the blue cheese mixture into the yolks,

then pour the yolk mixture into the saucepan, and whisk to blend. Cook, whisking, for 1 minute, then remove from the heat.

3. In a large mixing bowl, beat the egg whites until they are glossy with firm peaks, but not dry. Gently fold the yolk mixture into the egg whites until the soufflé mixture looks marbled. Pour the soufflé mixture into the prepared dish and bake for 40 to 45 minutes, or until the soufflé has pulled away from the

sides of the pan and has risen and begun to brown. Serve immediately.

BERRY GOOD BREAD PUDDING

Now that baking homemade bread is back in fashion, thanks in part to the automatic bread machine, recipes that use leftover

KANSAS FEVER

Between 1865 and 1880, Kansas attracted more immigrants than any other place in the nation; its population grew from about a hundred thousand to nearly a million in that time. "Kansas fevers" broke out in the most unexpected places, from New England and the deep South to Germany and the Russian steppes. The promise of virtually free land and a chance to start over again drew thousands to the rolling prairie. The first Homestead Act, passed by Congress in 1862, enabled the head of a family to claim 160 acres of land in Kansas for only a small filing fee and a promise to reside there for five years.

The Eastern Division of the Union Pacific Railroad had completed its swath across the state by 1868. Its rival, the Atchison, Topeka, and Santa Fe, stretched across Kansas by 1873. Both

railroads were given large tracts of land abutting their lines, and both were determined to find settlers who would grow crops that the railroads could transport. Railroad representatives aggressively promoted settlement by setting up land offices back East and even making trips to the Ukraine and other agricultural regions of Europe. The Santa Fe Railroad sponsored a railroad excursion to these new lands for newspaper editors from Ohio, Illinois, Indiana, Iowa, and Missouri, in the hopes that the publicity would draw new immigrants.

After the Civil War, freed slaves from Kentucky and Tennessee also made their way in droves to Kansas to found pioneer towns like Nicodemus in Graham County. For them, Kansas was the Promised Land, where they could own their own land and be free.

bread are popular as well. This bread pudding full of luscious berries is best made with homemade bread or bread from a good bakery. I have made the pudding with French Pear Bread (page 358), Saffron Bread (page 355), and Slavic Potato Bread (page 354), all with great results. Challah would be good, too. Although this makes a wonderful dessert, I'm partial to it as a breakfast or brunch dish.

SERVES 6

FOR THE PUDDING:

    2 cups milk
    ½ cup granulated sugar
    1 vanilla bean, split
    3 eggs, beaten
    ½ teaspoon ground cinnamon
    3 cups 1-inch cubes of day-old
        bread
    ¼ pound (1 stick) unsalted butter,
        melted
    2 cups mixed fresh berries, such as
        strawberries, blueberries,
        blackberries, mulberries, or
        raspberries

FOR THE SAUCE:

    1 cup fresh raspberries,
        blackberries, blueberries,
        or strawberries
    2 tablespoons confectioners' sugar

    Confectioners' sugar, for garnish

1. Preheat the oven to 350 degrees. Lightly oil a 1½-quart baking dish or 6 individual ramekins. In a saucepan over medium heat, bring the milk just to a boil. Remove from the heat, stir in the sugar and vanilla bean, and let the mixture steep for 20 minutes. Discard the vanilla bean. Whisk in the eggs and the cinnamon. Set aside.

2. Place the bread cubes in a bowl and toss them with the melted butter. Spread the buttered cubes evenly in the prepared baking dish or ramekins. Scatter the berries on top of the bread, then pour the milk mixture over all. Bake the large dish for 50 minutes to 1 hour or the individual ramekins for 35 minutes, or until the puddings are puffed and golden brown and the custard has set.

3. While the puddings bake, make the sauce: Puree the berries with the 2 tablespoons confectioners' sugar in a food processor or blender until smooth. Strain the mixture through a sieve to remove any seeds.

4. Serve the pudding hot, with some sauce drizzled on top and garnished with confectioners' sugar, and with additional sauce passed on the side.

ASPARAGUS, GOAT CHEESE, AND FRESH HERB BREAD PUDDING

As a brunch dish or casual supper, a savory bread pudding such as this one is comforting and delicious. For the bread, a hearty peasant loaf, a sourdough, a raisin-walnut bread, or even an olive bread, are all fine choices. Fresh strawberries or sliced melon are good accompaniments.

SERVES 6

1 pound asparagus, tough ends
    removed and cut diagonally
    into 2-inch pieces
2 cups 1-inch cubes of dry or day-old
    bread, preferably homemade
1/2 cup minced mixed fresh herbs,
    such as tarragon, chives,
    parsley, or thyme
8 ounces fresh goat cheese
2 cups milk
3 eggs, beaten
Salt and black pepper to taste

1. Preheat the oven to 350 degrees. Lightly oil or butter a 9-by-13-inch baking dish. Steam the asparagus until just barely tender, about 3 minutes.

2. Combine the bread cubes, cooked asparagus, and herbs in a large bowl. Spread this mixture evenly in the baking dish. Cut or crumble the goat cheese into small pieces and dot these over the bread mixture. In a separate bowl, whisk together the milk, eggs, salt, and pepper. Pour the milk mixture over the bread and cheese.

3. Bake for 45 to 50 minutes, or until the bread pudding is puffed and golden brown and the custard has set. Serve hot.

HAM AND CHEESE BREAD AND BUTTER PUDDING

Good-quality smoked ham, your favorite farmhouse cheddar cheese, and French bread make up a breakfast or brunch that is savory and satisfying.

SERVES 8

1 large baguette French bread
2 tablespoons unsalted butter
1 large leek, cleaned well and
    sliced thin
1/2 pound smoked ham, chopped
1 cup grated cheddar cheese
2 1/2 cups milk
4 eggs, beaten
1 tablespoon Dijon mustard

1. Lightly oil or butter a 1-quart soufflé dish or oval baking dish. Slice the bread into 20 to 24 slices and place half of the slices side by side in the bottom of the dish. Melt the 2 tablespoons butter in a small skillet over medium heat. Add the leek, and sauté it until it has softened slightly, about 5 minutes. Pour the sautéed leek over the bread in the dish. Sprinkle with the chopped ham and half the cheese. Top with the remaining slices of bread.

2. Whisk together the milk, eggs, and mustard in a bowl, and pour this mixture over the

bread in the dish. Sprinkle the remaining cheese evenly over the top. Cover and refrigerate for 3 to 4 hours or overnight to let the bread soften and the flavors blend.

3. Preheat the oven to 350 degrees. Bake, uncovered, for 45 minutes, or until the custard has set and the pudding is bubbly and golden brown. Serve hot.

HERBED SAUSAGE PATTIES

Here is an easy brunch or breakfast dish to make the night before. This homemade sausage is lower in fat than most store-bought varieties.

SERVES 4

1 pound ground turkey
1 egg
3/4 teaspoon ground dried sage
1/2 teaspoon crushed dried rosemary
1/2 teaspoon fresh-ground black pepper
1/4 teaspoon dried marjoram
1/4 teaspoon crushed dried thyme

1. Place all of the ingredients in a large bowl and mix thoroughly with a wooden spoon or by hand. Shape the mixture into 4 large or 8 small patties. Refrigerate, covered, for 1 hour or overnight.

2. Lightly oil a skillet. Pan-fry the patties over medium-low heat for about 10 minutes per side for large patties and 6 to 8 minutes per side for small ones, until the patties are browned. Serve hot.

VARIATION:

As an alternative to pan-frying, you can bake the patties at 350 degrees for 15 minutes, or until they are browned.

MORE SQUARES ON THE QUILT

As the Homestead Acts were amended and expanded in the latter half of the nineteenth century, new land opened up in North and South Dakota, Iowa, and Nebraska, bringing new groups of immigrants. Poles, Irish, Czechs, Bohemians, and Austrians, many of whom were unsettled by political upheaval at home, were lured by the generous terms of the Acts. Immigrants traveled by rail to Chicago, and from there to places north and west. By the 1880s, over sixty-seven thousand Czechs had settled in Nebraska alone. Norwegians and Swedes set out from Chicago to claim their acres in Wisconsin, Minnesota, and the Dakotas. And so the midwest began to be covered in the ever-changing quilt pattern we know today.

SWEDISH POTATO SAUSAGES

A mild-tasting favorite in Swedish communities throughout the Heartland, these sausages are nice for a big and hearty breakfast or for a casual dinner, perhaps with a creamy potato dish and a marinated vegetable salad.

SERVES 6 TO 8

3/4 cup ground beef
(about 1/2 pound)
3/4 cup ground pork
(about 1/2 pound)
1/2 cup shredded or ground
uncooked potato
1/2 cup diced yellow onion
3/4 teaspoon salt
1/4 teaspoon black pepper
1/8 teaspoon ground allspice
1/8 teaspoon crushed dried thyme

1. Place all of the ingredients in a large bowl and mix thoroughly with a wooden spoon or by hand. Shape the mixture into 6 to 8 patties. (The sausages may be prepared ahead to this point and refrigerated, covered, overnight.)

2. Lightly oil a skillet. Pan-fry the patties over medium-low heat until they are well browned, about 10 minutes per side. Check the inside of a patty to make sure there is no pinkness left in the meats. Serve hot.

ON THE MIGHTY MISSISSIP'

"Huck found a spring of clear cold water close by, and the boys made cups of broad oak or hickory leaves, and felt that water, sweetened with such a wild-wood charm as that, would be a good enough substitute for coffee. While Joe was slicing bacon for breakfast, Tom and Huck asked him to hold on a minute; they stepped to a promising nook in the river bank and threw in their lines; almost immediately they had a reward. Joe had not had time to get impatient before they were back again with some handsome bass, a couple of sun-perch and a small cat-fish—provisions enough for quite a family. They fried the fish with the bacon and were astonished; no fish had ever seemed so delicious before."

—MARK TWAIN, Tom Sawyer

SAUSAGE, APPLE, AND CHEDDAR PLAIT

This dish, called a plait because of its braided appearance, almost looks too pretty to eat. A fragrantly delicious dish perfect for a brunch or light supper, this savory plait can be baked and frozen, then warmed again in the oven. The recipe makes two pastries, so you can eat one and freeze one for later.

MAKES 2 SAVORY PASTRIES,
TO SERVE 12

1 tablespoon canola oil or corn oil
1 pound bulk pork or turkey
   sausage
1 large yellow onion, chopped
2 large tart apples, peeled, cored,
   and chopped
1 pound sharp cheddar cheese,
   shredded
3/4 cup dried herb stuffing,
   store-bought or homemade
2 eggs
1 17 1/4-ounce package (2 sheets)
   frozen puff pastry, thawed

1. Preheat the oven to 400 degrees. Lightly butter a large baking sheet.

2. Heat the oil in a large heavy skillet over medium-low heat. Add the sausage and onion, and sauté them until the sausage browns and the onions are translucent, about 10 minutes. Drain off the excess fat. Transfer the mixture to a large bowl, add the apples, cheese, and stuffing, and stir to combine well. Beat one of the eggs, add it to the sausage mixture, and stir to combine.

3. On a lightly floured work surface, roll out each of the 2 pastry sheets to a 14-by-18-inch rectangle. Spoon half of the sausage filling lengthwise down the center of each rectangle, starting 3 inches from the top and ending 3 inches from the bottom. Cut the pastry on either side of the sausage filling into diagonal strips about 1/2 inch wide. Fold the strips, alternately from each side, over the filling to create a lattice or braid effect. Repeat the process with the second pastry sheet.

4. Beat the remaining egg and brush the egg over both pastries. Bake for 30 minutes, or until the pastries are puffed and golden brown. Serve hot.

COUNTRY HAM ON WATERCRESS BISCUITS

The southern tradition of salt-curing hams traveled westward to Missouri, where, in this traditional dish for a spring breakfast or brunch, wafer-thin slices of ham go well with the fresh taste of the green-flecked biscuits. Creamy scrambled eggs, smoked turkey or chicken breast, or smoked salmon also make good fillings in place of the ham.

MAKES ABOUT 1 DOZEN BISCUITS

FOR THE BISCUITS:
  2 cups all-purpose flour
  3 teaspoons baking powder
  1/4 teaspoon salt
  1/8 teaspoon cayenne pepper
  2/3 cup minced watercress leaves
      and stems
  2 tablespoons minced fresh chives
  1/3 cup melted butter
  About 3/4 cup milk

  1/2 cup mayonnaise or
      4 tablespoons unsalted
      butter, softened
  1/2 pound country ham, sliced
      paper thin

1. Preheat the oven to 450 degrees. Sift the flour, baking powder, salt, and cayenne together into a mixing bowl. With a tea towel or paper towels, gently squeeze excess moisture from the watercress and chives. Add the watercress and chives to the flour mixture, and stir to combine. Gradually add the butter, stirring with a fork to blend. Add the milk a little at a time, continuing to stir with the fork; add just enough milk to form a soft, workable dough, neither runny nor thick and sticky.

2. Gather the dough into a ball and, on a lightly floured work surface, roll it out to a thickness of 1/2 inch. Cut the dough with a

2-inch biscuit cutter and place the biscuits on an ungreased baking sheet. Bake for 12 minutes, or until the tops have begun to brown. Remove from oven and let cool.

3. When the biscuits are cool enough to handle, carefully cut each one in half and spread the inside with the mayonnaise or softened butter. Place a very thin slice of country ham on one half and top with the other half of the biscuit. Serve immediately; or cover with plastic wrap, refrigerate until 1 hour before serving, bring to room temperature, and serve.

SMOKED TURKEY HASH

According to the Ohio women who compiled *Buckeye Cookery and Practical Housekeeping*, in the late nineteenth century, hash should not taste like "boarding house skillets, hotel coffee, garden garlics, or bologna sausage." Instead, "it is made so nicely, seasoned so delicately, and heated through so quickly, that the only trouble is, 'there is never enough to go around.'" With a side of scrambled eggs or topped with a poached egg, this midwestern take on corned beef hash will win converts at your breakfast table. Smoked whitefish or trout would be delicious in place of the turkey.

SERVES 4

4 potatoes, baked
3 tablespoons canola oil or corn oil
1 large red onion, chopped
1 cup chopped smoked turkey
　　(from about 1/2 pound)
Salt and black pepper to taste
2 tablespoons minced fresh dill or
　　1/2 teaspoon dried dill

1. Slice the potatoes thin and chop the slices into smaller pieces. Heat the oil in a large skillet over medium heat. Add the potatoes and onions, and sauté them, turning them occasionally, until browned, about 15 minutes.

2. Add the turkey and cook for 5 minutes more, or until the turkey is heated through. Add the salt, pepper, and dill, stir well, and serve.

THE BEST OF THE WURST

German immigrants to the midwest brought with them their love of sausages, and bratwurst in particular. I understand why. When I was in graduate school at Ohio State, my friends and I made many pilgrimages on summer nights to German Village, a section of Columbus that was settled by German immigrants in the nineteenth century. We would sit out in the cool shade of the beer gardens, at the back of narrow brick taverns, with frosty mugs of beer and with plates of savory grilled brats topped with fresh-ground horseradish.

Recipes for bratwurst vary from family to family and town to town. The small city of Sheboygan in southeastern Wisconsin claims to be the country's bratwurst capital. Soft, moist, mild, and delicate, bratwurst is made of pork or veal, or both, ground fine and blended with seasonings that might include parsley, nutmeg, white pepper, salt, and grated onion. In Minneapolis and the rest of southern Minnesota, a stronghold of German and Eastern European cuisine, you get your bratwurst sandwich on a thick hunk of sourdough rye bread along with a tangy mound of sauerkraut. If you order a bratwurst plate at restaurants like the Kaiserhoff in the town of New Ulm, you get a couple of steamy links along with a mound of homemade German potato salad and braised red cabbage. In nearby Lanesboro, Arv Fabian of the Wurst Haus makes his own bratwurst of secret seasonings, grills them, then marinates them in a vat of hot beer before plunking them down on toasty hard rolls called brotchen.

The beverage of choice with bratwurst? It's a good German beer or a fine midwestern microbrew for the hearty, a chilled glass of crisp white Liebfraumilch for the gentler soul.

GOETTA

Pronounced "gett-ah," this Cincinnati breakfast staple may not, to some, sound pleasant on paper, but eating it is another thing altogether. Made like polenta or scrapple and left in the loaf pan to cool, goetta is then sliced and fried for breakfast or for a light supper. In Cincinnati, you can buy goetta ready-made. As with Cincinnati chili, everyone has his or her own favorite versions—made with beef or pork or a mixture of the two; made with ground or shredded meat; made with onion or without. All agree, however, that goetta should be made with pinhead oatmeal from the Dottie Dorsel Company across the river in Kentucky. Pinhead oatmeal is made of whole oat kernels before they are flattened into rolled oats. Outside of Cincinnati, steel-cut oats are a fine substitute.

Whether this is a German dish, as I suspect, or an Irish one, as some believe, is a much-debated question in Cincinnati. In New Ulm, Minnesota, the Randall Smokehouse makes a similar German dish called Gritz-wurst: oatmeal and pork sausage cooked together, formed into a loaf, then sliced and fried. Here is my mother's Cincinnati-style goetta that she makes every autumn.

MAKES 4 SMALL OR 2 LARGE LOAVES

2 to 2½ pounds fresh pork
shoulder or Boston butt
1 large yellow onion, chopped
1 or 2 bay leaves
2 to 3 teaspoons salt
Black pepper to taste
2½ cups uncooked pinhead
oatmeal or steel-cut oats

1. Place the pork, onion, bay leaves, salt, and pepper in a large saucepan or stockpot. Cover with 2 quarts of water, bring to a slow simmer, and cook, covered, until the meat is cooked through and tender, about 1½ hours. Remove the pork, and reserve it.

2. Add the oatmeal to the broth and bring to a boil. Reduce the heat to low and simmer, covered, for ½ hour, stirring frequently. Remove the cover, and continue cooking the oatmeal until it is soft and very thick, about 15 minutes more.

3. While the oats cook, use your fingers or 2 forks to pull the pork apart into small pieces. Add the pork to the cooked oatmeal and cook for 10 minutes more, stirring often so the mixture does not stick to the bottom of the pan. Taste, and adjust the seasonings. Turn the goetta out into greased loaf pans to cool slightly. Transfer the pans to the refrigerator, and chill for at least 2 hours.

4. Slice the goetta ½ inch thick and sauté it on both sides in a lightly oiled skillet over medium heat until it is brown and crisp on the outside and tender in the middle, about 5 minutes per side. Serve hot, plain or with catsup.

A
Prairie
Pantry

A Prairie Pantry

FRESH FARMHOUSE CHEESE

1 rennet tablet
Cream, sour cream, or milk, optional

Molly O'Neill, the *New York Times* food columnist, writes that when her father was recuperating in a body cast during World War II, he dreamt of the cottage cheese "that his mother hung in gauze bags from the back porch" on their farm in Nebraska. Back when most Midwestern family farms grew, raised, or made most of their own table foods, cottage cheese was made at home. Many people still remember cheesecloth bags of curds draining whey from the clothesline in the backyard. Although making your own farmhouse cheese takes about 24 hours, it is not labor-intensive and it yields a superior product. You will end up with a creamy white cheese with a tender curd and a fresh, tangy flavor. I mix it with cream for a creamed fine-curd cottage cheese to eat fresh, perhaps flavored with snipped fresh chives or lemon balm. Or I use it (without the optional cream) for baking German Cheese Tart (page 393) or making Verenicke (page 266). I am indebted to Stephen Langlois, formerly the guiding light at Chicago's Prairie, for the recipe blueprint. You can find rennet tablets in the baking section of the grocery store.

MAKES 8 CUPS CHEESE

1½ gallons homogenized whole milk
1 cup buttermilk

1. Warm the whole milk and buttermilk over low heat in a large saucepan or stockpot until they reach 90 degrees on an instant-read thermometer. Pour ¼ cup of this mixture into a glass measuring cup and heat it in the microwave for 10 seconds on high, or until it is 115 degrees; alternatively, heat the ¼ cup milk in a small saucepan until it reaches the same temperature. Crumble the rennet tablet into the warm milk in the measuring cup and stir to blend. Pour this mixture back into the large saucepan and stir well. Remove from the heat, cover the pan, and let the mixture sit overnight, for at least 14 hours.

2. In the morning, return the pan to the heat and remove its cover. For a larger curd cheese, bring the mixture to 130 or 140 degrees over medium heat; for a smaller curd cheese, bring the mixture to about 115 degrees over low heat. Continue cooking, stirring occasionally, at the desired temperature for 1 to 1½ hours, or until the curds have separated from the whey.

3. Meanwhile, line two colanders with a double thickness of cheesecloth. Tie or clip the cheesecloths to the perimeters of the colanders to keep them from slipping in. Gently pour half of the mixture through 1 colander and half through the other. Let the whey drain off the cottage cheese for about 1 hour.

4. Spoon the drained cheese into two 1-pint containers. Stir in some fresh cream, sour cream, or whole milk, if you like, for a softer consistency and flavor. The cheese will keep covered in the refrigerator for up to 1 week.

HOME-CHURNED BUTTER

"No sloven can make good butter," declares the anonymous compiler of *Buckeye Cookery and Practical Housekeeping* (1877). She urges the reader to practice "neatness, neatness, neatness" as she goes through all the steps from keeping the cow clean to maintaining the proper temperature in the milking room to scalding the churn and dash. Luckily, we don't have to go through such a production to make home-churned butter, now that the food processor easily replaces the old wooden churn. Make this pale yellow unsalted butter as a treat for brunch guests or for your family as part of a special breakfast. After you've just made the butter, you can also spoon it into decorative molds. In Polish neighborhoods of Chicago around Easter, butter "lambs" are available in mom-and-pop groceries and delis; butter "cows," too, often turn up at midwestern county fairs. Use pasteurized rather than ultra-pasteurized cream, because the latter takes twice as long to churn. Because home-churned butter contains no salt (the small amount you add leaches out in the whey) and no preserva-

tives, it won't last as long as store-bought butter in the refrigerator. Chances are you won't have it around long enough for that to be a problem.

MAKES ABOUT 1 CUP,
THE EQUIVALENT OF
1/2 POUND OR 2 STICKS

2 cups pasteurized (not ultra-pasteurized) heavy cream

1. Line a sieve with a single layer of cheesecloth and place the sieve over a bowl. Pour the cream into a food processor and process for about 5 minutes, or until the butter forms a mass and separates from the whey (which appears as a milky liquid).

2. Transfer the butter and whey to the sieve and work the butter with a wooden spoon or spatula to release more of the whey, until you have a fairly solid mass, like whipped butter. Scoop the butter out from the sieve, wrap it in plastic wrap, and serve immediately or refrigerate. Or, if you like, spoon it into a metal or plastic mold and refrigerate.

VARIATIONS:

To make a Honey Butter, mix 1 cup softened butter with 1 tablespoon, or more to taste, wildflower or other medium-colored honey. For Herb Butter, mix 2 tablespoons fresh herbs with 1 cup softened butter. For a Strawberry Butter, particularly good with pancakes or waffles, mash 1 cup strawberries and blend with 1 cup softened butter.

IN PEARLENA'S KITCHEN

Short and tender-hearted, Pearlena Moore sits back in her kitchen and reminisces about the foods of her childhood in the 1930s and '40s, when everyone in her town of Nicodemus, Kansas, "raised a garden." Her dark eyes light up as she remembers gathering wild prairie greens and cooking them with a home-smoked hog jowl or a ham hock for seasoning; frying up jackrabbit legs to serve with milk gravy and boiled potatoes; and churning butter at home. "We used to have a little song we sang when we was churning butter," Pearlena says. "Come, butter, come./ Mama wants you come,/ Baby wants you come,/ Come, butter, come."

Her family's neighbors had a peach orchard. "One year," Pearlena recalls, "I canned fourteen bushels of peaches!"

These days, peaches come from the grocery store, for the orchard is gone. Pearlena still has a large glass preserve jar full of her prize-winning wild plums, dark purple but still good after many years. Her husband, Donald, has sixty-nine acres in wheat, and their four children, grown and gone, still come over for dinner on occasion. The grown children of her siblings call her "Aunt Teenie," and they still ask her for the rolled butterscotch cookies and homemade gingerbread cookies she used to make. "We got the molasses for the gingerbread cookies from my husband's family, who made molasses every year," she told me. "We made our own P&G soap, too," she laughs. "Only our P&G stood for 'push and grunt.'"

HOMEMADE CROUTONS

With the popularity of baking bread at home, whether by hand or with a bread machine, come lots of possibilities for what to do with all the delicious leftovers. Our great-grandmothers had a trove of recipes, many deserving of a revival, that made use of stale bread, old crusts, dried breadcrumbs, and so on. A salad made from fresh, crisp greens dressed with a simple vinaigrette and tossed with homemade croutons will remind you that simple things done well can be a revelation. Use stale or leftover bread of any flavor or variety, and vary the herbs or flavorings to suit the bread.

MAKES 2 CUPS SMALL CROUTONS

2 cups ½-inch cubes of bread
¼ pound (1 stick) unsalted butter
1 teaspoon minced fresh parsley

1. Melt the butter in a large skillet over medium heat. Add the bread cubes, and cook them, tossing them frequently, until they are lightly toasted on all sides, about 4 minutes.

2. Add the parsley, and toss briefly until most of the greens adhere to the bread cubes. Remove the croutons with a slotted spoon, and set them aside to cool to room temperature. Serve immediately, or store in an airtight container in the refrigerator or freezer.

VARIATIONS:

Instead of parsley, use 1 teaspoon dried herbs such as dill, thyme, tarragon, or basil. Or add 1 to 3 minced garlic cloves to the butter.

OVEN-DRIED TOMATOES

In many midwestern households, oven-dried tomatoes preserved in oil have supplanted jars of corn relish as the homemade staple you never should be without. Tossed with pasta, added to savory breads and muffins, or blended with goat cheese, these preserved tomatoes are well worth preparing when the August garden offers up a surplus. As the tomatoes dry out in the oven, they shrink dramatically and their flavor intensifies. The oil itself becomes flavored and can be used in salad dressings or wherever you want a tomato flavor.

MAKES I CUP DRIED TOMATOES

4 cups cherry or plum tomatoes, cut in half lengthwise
¾ cup olive oil, or more

1. Preheat the oven to 200 degrees. Lightly oil a baking sheet and place the tomatoes, cut side up, on the sheet. Drizzle with 4 tablespoons of the olive oil. Bake the tomatoes for 2 to 4 hours (the larger they are, the longer they will take), or until they have shrunk to about ¼ of their original size and are just dry but still somewhat soft to the touch.

2. As they get done, use a spoon to transfer the tomatoes to a sterilized 8-ounce jar. Pour in the remaining ½ cup oil, or more if necessary, to cover the tomatoes. Cap the jar, and store the tomatoes in the refrigerator. Make sure the tomatoes are always covered by the oil; if necessary, add more to the jar. The tomatoes will keep indefinitely.

OVEN-DRIED TOMATO MAYONNAISE

People from the east and west coasts think that midwesterners are unduly fond of mayonnaise. Here is a version that will show them why. Keep this homemade condiment on hand for hamburgers, grilled vegetable sandwiches, or a grilled chicken salad.

MAKES ABOUT 1½ CUPS MAYONNAISE

> 2/3 cup mayonnaise
> ½ cup diced fresh tomatoes
> ¼ cup Oven-Dried Tomatoes (page 42), with their oil
> 1 (2-ounce) jar diced pimientos, drained
> 1 medium garlic clove, minced
> ¼ teaspoon cayenne pepper
> Olive oil, to make ¼ cup total when combined with the oil from the Oven-Dried Tomatoes
> Salt and white pepper to taste

1. In a blender or a food processor fitted with a steel blade, blend together the mayonnaise, fresh tomatoes, dried tomatoes, pimientos, garlic, and cayenne. With the machine still running, pour in the reserved oil from the dried tomatoes plus the additional olive oil. If the mixture is too thick for a mayonnaise, add a few drops of water and run the machine to incorporate.

2. Stir in the salt and white pepper, taste, and adjust the seasonings. Transfer the mayonnaise to a clean pint jar or plastic container. Covered and refrigerated, the mayonnaise will keep for up to 1 month.

SPICED TOMATO CATSUP

Mrs. Seebohm, my grandmother's neighbor in Cincinnati, remained quite active well into her eighties. Wearing a floral print housedress and her white hair in a bun, Mrs. Seebohm kept pace with the rhythms of the day and of the year. She flung open her green shutters every morning, a sign to my grandmother and the other neighbors that she was up and about, and she closed them again when she went to bed at night. In spring and summer, she tended her sizable rose garden, and when her son brought her a bushel of garden tomatoes every August, she would make homemade catsup. My mother still recalls standing near Mrs. Seebohm's kitchen window to catch the savory aroma of the spicy tomatoes cooking down to a thick and zesty sauce. There's no finer catsup to slather on a good homemade meatloaf or to put on a roast beef sandwich fit for a homecoming.

MAKES ABOUT 2½ CUPS CATSUP

4 cups peeled and chopped very
    ripe fresh tomatoes (from 6 to
    8 large tomatoes), or 4 cups
    drained and chopped canned
    peeled tomatoes
1 yellow onion, chopped
1/3 cup cider vinegar
2 tablespoons sugar
1/2 teaspoon dry mustard
1/2 teaspoon black pepper
1/4 teaspoon ground nutmeg
1/2 teaspoon ground cinnamon
1/4 teaspoon ground cloves
1/4 teaspoon ground allspice
1/4 teaspoon cayenne pepper
1/2 teaspoon garlic salt

1. Cook the tomatoes and onion in a saucepan over medium-low heat for 20 to 25 minutes, or until both are very soft. Transfer them to a food processor or blender, and puree until nearly smooth.

2. Place a sieve over a clean saucepan and pass the puree through the sieve into the saucepan, pressing the puree with the back of a spoon or a rubber spatula to remove the seeds and to smooth out any lumps. Place the saucepan on the stove and add the rest of the ingredients. Bring to a simmer over medium heat, reduce the heat to low, and simmer, uncovered, for 1 hour to blend the flavors and thicken the catsup.

3. Pour the hot catsup through a funnel into a clean bottle. Cover the bottle, let the catsup cool slightly, then refrigerate the bottle. The catsup will keep indefinitely in the refrigerator.

TOMATO CHUTNEY

Make this richly flavored preserve when your late summer tomato garden is at its most productive. Serve the chutney as a condiment or side dish with grilled or roasted meats; on a sandwich, alone or with meats; or, as an appetizer, over cream cheese or brie.

MAKES 8 PINTS CHUTNEY

12 ripe tomatoes, peeled and
    chopped
4 yellow onions, chopped
2 large green bell peppers, chopped
6 tart apples, peeled and chopped
2 garlic cloves, minced
1 tablespoon grated fresh ginger
3 cups brown sugar
3 cups cider vinegar
1 cup dried cherries or raisins
2 teaspoons salt
1 teaspoon chili powder
1 teaspoon ground cinnamon

1. Place all of the ingredients in a large nonreactive stockpot and bring the mixture to a boil. Reduce the heat to low and simmer, uncovered, stirring occasionally, for 20 minutes, or until the chutney is thick.

2. Spoon or ladle the chutney into clean jars. Cap the jars. Refrigerated, the chutney will keep indefinitely.

GROUND CHERRY PRESERVES

A ground cherry is not a cherry but a relative of the tomato and tomatillo. Also called a husk tomato, strawberry tomato, or cape gooseberry, it is a small yellow or orange fruit enclosed in a papery husk. Europeans dip these sweet but acidic fruits in chocolate to garnish desserts, but they're also wonderful in preserves. Try the preserves spread on toasted bread that has first been spread with Maytag Blue cheese or another good blue cheese.

MAKES 6
8-OUNCE JARS OF PRESERVES

3 pounds ground cherries
1½ pounds sugar
Juice of 1 lemon
Grated zest of ½ lemon

1. Remove and discard the husks from the ground cherries and rinse the fruit well. Place the ground cherries in a large nonreactive pot or preserving kettle with 2 tablespoons of water and bring to a rapid boil (the tomatoes will render additional liquid). Boil steadily for 10 minutes, then gently stir in the sugar gradually.

2. When the sugar has been blended in, add the lemon juice and zest. Boil the mixture for 10 to 15 minutes more, or until the preserves begin to set. Spoon or ladle into sterilized 8-ounce canning jars, leaving ¼ inch of headspace. Cap the jars according to the manufacturer's directions. Process the jars for 10 minutes in a boiling-water bath. Let the jars cool and test for a seal. Stored in a cool, dry, dark place, the preserves will keep indefinitely.

VARIATION:

If you cannot find ground cherries, or if you have a bumper crop of pear tomatoes, substitute 3 pounds small yellow pear tomatoes.

GROUND CHERRIES

Ground cherries, *Physalis pubescens, are relatives of the tomatillo. Favored by German immigrants in the nineteenth century, ground cherries are still sown by Heartland gardeners among their corn plants. The small, round, yellow fruit is enclosed in a papery husk and grows on what looks like a tomato plant. It may be used in preserves, pies, chutneys, and salsas. Ground cherries ripen in early August.*

FRESH HORSERADISH SAUCE

Fresh horseradish sauce has a cleaner yet more pungent taste than a store-bought sauce. Mix this traditional condiment with lightly whipped cream to accompany a standing rib roast, or serve it as is with grilled bratwurst or a cottage ham. Most midwestern groceries now carry horseradish roots that you can peel and grind at home. Some farmers' markets offer fresh-ground horseradish in late summer and into the fall.

MAKES 4 1-CUP JARS SAUCE

½ pound fresh horseradish root, peeled
1¼ teaspoons salt
1 teaspoon sugar
2 cups white wine vinegar

1. Finely shred the horseradish with the shredding attachment on a food processor or by hand with a grater. (Be careful: As onions do, horseradish can make your eyes water.) Transfer the shredded horseradish to a large bowl, add the rest of the ingredients, and stir to blend evenly.

2. Funnel or spoon the sauce into four clean jars and cap the jars. Refrigerated, the sauce keeps for up to 1 year.

ITALIAN MARKET GARDEN RELISH

Many Italians who emigrated to the midwest came from Sicily. In Chicago and other big cities where they settled, they built neighborhood enclaves of "shotgun"-style homes—one room across and several rooms deep—with tidy fenced-in yards. However tiny the yard, a garden patch was always a must for the household. Many immigrants also became market gardeners, selling what they would grow on small plots of land they intensively farmed on the outskirts of the neighborhood. Today many of the largest produce suppliers to restaurants and groceries are the offspring and descendants of these market gardeners. This simple recipe, once made by market gardeners' wives to sell at market, makes a perfect picnic or potluck relish, especially attractive when packed into individual small canning jars.

MAKES 2 PINTS RELISH

½ small head of cauliflower, cut into small florets
2 carrots, peeled and cut into 2-inch-long, 1-inch-wide strips
2 celery ribs, diced fine
1 green bell pepper, cut into thin strips
4 ounces bottled pimientos, drained and cut into thin strips
3 ounces pitted green olives

¾ cup white wine vinegar
½ cup olive oil
½ teaspoon dried oregano
¼ teaspoon red pepper flakes
2 tablespoons sugar
1 teaspoon salt

1. In a large nonreactive skillet, bring all the ingredients plus ¼ cup water to a boil. Reduce the heat and simmer, covered, for 5 minutes. Remove the skillet from the heat, and let the relish cool slightly.

2. Spoon the relish into 2 clean pint jars and cap the jars. Refrigerate for at least 24 hours before serving. The relish will keep, covered in the refrigerator, for 3 to 4 days.

AMANA RADISH RELISH

Bunches of radishes always look so tempting piled high at farmers' markets or at the grocery store. But what do you do with them besides eating them raw, alone or in a salad? This zippy relish, a recipe from the Amana Colonies in Iowa, offers one tasty possibility. Serve it alongside pork chops, bratwurst, burgers, or fish.

MAKES 2 CUPS RELISH

1 pound radishes, trimmed
1 medium yellow onion, cut into
    thin strips

2 tablespoons whole allspice
    berries
¼ teaspoon whole cloves
1 teaspoon mustard seeds
1 cup distilled white vinegar
¾ cup sugar
½ teaspoon salt

1. By hand or with a food processor, cut the radishes into julienne strips. Place the radish and onion in a large metal bowl. Toss to blend, and set aside.

2. Make a spice bag by cutting out a square of cheesecloth, putting the allspice, cloves, and mustard seeds in the middle, and tying the corners of the cloth together with kitchen string. Place the bag in a saucepan, and add the vinegar, sugar, salt, and ¾ cup water. Bring the mixture to a boil, reduce the heat, and simmer, uncovered, for 10 minutes.

3. Pour the hot liquid over the radish and onion in the bowl. Let steep for 15 minutes. Pour the relish into a clean pint jar and let cool slightly. Cap the jar. The relish will keep, covered in the refrigerator, for 2 weeks.

PARADISE FOUND

Seeking a simpler, more perfect way of life, over a hundred utopian communities, founded by religious separatists or social reformers, sprang up in the Heartland in the nineteenth century. All of them made enduring contributions to the culture and ways of life, including the foodways, of the region.

The Shakers, a religious sect founded in England in 1774 by Mother Ann Lee and brought to New York in 1776, established communities in Ohio at Union Village (now Lebanon) and Watervliet (now Dayton) in 1812 and 1813. On the western outskirts of Cincinnati, the ghost buildings of the former Whitewater Shaker community (1824) stand stark and mute on a country lane. North Union (1826), in Cleveland, Ohio, continues its life as a museum, but the community founded in Busro, Indiana (1810), has been lost to time. The Shakers believed in a celibate life, with separate but equal housing, facilities, and employment for men and women. They lived in "families," in spacious center-hall homes divided in half, with men on one side and women on the other. Their communities were entirely self-supporting, and they also entertained any guests or outsiders who stopped by at mealtimes. The Shakers gained a reputation for their good food (see the Index for several Shaker-inspired recipes in this book) as well as their facility with medicinal herbs, their gracefully simple architecture, and their spare furniture styles.

The Mormons escaped religious persecution in New York and resettled in Nauvoo, Illinois, in 1839. Gradually, they went farther west, to Independence, Missouri, and then, of course, to Utah.

The Amana Colonies in southeastern Iowa were founded in 1855 by a religious group with a belief in a tight-knit communal life. Seven villages on twenty-six thousand acres once shared the bounty of the rich, rolling farmland. The communal way of life ceased in 1932, but the Colonies are still a destination, with four hundred historic buildings and many restaurants, shops, galleries, and museums open to the public.

Numerous Amish and Mennonite societies have found a haven in the midwest, in Ohio and Indiana, central and western Kansas, central Missouri, southwestern Minnesota, and northern Iowa. The simple abundance of their farm tables (see the Index for recipe examples) offers us all a taste of the not-too-distant agricultural past of many families.

For many, the Heartland is still a beacon, offering, in its small-town life, a slower pace and a place to grow a garden and a family.

WILD LEEK VINEGAR

When the lance-shaped leaves of wild leeks, also called ramps, peek out of the cold and damp soil of spring in the Upper Peninsula of Michigan, they are gathered by local foragers, much as morels are. With a sharper and more pungent flavor than domestic leeks, the wild variety is ideal to flavor a vinegar. Use this assertive condiment—a little goes a long way—to add a hint of leek to salads that include potatoes, cabbage, or beef. An empty tall bottle from a store-bought vinegar is ideal for this recipe, but you can use any lidded bottle you have on hand.

MAKES 1 CUP VINEGAR

4 wild leeks, cleaned well and trimmed to fit the size bottle you have
1 cup white wine vinegar

1. Stuff the leeks snugly into a glass bottle. Set aside.

2. Heat the vinegar in a nonreactive saucepan over medium-high heat until it is very hot, but not boiling. Using a funnel, pour the hot liquid into the bottle until the leeks are completely covered. Let the flavored vinegar cool to room temperature, cap the bottle, and let it sit for 2 weeks before using. If you want to keep the flavor from getting too strong, remove the leeks from the bottle after 2 or 3 weeks. Stored in a cool, dry, dark place, the vinegar will keep indefinitely.

VARIATIONS:

If you cannot find wild leeks, garlic chives, or long, thin wild onions, are good substitutes.

RED AND YELLOW PEPPERS IN WHITE WINE VINEGAR

Here is an appetizing way to preserve a summer's bounty of peppers. Dress the peppers with olive oil for a simple but vibrant salad, or use them instead of unflavored peppers in soups or stews.

MAKES 2 PINTS PEPPERS

5 cups white wine vinegar
1/2 teaspoon salt
2 medium red bell peppers, cut lengthwise into quarters
2 medium yellow bell peppers, cut lengthwise into quarters
4 bay leaves, as fresh as possible

1. Bring the vinegar and salt to a gentle boil in a large nonreactive saucepan. Add the peppers, and cook them, uncovered, just between a boil and a simmer for 15 minutes.

2. Remove the peppers with tongs and divide them between 2 clean pint jars. Using the tongs, tuck in 2 bay leaves on the sides of each jar. Fill the jars with the hot vinegar, making sure the vinegar completely covers the peppers. Let cool slightly, cap the jars, and keep in the refrigerator for 1 month to let the flavors develop. Refrigerated, the peppers will keep indefinitely.

ICICLE PICKLES

I first tasted these pickles in Ernestine Van Duvall's kitchen in Nicodemus, Kansas, when the temperature outside was 106 degrees in the shade. She had made them to accompany a barbecued rib dinner for Emancipation Days, held in late July. Cold, crisp, crunchy, and slightly sweet, they were just what my parched tastebuds wanted. Good home cooks all over the Heartland keep a tub of pickles like these in the refrigerator for days when temperatures soar and appetites flag. If you are a novice pickler, these quick pickles are a simple place to start. Sliced with a crinkle-cut slicer, they will stay even crisper. If you buy waxed cucumbers at the grocery store, carefully wash them with soap and water first to remove the protective coating.

MAKES ABOUT 3 QUARTS PICKLES

10 cups sliced (cut in 1/2-inch slices with a knife or a crinkle-cut slicer) pickling cucumbers

2 medium yellow onions, chopped
4 cups sugar
4 cups distilled white vinegar or cider vinegar
1/2 cup pickling salt
1 rounded teaspoon mustard seeds
1 rounded teaspoon celery seeds

1. Gently mix together the cucumbers and onions in a 3-quart plastic tub or container. Bring the remaining ingredients to a boil in a large nonreactive saucepan.

2. Pour the hot pickling liquid over the cucumbers. Let the pickles cool, then cover and refrigerate them for at least 24 hours so that the flavors will blend. Refrigerated, the pickles will keep indefinitely.

POLISH GARLIC DILL PICKLES

These crunchy dills are the pickles of choice to serve with a pastrami sandwich, a grilled brat, smoked ham on rye, or a big, sturdy midwestern cheese, like Mossholder or Klondike from Wisconsin. Use cucumbers from the garden or the farmers' market, if possible, for freshness and to avoid wax. (If you do buy waxed cucumbers, wash them well with soap and water to remove the protective coating.)

MAKES 9 PINTS PICKLES

4 pounds small (about 3-inch)
     pickling cucumbers
6 cups cider vinegar
2/3 cup pickling salt
1 whole head of garlic, cloves
     separated and peeled
4 tablespoons dill seeds
1 tablespoon whole black
     peppercorns

1. Sterilize 9 pint jars and lids and keep them hot. Wash the cucumbers well and trim off the blossom ends; do not peel. Combine the vinegar, pickling salt, and 6 cups water in a large nonreactive saucepan and bring to a boil.

2. Pack the cucumbers and garlic cloves into the hot jars. Divide the dill seeds and peppercorns evenly among the jars. Pour in the hot vinegar mixture, leaving 1/2 inch headspace so that the pickles do not touch the lid of the jar. Remove air bubbles with a plastic spatula. Cap the jars according to the manufacturer's directions.

3. Process the filled jars for 15 minutes in a boiling-water bath. Let the jars cool and test for a seal. Store in a cool, dry, dark place for 3 to 4 weeks so that the flavors will blend. The pickles will keep indefinitely.

BREW PUB
PICKLED ONIONS

The brew pubs that you find everywhere now in the midwest have helped revive regional cooking. In addition to the locally crafted beers and ales that are their specialty, they serve up lots of good and homey food, from artisan breads and regional cheeses to English condiments like this one. A crusty loaf of bread, a small pot of Home-Churned Butter (page 40), a tangy midwestern cheddar, a glass of a slightly bitter ale, and some of these pickled onions make a fine lunch.

MAKES 6 TO 8 8-OUNCE JARS

1/2 cup salt
2 pounds small white boiling or
     creamer onions, about 1 inch
     in diameter
5 cups malt vinegar
1/2 cup sugar
2 tablespoons mixed pickling spice
5 whole cloves
10 to 12 whole black peppercorns

1. The day or night before, place the salt in a bowl. Peel the onions, add them to the bowl, and toss gently to distribute the salt. Let the onions cure in the salt overnight.

2. The next day, wash the onions in cold water to remove the salt. Drain them and pat them dry. Bring the vinegar, sugar, pickling spice, cloves, and peppercorns to a boil in a

large nonreactive saucepan. Boil gently for 5 minutes, then add the onions. Bring the mixture back to a boil, reduce the heat, and simmer the onions for 8 minutes, or until they begin to be tender but still are crisp. Avoid overcooking them.

3. Transfer the onions to 6 to 8 hot, sterilized 8-ounce canning jars. Top up with the spiced liquid, leaving 1/4 inch headspace. Cap the jars according to the manufacturer's directions.

4. Process the jars for 10 minutes in a boiling-water bath. Let the jars cool and test for a seal. Let the onions steep for 3 weeks in a cool, dry, dark place before using. The onions will keep indefinitely.

PICKLED BEETS

Pickled beets are one of the "seven sours" that Eastern European immigrants brought to the midwest. The list varies by country of origin, but often includes sauerkraut, garlic dill pickles, pickled herring, pickled plums, horseradish, and marinated cucumbers. In some households, the pickled beets are blended with horseradish.

MAKES 1 TO 2 PINTS BEETS

2 pounds uncooked beets, peeled
1/2 cup vinegar
1 cup water
1 bay leaf
4 allspice berries
4 black peppercorns
1 whole clove
1 tablespoon sugar
1/4 teaspoon salt

1. In a 2-quart nonreactive saucepan, combine all of the ingredients except the beets. Bring to a boil, remove from the heat, and let cool while the beets cook.

2. Place the beets in a large saucepan, cover them with cold water, and bring them to a boil. Cook at a slow boil until they are tender, 45 minutes to 1 hour. Drain the beets and, when they are cool enough to handle, slice them thin. Discard the bay leaf from the marinade. Combine the beets and marinade and pour into clean jars. Cap the jars and refrigerate for 24 hours to let the flavors blend. The beets will keep indefinitely in the refrigerator.

AUTUMN IN MISSOURI

"Autumn in Missouri broke your heart. The tree-banked hillsides turned brilliant reds and oranges against the wide green slopes. In the event of an early snow, the grass, arrested by the cold, might stay green all winter. The streets, sidewalks, driveways, lawns, even the river, took on a slow mosaic until everything was covered with leaves."

—DEBORAH DIGGES, *Fugitive Spring*

PICK A PECK OF PEPPERS SAUCE

When fresh peppers of all varieties dominate your garden or the farmers' market, turn them into this satisfying sauce. Caramelizing the peppers and onions deepens and enriches the natural sweetness of the vegetables. Serve the sauce on pasta with parsley and grated Parmesan, spread it over a wheel of warm brie for an appetizer, or enjoy it as a sandwich filling.

MAKES 2 TO 3 CUPS SAUCE

1/2 cup olive oil
9 cups thin-sliced bell peppers
(from about 12 large peppers),
red, green, yellow, purple, or a
mix of colors
3 cups sliced mild to medium chile
peppers
9 cups thin-sliced yellow onions
(from about 9 large onions)
2 heads of garlic, cloves separated
and peeled

1. Heat the oil in a large stockpot over medium-high heat. Add the peppers, onions, and garlic, and cook, stirring frequently, until the vegetables are just beginning to brown, about 10 minutes.

2. Reduce the heat to low and cook for 1 to 1½ hours more, or until the peppers and onions are a dark, rich brown. Stir frequently to prevent burning. Serve immediately, let the sauce cool, transfer it to a covered container, and refrigerate for up to 2 weeks until ready to serve, or freeze.

HEARTLAND PARSLEY PESTO

As mainstream now as catsup, fresh pesto enriches sandwich fillings, pastas, and hors d'oeuvres of all kinds. Farmers' markets in and around the cities of the midwest often have vendors who make pesto fresh and sell it—sometimes the original Italian basil-and-pine nut version, and sometimes newer twists, like this midwestern parsley-and-pecan rendering, which takes only a few minutes to make. You can toss it with hot homemade noodles, slather it on toasted bread and top it with fresh tomatoes for an appetizer, or use it as a filling for grilled stuffed pork chops.

MAKES I CUP PESTO

1¼ cups packed fresh Italian
parsley leaves and stems
1/3 cup extra-virgin olive oil
2 tablespoons toasted chopped
pecans
2 tablespoons fresh-grated
Parmesan
1 teaspoon minced garlic
1/4 teaspoon salt

THE MIDWESTERN PANTRY

My grandparents lived in a Victorian shotgun-style house with one room behind the other. One of its fascinations for my sister and me was the pantry, a small room off the kitchen that had a wonderful, spicy smell. In the paneled pantry's built-in cabinet, my grandmother kept her kitchen essentials: flour, sugars, and salt; herbs and spices; home-canned goods; tins of crackers and cookies; shortening and oils; homemade dried egg noodles; dried beans; and potatoes and onions. In her large, light, airy kitchen, her big stove stood against one wall and diagonally across the room was her large porcelain sink with its grooved draining board. In the kitchen itself was little storage; that was the function of the pantry.

And that has been the function of the pantry ever since the Middle Ages.

Midwestern kitchens were the workhorses of the home, where food preparation, cooking, canning, laundry, and ironing were often done. Before modern convenience foods and twenty-four-hour supermarkets, food preparation took a lot of time. For a Sunday fried chicken dinner, the chicken had to be taken from the coop behind the house, killed, dipped in boiling water, plucked, singed, jointed, and fried. Homemade bread required hand kneading and two risings. Seasoned green beans were picked in the garden, cleaned, trimmed, and then simmered for hours. (Our taste for quickly sautéed or steamed vegetables is a recent one.) Potatoes had to be peeled and cut into pieces, but could be kept in cold salted water in a pan on the stove. Pies required cleaning and perhaps cutting the fruit, rolling out the pie crust, and mixing the filling ingredients together. A separate

Place all of the ingredients in a blender or food processor and process until smooth, if you like, or nearly smooth, if you prefer a pesto with some texture. Store in a jar with a tight-fitting lid in the refrigerator. The pesto will keep indefinitely.

CHILI SAUCE

The first fresh tomato from the garden is cause for celebration after all the pallid tomatoes of winter and spring. By the fiftieth or hundredth tomato, the celebration begins to wear thin and the law of marginal utility takes over. You're less thrilled. I first made this sauce one August day when we were moving into a new house and I had to do something with a "use it or lose it" tomato harvest. Whether you grow your own tomatoes or buy them by the bushel at farmers' markets, you'll be happy you invested a few hours to make this sauce. It is terrific on meatloaf or Santa Fe Trail Smothered Steak (page room for storage left the kitchen workspace uncluttered and ready for the next task.

After working hard on most of a meal, a cook could breathe a sigh of relief that she might choose from an array of pickled and preserved foods in her pantry to provide the first course. Perhaps pickled watermelon, beets preserved with horseradish, a jewel-toned homemade jelly for the bread, and a bowl of colorful corn relish would look pretty on the table and stave off appetites until the chicken was on the platter and the mashed potatoes in the bowl, ready to be carried to the table.

My own idea of a well-stocked prairie pantry includes a few items, both home-made and commercial, that I just have to have: good canned tomatoes, black beans, chicken broth, hominy, and evaporated milk; herbs and spices; wildflower honey; flours, sugars, and salt; a variety of dried pastas plus my own Homemade Egg Noodles (page 259), rolled very thin and dried; jellies and preserves I have made the previous summer and fall; garlic, pota-toes, and onions; dried beans, rice, cracked wheat, and oatmeal; and peanut butter. My larder also extends to the refrigerator, where I keep the homemade condiments presented in this book, a jar or two of lemon curd that seems to last indefinitely, a jar of yeast, homemade syrups, dried fruits like cherries and raisins, and my Amish Friendship Starter (see page 347). In the freezer, I count on at least one good pie, frozen homemade yeast rolls, a jar of fresh-squeezed lemon juice that I make up when lemons are inexpensive dur-ing the winter, packages of frozen berries and shoepeg corn, homemade applesauce and pear sauce, plus frozen meats and chicken. With a well-stocked dry pantry, refrigerated pantry, and frozen pantry, a fine dinner is always just minutes away from reality, even if you haven't had time to get to the supermarket.

---

181), as a marinade for other steaks, or as a condiment on sandwiches.

MAKES 9 TO 10
HALF-PINT JARS

6 pounds tomatoes
4 large green bell peppers, chopped
3 medium yellow onions, chopped
1/4 cup salt
1 cup sugar, or to taste
1/2 cup cider vinegar

1 to 2 tablespoons Fireworks Rub
(page 56)

1. Bring a large pot of water to a boil. Put the tomatoes in the boiling water, several at a time, until the skins begin to crack. Remove the tomatoes with a slotted spoon, let them cool, and peel and chop them.

2. Pour out the water from the pot, return the pot to the stove, and add the tomatoes and the rest of the ingredients. Bring to a boil,

reduce the heat, and simmer gently, uncovered, for about 2½ hours, or until the sauce is thick but not dry. Funnel the sauce into clean half-pint jars and freeze or keep in the refrigerator.

BREW PUB MOP

When meats are cooking slowly over a low outdoor fire, an occasional basting with a flavorful liquid makes the food taste better and helps retain moisture. That's where a good mop comes in. A mop can be as simple as coffee or cola administered to the meat with a dish mop, or as fancy as a complex creation brushed on with a brand new paintbrush. You can also use a mop as a marinade to flavor the meat before cooking; if you do so, play it safe and make up separate batches for marinating and basting. If you like, use your favorite local microbrew for a richer and more interesting taste.

MAKES 1 PINT MOP

1 12-ounce bottle of ale, lager, or
    wheat beer
½ cup canola oil or corn oil
¼ cup minced onion
Zest of 1 lemon
3 tablespoons sugar
1 tablespoon garlic salt

Stir together all of the ingredients in a large bowl. Pour the mop into a lidded glass jar to

store. Shake before using to baste flank steak, pork tenderloins, or chicken breasts on the grill or in the smoker. Or use it as a marinade, for the same foods. Refrigerated, the mop will keep indefinitely.

FIREWORKS RUB

A rub is a mixture of herbs, spices, and sugar that is rubbed into meat, chicken, or fish, usually for grilling or smoking. The rub creates a charry crust that seals in flavors and adds its own accents. This rub, which has a medium level of heat, goes well with grilled firm-fleshed fish, hamburgers, and pork chops, or with smoked brisket, pheasant, and baby back spareribs. You can also enjoy a savory dash of flavor by adding a tablespoon or two of this mixture to baked beans, cream cheese, or your favorite bread recipe.

MAKES ABOUT 1 CUP RUB

4 tablespoons chili powder
4 tablespoons ground cumin
4 tablespoons ground coriander
1 tablespoon ground cinnamon
2 tablespoons packed brown sugar
1 tablespoon salt
1 tablespoon red pepper flakes
2 tablespoons fresh-ground black
    pepper

Stir together all of the ingredients in a bowl. Transfer the rub to a lidded glass jar, and shake to blend more. Stored in a cool, dry, dark place, the rub will keep indefinitely, although the flavors will decline slowly over time.

Aromatic Herb Rub

Newfangled grillers and barbecuers in the prairie states like to blend old-time, down-home BBQ flavorings—the first four ingredients listed—with more exotic Old World tastes—the last three ingredients. Keep this blend on hand to rub on duck or chicken before it goes in the oven to roast, on meatloafs and pâtés, or on vegetables that are headed for the grill.

Makes 3 cups rub

1/4 cup garlic powder
1/4 cup white pepper
1/4 cup salt
1 tablespoon paprika
1/4 cup dried rosemary
1/4 cup fennel seeds
1/4 cup anise seeds

Stir together all of the ingredients in a bowl; or, if you prefer, grind together all of the ingredients in a spice grinder. Transfer the rub to a lidded glass jar or jars. Stored in a cool, dry, dark place, the rub will keep indefinitely, although the flavors will decline slowly over time.

Smoky, Spicy Barbecue Sauce

Homemade barbecue sauce has a fresher, richer taste than commercial varieties, and you can give it the signature flavor you want. This particular recipe makes a smoky, tangy, zippy sauce perfect for barbecued brisket and ribs. Or you may use it instead of catsup, over meatloaf for example.

Makes 1 pint sauce

1 large yellow onion, chopped
3/4 cup cider vinegar
3/4 cup packed brown sugar
1/2 cup honey
1/4 cup molasses, sorghum, or corn syrup
12 ounces tomato paste
1/4 cup brown mustard
1 teaspoon celery seeds
1 teaspoon ground cumin
1 teaspoon ground coriander
1 teaspoon garlic powder
1/4 teaspoon cayenne pepper
1/4 teaspoon bottled hot sauce
3 to 4 teaspoons liquid-smoke flavoring
1/4 teaspoon black pepper

1. Puree the onion, vinegar, brown sugar, honey, and molasses in a food processor or blender. Put the tomato paste in a large non-reactive saucepan over medium-low heat. Pour the onion puree into the tomato paste

KANSAS CITY BARBECUE

Traveling up from South America, the barbecue tradition has its roots in the foodways of rainforest Indians who smoked meats over green wood to preserve them for later use. Over time the technique spread to the South and from there to Missouri, where African-American residents used pit barbecues to smoke lesser and cheaper cuts of meat like spareribs and brisket. In 1916, Kansas Citian Henry Perry began selling barbecued turkey, duck, pig, and goose, and by 1929 he had three popular barbecue stands. As Perry's fame spread, he taught others the secrets of slow-smoking. One of his students was Charlie Bryant, the brother of soon-to-be-famous Arthur Bryant. The Bryants eventually took over Perry's business, calling it Charlie Bryant's. When Charlie died in 1952, it became Arthur Bryant's, whose barbecue rose to fame when Calvin Trillin extolled it as "the single best restaurant in the world." Today, Kansas City has over a hundred thriving barbecue joints, from your basic shack to the high-style K.C. Masterpiece, and thousands of Kansas Citians cook their own home-style "Q" on backyard smokers.

and stir to blend. Bring to a simmer. Add the rest of the seasonings, and simmer the sauce for 30 minutes, stirring occasionally.

2. Remove the saucepan from the heat and ladle the sauce into a sieve placed over a bowl. Press the sauce through the sieve with the back of a spoon. Transfer to a lidded jar. Refrigerated, the sauce will keep indefinitely. Reheat before using.

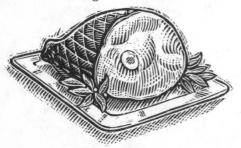

RED CURRANT SYRUP

Eastern Europeans brought to the midwest the practice of preserving red currants in syrups and jellies to last the long winter. A well-stocked pantry full of wonderful things the lady of the house has "put up" remains one of the glories of prairie home cooking. When the put up things are as easy to make as a homemade syrup, anyone can achieve some of that glory. I first made this when the three red currant bushes I had recently planted yielded only one cup of good fruit for me—the rest had been taken by the birds. Raspberries, blackberries, blueberries, or even wild fruits, such as elderberries, also would work well in this recipe. Serve over pancakes, rice pudding, pound cake, or ice cream, or use the syrup when you make your own sorbet.

MAKES 1 GENEROUS CUP SYRUP

1 cup red currants
1 cup sugar
Juice of 1/2 lemon

1. Bring the currants, sugar, and 1 cup water to a boil in a saucepan over medium heat. Reduce the heat and simmer, stirring occasionally, for 20 minutes. Make sure the sugar is completely dissolved.

2. Add the lemon juice and stir to blend. Strain through a fine-meshed sieve into a lidded bottle or jar, and let cool slightly. Cap the bottle. This brilliant red syrup keeps indefinitely in the refrigerator.

MIDSOMMERSDAG ELDERBERRY SYRUP

Midwestern communities that still keep alive their Swedish origins, such as Bishop Hill, Illinois, and Lindsborg, Kansas, honor the turnings of the traditional Swedish year with festivities that date back hundreds of years. St. Lucia Day, during the darkest days of mid-December, brings light into the winter gloom, and Midsommersdag, in June on the longest day of the year, turns the long hours of sunshine into a summer celebration. In Lindsborg, Swedish dancers perform their traditional steps in the street, children fashion flowering May crowns, and adults gobble up *ostkaka*, a cheesecake-like Swedish dessert. At the festival grounds, a large Maypole is festooned with cottonwood limbs and the young dancers clutch the garlands and swirl around each other, weaving a colorful pattern. In the Old Country, Midsommersdag celebrants enjoy a splash of this syrup with vodka or sparkling wine for a toast to summer. In the wheat-farming community of Lindsborg, however, when the wheat harvest is imminent at this time of year, elderberry syrup is more likely to be served over *ostkaka* or Swedish pancakes.

MAKES 1 GENEROUS CUP SYRUP

1 cup fresh elderberries or
   blackberries
1 cup sugar
1/2 teaspoon ground cinnamon
1/2 teaspoon fresh-grated nutmeg
Juice of 1/2 lemon

1. Bring the elderberries, sugar, cinnamon, nutmeg, and 1 cup water to a boil in a saucepan over medium heat. Reduce the heat and simmer, stirring occasionally, for 20 minutes. Make sure the sugar is completely dissolved.

2. Add the lemon juice and stir to blend. Strain the syrup through a fine-meshed sieve into a lidded bottle or jar. Let cool slightly,

AUGUST IS STATE FAIR TIME

During the 1850s, when the region was predominantly agricultural, state fairs became established throughout the Heartland. The first was the Ohio State Fair, held in Cincinnati in 1850. In 1859 Nebraska held a state fair before it was even a state.

The tradition continues, even though most midwestern states' economies are no longer primarily agricultural. The fairs run at different times from early August through Labor Day. Although livestock competitions remain popular, other events lack the participation they once had. There are far fewer farm wives who are full-time homemakers, and the ones who remain are not as given to entering their jams, jellies, preserves, and pies in the fairs' contests.

Still, fairgoers find plenty with which to keep themselves occupied. There's always the Butter Cow to view, a traditional state fair attraction that began at the Ohio State Fair in 1903. Today, the reigning queen of midwestern butter sculptors is Norma Duffield Lyon of Toledo, Iowa, who took up her craft in 1960. At the Iowa State Fair, she sculpts a life-size cow out of more than a quarter-ton of low-moisture sweet butter. She fashions it by hand in about sixteen hours, and then it is displayed in a 40-degree showcase in the Agricul-

ture Building. In 1994, "Duffy," as Lyon is known, gained national fame by sculpting a four hundred pound likeness of country music superstar Garth Brooks. In honor of Iowa's Sesquicentennial in 1996, she recreated Grant Wood's famed "American Gothic" in butter. In 1997 she sculpted Elvis Presley, marking the twentieth anniversary of the entertainer's death.

At the Iowa State Fair, visitors can watch competitions in areas as diverse as Apiary, Auctioneering, Auto Racing, Banjo, Guitar and Mandolin, Beef Cattle, Bench Press, Cats, Checkers, Chess, Cookout, Dairy Cattle, Dairy Goats, Dogs, Fiddlers, 4-H and FFA, Horses, Horseshoe Pitching, Horticulture and Floriculture, Llamas, Pigeons, Poultry, Rabbits, Sheep, State Fair Queen Pageant, Twins, and more.

Then there are the midway attractions. "It slices, it dices, it chops in seconds" and similar pitches entice fairgoers with the latest gadgets. Concessions offer special state fair food, from pork chop dinners in Iowa, barbecued rib dinners in Missouri, fried chicken dinners in Ohio, Indian tacos in Nebraska, and anything you want on a stick: cheese-on-a-stick, bamboo beef, smoked turkey legs, chocolate-covered frozen bananas, roasted corn, corn dogs, and kebabs.

cap the bottle, and store in the refrigerator. Refrigerated, this reddish-purple syrup keeps indefinitely.

Honeysuckle Syrup

The scent of honeysuckle seems to be the perfume the Heartland wears in late May and early June. It is so intoxicating that I've often wondered how I could capture the scent and flavor and keep it for the rest of the year. When I mentioned this once to my mother, she gave me this recipe, which she concocted after she gathered enough honeysuckle blossoms along the pathway where she walks every day. I gather my own honeysuckle from my backyard, where it makes a green "fence" for most of the year. Drizzle this syrup over luscious strawberries or use it to sweeten homemade lemonade. You can tailor this recipe to the amount of blossoms you gather. (If you do not have honeysuckle blossoms, then make Honey Syrup, similar in flavor, which follows as a Variation.)

MAKES ABOUT 4 CUPS SYRUP

4 cups packed honeysuckle
blossoms
Sugar
Lemon juice

1. Rinse the honeysuckle blossoms gently. Put the blossoms in a large saucepan and pour over enough boiling water to cover. Cover the saucepan, remove it from the heat, and let the mixture steep for 24 hours.

2. The next day, strain the cooled liquid into a large bowl, discarding the blossoms. Measure the liquid and pour it into a large saucepan. For each cup of the infusion, add 2 cups sugar and the juice of ½ lemon to the saucepan. Bring this mixture to a boil, reduce the heat, and simmer for 10 to 15 minutes, until the sugar is dissolved and the mixture has a syrupy texture. Remove the pan from the heat, let the syrup cool slightly, and pour into lidded glass bottles or jars. Refrigerated, the syrup will keep indefinitely.

VARIATION:

To make Honey Syrup, bring the juice of 2 lemons, 2 cups clover or blossom honey, and 2 cups water to a boil in a saucepan. Reduce the heat and simmer until the syrup is thick, about 15 minutes. Serve immediately, or store, covered, in the refrigerator.

Watermelon Syrup

In Russian Mennonite communities that dot the prairie from central Kansas up through the Dakotas to Saskatchewan and Manitoba, the love of watermelons is legendary. Farmers and gardeners prefer to grow the small, thick-skinned varieties that will keep well, wrapped in newspaper in a cool cellar, until they are served for the last time at Christmas. They also make this syrup of these sweet melons to use (in place of sugar) in making pfeffernüesse, or to drizzle on pancakes or coffeecakes.

MAKES ABOUT 2 CUPS SYRUP

3 small ripe watermelons or 1
large ripe watermelon
1 tablespoon sugar, or to taste

1. Cut the rind and green part off the watermelon and cube the red flesh. Discard the seeds. Transfer the flesh to a large stockpot. Cook the watermelon over medium-high heat, stirring occasionally, for 30 minutes, or until it has released nearly all of its juice and the pulp has cooked down. Remove from the heat and strain the juice through a cheesecloth-lined strainer or colander into a bowl.

2. Measure the juice in the bowl. For each 4 cups of juice, add 1 tablespoon of sugar to the bowl. Pour the juice and sugar into a saucepan, bring to a boil, reduce the heat, and simmer until the syrup has thickened and darkened, 1½ to 2 hours. Remove from the heat, let cool slightly, and pour into a lidded glass bottle. Refrigerated, the syrup keeps indefinitely.

PEACH LEAF SYRUP

When you make this delicate almond-flavored brew, make sure you use organic or unsprayed peach leaves. Use the leaves shortly after they are picked (if they dry out, the syrup will taste like tea). Or you can freeze them in a plastic bag; you do not need to thaw them before you make the syrup. Pears or peaches poached in this syrup are heavenly, and it also makes a refreshing sorbet.

MAKES ABOUT 3 CUPS SYRUP

24 fresh peach leaves
2 cups boiling water
Juice of 1 lemon
2 cups sugar

1. Rinse the peach leaves gently and let them drain for 10 to 15 minutes in a colander. Place the leaves in a small saucepan and pour the 2 cups boiling water over them. Cover the saucepan and let the mixture steep for 24 hours.

2. The next day, strain the steeped liquid through a sieve into a bowl. Discard the leaves. Add the lemon juice and sugar. Transfer the mixture to a large saucepan, bring to a boil, reduce the heat, and simmer for 10 to 15 minutes, or until the temperature of the syrup reaches 220 degrees on a candy thermometer (or until a drop placed on a

chilled saucer and refrigerated for 1 minute is thick and syrupy). Remove the syrup from the heat, let it cool slightly, and pour it into lidded glass bottles. Refrigerated, the syrup will keep indefinitely.

PRESERVED WATERMELON RIND

When I was a child in Cincinnati, my family took Sunday drives. Maybe we'd go to a farm auction, where my parents sought out country antiques. Or we might go to an orchard to pick apples and enjoy a cup of cider. Sometimes we would head across the border to Evansville, Indiana, where there was a restaurant we liked to go to for Sunday dinner. While everyone else anticipated the wonderful fried chicken dinner ahead of us, my sister and I had our eyes on the relish tray, of all things. That's because we loved watermelon pickles. When the little dish of these satin-smooth, tart yet sweet morsels was placed on the table, we'd wait until the adults started up their conversation again, then we'd try to sneak as many pickles as we could before someone could give us a look and say, "You'll spoil your dinner."

MAKES 7 PINTS

7 pounds watermelon rind
(from about 1 large melon),
with a small amount of pink
flesh left on
7 pounds sugar
1 quart apple cider vinegar
1 teaspoon clove oil
1 teaspoon cinnamon oil

1. Prepare the watermelon rind by peeling off most but not all of the dark green outside skin. You want the striped appearance of just a little pink fruit, pale green rind, and a slight darker green edge. Cut the rind into 1-inch-square pieces.

2. Put the rind pieces into a large saucepan or stockpot and add enough water to cover. Bring to a boil, reduce the heat, and simmer the rind until you can pierce it through with a fork, about 30 minutes. Remove from the heat and drain.

3. Bring the sugar and vinegar to a boil in a large saucepan. Add the oils, and stir to blend. Add the cooked watermelon rind, reduce the heat, and simmer for about 15 minutes, until the pieces are shiny and nearly transparent. Pack the rind in hot, sterilized canning jars. Top up with syrup, leaving 1/4 inch of headspace. Cap the jars according to the manufacturer's directions. Process the jars for 10 minutes in a boiling-water bath. Let the jars cool and test for a seal. Stored in a cool, dry, dark place, the pickles will keep indefinitely.

NOTE: Clove oil and cinnamon oil are available at specialty food stores and at larger drugstores.

HEARTLAND WINES

Before Prohibition, America's most productive winemaking state was not California but Missouri. Now wines from midwestern states are making a comeback. With European grapes grafted onto native varieties better equipped to withstand the hot summers and cold winters, varietals such as the Chardonnay-like vidal and seyval blanc, the Riesling-like vignole, and the full-bodied red Chambourcin are gaining an appreciative audience.

Founded in Hermann, Missouri, in 1847, the Stone Hill Winery produces a crisp white vidal and a pair of robust dry reds called Schoolhouse Red and Norton. In nearby August, Missouri, the Mount Pleasant Winery makes a delicious port. At Wisconsin's Wollersheim Winery, founded in the 1840s, a Prairie Fumé made from seyval blanc is the most popular wine. The lake effect in Michigan produces a microclimate favorable to the same grape varieties grown in Missouri, and seyval blancs, vignoles, and Chambourcins from Michigan are worth seeking out. Reds worth noting from Peterson and Sons winery in Kalamazoo include the Bonamego Red and the Chancellor Noir Dry; whites from the same producer include a Niagara-Delaware Dry and a Seyval Blanc Dry.

Sweeter "country wines," such as the rhubarb wine from the Amana Colonies in Iowa, the apple wine from Pirtle's Vineyard in Weston, Missouri, and the elderberry or cranberry wines from Peterson in Michigan, are good for sipping chilled or for poaching fruit.

CRABAPPLES IN CHAMBOURCIN

Once the province of farm wives and small-town homemakers, canning now is popular among big-city home cooks and even in upscale restaurants, where creative chefs take pride in producing their own signature salsas, vinegars, catsups, pickles, and preserves. As their colleagues do in other regions, midwestern chefs like to cook with local produce, and canning solves the problem of how to make the bounty last through the cold months. These crabapples, preserved in a spiced red wine that is made in Missouri and in Michigan, are a new take on traditional spiced crabs. Tiny lady apples and a cabernet sauvignon can be substituted in this recipe, which is a delicious accompaniment to roast pork, turkey, or game, or simply as part of a relish tray.

MAKES ABOUT 3 PINTS

2½ quarts crabapples or lady
   apples
1 bottle (750ml) Chambourcin
   wine or cabernet sauvignon
   wine
2 bay leaves
1 tablespoon juniper berries
3 cups cider vinegar
3 cups sugar
4 cinnamon sticks
1 tablespoon whole cloves
1 tablespoon whole allspice berries
1 whole nutmeg, cracked open with
   a nutcracker or hammer

1. Prick each of the crabapples several times with a fork to keep them from bursting. In a large stockpot, combine the wine, bay leaves, juniper berries, vinegar, sugar, and whole spices. Bring the mixture to a boil, then reduce the heat to a simmer. Poach the crabapples in batches until they are hot all the way through but still firm to the touch, about 5 minutes for each batch. Remove the crabapples with a slotted spoon and set them aside in a heatproof bowl until all the batches have been poached.

2. Bring the wine and spice mixture to a boil again. Boil for 5 minutes. Pour the hot liquid over the crabapples in the bowl and let sit for 8 hours or overnight.

3. Sterilize 3 1-pint canning jars and keep the jars hot. Remove the crabapples with a slotted spoon and pack them in the jars. Pour the wine and spices back into a saucepan and bring to a boil. Once the liquid is boiling, remove the pan from heat and strain the liquid through a sieve into a bowl or a large measuring cup with a spout. Pour the strained liquid over the crabapples in the jars, adding enough liquid to cover the fruit but leaving ¼ inch of headspace. Remove air bubbles with a plastic spatula, then cap the jars according to the manufacturer's directions.

4. Process the jars for 15 minutes in a boiling-water bath. Let the jars cool and test for a seal. Store in a cool, dry, dark place for 3 to 4 weeks to let the flavors blend. The crabapples will keep indefinitely.

PRESERVED PEARS WITH WINE, DRIED CHERRIES, AND LEMON

When my friend and fellow barbecue queen Karen Adler gave me a bag of dried cherries from Michigan last fall, her gift coincided with a glut of pears from my two pear trees. My family had already eaten pears in every conceivable way, and I had made a quart of French Valley Spiced Pear Cordial (page 112). That's when I dreamed up this recipe, which is like a deluxe version of poached pears. Over time, the dried cherries plump up and give a hint of almond flavor to the pears. Serve these pears as a quick dessert accompanied by a crisp cookie, or as a compote for a brunch. Or give them as a gift from your kitchen.

MAKES 6 8-OUNCE JARS PEARS

2 cups dry white wine
2 cups sugar
1 vanilla bean
Juice of 1 lemon
8 to 10 firm, ripe pears, peeled,
    cored, and sliced thin
6 tablespoons dried cherries
6 long strips of lemon zest

1. Sterilize 6 8-ounce canning jars and keep them hot.

2. Bring the wine, sugar, vanilla bean, lemon juice, and 2 cups of water to a boil in a large saucepan over medium-high heat. Continue to boil the mixture until it reaches a temperature of 200 degrees on a candy or instant-read thermometer and has thickened, 15 to 20 minutes.

3. Add the pear slices and cook them for 5 to 10 minutes, or until they have softened somewhat but still are firm. Remove the pears with a slotted spoon and pack the hot jars half full with the pears. Place 1 tablespoon of dried cherries and 1 strip of lemon zest over the pears in each jar, then fill the jar with more pears. Pour the hot cooking liquid over the pears in the jars, adding enough liquid to cover the fruit but leaving ¼ inch of headspace. Remove air bubbles with a plastic spatula, then cap the jars according to the manufacturer's directions.

4. Process the jars in a boiling-water bath for 10 minutes. Let the jars cool and test for a seal. Store in a cool, dry, dark place for 3 to 4 weeks to let the flavors blend. The pears will keep indefinitely.

LIKE A WILD CREATURE

"**P**reserving was almost a mania for Mrs. Bergson. Stout as she was, she roamed the scrubby banks of Norway Creek looking for fox grapes and goose plums, like a wild creature in search of prey. She made a yellow jam of the insipid ground-cherries that grew on the prairie, flavoring it with lemon peel."

—WILLA CATHER, O Pioneers!

GINGERED PEAR BUTTER

Fruit "butters" are a traditional European way of preserving fruits that results in a dark, sweet puree that may be spread on bread or other baked goods. Most Americans have had apple butter, but in the midwest, especially, fruit butters are made from all kinds of fruits—crabapple, peach, pear, quince, plum, and cherry, as well as apple, all are common—or from combinations of fruits. You can use this recipe as a model to experiment with your own fruit butters. Typical flavorings are spices such as cinnamon, allspice, and cloves; grated citrus peel or citrus juice; liqueurs; and extracts. For a light-colored butter, tie whole spices loosely in a cheesecloth bag; remove the bag after the butter is cooked. White or brown sugar may be used; note that brown sugar darkens butters made from light fruits and adds a more pronounced flavor. Any variety of pear works well in this recipe.

MAKES ABOUT 2 PINTS PEAR BUTTER

16 cups quartered peeled and
*   cored pears, from about 16 to*
*   20 large pears*
Sugar
2 tablespoons grated fresh ginger

1. Bring the pears and 8 cups of water to a boil in a large saucepan or stockpot. Reduce the heat and simmer, uncovered, for 15 to 20 minutes, or until the pears are quite soft. Remove the fruit with a slotted spoon and pass it through a food mill or press it through a fine sieve into a bowl. Discard the cooking liquid.

2. Preheat the oven to 300 degrees. Measure the sieved pear pulp and return it to its bowl. Add ½ cup sugar for each cup of pulp. Stir well to blend, then stir in the ginger. Spread out the sweetened pulp in a shallow non-reactive baking pan. Bake for 2 to 2½ hours,

stirring occasionally, until the butter is thick and has a spreadable consistency. Or test for doneness by placing a spoonful on a chilled saucer: If no rim of liquid forms around the edge of the butter, it is done. While the pears are baking, sterilize 4 half-pint canning jars and keep them hot.

3. Working quickly, ladle the pear butter into the hot jars, leaving ½ inch of headspace. Cap the jars according to the manufacturer's directions. Process in a boiling-water bath for 10 minutes. Let the jars cool and test for a seal. Stored in a cool, dry, dark place, the pear butter will keep indefinitely.

PLUM BUTTER

You can make this butter with wild plums or with domestic ones. Domestic plums are sweeter, so you use less sugar. This sweet spread is delicious on toasted homemade bread or as a filling for kolache. This recipe requires a slow-cooker.

MAKES 1 PINT PLUM BUTTER

1 quart wild or domestic plums
Sugar to taste, about 1 cup sugar
*   to 3 cups pulp for wild plums*
*   or ¾ cup sugar to 3 cups pulp*
*   for domestic plums*
¼ teaspoon fresh-grated nutmeg
¼ teaspoon ground cinnamon

1. Bring the plums and 2 cups of water to a boil in a large stockpot. Reduce the heat and simmer, covered, for 5 minutes. Continue simmering, but after 5 minutes begin stirring occasionally and checking the plums to see if their skins are bursting. Once the skins of half the plums have burst, turn the plums out into a colander to drain.

2. In batches, press the plums through a sieve or pass them through a food mill into a bowl. You want the plum flesh, not the skin and pit.

3. Measure the plum pulp and return it to its bowl. For wild plums, add 1 cup sugar for every 3 cups of pulp; for domestic plums, add ¾ cup sugar per 3 cups of pulp. Stir to blend, then stir in the nutmeg and cinnamon.

4. Transfer the seasoned pulp to a slow cooker. Cook, uncovered, for 8 hours on low heat until the plum butter has darkened and has thickened to a spreading consistency. Transfer the butter to a lidded glass jar. Refrigerated, the butter will keep indefinitely.

GOOD AND SIMPLE APPLESAUCE

Every year in the late summer and early fall my mother visits the orchards near her home in Ohio, looking for the best apples from which to make homemade applesauce. When you taste hers, which this recipe is, or another good homemade one, and then taste most commercial varieties, there's no comparison. You'll want a good cooking apple that melts down to a fine puree: Transparent, Lodi, Duchess, or Rhode Island Greening are all good prospects, but you also can use Jonathans or Golden Delicious. You can mix apple varieties, too, if you like. For a wintertime breakfast treat, serve this applesauce warm, sweetened with a little sugar and mellowed with a little vanilla.

MAKES 3 QUARTS APPLESAUCE

6 cups unsweetened apple cider
5 pounds cooking apples, cored
and quartered
Pinch of salt

1. Bring the cider to a boil in a large stockpot. Boil until the cider is reduced by half, 8 to 10 minutes. Add the apples and salt, and bring the liquid back to a boil. Reduce the heat and simmer, stirring occasionally, for about 45 minutes, until the mixture is a thick puree.

2. While the apples cook, sterilize 3 1-quart canning jars and keep them hot.

3. Remove the apple skins and any remaining seeds by passing the pulp through a fine-meshed sieve over a bowl.

4. Funnel the applesauce into the jars and cap them according to the manufacturer's directions. Process the jars in a boiling-water bath for 10 minutes. Let the jars cool, then test for a seal. Stored in a cool, dry, dark place, the applesauce will keep indefinitely.

NOTE: Instead of canning the applesauce, you may funnel it into plastic containers and freeze it.

ANTIQUE APPLES

Thank goodness for John Chapman, a.k.a. Johnny Appleseed, who wandered the wilderness that was the midwest, dropping apple seeds as he went. Born in Massachusetts in 1774, he died in Fort Wayne, Indiana, in 1845. By the late nineteenth century, orchards were common and apples were the midwest's favorite fruit. Apple cider, butter, dumplings, pies, and charlottes, and, of course, applesauce, have long been part of the Heartland's culinary repertoire.

Some midwestern apples, including heirloom varieties recently receiving new attention:

* *BLACK AMISH. An extra-tart variety delicious as a baked apple or eaten out of hand.*

* *LODI. A light-green summer apple, for cooking, especially applesauce.*

* *MISSOURI PIPPIN. Planted extensively in the midwest after the Civil War. Bright red with a firm texture, it is easy to grow and has a mild flavor.*

* *PLUMB CIDER. A yellow apple, shaded with red, that ripens in October. First recorded in Milton, Wisconsin, in 1844, it "disappeared" until 1989, when it was rediscovered. As its name implies, a good apple for cider.*

* *PRAIRIE SPY. Developed in 1940 at the University of Minnesota, a crisp and intensely flavored apple wonderful for pies.*

* *TRANSPARENT. A green apple common to Heartland farms but not widely known outside the midwest. Cooks up to a fine paste, making it perfect for applesauce or apple butter.*

* *WHITE WINTER PEARMAIN. A nineteenth-century variety from Indiana, yellow with a pink blush. Its fine, crisp, aromatic flavor is wonderful for eating out of hand, but it does not keep well.*

* *WHITNEY CRAB. Bears sweet crabapples in July and August that are delicious for eating out of hand, or for canning, coddling, or pickling.*

ORCHARD APPLE CHUTNEY

The apple season in the Heartland begins when the green Transparent apples ripen in late June and early July. Transparents are good for applesauce and pies, but they taste too "green" to eat out of hand. Jonathan, McIntosh, or Granny Smith, work best in this recipe. The chutney is a great accompaniment to smoked turkey or pheasant, and goes well alongside Quiltmaker's Cakes (page 86) or Herbed Sausage Patties (page 29).

MAKES ABOUT 2 CUPS CHUTNEY

2 cups rice vinegar
3/4 cup packed brown sugar
1/2 large red bell pepper, diced
2 large jalapeño peppers, seeded
    and diced
2 tablespoons diced yellow onion
3 tart, firm apples, peeled, cored,
    and diced
Juice of 1 lemon

1. Sterilize 2 half-pint canning jars and keep them hot.

2. Bring the vinegar and sugar to a boil in a large saucepan. Stir to dissolve the sugar completely. Add the bell pepper, jalapeños, and onion, and continue to boil for 8 minutes. Add the apples, reduce the heat, and simmer until the apples are tender, about 10 minutes more. Remove from the heat and stir in the lemon juice.

3. Spoon or ladle the chutney into the jars. Cap the jars according the manufacturer's directions. Process for 10 minutes in a boiling-water bath. Let cool and test for a seal. Stored in a cool, dry, dark place, the chutney will last indefinitely.

VARIATION:

If you do not want to process and can the chutney, spoon or ladle it (in step 3) into sterilized lidded jars. Let cool slightly, and refrigerate. This version will keep for 2 weeks in the refrigerator.

BLUE RIBBON MINCEMEAT

In the 1945 film "State Fair," the fortunes of the Frake family at the Iowa State Fair revolve around Blue Boy, the prize Hampshire boar, and Mrs. Frake's pickles and mincemeat. Blue Boy wins the top prize, perking up for the judges at the last minute, thanks to the prize Hampshire sow he has his eye on. And Mrs. Frake wins a special award of distinction when one of the judges just can't get enough of her mincemeat, liberally enlivened with brandy. I like to think this is Mrs. Frake's secret recipe. I use this rich mincemeat as a filling in miniature tarts for hungry carolers at Christmas. You can put a small dollop of mincemeat on top of a sliver of smoked ham, turkey, or pheasant for a cock-tail nibble. A jar of this prize mincemeat makes a great hostess gift, too.

MAKES ABOUT 10 CUPS MINCEMEAT

1 lemon
1 orange
¼ pound shredded beef suet
    (order from the butcher)
1 cup chopped hardshell or
    softshell pecans
1 cup chopped almonds
¾ cup dark raisins
¾ cup golden raisins
1 cup dried cherries
¼ cup sorghum or molasses
1¼ cups packed dark brown
    sugar
1 tablespoon ground cinnamon
3 teaspoons ground allspice
1½ teaspoons fresh-grated
    nutmeg
¼ teaspoon salt
1 cup brandy
4 tart apples, peeled, cored, and
    chopped

1. Grate the zests of the lemon and the orange into a large bowl. Squeeze the juice of the lemon and orange over the zest. Add the remaining ingredients and stir well to blend.

2. Transfer the mincemeat to covered plastic or glass pint containers. Refrigerate, and let the flavors blend for at least 2 days, and preferably 1 week, before using. The mince-meat will keep, covered in the refrigerator,

for 3 to 4 months; the flavor gets better with longer storage.

STAR-SPANGLED GOOSEBERRY AND ELDERFLOWER CONSERVE

Happily for us, the wild elderberry bush blossoms into large, lacy white flowers in June, at just the same time that gooseberries ripen. The tart flavor of gooseberry and the mellow vanilla scent of elderflowers combine very nicely. I pick my elderflowers along country lanes not far from where I live, but you also can grow the plant in your garden for a ready harvest of elderflowers and, later, elderberries. Use this as a filling for a jelly roll, spread it on homemade rolls, or serve it atop a wheel of brie that you have warmed to just melting in the oven.

MAKES 4 CUPS CONSERVE

4 pounds ripe green gooseberries
4 cups sugar
2 large elderflower heads, gently
    rinsed and patted dry
Juice of ½ lemon

1. Trim the stems and the knobby ends from the gooseberries. Place them in a large sauce-pan or stockpot with the sugar and 2 cups of

ELDERFLOWERS AND ELDERBERRIES

In late spring the white flower heads of the bushy elder tree, Sambucus canadensis, have a taste that resembles vanilla; add them when you cook gooseberries for pies, or when you make the conserve on page 71. Or use them to make an elderflower cordial. Dark purple elderberries, which you can pick from late July on, make a flavorful jelly or a sweet wine. Look for elder bushes along fences or the edges of fields, but do not gather them if there is a chance they have been sprayed. Rinse elderflower heads carefully after you gather them to remove any unwanted bugs. Nurseries specializing in prairie plants and wildflowers now have native elder for you to plant in your garden at home.

water. Bring to a boil, reduce the heat, and simmer, uncovered, until the gooseberries are soft and the syrup has thickened, about 15 minutes. Gently stir in one of the elderflower heads and simmer for 5 minutes more.

2. Stir in the lemon juice and remove the pan from heat. Remove and discard the elderflower head. Using kitchen shears or your fingers, remove some of the star-shaped blossoms

from the remaining elderflower head. Gently stir the blossoms into the conserve.

3. Spoon or ladle the conserve into lidded jars or jam pots. Let cool slightly, cover, and refrigerate. The conserve will keep indefinitely.

NOTE: You may substitute 1 vanilla bean for the elderberry flowers. Stir it in when the first elderflower head is added, in step 1.

OLD WORLD RED CURRANT JELLY

When German, Polish, and Bohemian immigrants first came to the prairie and endured the long, cold winter in a sod hut in Nebraska, a dugout in a creek bank in Kansas, or a flimsy shanty in the Dakotas, they dreamed of the fields they would plant and the gardens they would tend when warm weather came. Enterprising immigrants brought seeds of their favorite Old World plants with them to start in gardens an ocean and a prairie away. Because red currant jelly features in many northern European dishes, that custom continues today. Red currants bear fruit just once a year, and thus are very expensive to buy—when you can find them. Most midwesterners who love red currants grow their own, and many prepare this deep red jewel-like jelly, so simple to make, with their harvest. The pectin that gels the juice is in the red currant skins; if you let the fruit sit in water for too long, the jelly will not gel. This recipe uses equal weights of berries and sugar, so adapt it to the amount of red currants you have. Use it to flavor braised red cabbage, add it to a cream sauce with roast pheasant, pair it with a custard filling in an old-fashioned jelly roll, or spread it on toasted homemade bread.

MAKES 3 CUPS JELLY

*1 pound red currants, rinsed but
not stemmed
1 pound sugar*

1. Have ready 3 clean 8-ounce glass jars and lids.

2. Place the red currants and the sugar in a heavy-bottomed preserving pan or saucepan and pour 1 cup of water over all. Bring the mixture to a boil over medium-high heat, stirring to dissolve the sugar. Let the mixture boil for exactly 8 minutes.

3. While the red currants are cooking, line a sieve with a double thickness of cheesecloth and place the sieve over a bowl. When the 8 minutes are up, remove the mixture from the heat and carefully pour the berries and the cooking liquid into the lined sieve. Let the juice drain into the bowl for about 15 minutes, then press very lightly on the berries caught in the sieve. (If you press too hard, the jelly will become cloudy.) Remove the sieve and discard the cheesecloth and cooked red currants. Funnel the hot juice into the jars.

Let the jelly cool; it will set as it does so. When the jelly is cool, put on the lids and refrigerate until ready to use. The jelly will keep indefinitely.

CHOKECHERRY AND BUFFALO BERRY JELLY

Both of these tasty wild fruits ripen in July in the northern Plains, and together they make a delicious jelly. Chokecherries do not contain pectin, and so need help from other fruits that do.

MAKES 4 TO 5 PINTS JELLY

*4 cups ripe chokecherries
4 cups ripe buffalo berries
Sugar
Lemon juice to taste*

1. The day before you make the jelly, place the 2 fruits in a kettle or stockpot with just enough water to cover. Bring to a boil over medium-high heat, reduce the heat, and simmer, uncovered, until the fruits are tender, about 15 minutes. Remove the kettle from the heat. Set a jelly bag or colander lined with a double thickness of cheesecloth over a bowl or pot. Pour the contents of the kettle into the jelly bag. Let the juices drain through overnight.

2. The next day, sterilize 8 to 10 half-pint jelly jars and lids and keep them hot. Measure the amount of drained juice. Transfer the juice to a saucepan and, for each cup of juice, add 1 cup of sugar. Bring the mixture to a boil, stirring to dissolve the sugar. Boil the mixture rapidly until the set stage, about 20 minutes. To test for readiness to set, place a spoonful of the mixture on a chilled plate; if it holds its shape and does not run, it is ready.

3. Spoon or ladle the jelly into the hot jars. Cap the jars according to the manufacturer's directions. Process the jars in a boiling-water bath for 10 minutes. Let cool and test for a seal. Stored in a cool, dry, dark place, the jelly will keep indefinitely.

WILD PLUM JELLY

Wild plums grow abundantly on the western prairie, in thickets in low-lying areas near creek banks where moisture is more reliable. About the size of large cherries, and varying in color from orange to fuchsia to burgundy, wild plums ripen in July.

MAKES 4 TO 5 PINTS JELLY

8 cups wild plums
Sugar

1. The day before you make the jelly, wash the plums well and discard any damaged fruit.

Place the plums in a large preserving kettle or stockpot. Add water to a level just below the top layer of the fruit. Bring to a boil over medium-high heat, reduce the heat, and simmer, uncovered, until the fruit is quite soft, about 15 minutes. As the plums cook, use a potato masher or another utensil to break their skins and to separate the flesh from the stone.

2. Meanwhile, set a jelly bag or colander lined with a double thickness of cheesecloth over a bowl or crock. When the plums are cooked, pour the contents of the kettle into the jelly bag. Let the juices drain through overnight. (Do not press the mixture; that will make the jelly cloudy.)

3. The next day, sterilize 8 to 10 half-pint jars and lids and keep them hot. Measure the drained juice and transfer it to a saucepan. Bring to a boil over medium-high heat, and boil for 3 minutes. Add ¾ cup sugar for each cup of juice, stir, and bring to the boil again. Boil briskly, uncovered, until the sweetened juice reaches the jelly stage—when it coats the back of a spoon—about 20 minutes.

4. Spoon or ladle the jelly into the hot jars, leaving ¼ inch headspace. Cap the jars according to the manufacturer's directions. Process the jars in a boiling-water bath for 10 minutes. Let cool and test for a seal. Stored in a cool, dry, dark place, the jelly will keep indefinitely.

WILD PLUMS

The wild plum, Prunus americanus, known in the prairie states also as the sand hill plum, is a favorite among midwesterners who like to make their own jelly. These tasty native fruits were recognized and prized by early travelers and homesteaders in the midwest.

Lewis and Clark noted the wealth of wild fruit along the banks of the Missouri River in what is now Jackson County, Missouri, in June of 1805: "The prairies here approach the river and contain many fruits, such as plums, raspberries, wild apples, and, nearer the river, vast quantities of mulberries." Laura Ingalls Wilder introduced young readers to the shrub in her novel On the Banks of Plum Creek, in which she wrote that one knew spring had come in Minnesota when "willow and cottonwood and plum thickets put out leaves again." In the 1860s, the vegetarian pioneer Miriam Colt Davis wrote in her first-person narrative, Went to Kansas, that "our neighbors keep us well supplied with wild red plums; they are very sweet and delicious, as are the strawberry tomatoes [ground cherries] which are indigenous to the soil." Mary Hartwell Catherwood, in her novel Steven Guthrie, wrote about playing in an Indiana plum thicket: "She stood again in the thick grove which was like an oasis in the prairie and saw the horizon-bounded plain sweeping off to the ends of the earth. . . . Again she felt the plums rattle down on her sunbonneted head and gathered her apron full, shouting with the other children."

The bushy wild plum shrub grows in low-lying areas along creek or river banks where there is plenty of moisture in the otherwise dry prairie. The small apricot-sized fruits range in color from a bright pink mottled with gold to a dark purple. They ripen in the latter half of July. Eaten out of hand, the wild plum does not have much pulp and can be rather bitter. That is why the preferred method of using them is to boil them to extract the juice, and then to mix the juice with sugar to make delicious jellies that range in color from a deep pink to a dark purple. Because the plums ripen when the temperature can soar over a hundred degrees, some cooks freeze the juice and make jelly later on, when the kitchen is cooler. Regional wild plum jellies are also available in midwestern grocery stores and specialty food stores, and by mail-order.

DOOR COUNTY CHERRY JAM

On this Wisconsin peninsula, which juts out into Lake Michigan south and east of Green Bay, over seven hundred thousand sour-cherry trees burst into blossom in May, an unforgettable sight. Once the cherries start to ripen in mid July, a frenzy of activity begins, in which cherry-picking alternates with pie-baking and jam-making, all to get the best of these bright red jewels. If you do not have a cherry orchard nearby, substitute whole sour cherries frozen without syrup.

MAKES 3 PINTS JELLY

3½ cups chopped pitted sour
    cherries
4½ cups sugar
½ cup amaretto liqueur
3 ounces liquid pectin

1. Sterilize 6 half-pint jars and lids and keep them hot.

2. Combine the cherries, sugar, and amaretto in a large kettle or stockpot. Bring the mixture to a full rolling boil over high heat, stirring constantly. Continuing to stir, boil hard for exactly 1 minute. Remove the kettle from the heat and stir in the pectin. Skim off any foam with a large metal spoon.

3. Ladle the jelly immediately into the hot jars, leaving ¼ inch headspace. Cap the jars according to the manufacturer's directions. Process the jars for 10 minutes in a boiling-water bath. Let cool and test for a seal. Stored in a cool, dry, dark place, the jelly will keep indefinitely.

SUMMER PEACH JAM

For me, this jam defines summer. It seems magical how these few simple ingredients come together to create something so splendid.

MAKES 4 PINTS JAM

10 cups chopped peach flesh, from
    about 5 pounds (or 12 large)
    firm, ripe, peeled peaches
3 tablespoons fresh lemon juice
5 cups sugar

1. Place the peaches, lemon juice, and sugar in a large bowl and let sit for 1 hour. Meanwhile, sterilize 8 half-pint jars and lids and keep them hot.

2. Transfer the peach mixture to an 8-quart or larger pot. Bring to a boil, reduce the heat, and simmer, uncovered, until the sugar is dissolved, about 15 minutes.

3. Bring the mixture to a full boil over medium-high heat, and boil constantly until

the jelly stage is reached, about 25 minutes; stir occasionally at first and then constantly as the mixture nears the jelly stage. To test for doneness, place a small spoonful of jam on a chilled saucer; if the jam holds its shape and no ring of moisture forms, it is ready.

Remove from the heat and skim off any foam with a large metal spoon.

4. Ladle the jam quickly into the hot jars, leaving ½ inch headspace. Cap the jars according to the manufacturer's directions. Process

CANNING

For early settlers in the midwest, putting foods by was a necessity for survival through the winter. At first, salt, sugar, smoke, and dehydration were the most common preservation agents. Other foods were kept in crocks under thick layers of lard, and still others were preserved in corked bottles sealed with wax.

Canning—preserving food in a vacuum-sealed container—was invented in the early nineteenth century. Napoleon's army used canned foods on the march, but it was a labor-intensive process at first. A cooper or tinsmith would have to make each can by hand, forming a sheet of tin into a cylinder, then soldering on the bottom and top lids. A hole was left in the top lid and food was funneled into the can. Then the can was sealed and the whole thing boiled to sterilize the contents.

Cans were opened by punching holes in them or by removing a strip of metal around the can. The earliest can openers were invented by 1858. By the time of the great push westward in the 1840s and beyond, canned goods were a part of every chuckwagon and prairie schooner headed west, along with bacon, cornmeal, flour, coffee, and beans. Because fresh milk was hard to come by, pioneers and homesteaders developed a taste for canned milk, for stirring into their coffee or whipping into their mashed potatoes. Canned tomatoes and peaches also were welcome additions to the basic chuckwagon staples.

The glass Mason jar was not as portable if you were hitting the trail, but it became a fixture of the well-stocked midwestern larder. In 1858, John L. Mason invented a glass jar with a threaded opening that allowed a metal cap to be screwed on for a tight seal; a rubber ring was added as a gasket to make the seal airtight. In 1903, Alexander H. Kerr refined the technology with a lid that included the rubber gasket. In 1915, Kerr invented the two-piece cap, which allowed air to escape when heated and created a seal when cooled.

the jars for 10 minutes in a boiling-water bath. Let cool and test for a seal. Stored in a cool, dry, dark place, the jam will keep indefinitely.

HONEYED CARROT-GINGER MARMALADE

Tasting this simple yet extraordinary conserve is like eating a spoonful of sunshine. By making this with wildflower honey, you get a taste of summer all year long. Use this marmalade as filling for a cake or for jelly rolls, serve it with cream cheese in a delicate tea sandwich, or simply spread it on good bread. Or just sneak a spoonful straight out of the jar!

MAKES 8 CUPS MARMALADE

8 cups peeled and finely shredded carrots
1 4-inch-long piece of fresh ginger, peeled and shredded
4 cups wildflower or other medium-colored honey
Juice of 2 lemons

1. Stir together the carrots, ginger, and honey in a bowl. Let sit for several hours or overnight.

2. Transfer the mixture to a saucepan or stockpot and cook over very low heat for 1½ to 2 hours, or until the carrots are translucent. (You can do this in a slow-cooker set on low, too.) Add the lemon juice and stir to blend well.

3. Spoon the marmalade into 8 half-pint jars, cap the jars, and refrigerate. Refrigerated, the marmalade will keep indefinitely.

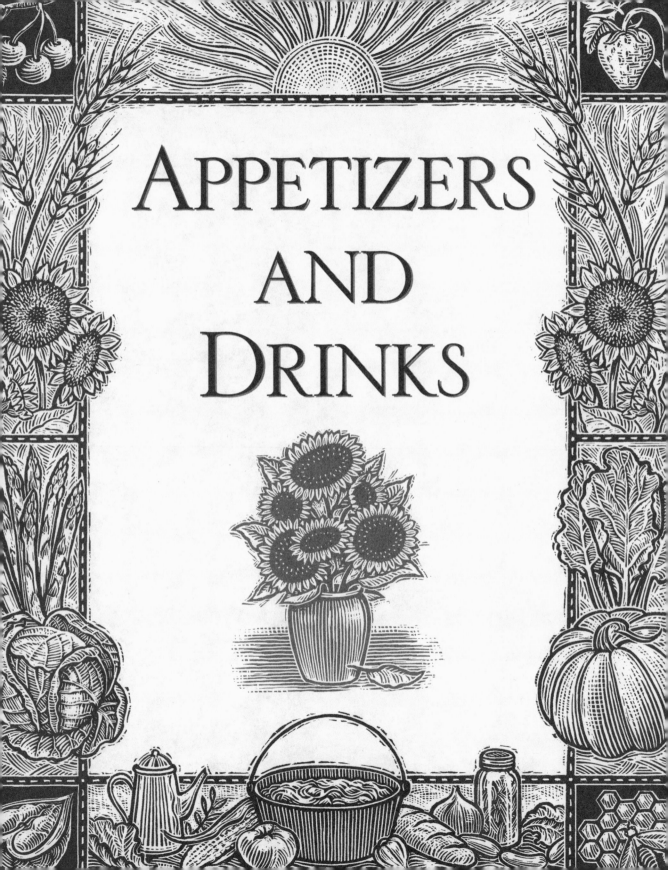

APPETIZERS
AND
DRINKS

APPETIZERS AND DRINKS

APPETIZERS

DRINKS

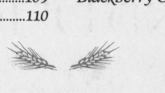

TARRAGON PICKLED VEGETABLES

Choose the freshest and tiniest vegetables for this recipe, a wonderful accompaniment to grilled meats, Prairie Pâté (page 101), and just about any light summer or picnic fare. You can bottle them up in individual canning jars or you can make a single large batch in a plastic container.

MAKES 8 1-CUP JARS OR 2 QUARTS

2 pounds haricots verts or other
  thin green beans, stem ends
  trimmed, or 2 pounds thin
  asparagus, tough ends
  removed
1 pound baby carrots, with some of
  tops left on for decoration, if
  you like
1 pound mushrooms, stems
  trimmed
8 sprigs fresh tarragon
4 cups tarragon vinegar
4 teaspoons dried tarragon
Juice of 2 lemons
3 cups sugar

1. In separate saucepans, steam each of the vegetables until they are just tender. Drain, refresh under cold water, pat dry, and let cool slightly. If you are using 1-cup canning jars, cut the beans or asparagus to lengths that fit the height of the jars. If not, leave the beans or asparagus as they are.

2. Arrange the vegetables decoratively in the 8 individual jars, adding a sprig of tarragon to each; or assemble the vegetables and tarragon sprigs in a large sealable plastic container. Combine the vinegar, dried tarragon, lemon juice, and sugar in a saucepan, bring to a boil, and stir until the sugar has dissolved. Pour some of the mixture into each canning jar, or pour all of it into the plastic container. Cover and refrigerate for 3 to 4 hours or overnight. Serve cold or at room temperature. The pickles will keep, refrigerated, for 2 to 3 days.

PRAIRIE SAGE POTATO CRISPS

You can serve these thin, nearly translucent potato "sandwiches," with their hints of green sage inside, as an appetizer or as a casual side dish, perhaps with chicken or a game bird.

SERVES 4

4 large baking potatoes, peeled and
  sliced very thin lengthwise
1/2 pound (2 sticks) butter, melted
32 fresh sage leaves
Salt and white pepper, preferably
  fresh-ground, to taste

1. Preheat the oven to 350 degrees. Lightly oil or butter a large baking sheet. Select the

longer and better-looking potato slices and discard any discolored ones. Transfer the melted butter to a small dipping bowl.

2. Dip a potato slice into the butter and place the slice on your work surface. Top the slice lengthwise with a sage leaf, and add a pinch of salt and a sprinkling of white pepper. Dip a second potato slice in the butter and place it on top of the first slice to make a sandwich. Transfer the sandwich to the baking sheet, and continue making sandwiches until all the sage leaves are used.

ON THE RANGE

In the northwestern corner of Nebraska, along the Wyoming and South Dakota borders, the Oglala National Grasslands give the traveler a peek at what "Home on the Range" was really like. Although the lyrics to the song were written by Smith County, Kansas, homesteader Brewster Higley in 1871, the Grasslands are the place to go nowadays if you want to see the deer and the antelope play. Perhaps the country's most important intact prairie wilderness, the Grasslands, which once were part of the Oglala Sioux domain, are home to pronghorn antelopes, black-tailed prairie dogs, eagles, foxes, coyotes, prairie hawks, and a wealth of rare native grasses and wildflowers.

3. Bake for 15 to 20 minutes, turning the sandwiches 2 or 3 times, until the potatoes are crisp and golden brown. Let them cool to room temperature, and serve.

HICKORY-SMOKED PECANS

Groves of black walnut, hickory, and native pecan trees line river banks throughout the central midwest. In the fall, the nuts are harvested and sold at farmstands and farmers' markets. If you cannot use fresh nuts within a week or two, freeze them so they stay fresh. Or make several batches of these savory nuts and store them in an airtight container.

MAKES 4 CUPS NUTS

1 tablespoon Fireworks Rub
   (page 56)
2 garlic cloves, minced
¼ cup Worcestershire sauce
1 teaspoon sugar
4 cups whole pecans (see Note)

1. Combine the rub, garlic, Worcestershire, sugar, and ½ cup water in a medium bowl. Add the pecans and stir or toss to coat them. Let them marinate for at least 1 hour at room temperature. If you have a smoker, soak 3 to 4 chunks of hickory wood in water for 30 minutes; if you have a covered charcoal or gas

grill, soak 2 handfuls of hickory chips in water for 30 minutes.

2. If you have a smoker: Add the hickory chunks and bring the temperature to 225 degrees. If you have a covered charcoal or gas grill: Build a low-heat indirect fire and bring the temperature to 225 degrees. Wrap the chips in foil, perforate the foil several times, and, when you are ready for the next step, place the foil wrapper(s) on the coals or lava.

3. Drain the pecans and arrange them on a disposable aluminum baking sheet. Place the baking sheet on the smoker or grill and smoke, covered, for 1 hour, or until the pecans are crisp and taste lightly smoked. Serve immediately, or store in an airtight container until ready to serve.

NOTE: I prefer this recipe with pecans, but almonds, hickory nuts, or walnuts are also very good prepared this way.

RYE BREAD TOASTS WITH ACORN SQUASH AND FRIED SAGE

Sauerkraut Rye Bread (page 353) or a good store-bought rye work particularly well in this tasty appetizer, but you can use pumpernickel, too. For a festive presentation, use cookie or biscuit cutters, perhaps in a leaf shape, to cut out the bread before you toast it.

MAKES ABOUT 2 DOZEN TOASTS

1 large acorn squash, cut in half and seeded
1 loaf Sauerkraut Rye Bread (page 353), store-bought rye bread, or pumpernickel bread, sliced
1/8 teaspoon fresh-grated nutmeg
2 tablespoons unsalted butter
1/2 cup fresh-grated Parmesan or Asiago cheese
2 tablespoons canola oil or corn oil
24 fresh sage leaves

1. Bake the squash in an oven or microwave. For the oven, preheat to 350 degrees. Cover the cut sides of the squash halves with heavy foil and place them, cut side down, on a baking sheet. Bake for 45 minutes to 1 hour, or until the squash is tender. For the microwave, cover the cut sides of the squash halves with microwave-safe plastic wrap and place them, cut side down, in a glass dish. Microwave on high for 7 minutes, or until the squash is tender. Set the cooked squash aside until it is cool enough to handle.

2. Spread out the bread slices on baking sheets and toast them in a 350 degree oven for 5 to 10 minutes, or until the tops begin to brown. Turn them over and toast them for 5 minutes more, or until they are browned and just crisp.

3. Scrape out the squash flesh and transfer it to a food processor. Add the nutmeg, butter, and cheese, and puree.

4. Heat the oil in a large skillet over medium-low heat. Add the sage leaves, and pan-fry them until they are sizzling and have turned a darker green, about 1 minute. Remove the leaves and drain them on absorbent paper. Spread each toast with the squash puree, top with a fried sage leaf, and serve.

QUILTMAKER'S CAKES WITH ROASTED RED PEPPER SAUCE AND PARSLEY SAUCE

In the tradition of prairie farmhouse cooks, from Amish and Mennonite to Volga German and thrifty Scottish, nothing goes to waste. Leftovers are simply recycled into tomorrow's lunch or dinner. These delicious cakes, which you can make from leftover mashed potatoes, are good examples. Formed into patties, then drizzled with flavorful sauces in quiltlike patterns, they're a nice way to exercise a little creativity—or at least to play with your food.

SERVES 4 AS AN APPETIZER OR LIGHT LUNCH

1 whole head of garlic
1 teaspoon olive oil
2 cups mashed potatoes
1 egg, beaten

½ to ¾ cup all-purpose flour
Salt and fresh-ground black
    pepper to taste
1½ cups breadcrumbs, preferably
    homemade
2 tablespoons butter
2 tablespoons canola oil or corn oil
⅔ cup Roasted Red Pepper Sauce
    (recipe follows)
⅔ cup Parsley Sauce (recipe
    follows)
¼ cup minced fresh parsley,
    for garnish

1. Preheat the oven to 350 degrees. Cut about ¼ inch deep across the pointed end of the garlic head. Drizzle the garlic with the olive oil, place it in a small baking pan, and roast it for 30 minutes, or until it is soft. Set the garlic aside until it is cool enough to handle.

2. Place the potatoes in a medium bowl. Squeeze out the pulp from each garlic clove and mix the pulp with the potatoes. Mix in the egg, ½ cup of the flour, and the salt and pepper. Add more flour if necessary to make a stiff dough or paste.

3. Spread out the breadcrumbs on a plate. Form a patty by flattening about ⅓ cup of the potato mixture between your hands until you have a patty about 3 inches wide. Place the patty on the plate with the breadcrumbs and carefully coat both sides. Continue forming the patties until there is no more dough.

4. Heat the butter and oil in a large skillet over medium heat. Add as many patties to the

skillet as will fit without crowding. Pan-fry the patties on both sides until browned, about 5 minutes per side. Keep the patties warm in a low oven until ready to serve.

5. Drizzle each patty, using a squeeze bottle if you have one, with one or the other of the sauces in a decorative pattern, such as diamonds, stripes, or overlapping circles. Garnish with the minced parsley, and serve.

ROASTED RED PEPPER SAUCE

MAKES ABOUT ⅔ CUP

2 tablespoons chopped roasted red
    pepper or bottled pimiento,
    drained
½ cup mayonnaise
Milk

Puree the pepper or pimiento in a blender or food processor. Add the mayonnaise, and puree until smooth. Thin to a pouring consistency with milk.

PARSLEY SAUCE

MAKES ABOUT ⅔ CUP

½ cup chopped fresh parsley
1 tablespoon fresh lemon juice
½ cup mayonnaise
Milk, if necessary

Puree the parsley with the lemon juice in a blender or food processor. Add the mayonnaise, and puree until smooth. Add milk, if necessary, to reach a pouring consistency.

GRILLED PEPPER AND TOMATO SPREAD WITH TWO CHEESES

Here is a late-summer dish that's superb with garden-fresh produce. Perfect for a casual porch supper, it's a good choice when you're serving a crowd.

SERVES 10

Olive oil
Salt and black pepper
2 red bell peppers
2 yellow bell peppers
2 orange bell peppers
6 plum tomatoes
6 ounces goat cheese
1 cup Fresh Farmhouse Cheese
    (page 39) or fromage blanc
Arugula leaves and basil leaves,
    for garnish
1 loaf French bread, sliced thin

1. Prepare a medium-hot fire in a grill. Lightly oil, salt, and pepper the bell peppers and the tomatoes. Grill the vegetables, turning them frequently, until the skin is blackened all over, about 15 minutes. Remove the vegetables

from the grill, set them aside until they are cool enough to handle, then seed and chop them; do not peel them. Transfer the chopped vegetables to a bowl and stir gently to blend.

2. Preheat the broiler. Blend the goat cheese and farmhouse cheese together in a medium bowl. Spread out the pepper-and-tomato mixture on a lightly oiled baking dish and top with dollops of the cheese mixture. Drizzle olive oil over all and then place briefly under the broiler until the top is bubbly, 5 to 7 minutes. Transfer to a serving bowl, garnish

with the arugula and basil leaves, and serve, with French bread alongside.

GERMAN CARAWAY CHEESE

My friend Vicki Johnson is a professional food stylist (someone who prepares food for food photographers) who grew up in a German-American family in Russell,

PRIDE OF THE DAIRY STATE

Just outside of Appleton, Wisconsin, on State Highway 47, is the farm of Herbert and Dorothy Mossholder and the home of Mossholder Cheese, dubbed "an American Treasure" by cheese expert Steven Jenkins. Surrounded now by suburban sprawl, the farm once had a painted sign, FOR SALE: MOSS-HOLDER'S HOME MADE CHEESE, nailed to a tree in the front yard, and, on the porch, a similar sign that read RING DOORBELL FOR CHEESE. A red barn shelters the family's cattle, but the cheeserie is hidden from view in the green- and white-tiled basement of the farmhouse.

Otto Mossholder created the first Mossholder Cheese in the 1920s on a stove in the farmstead's kitchen. Today,

the cheese is still made in small batches from milk from the family's own Holsteins. Made with unpasteurized cheese, the final product is aged sixty days before it is sold. Pale ivory in color and with a creamy, buttery, nutty flavor, Mossholder Cheese tastes like a cross between a very good cheddar and an equally fine Swiss. Its flavor is perfect alongside other Wisconsin specialties like handcrafted sausages and beers.

The fate of farmstead cheeses like this one, no matter how well they are regarded, is threatened by government regulations and by a market that seems to be content with inferior or artificial cheeses. Mossholder Cheese is a treasure to be savored now.

Kansas. She remembers her mother making this homemade cheese and how good it tasted on homemade bread. It's just as good on Swedish Knackebrod (page 331) or on crackers.

SERVES 12

8 cups Fresh Farmhouse Cheese
    (page 39), pot cheese, or
    dry-curd cottage cheese
1/2 pound (2 sticks) unsalted butter
1 teaspoon baking soda
2 teaspoons salt
1 pint sour cream
2 tablespoons caraway seeds

1. Make sure the farmhouse cheese is drained well in cheesecloth. Place the butter, baking soda, and salt in the top of a double boiler over simmering water. When the butter is melted, add the cheese, and continue cooking, whisking occasionally, until the cheese has melted, about 1 hour. The butter and cheese will be separated.

2. Beat in the sour cream and caraway seeds until the mixture is blended well together. Pour into a large loaf pan or a crock. Cover, and refrigerate for at least 1 hour, until the cheese is firm. Turn out onto a serving dish, if you like, bring to room temperature, and serve.

PRAIRIE SAGE CHEESE

This simple cheese makes a great sandwich spread, with a hearty wheat or rye bread, or cracker topper. If you would like to serve it as a dip for crudités or crackers, thin the consistency by adding a little milk or some extra wine.

MAKES ABOUT 1 1/2 CUPS CHEESE

1 cup Fresh Farmhouse Cheese
    (page 39) or ricotta cheese
2 tablespoons shredded Parmesan
    cheese
1 tablespoon dry white wine
2 teaspoons minced fresh sage or
    1 teaspoon rubbed dried sage
1 teaspoon minced fresh savory or
    1/2 teaspoon dried savory
1 teaspoon Worcestershire sauce
1 tablespoon minced fresh chives
Minced fresh parsley or snipped
    fresh chives, for garnish

1. Vigorously stir all of the ingredients, except the garnish, together in a medium mixing bowl until they are thoroughly blended.

2. Transfer to a serving bowl and smooth the top with a rubber spatula. Cover, and refrigerate for at least 1 hour until the cheese is firm. Garnish with parsley or chives, and serve.

HUNGARIAN EASTER CHEESE

When Easter fell in April, Hungarian-American families in the Detroit area would reserve the first three days of the month for planting spring crops in the garden. The fourth day of the month was Cheese Day, when families prepared Easter Cheese. Made ahead and kept cold, Easter Cheese is meant to be enjoyed on Easter Sunday, when it is slathered on homemade bread and topped with pickled red beets mixed with horseradish.

SERVES 8 TO 12

2 dozen eggs
1/2 teaspoon salt
1/2 cup sugar
1 teaspoon vanilla extract
2 quarts milk

1. Beat the eggs, salt, sugar, and vanilla together in a large bowl. Heat the milk slowly over low heat in a large saucepan. When it is warm, add the egg mixture and stir well to blend. Cook, stirring occasionally, until the cheese comes together in a ball, about 10 minutes.

2. Line a colander with a double thickness of cheesecloth. Pour the contents of the saucepan into the lined colander. Drain the cheese for 2 hours. Pour the curds into a bowl and press them into a mass with the back of a spoon. Cover, and refrigerate at least 1 hour, or until firm. Refrigerated, the cheese will keep 3 to 4 weeks.

LIPTAUER CHEESE

This is a pungent and tasty Austro-Hungarian appetizer, still popular among immigrant families, that is delicious on rye bread, as it is traditionally served, or on homemade (page 331) or store-bought knackebrod.

MAKES 3 CUPS CHEESE

1/2 pound (2 sticks) unsalted butter, softened
16 ounces cream cheese, softened
1 tablespoon grated yellow onion
1 tablespoon Dijon mustard
1 1/2 teaspoons caraway seeds
1 tablespoon minced fresh parsley
1 tablespoon minced fresh chives
2 teaspoons chopped capers
Chopped fresh parsley, for garnish

1. Place all of the ingredients, except the garnish, in a large mixing bowl. Stir with a wooden spoon to blend well.

2. Turn the cheese out onto a serving plate and round its shape into a mound. Garnish with the chopped parsley, and serve.

BLUE CHEESE AND TOASTED PECAN SPREAD

I am a big fan of blue cheese, and I buy a small wheel of it every year. I usually freeze some of it. When it's thawed again, the texture is more crumbly than the original. That's when it's perfect to use in a savory spread like this one. A crock of this cheese served with knackebrod, French bread, or rye bread is the perfect nibble with a micro-brewed beer, a warm glass of *Julglogg* (a Swedish warm spiced wine), or a Missouri or Michigan claret. It makes a wonderful gift from your kitchen as well.

MAKES ABOUT 2½ CUPS SPREAD

*1 pound blue cheese, such as
    Maytag Blue from Iowa,
    crumbled
4 tablespoons unsalted butter,
    softened
¼ cup heavy cream
1 garlic clove, minced
1 cup pecans, toasted and chopped
    fine
¼ cup chopped green onions,
    white part and some green
    part
¼ cup chopped fresh Italian parsley*

1. Blend the cheese, butter, cream, and garlic to a smooth paste in a food processor.

Transfer the mixture to a bowl or crock and fold in the pecans, green onions, and parsley. Refrigerate, covered, for 2 hours or more, until the mixture has firmed up.

2. Remove the spread from the refrigerator an hour before serving. Serve at room temperature, with bread or crackers.

FRESH GOAT CHEESE WITH OVEN-DRIED TOMATO CONSERVE

This is a quick and fresh-tasting appetizer spread that's good with crusty French bread or whole wheat rolls.

SERVES 6 TO 8

*1 cup Oven-Dried Tomatoes
    (page 42), drained, or 6 ounces
    dry-packed sun-dried
    tomatoes, soaked in hot water
    for 15 minutes and drained
1 cup olive oil
2 large garlic cloves
5 fresh basil leaves
¼ teaspoon cayenne pepper
½ teaspoon salt
½ teaspoon sugar
1 green onion, white part and
    some green part, minced
8 ounces fresh goat cheese, in a log
    or logs*

A Prairie Cheeseboard

Although the regions overlap, the midwest may be divided roughly into three parts: the corn belt to the east, the dairy belt in the middle, and the wheat belt to the west. The dairy belt, from southern Ohio through Indiana and up into Wisconsin, is an area of grassy hills and green meadows, with humid summers and snowy winters. It is a perfect landscape for grazing dairy cattle, goats, and sheep, so it is not surprising that cheesemaking is a high art in the area. Many German, Belgian, and Dutch immigrant families brought their cheesemaking skills to the midwest, while other midwesterners learned the craft much later. To this day there are many very good cheeses made in the midwest that are sold only around one town or in a few adjacent counties. If I were to assemble a prairie cheeseboard from among the varieties that have wider or national distribution, these are the ones I might feature:

An assortment of goat cheeses, plain and flavored, ashed and unashed, fresh and aged, made by Capriole, Inc., in Greenville, Indiana.

An assortment of sheep's milk cheeses, smoked and unsmoked, from La Paysanne, Inc., in Hayward, Minnesota.

A creamy fromage blanc from Dancing Winds Farm in Kenyon, Minnesota.

A heady Gorgonzola from BelGioioso Auricchio Cheese in Denmark, Wisconsin.

Klondike Brick, a mellow, award-winning cow's milk cheese from the Klondike Cheese Company in Monroe, Wisconsin.

Maytag Blue cheese, one of the first and still one of the best midwestern handcrafted cheeses, from Maytag Dairy Farms in Newton, Iowa.

Mossholder Cheese, an aromatic, spicy, and full-flavored cow's milk cheese made by Mossholder Farm of Appleton, Wisconsin.

Pinconning, a mild cross between a Colby and a cheddar, from the Williams Cheese Company in Saginaw Bay, Michigan.

Pur Chèvre Bleu, a blue goat's milk cheese from Dietrich's Dairy in Fowler, Illinois.

1. Place all of the ingredients except the goat cheese in a food processor fitted with a steel blade. Process in quick bursts to chop but not puree the mixture. Let the conserve sit for at least 30 minutes to soften the tomatoes and allow the flavors to blend.

2. Place the goat cheese logs on a serving plate, pour the conserve over the cheese, and serve.

SORREL, GOAT CHEESE, AND CREAM CHEESE TART

Among early pioneers to the midwest, sorrel, or "sour grass," was a springtime favorite, a tart and refreshing taste after the stodgy fare of winter. Prairie pioneers gathered it wild, but sorrel is a very easy perennial plant to grow. To save time, you can bake and freeze the pastry ahead of time, then let it thaw before the final baking. I like to serve this on the same plate with a side salad of mixed greens dressed simply with olive oil and balsamic vinegar. Fresh-from-the-garden arugula or basil may replace the sorrel, if you like.

SERVES 10 AS AN APPETIZER OR
6 AS A LIGHT MAIN DISH

FOR THE PASTRY:
1¼ cups all-purpose flour
½ teaspoon salt
¼ teaspoon white pepper
¼ pound (1 stick) unsalted butter, cubed
¼ cup ice water

FOR THE FILLING:
1 tablespoon olive oil
1 yellow onion, chopped
1 cup packed fresh sorrel, chopped
¼ cup chopped fresh parsley
6 ounces fresh goat cheese
14 ounces cream cheese, softened
3 eggs
Salt and black pepper to taste

1. Make the pastry: Put the flour, salt, white pepper, and butter in a food processor and process until the mixture resembles coarse crumbs. Add the ice water a little at a time and process until the dough forms a ball. Transfer the dough to a work surface and pat it out into a disk shape. Wrap the dough in plastic wrap and refrigerate it for 15 minutes.

2. Preheat the oven to 400 degrees. Roll out the dough to a circle on a floured work surface, then line a 9-inch round tart pan with the pastry. Prick the dough all over with a fork. Put the lined tart pan in the freezer for 10 minutes (to keep the pastry from shrinking when it bakes). Remove the tart pan from the freezer and bake the pastry for 15 minutes, or until it is lightly browned. Remove from the oven and let cool slightly. (The

pastry can be prepared ahead to this point, and frozen.)

3. If you made the pastry beforehand, thaw it. Preheat the oven again to 400 degrees. Make the filling: Heat the olive oil in a skillet over medium-low heat, add the onion, and sauté it until it is translucent, 6 to 8 minutes. Spoon the onion onto the bottom of the pastry in the tart pan and top with the sorrel and parsley. In a food processor or blender, blend the goat cheese, cream cheese, eggs, salt, and black pepper to a smooth consistency, and pour or spoon this mixture into the tart pan. Bake for 20 to 25 minutes, or until the top is browned and a knife inserted in the center comes out clean. Cut into wedges, and serve hot.

FARMSTEAD CHEDDAR TARTLETS

Holiday gatherings at our house when I was growing up were not complete without my mother's savory cheese tartlets. They taste good served hot, at room temperature, or chilled. Vary the cheese, if you like; Gruyère, blue cheese, goat cheese, or smoked Gouda all are fine.

Note that in this recipe the sixty tartlets are baked in two batches. If your oven is large enough, you can bake in just one batch.

MAKES 5 DOZEN TARTLETS

FOR THE PASTRY:
2½ cups all-purpose flour
1 teaspoon salt
½ teaspoon white pepper
1 tablespoon fresh thyme or
   ½ teaspoon dried thyme,
   optional
½ pound (2 sticks) unsalted butter,
   cubed
¼ to ½ cup ice water

FOR THE FILLING:
1⅓ cups half-and-half
2 eggs, beaten
½ teaspoon salt
¼ teaspoon white pepper
¼ teaspoon bottled hot pepper sauce
1 teaspoon Maggi seasoning or
   Worcestershire sauce
1 pound sharp cheddar cheese,
   diced into 60 pieces

1. Make the pastry: Combine the flour, salt, white pepper, and, if you like, thyme in the bowl of a food processor fitted with a steel blade. Add the butter, 1 cube at a time, and process until the mixture resembles coarse meal. With the motor running, slowly pour in ice water until the dough forms a ball. Wrap the dough ball in plastic and refrigerate it until firm, about 30 minutes.

2. Make the filling: Whisk together the half-and-half, eggs, salt, white pepper, hot pepper sauce, and Maggi in a bowl. Set aside.

3. Preheat the oven to 425 degrees. Lightly oil 2 or 3 miniature muffin pans, with

1 tablespoon capers, minced
1 tablespoon minced fresh parsley
Fresh-ground black pepper to taste

1. Remove the skin and bones from the fish. Flake the fish into the bowl of a food processor. Add the remaining ingredients and pulse to blend.

2. Pack the spread into a serving bowl and refrigerate, covered, until ready to serve. Serve chilled or at room temperature, with crackers, French bread, or Swedish Knackebrod (page 331).

GREAT LAKES WHITEFISH TERRINE

This combination of smoky, creamy, and herby flavors is a perfect spring or summer appetizer. This recipe is adapted from a smoked trout recipe, with a different sauce, created by Larry Forgione. Look for the best smoked whitefish you can find.

SERVES 6 TO 8

1 (1/4-ounce) envelope unflavored
    gelatin
1/3 cup cold water
1/3 cup boiling water
1/2 cup mayonnaise
1/4 cup sour cream
2 tablespoons lemon juice
2 tablespoons minced red onion
1/4 teaspoon cayenne pepper
1/4 teaspoon black pepper
2 cups (about 10 ounces) flaked
    smoked whitefish
1/4 cup chopped fresh Italian parsley
2/3 cup heavy cream
4 cups watercress, for garnish

FOR THE SAUCE:
    1/2 cup sour cream
    1/2 cup mayonnaise
    1/4 cup tarragon vinegar
    1 teaspoon minced fresh dill
    1 tablespoon snipped fresh chives

1. In a large mixing bowl, soften the gelatin in the cold water for 5 minutes. Add the boiling water and stir until the gelatin has dissolved. Whisk in the mayonnaise, sour cream, lemon juice, onion, cayenne, and black pepper. Gently fold in the fish and parsley. In a separate bowl, beat the cream until it just starts to thicken. Fold the cream into the fish mixture.

2. Line an 8-by-4-by-2-inch loaf pan with plastic wrap. Pour the fish mixture into the lined loaf pan. Smooth the top with a rubber spatula. Cover and refrigerate for 6 hours or overnight.

3. Shortly before serving, stir together all of the sauce ingredients in a bowl. To serve, carefully unmold the terrine and slice it thin with a very sharp knife. Arrange the slices on individual plates, garnish with watercress, and top each serving with a dollop of sauce.

CHICKEN PÂTÉ WITH GOAT CHEESE AND HERBS

A homemade chicken loaf, usually served with a cream sauce, was a venerable part of the Heartland cook's repertoire in the 1930s and '40s. This updated and lighter version is based on a recipe by Kathy Carey of Lilly's in Louisville, right across the Ohio

---

AN AMISH SATURDAY FROLIC

In Harmony, a small town in the rolling farmland of southeastern Minnesota, over one hundred Amish families live simply according to their religious beliefs. They still use horsepower to raise corn, oats, soybeans, and hay. Their neat and spotlessly clean kitchens feature dry sinks, iceboxes, dropleaf tables, wood or coal cookstoves, zinc-topped worktables for kneading bread and preparing pastry, and kerosene lamps. Horse and buggy transportation takes them to town for supplies or to each other's homes for visits.

When a farmer needs help to build or repair farm buildings, thresh oats, or fill a silo, he will announce a "frolic" for a certain day and invite as many friends and family as can come to help out. Amish women, arriving with heaping bowls and platters of food they have prepared at home, set up long tables outdoors to feed the hungry men. There are always plenty of the mashed-potato doughnuts that are an Amish favorite. After the men have eaten and have stretched out to rest in the shade of an

old shagbark hickory, the children eat next and then ramble off to play. Finally, the women sit down to sample each other's cooking and enjoy their time together.

If you need to gather friends for your own frolic, or if you are organizing any other kind of potluck get-together for a hungry crowd, here is a menu you might try:

Orange-Mint Thresher's Drink
(page 108)

Firehouse Tomatoes (page 156)

Pickled Beets (page 52)

Baked Macaroni and Cheddar
(page 264)

Scalloped Peaches-and-Cream Corn
(page 308)

Buttermilk-Oatmeal Bread (page 350)

New Prague Meatloaf (page 186)

Norwegian Potato Doughnuts
(page 337)

Old-Fashioned Chocolate Cake with
Boiled Frosting (page 407)

River from the rolling bluff country near Greenville, Indiana, where Judy Schad makes her award-winning Capriole goat cheeses, which Carey uses in her dishes. Especially delicious in summer, this contemporary chicken loaf benefits from the additions of fresh herbs, goat cheese, and oven-dried tomatoes for extra flavor and color. Chilled and sliced thin, it's a great appetizer to take to a potluck or picnic, but you can also serve it warm and thick-sliced, as a main course.

SERVES 12 AS AN APPETIZER,
OR 6 TO 8 AS A LIGHT MAIN DISH

*2 pounds skinless, boneless chicken
    breasts, chopped fine*
2 eggs, beaten
1/4 cup minced fresh dill
1/4 cup minced fresh tarragon
2 teaspoons salt
*1/4 teaspoon fresh-grated
    nutmeg*
1/4 teaspoon cayenne pepper
2 cups heavy cream
*8 ounces fresh goat cheese,
    crumbled*
*1/2 cup dry-packed sun-dried
    tomatoes or Oven-Dried
    Tomatoes (page 42), chopped,
    soaked in hot water for 15
    minutes, and drained*

1. Preheat the oven to 350 degrees. Oil a 9-by-5-inch loaf pan or a longer pâté pan. Puree the chicken breasts in a food processor with the eggs, herbs, salt, nutmeg, and cayenne until the mixture is smooth. With the machine running, pour in the cream and process until the cream is incorporated.

2. Pour 1/3 of the chicken mixture into the bottom of the loaf pan. Sprinkle half of the goat cheese on top of the chicken, followed by half of the tomatoes. Pour in another 1/3 of the chicken mixture and top with the remaining cheese followed by the remaining tomatoes. Pour the remaining 1/3 of the chicken mixture on top.

3. Set the loaf pan in a larger pan with deep sides and pour in enough water to reach halfway up the sides of the loaf pan. Bake for 1 hour and 15 minutes, or until a knife inserted in the center comes out clean. Remove the pans from the oven and let the pâté cool slightly. To serve warm, turn out onto a serving platter, slice, and serve. Or chill for several hours until firm, turn out, slice, and serve.

BRANDING IRON BEEF

If you cook this recipe indoors, open the windows and turn on the exhaust fan, because you're going to get lots of smoke. The elegant results, however, are worth it.

SERVES 4

1 pound beef sirloin tip
Extra-virgin olive oil
Salt and black pepper to taste
1 small ancho chile, halved, stemmed, and seeded
1 cup mayonnaise
2 tablespoons capers, drained, for garnish

1. Brush all sides of the sirloin tip with olive oil, then salt and pepper the surface of the meat. If your outdoor grill has enough BTUs to blacken meat or fish, build a very hot fire in your grill. If not, heat a cast-iron skillet over high heat on your stove. When the grill or skillet is extremely hot, blacken the beef for about 1 minute on all sides. Set the meat aside to cool down.

2. While the beef is cooling, prepare an ancho mayonnaise. Heat a small skillet on high until quite hot. Add the ancho chile and toast it until it is fragrant, about 10 seconds on each side. Transfer the chile to a small bowl and pour over just enough hot water to cover. Let the chile steep for 10 minutes, then remove it

and pat it dry. Put the chile and the mayonnaise in a food processor and process until the mixture is smooth and slightly pink. Cover and refrigerate until ready to serve.

3. When the beef is cool to the touch, wrap it in plastic wrap and put it in the freezer to firm up (but not freeze), 20 to 30 minutes. Meanwhile, chill four appetizer serving plates. Remove the beef from the freezer and, using a mandoline if you have one, or a very sharp knife, cut the beef paper thin. Arrange the slices around the perimeter of the four plates. Drizzle the ancho mayonnaise attractively over the beef. Garnish each plate with capers, and serve immediately.

KANSAS CITY-STYLE BARBECUED BRISKET DIP

This is fusion cooking, Heartland-style, and a great way to use leftovers from a barbecued brisket. I've adapted this dip from a recipe given to me by Ardie Davis, one of Kansas City's best barbecuers.

SERVES 8 TO 10

1 pound barbecued brisket, chopped
1/2 cup chopped yellow onion
1 garlic clove, minced

1¼ cups tomato-based barbecue
    sauce
1 4-ounce can jalapeño peppers,
    chopped
8 ounces cream cheese, softened
⅓ cup grated Pecorino, Monterey
    Jack, or Parmesan cheese

1. Preheat the oven to 350 degrees. Lightly oil a baking dish or an ovenproof ceramic chafing dish.

2. Combine all the ingredients in a mixing bowl, stirring to distribute them evenly. Transfer to the baking dish. Bake for 20 to 30 minutes, or until just bubbly and completely heated through. Serve immediately, with slices of French bread.

BLT BITES

Really fresh cherry tomatoes and some good apple-smoked bacon will make this hors d'oeuvre awfully hard to pass up. Try to find cherry tomatoes that are on the large side.

SERVES 4

16 cherry tomatoes
½ pound apple-smoked bacon,
    cooked and crumbled
½ cup mayonnaise
⅓ cup minced green onions, white
    and green parts
2 tablespoons minced romaine
    lettuce

1. Cut a thin slice off the stem end of each tomato, and scoop out and discard the pulp. Drain the tomatoes, cut side down, on absorbent paper for 10 minutes.

2. Meanwhile, combine the remaining ingredients in a small bowl and stir gently to mix well. Spoon this mixture into the tomatoes. Refrigerate, covered, for at least 1 hour, but not overnight, and serve chilled.

PRAIRIE PÂTÉ

Hand-cranked meat grinders that clamped onto the kitchen table were a fixture in midwestern kitchens and a necessary utensil for turning out a simple but delectable meatloaf of beef, veal, or ham. Today we buy our meats already ground, and our tastes have gotten a little more sophisticated. This is a "next generation" recipe that harks back to the Old Country. Serve slices of this moist pâté at room temperature with a crusty homemade bread and, perhaps, with Coddled Crabapples (page 309) or little individual jars of Tarragon Pickled Vegetables (page 83) topped with lacy paper and tied with raffia.

SERVES 8 TO 12 AS AN APPETIZER OR
4 TO 6 AS SANDWICHES FOR LUNCH

½ pound ground turkey
1½ pounds bulk sweet Italian
    sausage

1 pound skinless, boneless
    pheasant breast or chicken
    breast, cut into 1-inch-wide
    strips
3 tablespoons minced green onion,
    white part and some green part
3 to 4 garlic cloves, minced
1/3 cup minced fresh parsley
1 bay leaf
3/4 teaspoon salt
1/2 teaspoon white pepper
1 cup dry white wine
2 eggs, beaten
1 1/2 cups fine breadcrumbs,
    preferably homemade

MAKING SAUERKRAUT

"*All day they chopped and shredded, washed and drained the
white winter cabbage. Then it was
packed into the barrel, with just the
right amount of pickling salt: nine
tablespoons for every fifteen pounds
of cabbage. . . . We reaped the benefits of that day all winter long. Every
Thursday our family, all ten of us,
looked forward to supper, knowing
exactly what it would be: a platter
piled high with roasted spareribs, a
mountain of fluffy mashed potatoes,
a small lake of smooth gravy, and a
heaping bowl of sauerkraut.*"
—RITA KLARER, SUGAR CREEK, MISSOURI

1. Place the turkey, sausage, pheasant or chicken, green onion, garlic, parsley, bay leaf, salt, pepper, and wine in a large bowl and stir to combine. Cover and refrigerate overnight.

2. Preheat the oven to 375 degrees. Lightly oil a long terrine or loaf pan. Transfer the meat mixture to a colander and drain off the liquid for 5 to 10 minutes. Remove the pheasant or chicken strips to a plate and set aside. Remove and discard the bay leaf. Return the meat mixture to a bowl, add the eggs and breadcrumbs, and mix well with a wooden spoon or your hands.

3. Spoon half of the meat mixture evenly in the bottom of the terrine or loaf pan. Place the pheasant or chicken strips over the sur-face and spoon the rest of the meat over the top. Cover tightly with foil and bake for 1 hour and 15 minutes, or until the pâté has begun to separate from the edges of the pan. Remove from the oven and let cool for 1 hour. Loosen the edges with a sharp knife, turn out onto a serving platter, and cut with a bread knife using a sawing motion. Serve at room temperature.

HERBED PORK PÂTÉ

S erve this earthy and, if you wish, lightly spiked spread on toast points or Swedish Knackebrod (page 331).

SERVES 8

*½ pound boneless pork loin, cut
    into ½-inch cubes*
*½ pound sliced bacon, cut into
    ½-inch pieces*
*2 teaspoons Aromatic Herb Rub
    (see page 57)*
1 bay leaf
2 tablespoons Cognac, optional

1. Combine the pork, bacon, herb rub, and bay leaf with 2 cups water in a large sauce-pan. Bring to a boil, reduce the heat, and simmer, uncovered, for 1 to 1½ hours, stir-ring occasionally. The meat should be tender and there should be about ¼ cup of liquid left in the saucepan.

2. Remove the pan from the heat, discard the bay leaf, and let the meat cool for 30 minutes. Transfer the meat and the cooking liquid (discard any cooking liquid beyond ¼ cup) to the bowl of a food processor or to a meat grinder. Process or grind until the pâté is fairly smooth. Stir in the Cognac, if you like. Spoon the mixture, packing tightly as you do so, into a crock or bowl and refrigerate, covered, for 12 to 24 hours to let the flavors blend. Serve chilled.

SAUERKRAUT BALLS

Popular in pockets of the midwest, these savory appetizers are always a hit, even if they are a little unusual. In Minnesota, they're usually made of finely chopped ham or corned beef. This Ohio version, made with sausage, is quicker, easier, and more deeply flavorful.

MAKES 2 DOZEN BALLS

*8 ounces pork sausage, finely
    crumbled*
¼ cup minced yellow onion
*16 ounces sauerkraut, drained well
    and chopped*
3 ounces cream cheese, softened
2 tablespoons minced fresh parsley
1 teaspoon mustard
¼ teaspoon garlic salt
⅛ teaspoon black pepper
*¾ cup plus 2 tablespoons fine
    breadcrumbs*
¼ cup all-purpose flour
2 eggs, beaten well
¼ cup milk
Vegetable oil for frying

1. Cook the sausage in a large skillet over medium heat. Once the meat has rendered some fat, after 1 to 2 minutes, add the onion, and continue cooking, stirring fre-quently, until the meat is browned and the onion is nearly translucent, about 6 minutes more. Drain the fat and add the sauerkraut, cream cheese, parsley, mustard, garlic salt, pepper, and 2 tablespoons of the breadcrumbs and stir to blend. Transfer the mixture to a bowl and refrigerate, covered, for 30 minutes.

2. Place the flour on one plate and the ¾ cup breadcrumbs on another plate. Beat the eggs

and milk together in a small bowl. Pinch off enough of the sauerkraut mixture to roll into

HEARTLAND SAUSAGES

Butcher shops and smokehouses in the midwest still make an astonishing array of homemade and home-smoked sausages, colorful and colorfully named, that continue Old World customs into the New. Here is a sampling of the wide variety you will find:

🐖 BOLOGNA. In handcrafted versions, but not always in mass-produced ones, a smoked mixture of beef, pork, and onion seasoned with salt, pepper, and ground ginger.

🐖 JATERNICE. A Czech version of head cheese, spiced with paprika.

🐖 KALBERWURST. A mild Swiss veal sausage that includes crackers and milk.

🐖 KIELBASA. A Polish pork and beef sausage that is amply spiced and then smoked. What you get when you order "a Polish" from a Chicago street vendor.

🐖 KRAKOWSKA. A Polish ham sausage that tastes like smoked ham and is delicious on sandwiches.

🐖 LANDJAEGER. A long, thin beef and pork sausage that is cured, smoked, and then dried.

🐖 LIVERWURST. A rich ground liver sausage spiced with salt, pepper, and, sometimes, garlic. Many varieties are available, from coarse-ground to the smooth, creamy texture of Braunschweiger.

🐖 NADLAVA. A Croatian Easter sausage made with cubed bread, bacon, green onions, ham, and beaten eggs stuffed into a casing and then baked.

🐖 POLTAVSKA. A Russian and Ukrainian sausage studded with large squares of creamy white fat.

🐖 POTATISKORV. A Swedish sausage made of beef, pork, onion, potato, and seasonings ground together.

🐖 SCHWARTENMAGEN. Made in the Amana Colonies in Iowa, a hearty mixture of beef heart and pork tongue, jowls, and skin.

🐖 SUMMER SAUSAGE. A dark pink sausage made of ground beef with spices. Cured rather than smoked.

a ball ¾ inch in diameter. Roll the ball in the flour, dip it in the egg mixture, and roll it in the breadcrumbs to coat. Repeat the process until all the sauerkraut mixture has been used.

3. Heat the oil to a depth of 2 inches in an electric skillet or deep fryer until it is 375 degrees. Fry the sauerkraut balls in batches for about 1 minute, or until they are golden brown. Drain on absorbent paper. Serve with toothpicks, either hot or at room temperature.

ITALIAN SAUSAGE, SPINACH, AND RICOTTA TOASTS

Whether you say bruschetta or simply "toast," you can make wonderful appetizers if you have great bread on hand. Although we now would buy the ingredients in the supermarket, dishes like this became a part of the Italian-American culinary repertoire as simple means to use up leftovers, such as sausage or ricotta, by combining them with common staples.

SERVES 8

8 ounces bulk sweet Italian sausage, crumbled

1 garlic clove, minced
1½ cups fresh spinach or 1 10-ounce package frozen spinach, thawed and squeezed dry
½ cup Fresh Farmhouse Cheese (page 39) or ricotta
Dash of fresh-grated nutmeg
Fresh-ground black pepper to taste
½ cup fresh-grated Parmesan
8 slices Italian or peasant bread, toasted

1. Cook the sausage, stirring frequently, in a large skillet over medium heat for 6 to 8 minutes, or until the sausage is browned. Add the garlic and spinach and continue to cook, stirring, until the spinach wilts, 1 to 2 minutes more. Remove the skillet from the heat and stir in the cheese, nutmeg, and pepper.

2. Preheat the broiler. Place the toast slices on a sheet or pan you can run under the broiler; you may need to do this in 2 batches. Spread the sausage-cheese mixture on each piece of toast, sprinkle with Parmesan, and broil for 3 to 4 minutes, or until the cheese is browned and the topping is bubbly. Serve hot.

THE SWEDISH TABLE

Flavors clean and pure like salt-tanged sea air, creamy and mild tastes, and lots of rich, buttery baked goods define the constellation of Swedish foods brought by immigrants and still made in the midwest. The crisp tastes of sillsalat, pickled herring, and pickled beets offer a taste counterpoint to the mildness of Swedish potato sausage, baked brown beans, and yellow pea soup. Fresh dill turns up in potato dishes and pickles of all kinds. But the highlight of a Swedish meal is always the baked goods: almond-flavored kringlor, saffron-flavored Lucia buns, or a tea ring for breakfast; hard and crispy knackebrod, served with soup for lunch; and mellow limpa rye bread with dinner. Milky desserts like ostkaka and rice pudding are very often served with a red fruit sauce, as much for a color contrast as for a taste complement. Indeed, the color of deep, dark red is a favorite punctuation mark in Swedish meals, whether it appears in the spiced drink gluhwein on special occasions, in beet dishes and sillsalat, or in lingonberry and red currant sauces for everything from lacy Swedish pancakes to roast goose.

Broths and soups are part of many meals. Christmas Eve is also called Dipping Day, in honor of the large pot of soup that provides sustenance on the last fast day of Advent. Children (and adults) are allowed to dip a piece of bread in the broth if they are impatient for dinner.

Swedes are not partial to smoky flavors. They prefer their ham, for example, to be on the sweeter and drier side. The unsmoked potato sausage is looser in texture and fresher-tasting than smoked sausage.

Every culture has an overripened, pungent dish that its people like–and outsiders do not. For the Swedes, as for Norwegians as well, it's lutefisk. Made from dried cod that has been soaked for an extended period in lye and then rinsed several times, lutefisk resembles a fish gelatin by the time it is done. Its taste is an acquired one, to be sure. But that doesn't prevent lutefisk-eating contests from drawing crowds of hearty eaters in Scandinavian strongholds from Lindsborg, Kansas, to, well, Lake Wobegon, Minnesota. Ironically, lutefisk, a poor man's dish in the Old Country, has become a desirable symbol of both cultural identity and abundance in the Heartland.

SMOKED SAUSAGE AND POTATO CAKES

These are savory and delicious appetizers that also might serve as a brunch dish or a light supper. Serve with a dollop of Orchard Apple Chutney (page 70), a good applesauce, or cranberry relish.

SERVES 4

1 pound baking potatoes, peeled
    and shredded
8 ounces smoked sausage, casings
    removed, minced
1/4 cup chopped green onions, white
    part and some green part
1/2 cup all-purpose flour
2 eggs, beaten
Salt and black pepper to taste
1 teaspoon fresh-grated nutmeg
Vegetable oil for frying
Orchard Apple Chutney (page 70),
    applesauce, or cranberry
    relish, for garnish

1. Combine the potato, sausage, green onions, flour, eggs, salt, pepper, and nutmeg in a mixing bowl. Stir to blend well.

2. Heat the oil to a depth of 1 inch in a large skillet over medium-high heat. Using a spoon or spatula, drop the mixture, 1/4 cup at a time, into the hot oil. Flatten the cakes with a spatula or turner as they are frying. Cook for about 4 minutes per side, or until both sides of the cake are golden brown, then remove the cake and drain it on absorbent paper. Continue until all of the batter has been used; you should have about 12 cakes. Serve hot, with a dollop of chutney for each cake.

DRINKS

PICNIC LEMONADE

Hot, humid summers in the eastern midwest and hot, dry summers on the prairie both demand lots of cool, refreshing beverages. Use honey as a sweetener, or a mixture of honey and sugar, for a delicious change of pace.

SERVES 10 TO 12

Juice of 12 lemons
1¼ cups sugar or 1 cup wildflower
  honey or 1 cup Honeysuckle
  Syrup (page 61)
3 quarts chilled spring water
Sprigs of fresh mint or lemon
  balm, for garnish

1. Heat the lemon juice and sugar or honey over medium heat in a saucepan until the sugar or honey completely dissolves. Set aside to cool slightly.

2. In a gallon container, stir together the lemon mixture with the spring water. Fill glasses with ice, add a sprig of mint or lemon balm, and pour in the lemonade.

ORANGE-MINT THRESHER'S DRINK

This is a modern day wheat harvester's drink from central Kansas. In late June the winter wheat is at last ripe, which means long, hot, dusty days getting the harvest in. This icy, invigorating beverage slakes the wheatcutters' thirst, but also stars at a brunch gathering or just for sipping on the porch.

SERVES 10 TO 12

2 cups sugar
1 12-ounce can frozen orange
  juice concentrate, thawed
1 12-ounce can frozen lemonade
  concentrate, thawed
Grated rind of 1 orange
1 cup packed fresh mint leaves
Sparkling water, for serving

1. Make a simple syrup: Add the sugar to 2½ cups water in a large saucepan and bring to a boil. Reduce the heat and simmer for about 10 minutes. The syrup should be clear and the sugar completely dissolved. Set aside to cool slightly.

2. Stir together the simple syrup, orange juice, lemonade, and grated orange rind in a large

pitcher. Add the mint leaves and stir well. Cover and let steep in the refrigerator for at least 1 hour. To serve, fill tall glasses with ice, pour in about 1 cup of the drink mixture, and add sparkling water to taste.

PRAIRIE SHANDY

Microbreweries throughout the prairie states have brought back wheat beer, with hundreds of rich and tasty varieties available. A shandy is a traditional drink, with origins in the British Isles, that combines a beer or ale with a lemon drink, such as lemonade.

SERVES 8

32 ounces ice-cold wheat beer
32 ounces ice-cold Picnic
    Lemonade (page 108)
8 lemon slices, for garnish

Frost 8 pilsner glasses or beer mugs in your freezer. Pour 4 ounces of the beer and of the lemonade into each glass, and give each glass a quick stir. Garnish with lemon slices, and serve.

WHEAT-COUNTRY BEER

The main ingredients in beer are hops and malted grains. Europeans have long made beers in which wheat malt is the dominant malt, but the style has caught on in the United States only recently, with the microbrewery revolution. Not surprisingly, a number of microbreweries in the wheat-growing midwest have a reputation for their fine wheat beers. Here are some of the best:

Bison Weizen, from Bricktown Brewery in Oklahoma City, Oklahoma

Harvester Wheat Beer, from Jones Street Brewing Company in Omaha, Nebraska

Hefe-Weizen, from Summit Brewing Company in St. Paul, Minnesota

Prairie Wheat, from Flatlanders Chophouse and Brewery in Lincolnshire, Illinois

Raspberry Wheat and Wilderness Wheat, from Firehouse Brewing Company in Rapid City, South Dakota

Wheat State Golden, from Free State Brewing Company in Lawrence, Kansas

Wildcat Wheat Beer, from Little Apple Brewing Company in Manhattan, Kansas

SWEDISH SPICED WINE

The festive spiced drink known as *glogg*, served during the Christmas season, can be made two ways: for adults and for children. In Lindsborg, Kansas, where many Swedish immigrants settled in the nineteenth century, families today make the kids' non-alcoholic variety to serve on St. Lucia Day with pepparkakor, thin ginger-spiced cookies. The grownups' more potent variety is served up on Christmas Eve, along with a ham baked with a sweet mustard glaze, anise-flavored rye bread, and rice pudding.

SERVES 6

1¾ *cups dry red wine*
   (or, for children, cranberry juice cocktail)
1½ *cups port (or, for children, additional cranberry juice cocktail)*
1½ *cups vodka (or, for children, pineapple juice)*
6 *cardamom pods*
4 *whole cloves*
Peel of 1 orange, in 1 continuous spiral strip
2 *cinnamon sticks*
6 *almonds, blanched*
18 to 24 *raisins*

1. Bring the wine, port, vodka, cardamom, cloves, orange peel, and cinnamon to a sim-mer in a nonreactive saucepan or stockpot. Simmer the mixture slowly for 15 minutes.

2. Place 1 blanched almond and several raisins in the bottom of each punch glass. Pour the warm wine mixture over (filtering out the spices, if you like), and serve. *Glogg* may be reheated.

MULLED WHITE WINE

The first time I had mulled wine was when I was in college, in Springfield, Ohio, at a holiday party at an English professor's house. As I sipped the spicy red wine and practiced what for me was the new art of small talk, I thought I was the epitome of sophistication. Now that I've got small talk down pat, mulled red wines seem too harsh to me, and I have longed for something that goes down a bit easier. The answer was practically in my own backyard. I make my mulled wine with white wines made from seyval blanc or vignole grapes, which are grown in the Missouri Valley near St. Louis and in Michigan, near the shores of Lake Michigan. Seyval blanc, a dry wine not unlike a chardonnay, and vignole, a slightly sweeter wine like a Ries-ling, taste wonderful cold—or warmed, as in this holiday recipe. Served in a glass bowl, this bracing drink is both beautiful to the eye and delectable to the palate. Propose a toast to salute friends and family, welcome carolers chilled from the wintry night, or sip as you sit by the fireside, happy to be at home.

SERVES 8 TO 10

¼ cup sugar
½ cup light rum or brandy
Peel of 1 small lemon, in 1
    continuous spiral strip

1 small lemon stuck with 10 whole
    cloves
2 bay leaves
1 bottle (750ml) white wine,
    such as a seyval blanc or
    chardonnay, or a vignole or
    Riesling

PEARS

The French brought their love of the pear, and their expertise in growing it and cooking it, to the places they settled in the Mississippi Valley, in what are now Illinois and Missouri. In the former Fort Cahokia, across the river from St. Louis, the largest pear tree in the United States once grew. Today, the hardier fall- and winter-ripening pear varieties, like Anjou, Bosc, and Comice, do well in the midwest. The ubiquitous Bartlett pear, harvested in summer, is not as reliable in the Heartland because of the vagaries of summer rainfall.

Smaller and harder pear varieties, such as Seckel and Kieffer, also grow well in the midwest. Not common in supermarkets, and not particularly good to eat out of hand, these are very fine cooking pears worth picking up when you see them at a farmstand or farmers' market. They keep well in the refrigerator and make delicious pear preserves. I use them to make a homemade pear sauce, prepared like applesauce, to serve with Gingerbread Waffles (page 19) on winter mornings.

My own pair of Kieffer pear trees froth into white blossoms in April, bear tiny green fruits that grow to three or four inches long, and are ready for harvest in early to mid-September. Pears must be picked before they ripen, because they will become granular and mushy if left to ripen on the tree. I judge by the color: When the mild chartreuse green begins to mellow and turn slightly yellow, I pick them. If they are picked too early, the pears will not convert enough starches to sugar and be sweet and juicy. If picked too late, they are gritty. Another clue that it is time to pick is if a few pears have already ripened and fallen from the tree. Once you have picked your pears—or brought them home from the grocery store, where they will also be unripe—let them sit out at room temperature to finish ripening for several days before eating.

1. Put the sugar in a punch bowl, pour in the rum, and stir to blend. Add the lemon peel, the lemon, and the bay leaves. Let the mixture steep for 1 hour.

2. Bring the wine to a simmer in a saucepan, then pour it into the punch bowl. Stir, and ladle into punch glasses.

FRENCH VALLEY SPICED PEAR CORDIAL

P ear trees have been grown in southern Illinois along the Mississippi River for more than two centuries. That portion of the valley has many French settlements, most of which date from the eighteenth century, and is casually known as the French Valley. A sip of this amber nectar as you sit by the warm fireside on a cold winter night will banish any worries. Bartlett, Kieffer, or Seckel pears are excellent choices for this cordial. Besides sipping it straight up, you can add a tablespoon or two of the cordial to beaten eggs to make a really French French toast, or mix the cordial in equal parts with a dry white wine for a mulled pear wine.

MAKES 1 GENEROUS
QUART

3 *large or 6 small ripe but still firm*
  pears
2 *cups Cognac*
2½ *cups vodka*
1¼ *cups sugar*
1 *teaspoon whole cloves*
2 *cinnamon sticks*
1 *small whole nutmeg*

1. Place the pears in a 2-quart widemouth jar. Bring the Cognac, vodka, and sugar to a simmer in a large saucepan, and continue simmering until the sugar dissolves, about 10 minutes.

2. Pour the hot liquid over the pears. Add the cloves, cinnamon, and nutmeg, distributing them evenly in the jar. Let the mixture cool down, then close tightly and let sit for 6 weeks in a cool, dry place. Serve at room temperature or, if you like, reheat it for a mulled pear wine.

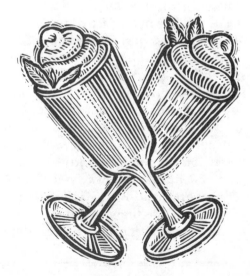

BLACKBERRY CORDIAL

A profusion of blackberries, in the wild, on farms, and in backyards, ripens throughout the midwest in the late summer. You can drink this cordial straight up, but I prefer to use it to make what I call a Prairie Kir: I place a tablespoon of the cordial and a fresh or preserved blackberry in the bottom of a wine glass and top up with a dry white wine.

MAKES 1 GENEROUS QUART

1 quart fresh blackberries or
    4 cups frozen blackberries,
    thawed
1 quart vodka
1½ cups sugar

Put the blackberries in the bottom of a large widemouth jar. Pour the vodka and sugar over the blackberries, tighten the lid, and shake gently to blend. Store for at least 2 months in a cool, dry place before using. To decant, pour the liquid through a cheesecloth-lined strainer into a bowl, then funnel the cordial into a decanter.

A TASTE OF HONEY

With their abundance of wildflowers, sunflowers, and blossoming clover, it is no surprise that the prairie states are among the largest producers of honey in the United States. North and South Dakota alone account for almost sixty million pounds of honey each year. The two main honey varieties from the midwest are blossom honey, also called clover honey, and wildflower honey.

Blossom honey, produced from early spring to mid-summer, is light in color and mildly sweet in flavor. It is made by honeybees that favor wild plum blossoms, on scrub trees that line creek beds, or cone-shaped clover blossoms, which grow amid other prairie grasses.

Wildflower honey is darker, richer, and less sweet. This midsummer to early fall honey has become a favorite with chefs because it gives a distinct honey flavor without too much sweetness. An abundance of prairie wildflowers gives the bees a lot of choice: black-eyed Susan, prairie flax, blue grama, annual phlox, blanket flower, and evening primrose.

In prairie kitchens, honey sweetens desserts of all kinds, from spice cookies to cobblers and ice creams. But the undeniable favorite is to drizzle honey over split and buttered biscuits hot from the oven.

SIMMERING SOUPS

SIMMERING SOUPS

AUGUST CORN AND TOMATO BISQUE

Fresh sweet corn and tomatoes ripen together in midwestern gardens at the beginning of August, so a lot of cooks have recipes for corn and tomato bisques. But this is a soup you can make at other times of the year, too. At our last organic farmers' market of the growing season, in November, I bought some beautiful Big Rainbow heirloom tomatoes, which have salmon and gold stripes, and I used these and frozen shoepeg corn to make the soup. Take care not to boil this soup; the acids in the tomatoes and wine will cause the soup to separate if you do.

SERVES 4

2 tablespoons unsalted butter
⅓ cup chopped yellow onion
⅓ cup chopped green bell pepper
1 tablespoon all-purpose flour
2 cups finely chopped peeled
    tomatoes
1½ cups half-and-half, scalded, or
    evaporated lowfat milk
1 cup kernels fresh or frozen sweet
    corn or shoepeg corn
⅓ cup dry white wine
Salt and white pepper to taste
Fresh parsley, for garnish

1. Melt the butter in a stockpot or large saucepan over medium heat. Add the onion and bell pepper, and sauté them until the onion is translucent, 6 to 8 minutes. Reduce the heat to low, and stir in the flour.

2. Add the tomatoes, half-and-half, and corn. Bring to a simmer over medium heat, but do not boil. Simmer, uncovered, for 10 minutes, until the corn is tender. Add the white wine and simmer for 5 minutes more. Season with salt and white pepper, taste, and adjust the seasoning. Serve hot, garnished with parsley.

CHILLED YELLOW TOMATO SOUP WITH BLACK OLIVE CREAM

When the tomato glut hits in late August, make up a batch of this vibrant soup and revel in the season. Yellow tomatoes are lower in acidity than red ones, so if you substitute red tomatoes you may want to add a little sugar to balance the flavor. This recipe is adapted from one by Michael McLaughlin, who has a real feel for regional American food, that appeared in the *Chicago Tribune*. Accompany this refreshing soup with very good artisan or homemade bread and a leafy green salad. For a fancy light dinner, add a German Cheese Tart (page 393).

SERVES 8

5 tablespoons unsalted butter

2 large leeks, white part only,
    cleaned well and sliced thin

1 tablespoon minced fresh thyme

2 bay leaves

2 pounds yellow tomatoes,
    preferably, chopped, or 2
    pounds red tomatoes, chopped

3½ cups chicken stock

2 teaspoons sugar

·1 tablespoon salt

1 teaspoon fresh-ground black pepper

FOR THE OLIVE CREAM:

⅓ cup bottled or homemade black
    olive puree

¼ cup heavy cream or evaporated
    skim milk

1. Melt the butter in a nonreactive pot over low heat. Add the leeks, thyme, and bay leaves, and cook, covered, for 20 minutes, stirring several times. Stir in the tomatoes, stock, sugar, salt, and pepper. Bring to a simmer and cook, uncovered, stirring once or twice, for 25 minutes, until the tomatoes are very tender and the soup has thickened. Remove from the heat and let cool slightly. Remove and discard the bay leaves.

2. Puree the soup in a food processor or blender. Transfer to a bowl, cover, and refrigerate until well chilled, at least 4 hours. (The soup may be prepared to this point up to 2 days ahead.)

3. Make the olive cream by whisking together the black olive puree and the cream in a small bowl.

4. Taste the soup and adjust the seasoning. Ladle the soup into chilled bowls and drizzle the olive cream over each serving.

IN EL·A·NOY

Way down upon the Wabash
Such land was never known,
If Adam had passed over it,
The soil he'd surely own.
He'd think it was the garden
He'd played in when a boy,
And straight pronounce it Eden
In the state of El-a-noy.

—FOLKSONG

SHAKER FRESH HERB SOUP

In the nineteenth century, the herb garden was a household's pharmacy. No group was better known for their herbal knowledge than the Shakers, some of whom settled in Ohio, near what is now Cleveland, in a community they called North Union. The Shakers were ahead of their time in espousing a "preventive medicine" approach, with a variety of good and healthy food, fresh air, physical exercise, keeping busy, and living with a sense of purpose. Just savoring the aroma of this fresh-tasting soup makes you feel better, a welcome back to a sense of well-being after a stressful week or a bout with a cold.

SERVES 4 TO 6

1 tablespoon unsalted butter
2 tablespoons snipped fresh chives
2 tablespoons chopped fresh sorrel
2 tablespoons chopped fresh
    chervil (see Note)
1 teaspoon chopped fresh tarragon
1 cup minced celery
4 cups chicken stock
Salt and fresh-ground black
    pepper to taste
2 cups Homemade Croutons
    (page 41)

1. Melt the butter in a stockpot over medium heat. Add the herbs and celery, and sauté, stirring, for 2 to 3 minutes, until the celery is just soft.

2. Add the stock, salt, and pepper. Bring to a simmer over medium-high heat, reduce the heat, and simmer, partially covered, for 20 minutes. Taste the soup and adjust the seasoning. Portion out the croutons into serving bowls and ladle the soup over the toasted bread. Serve hot.

NOTE: If you cannot find fresh chervil, substitute an additional 2 tablespoons chopped fresh tarragon.

GINGERED CARROT AND PARSNIP SOUP

In the upper midwest, cold-hardy root crops like carrots and parsnips were the only reliable winter vegetables in the early days of settlement. The pleasingly sweet flavor of this creamy soup gets a lift from fresh ginger and lemon juice. Serve with warm bread and fresh fruit for a simple midweek dinner.

SERVES 4

3 cups shredded carrots
3 cups shredded parsnips
1 1-inch-long piece fresh ginger,
    peeled and shredded
2 cups chicken stock or vegetable
    stock
1/2 to 3/4 cup heavy cream or
    evaporated skim milk
Salt and white pepper to taste
1 teaspoon fresh lemon juice
Snipped fresh chives, optional, for
    garnish

1. Bring the carrots, parsnips, ginger, and stock to a boil in a large saucepan over medium heat. Reduce the heat and simmer, partially covered, for 30 minutes, or until the vegetables are very tender. Remove from the heat and let cool slightly.

2. Transfer the contents of the saucepan to a blender or food processor. Puree the soup until it is nearly smooth, then pour the puree

back into the saucepan. Add the cream, and bring to a simmer again over medium heat. Stir in the salt, white pepper, and lemon juice. Taste, and adjust the seasonings. Garnish with chives, if you like. Serve hot, or refrigerate, covered, for several hours and serve chilled.

SALSIFY SOUP

A favorite in old-time gardens, salsify is a long root vegetable that is available in markets at holiday time. Its pale coloring and mild oysterlike flavor—it's also called *oyster plant*—make it perfect for a creamy bisque. The lemon juice adds flavor and keeps the salsify from discoloring.

SERVES 4 TO 6

5 medium (7 to 9 inches) salsify
  roots
Juice of 1/2 lemon
4 cups whole milk or half-and-half
Salt and white pepper, preferably
  fresh-ground, to taste
Snipped fresh chives, for garnish

1. Peel the salsify roots and slice them thin. Immediately put them into a saucepan with enough cold water to cover. Add the lemon juice. Bring to a boil and cook, uncovered, until tender, about 10 minutes. Remove the pan from the heat.

2. Mash the salsify with a potato masher against the bottom of the pan; or, for a smoother soup, puree it with the cooking liquid in batches in a food processor or blender, and return the puree to the pan. Add the milk, adjusting the quantity of milk up or down to vary the thickness to your liking. Bring to a simmer over medium heat, and stir in the salt and white pepper. Simmer gently, stirring, until heated through, 2 to 3 minutes. Taste the soup and adjust the seasonings. Serve hot, garnished with chives.

HOMINY SOUP WITH CRÈME FRAÎCHE

Early settlers on the prairie learned from Native Americans how to make hominy from dent corn soaked in lye. Other homesteaders who came to the midwest from the East or the South brought hominy with them as a preserved food. Midwesterners still like their hominy today. Its unique flavor blends well with warm spices such as cumin or coriander and with mellow crème fraîche.

SERVES 6 TO 8

1 cup heavy cream
1 cup sour cream
2 tablespoons corn oil or canola oil
1 cup minced yellow onion

2 garlic cloves, minced
¼ cup chopped green bell pepper
¼ cup chopped red bell pepper
2 teaspoons ground cumin
2 teaspoons ground coriander
10 cups chicken stock
28 ounces canned white hominy
28 ounces canned yellow hominy
Salt and black pepper to taste

1. Make a simple version of crème fraîche by whisking together the heavy cream and sour cream in a bowl and letting the mixture stand, covered, at room temperature for several hours.

2. Heat the oil in a stockpot or large saucepan over medium heat. Add the onion, garlic, and bell peppers, and sauté until the vegetables have softened, about 5 minutes. Stir in the cumin and coriander and cook, stirring, for 1 minute more.

3. Add the stock and the 2 kinds of hominy. Bring to a boil, reduce the heat, and simmer, partially covered, for 15 to 20 minutes to let

FEAST OF THE HUNTER'S MOON

In 1717, Fort Ouiatenon, near the Wabash River in present-day Lafayette, Indiana, was a French outpost amid a number of Indian villages. The fort was home to a standing military presence, along with the soldiers' wives and children. The Fort also served as a way station for French-Canadian voyageurs, the compact-bodied and boisterous truck drivers of the eighteenth century, who brought trade goods down from Canada to the early river settlements and left, in their huge birchbark canoes, with furs collected and sold by Native Americans. The voyageurs paddled the riverways, often kneeling among bales of furs. When the rivers ended, the voyageurs had to portage their canoes and freight over difficult terrain until another waterway was reached.

Fort Ouiatenon was taken over by the British in 1763, after the French and Indian War, ending the official French presence in Indiana.

Each October, this period in Lafayette's history is celebrated with the Feast of the Hunter's Moon. A variety of old French and Native American foods are cooked over open fires, men dress as voyageurs and sing bawdy songs—in French, so the children cannot understand—and eighteenth-century military buffs camp out. If you have never tasted hominy cooked over a wood fire or roasted apples, come to Lafayette for this open-air fall celebration.

the flavors blend. Season with salt and pepper to taste. Serve hot, with a dollop of crème fraîche atop each bowl.

WILD MUSHROOM POT DE BOUILLON

In early French settlements along the Mississippi and Missouri rivers, no party was complete without a *pot de bouillon*, a warm and hearty broth strengthened with spirits and drunk in a cup with a handle. This updated recipe makes enough for a gathering of après-skiers, sledders, or New Year's Eve partygoers. You can serve this *pot de bouillon* as a soup at suppertime or as a punch for a party.

SERVES 12

2 ounces dried wild mushrooms,
    such as morels or porcini
16 cups canned or homemade beef
    consommé
1/2 cup dry sherry or cognac
Juice of 1 lemon
1/2 teaspoon fresh-ground black
    pepper

1. Bring the wild mushrooms and the consommé to a boil in a stockpot or large saucepan. Reduce the heat and simmer, partially covered, until the mushrooms are soft, about 20 minutes. Remove the mushrooms with a slotted spoon and discard them.

2. Just before serving, stir in the sherry, lemon juice, and pepper. Taste the soup and adjust the seasonings. Serve hot in soup bowls or, as a punch, with drinking cups.

POLISH WILD MUSHROOM AND POTATO SOUP

When the winter winds howl through Chicago, frozen urbanites huddle over bowls of this soup in any number of Polish cafés and homestyle restaurants. With a green salad, a big chunk of dark peasant bread, and a wheat beer, you'll forget the cold.

SERVES 4 TO 6

1 1/2 cups (about 3/4 ounce) dried
    wild mushrooms, such as
    morels or porcini
2 tablespoons unsalted butter
3/4 cup chopped yellow onion
1 cup chopped celery
1 teaspoon caraway seeds
4 large potatoes, peeled and diced
1/4 cup all-purpose flour
1 quart milk
1/2 cup heavy cream
Salt and black pepper to taste
Snipped fresh chives or minced
    fresh parsley, for garnish

1. Combine the mushrooms and 3 cups of water in a large saucepan. Bring to a boil, reduce the heat, and simmer, partially covered, for 15 to 20 minutes, or until the mushrooms have begun to soften (the time depends on the type of mushroom you use). Drain the mushrooms and reserve the cooking liquid. Chop the mushrooms fine.

2. Melt the butter in the same saucepan. Add the onion, celery, caraway, and mushrooms, and sauté over medium-low heat until the celery is almost tender, about 6 minutes. Meanwhile, in a large stockpot, bring the reserved mushroom liquid to a boil.

3. Add the potatoes to the mushroom liquid and cook, covered, at a gentle boil until the potatoes are tender, 10 to 15 minutes. Add the sautéed vegetables to the soup and return to a boil. Mash about half the potatoes against the side of the pot with a spoon.

4. Whisk or stir together the flour and 1 cup of the milk in a bowl until smooth. Stir the flour mixture into the soup, then add the remaining milk and the cream. Reduce the heat and simmer until the soup is heated through. Season to taste with salt and pepper. Serve hot, garnished with chives or parsley.

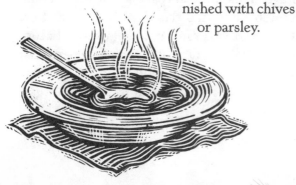

WISCONSIN CHEDDAR BEER SOUP

In Wisconsin, they'll cook just about anything with beer. Soups of cheddar and beer have taken off nationally, in brew pubs and among home cooks; this is my take on the Badger State original. This hearty soup is delicious to serve when there's a nip in the air.

SERVES 4

2 tablespoons unsalted butter
1/4 cup chopped yellow onion
1/2 cup thin-sliced celery
2 tablespoons all-purpose flour
1/4 teaspoon cayenne pepper
1/4 teaspoon dry mustard
1 cup milk
1 1/2 cups full-bodied beer
2 to 3 cups shredded cheddar
    cheese
1 tablespoon paprika

1. Melt the butter in a stockpot or large saucepan over medium heat. Add the onion and celery, and sauté them until they have softened, 6 to 8 minutes. Stir in the flour and cook, stirring constantly, for 2 minutes more. Add the cayenne and mustard, and stir to blend.

2. Whisk in the milk and beer. Whisking constantly, bring the soup to a boil over

1 pickled pig's foot
½ teaspoon salt
½ teaspoon black pepper
Red wine vinegar or white wine
vinegar, optional

1. Bring all of the ingredients, except the vinegar, and 3 quarts of water to a boil in a large stockpot. Reduce the heat, and simmer, covered, over low heat until the beans are tender, about 1 hour. Stir occasionally as the beans cook.

2. Serve hot, with vinegar at the table, if you like. Swedish rye bread and fresh fruit are traditional accompaniments.

medium-high heat. Reduce the heat and simmer, uncovered, until the soup is thick, about 15 minutes. Remove the soup from the heat. Add the cheddar and paprika, and stir them through the soup until the cheese has melted. Serve hot.

HOMESTEADERS' BEAN SOUP

During the long winters, a robust pot of bean soup simmering on the wood stove kept up the spirits of many a Dakota homesteader from Scandinavia. The pickled pig's foot is traditional, but you may substitute a ham hock, smoked or not, instead. Old-timers serve this with a cruet of vinegar to splash on the soup at the table.

SERVES 6 TO 8

16 ounces dried white or navy
beans, picked over and rinsed
well
2 to 3 bay leaves

MILWAUKEE GERMAN LENTIL SOUP

Nestled on the western shore of Lake Michigan an hour north of Chicago, Milwaukee takes pride in its German heritage. This thick and smoky-flavored soup, which I adapted from one served at Karl Ratzch's restaurant in Milwaukee, a fixture since 1904, is a favorite warmer-upper when winter winds come howling in off the lake. Homemade croutons and fresh parsley garnish each bowl.

SERVES 6 TO 8

16 ounces dried lentils, picked over
    and rinsed well
3 quarts chicken stock or ham stock
1 bay leaf
½ teaspoon Worcestershire sauce
1 garlic clove, minced
¼ teaspoon fresh-grated nutmeg
4 drops bottled hot pepper sauce
¼ teaspoon caraway seeds
½ teaspoon celery salt
1 cup chopped carrots
1 cup chopped celery
1 cup chopped yellow onion
½ pound smoked ham, chopped
2 tablespoons bacon grease
2 tablespoons all-purpose flour
Homemade Croutons (page 41)
    and chopped fresh parsley,
    for garnish

1. Place the lentils, stock, bay leaf, Worcestershire, garlic, nutmeg, hot pepper sauce, caraway, and celery salt in a large stockpot. Bring to a boil, reduce the heat, cover, and simmer, stirring occasionally, for 30 minutes. Stir in the carrots, celery, onion, and ham, and cook for 10 minutes more, until the vegetables have softened.

2. Meanwhile, melt the bacon grease in a skillet over medium-low heat. Whisk in the flour to make a roux. Whisk the roux into the hot soup, a teaspoon or so at a time, until the soup is thickened to your liking. Serve hot, garnishing each bowl with croutons and a sprinkling of parsley.

THREE GENERATIONS, SAME SOUP

"We can trace three generations of German recipes in our family," says Micheline Burger of Kansas City. "My grandmother, Oma, my mother, Anja, and I have all cooked the same things, but maybe not in the same ways." In Oma's time in Bavaria, the family's favorite lentil soup was a wash-day meal that would simmer all day long on a coal stove in a heavy iron pot. When Anja made the soup in Wichita, Kansas, she used a stainless steel pot on a new gas range. Now, when Micheline makes the dish, she puts all the ingredients in a slow-cooker and lets the soup simmer all day while she is at work.

SWEDISH YELLOW PEA SOUP

This soup, bordering on a stew, makes for a hearty one-dish meal. It is an old-style peasant dish well suited for a cold-weather wash day when an easy dinner simmering on the fire was the housewife's requirement. Today, this soup can simmer away on a

Sunday afternoon, with enough left over to reheat on a more hectic Monday.

SERVES 6 TO 8

16 ounces dried whole Swedish
 yellow peas (see Note)
1½ pounds boneless pork loin
1 medium yellow onion, chopped
1 bay leaf
3 quarts chicken stock
1 teaspoon salt
1 teaspoon fresh-ground black
 pepper
4 medium potatoes, peeled and
 quartered

1. Soak the peas in water to cover overnight; or put them in a saucepan with water to cover, bring to a boil, remove from the heat, and let soak for 1 hour. Drain the peas.

2. Place the pork loin in the bottom of a stock-pot or large saucepan. Add the peas, onion, and bay leaf. Pour in the stock and season with salt and pepper. Bring to a boil, reduce the heat, cover, and simmer gently for at least 4 hours, stirring occasionally and skimming off any foam. After 3 hours, add the potatoes, and stir well. Add water if necessary to make sure the soup does not scorch.

3. Taste the soup and adjust the seasonings. To serve as a soup: Remove the pork loin and shred it fine, and remove the potatoes and chop them. Return the pork and potatoes to the soup, stir, heat through for 3 to 4 minutes, and serve. To serve as a stew: Slice the pork loin, 1 slice for each bowl, and put a slice and some potatoes in each bowl. Pour the soup over, and serve.

NOTE: These heirloom peas are becoming more widely available in Swedish communities in the midwest and in specialty stores. If you cannot find them, substitute split yellow peas, and omit the first step and reduce the cooking time in step 2 to 2 hours.

SPRING GREENS BORSCHT

Here is a spring tonic popular in Russian Mennonite communities throughout the prairie. *Borscht* for the Mennonites is synonymous with vegetable soup—not just beet soup—and the kinds of borscht they serve change throughout the year. First come the borschts made with wild spring greens or the first greens from the garden. In summer, borschts will have cabbage and tomato, perhaps corn and squash. In the fall and winter months, borschts feature cabbage, beets, and potato. Not a delicate soup, this one is meant to wake up the tastebuds.

SERVES 6 TO 8

2 ham hocks, preferably smoked
3 medium potatoes, peeled and
 diced

8 cups mixed greens, such as
  spinach, beet greens, sorrel,
  chard, and wild greens (such
  as burdock, lamb's quarters,
  wild mustard, pig weed, or
  dandelion greens), rinsed well
  and torn into small pieces
1 medium yellow onion, chopped
2 cups snipped fresh chives or 2
  cups green onions, white and
  green parts
2 bay leaves
1/2 cup chopped fresh dill
1/4 cup chopped fresh parsley
1/2 cup light cream, for garnish

1. Place the ham hocks with water to cover in a stockpot. Bring to a boil, reduce the heat, and simmer gently, partially covered, for 1 hour. Measure the liquid in the pot, and add additional water to total 3 quarts water.

2. Add the potatoes, greens, yellow onion, chives, bay leaves, dill, and parsley. Bring to a boil, reduce the heat, and simmer, uncovered, for 30 minutes more. Stir the soup occasionally as it cooks. Serve hot, preferably in wide soup bowls. Garnish with a swirl of cream in the center of each bowl.

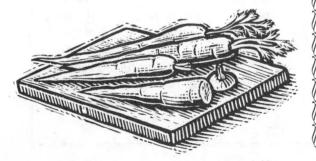

HEARTY SAUSAGE AND KALE SOUP

Growing up in Ohio, my sister and I used to enjoy a one-dish meal of dark and leafy kale, smoked sausage, and chopped turnips and onions, which my mother would simmer all day for a winter supper. This soup combines similar flavors in a quicker preparation.

SERVES 4

1 pound Italian sausage links
1 tablespoon olive oil
3/4 cup diced yellow onion
2 garlic cloves, minced
2 medium potatoes, peeled and
  diced
1 quart chicken stock
2 cups shredded kale leaves
1/3 cup heavy cream, optional

1. Preheat the oven to 300 degrees. Place the sausage links on a baking pan and bake for 25 minutes, or until they are just cooked through. Cut into half lengthwise, then cut the halves diagonally into 1/2-inch lengths.

2. Heat the oil in a stockpot or large saucepan over medium heat. Add the onions, and sauté them until they are just translucent, about 6 minutes. Add the garlic and sauté for 1 minute more. Add the potatoes and stock,

bring to a boil, reduce the heat, and simmer, uncovered, for 15 minutes. Add the sausage, kale, and, if you like, the cream. Simmer for 5 minutes more, or until the soup is completely heated through. Serve hot, with a crusty bread alongside.

THE MIDWEST

The term midwest first appeared in print in 1880 and was used to describe the Kansas-Nebraska region. By 1910 it had come to include all twelve of what most people now agree are the midwestern states: Ohio, Indiana, Michigan, Illinois, Wisconsin, Minnesota, Iowa, Missouri, North Dakota, South Dakota, Kansas, and Nebraska.

The geography of the midwest encompasses wide and fertile river valleys, limestone bluffs overlooking waterways and lakes, broad expanses of grasslands on the Great Plains and along the shores of the Great Lakes, the dry and rocky Badlands of the Dakotas, the deciduous woodlands in the northern Midwest and southern Missouri, the sand hills of Nebraska, and extensive wetlands that attract migrating wildfowl. Despite the wide divergence in geography, not to mention politics, ethnicity, and economics, the midwest is united in believing, like Dorothy in The Wizard of Oz—written about midwesterners by a midwesterner—that what's really important in life is no farther than your own backyard.

According to the geographer James Shortridge, midwestern connotes pastoralism, small-town life, hospitality and friendliness, traditional values, yeoman society, and the Jeffersonian ideal. "The Midwest is America's pastoral face," he writes, "etched into our consciousness as a permanent physical location, despite the presence of industrial cities," which latter are accepted, nonetheless, as exceptions to the rule.

Midwesterners have a grounded sense of who they are because they are still close to the land. Many families are only a generation or two removed from the family farm, and, even in a big city, many still feel that summer is not summer without canning tomatoes or making homemade jelly. Outlying farms surround most metropolitan areas, and urban midwesterners know they don't have to go far to breathe a little fresh air and be out in the country. They never really left their roots.

ITALIAN SAUSAGE AND ARTICHOKE SOUP

Fifty years ago, neighborhood Italian mom-and-pop grocery stores often made their own sausage, typically in mild and hot versions, for their customers. As the big grocery stores nudged them out, some enterprising families began to concentrate on making—and selling to the big stores—homemade sausages from family recipes centuries old. In Chicago, St. Louis, and Kansas City, or in other cities with Italian communities of long standing, locally made Italian sausages are worth seeking out and transforming into this soup.

SERVES 6

1 pound Italian pork sausage links
 or chicken florentine sausage
 links
1 large red onion, chopped
1 14-ounce can artichoke hearts,
 drained and chopped, or
 1 9-ounce package frozen
 artichoke hearts, thawed and
 chopped
1 28-ounce can plum tomatoes,
 chopped, with juice reserved
3 cups chicken stock
1 teaspoon dried oregano
1 teaspoon dried basil
1 teaspoon fennel seeds
1/4 pound penne pasta

Salt and fresh-ground black
 pepper to taste

1. Remove the sausage from its casings, if necessary, and crumble it. Brown the sausage, stirring often, with the chopped onions in a stockpot over medium heat for 6 to 8 minutes, or until the sausage is cooked through and the onions are translucent. Add the artichoke hearts and the tomatoes with their juice, then pour the stock over the sausage and vegetables. Stir in the the oregano, basil, and fennel seeds.

2. Bring to a boil over medium-high heat, reduce the heat, and simmer, uncovered, for 30 minutes. Add the pasta, and simmer for 15 minutes more, or until the pasta is al dente. Add salt and pepper. Serve hot.

NOTE: Omit the pasta, if you like, for a less filling soup. Simmer the soup for a total of 40 to 45 minutes.

DIP-IN-THE-POT SOUP

Dopp I Grytan, "dip-in-the-pot soup," remains a Christmas Eve tradition in many midwestern households of Swedish descent. Long ago in the Old Country, a kettle of this rich broth was kept simmering on the back of the stove. As the busy housewife made last-minute preparations for the holiday meal, her family would help themselves to homemade rye bread and dip it in the meaty broth whenever they became hungry.

SERVES 6 TO 8

1½ pounds lean veal or beef chuck
1½ pounds lean pork shoulder
2 tablespoons plus ½ teaspoon salt
½ teaspoon fresh-ground black
    pepper
1 teaspoon ground allspice
Rye bread croutons, preferably
    homemade (see page 41),
    for garnish

1. Two days before serving, rub the 2 tablespoons of salt into the surfaces of the meats. Cover, and let rest in the refrigerator overnight.

2. The next day, rinse off the salt, pat the meats dry, and put them in a stockpot or kettle with water to cover. Add the ½ teaspoons each of salt and pepper and the allspice. Bring to a boil, reduce the heat, and simmer gently for 2 to 3 hours, until the meats are quite tender. Remove the soup from the heat and remove the meats to cool slightly; do not drain or discard the broth. Cut the meats into small cubes, return them to the pot, cover, and refrigerate overnight.

3. On the day you wish to serve the soup, skim the congealed fat off the top of the soup and bring it to a boil again. Reduce the heat and simmer, uncovered, for 30 minutes. Taste the soup and adjust the seasonings. Place the croutons in the bottoms of individual bowls, pour the soup over, and serve.

MOCK TURTLE SOUP

This spicy and sweet-and-sour soup has long been a favorite in German immigrant communities in southern Ohio and Indiana. In the nineteenth century, river turtles were used for this recipe, but today ground beef takes their place. During the annual Chicken Dinner Trail festivities (see box, page 133), this soup is a featured item in many church suppers. With affinities to today's famous Cincinnati chili, this thick brew may be what prepared local palates for the area's chili fixation in the twentieth century.

SERVES 6 TO 8

2 tablespoons all-purpose flour
1 pound lean ground beef
16 ounces catsup, preferably a
    spicy variety
1 medium yellow onion, chopped
1 lemon, sliced very thin
2 celery ribs, chopped fine

1 tablespoon pickling spice, tied up
    in a muslin or cheesecloth bag
Salt and fresh-ground black
    pepper to taste
2 hard-cooked eggs, chopped fine,
    for garnish
Chopped fresh parsley, for garnish

ON THE CHICKEN DINNER TRAIL

Hungry folks in the Cincinnati area look forward all year to a springtime announcement in the regional Catholic Telegraph Register. Catholic readers are happy to spread the word to their friends of other faiths, because the news is just too good to keep to themselves. What's the fuss about? It is nothing less than the schedule of chicken dinners, open to the public, to be held at small churches in the southwestern Ohio countryside and across the state lines in southeastern Indiana and northern Kentucky.

On most weekends in the summer and early fall, these tiny Catholic churches gear up to feed the multitudes. The home-style fried chicken dinners have made converts—at least to the worthiness of driving miles into the country for dinner—out of staunch atheists and skeptical restaurant critics.

Imagine sitting down at a long school-cafeteria table to platters of crispy, golden chicken fried in lard, a huge bowl of real mashed potatoes, and that authentic chicken gravy that has no peer. The chicken, potatoes, and gravy are the ubiquitous standards; beyond them, each congregation contributes its own unique flavor to the rest of the offerings. At St. Cecilia's in Dover, Ohio, veteran attendees know they will also get homemade egg noodles and baked beans. At Holy Family Church in Oldenburg, Indiana, and at St. Peter's in Brookville, Indiana, the mock turtle soup is a draw (see the recipe, page 132). At St. John's in Dry Ridge, Ohio, the temptation is the fresh creamed corn. Marinated cucumbers, seasoned green beans, celery-seed coleslaw, sliced fresh tomatoes, and squash casserole appear and disappear, as the repertoire of side dishes follows the progress of local gardens. And the pies! Blackberry, cherry, custard, sugar cream, apple, peach, and everything in between. No pilgrims to Canterbury were ever as devout as the crowds that seek the perfect fried chicken dinner in the rolling farmland of the Ohio River Valley.

1. Brown the flour, whisking often so that it browns evenly, for about 5 minutes in a large saucepan over medium heat. Add the beef, catsup, onion, lemon, celery, spice bag, and 6 cups of water. Bring to a boil, reduce the heat, and simmer uncovered, stirring occasionally, for 1 hour.

2. Remove and discard the spice bag. Stir in the salt and pepper, taste the soup, and adjust the seasonings. Serve hot, garnishing each bowl with chopped eggs and parsley.

BLACK HILLS BISON CHILI IN A CORNBREAD BOWL

The term *bison* rather than *buffalo* is preferred by ranchers, because this native range animal is in the bison rather than the buffalo family. Nonetheless, the meat of this animal is almost always sold as *buffalo*. You might be served this chili dish, or a simple feast of buffalo burgers and corn on the cob, at the Nu 'Eta Corn and Buffalo Festival at Fort Lincoln State Park in Mandan, North Dakota, the first weekend in August. The Mandan tribes have grown corn along the Missouri River in North Dakota for a thousand years, as long as they have hunted the buffalo. You may substitute beef, if you prefer, for the buffalo.

SERVES 4 TO 6

FOR THE PICO DE GALLO:
  1/2 cup chopped fresh tomato
  1/2 cup chopped onion
  1/2 cup chopped fresh cilantro
  1/2 cup chopped jalapeño peppers

FOR THE CHILI:
  1 tablespoon canola oil or corn oil
  2 garlic cloves, minced
  1 large yellow onion, chopped
  1 pound ground buffalo or ground beef
  1 pound dried black turtle beans (see Note)
  1/2 cup chopped celery
  1 green bell pepper, diced
  1 cup chopped fresh or canned peeled and seeded tomatoes
  2 teaspoons dried thyme
  1 teaspoon fresh-ground black pepper
  2 bay leaves
  Sour cream, for garnish

FOR THE CORNBREAD BOWL:
  1/2 cup cornmeal
  1/2 cup all-purpose flour
  1 tablespoon sugar
  3/4 teaspoon baking powder
  1/2 teaspoon baking soda
  1 teaspoon salt
  2 tablespoons canola oil or corn oil
  1 egg, beaten
  1/2 cup buttermilk

1. Make the pico de gallo: Combine all of the ingredients in a small bowl, cover, and refrig-

erate until ready to serve. Bring to room temperature before serving. (The pico de gallo is best if made no more than a day ahead.)

2. Make the chili: Heat the oil in a large stockpot over medium-low heat. Add the garlic and onion, and sauté them until they are softened, 6 to 8 minutes. Add the buffalo and the beans, celery, bell pepper, tomatoes, thyme, black pepper, bay leaves, and 1 quart of water. Bring to a boil over medium-high heat, reduce the heat, cover partially, and simmer, stirring frequently, for 1½ hours or until the chili is very thick but not dried out.

3. While the chili is simmering, prepare the cornbread bowl. Preheat the oven to 400 degrees. Stir together the cornmeal, flour, sugar, baking powder, baking soda, and salt in a medium bowl. Mix in the oil, egg, and buttermilk; do not overmix. Lightly oil or butter a 1-quart round glass baking dish. Find a pot (the top of a standard-size double boiler works well; don't worry about the handle, as long as it is heatproof) or a smaller heatproof mixing bowl that fits into the baking dish with about 1 inch all around to spare; this pot or bowl will form the bowl shape of the cornbread. Cover the bottom and sides of the pot or bowl with aluminum foil and spray the foil with nonstick cooking spray or lightly oil it. Pour the batter into the outer glass baking dish, then place the foil-covered pot or bowl in the center of the batter. Push down gently

WINTER ON LAKE MICHIGAN

In 1982, Justin Rashid co-founded, with Larry Forgione, American Spoon Foods, a very fine maker and catalog retailer (see Resources, page 416) of regional specialty foods such as jams, preserves, fruit butters, and dried fruits. Born and raised in Michigan, Rashid brings a touch of the poetic to the American Spoon Foods catalogs. Here is an excerpt:

"Winter comes to our edge of Northern Michigan on winds that have crossed one hundred miles of open water. Perched on hills above Lake Michigan's vast plain, we can see it coming a long way off. We often stand above the lake, transfixed by the force of the wind and the endless play of colors in sky, water, and the distant hills to the north. . . . Towering gray clouds appear to be bringing snow down from Canada. The northwest wind that carries them has undressed the hills across Little Traverse Bay. There is no end to the wind and no end to the seasons that circle us again and again. It is up to us to celebrate the beauty of the days that visit and the love of people that bring us joy and peace."

so that the batter rises up the sides of the baking dish. Bake for 20 to 25 minutes, or until the cornbread is golden brown and a toothpick inserted in it comes out clean. Remove the foil-covered pot or bowl and let the cornbread cool slightly before filling it.

4. Pour the chili in the cornbread bowl, and spoon the chili and cornbread into individual bowls at the table. Pass the sour cream and pico de gallo in serving bowls.

NOTE: You may substitute 2 cups canned and drained black beans, if you like. If you do so, use 2 cups water rather than 1 quart in step 2, and simmer the chili for just 1/2 hour.

RUSSIAN MENNONITE CHICKEN NOODLE SOUP

This is a simple, traditional soup served in Mennonite communities in Saskatchewan. The use of star anise, the surprising ingredient here, dates to the years the Mennonites spent in the Netherlands. The homemade noodles should be cut very thin.

SERVES 8 TO 10

4 whole star anise
10 whole black peppercorns
6 bay leaves

10 cups good-quality chicken stock, preferably homemade
2 to 3 cups uncooked Homemade Egg Noodles (page 259) or 12 ounces uncooked dried egg noodles
1/3 cup chopped fresh parsley
Salt, optional

1. Tie together the star anise, peppercorns, and bay leaves in a cheesecloth bag. Pour the stock into a stockpot and add the spice bag. Bring to a boil over medium-high heat, reduce the heat, and simmer, partially covered, for 20 to 30 minutes; the longer the simmer, the stronger the flavor.

2. Remove the spice bag and discard it. Add the noodles and parsley, and bring to a boil again over medium-high heat, reduce the heat, and simmer until the noodles are cooked (the time will vary depending on the kind of noodles you have). Remove from the heat, and season to taste with salt, if you like, if your stock is not particularly salty. Serve hot. This soup freezes well, too.

HEARTLAND SMOKED CHICKEN AND CORN CHOWDER

Midwestern specialty meat purveyors, particularly in upper midwest states like Wisconsin, now produce a range of deep-flavored wood-smoked bacons, which they sell through grocery stores and by mail-order. This comforting and colorful chowder, which you can serve hot or cold, is a fine platform for serving up your favorite variety.

SERVES 6 TO 8

1/2 pound bacon, preferably apple-smoked, diced
1 medium yellow onion, chopped
1 red bell pepper, chopped
1 green bell pepper, chopped
6 cups fresh, preferably, or frozen corn kernels
2 cups chopped cooked Smoked Herbed Chicken (page 222) or other smoked chicken
4 potatoes, peeled and diced
3 cups half-and-half
1/4 teaspoon cayenne pepper
Salt and fresh-ground black pepper to taste

SMOKY SOUPS

One redeeming quality of the cold and dreary days of winter is that they make us appreciate the therapeutic and culinary value of a great bowl of soup. For a few brief minutes, we can cup our hands around the warm bowl and breathe in the aromatic steam that rises in the chilly air. And when the soup spoon reaches the tongue, we appreciate a taste that is hearty, not delicate—the difference between a bulky sweater and a silk scarf.

Prairie food is all about heartiness and comfort. Winters in the Heartland test everyone's mettle, with ice storms, blizzards, and endless gray days of bone-chilling cold. When the icicles form, we want a flavor that evokes the warmth and comfort of the fireplace and the hearth. Soups with smoked foods do the trick.

Smoked foods are a staple of midwestern cuisine, whether cold-smoked ones like Polish sausages or smoked whitefish, or hot-smoked ones, like authentic Kansas City barbecue. Smoked foods are great straight up, but they really star as ingredients in cold-weather soups.

1. Sauté the bacon in a large saucepan over medium-low heat. After about 2 minutes, when the bacon has rendered some fat, add the onion and bell peppers. Continue sautéing until the vegetables are crisp-tender, 4 to 5 minutes more. Add 4 cups of the corn along with the chicken and the potatoes. Add water just to cover. Bring to a boil over medium-high heat, reduce the heat, cover, and simmer, stirring several times, for 1 hour.

2. Puree the remaining 2 cups of corn with 1 cup of the half-and-half in a food processor or blender. Stir this puree into the soup, and simmer for 30 minutes more. Just before serving, add the remaining half-and-half, the cayenne, and salt and pepper. Heat through for a minute or two, taste, and adjust the seasonings. Serve hot; or let cool, cover, and refrigerate for several hours to serve chilled.

GREAT LAKES POTATO AND WHITEFISH CHOWDER

Near the shore towns of the Great Lakes, from Sandusky in Ohio to Sturgeon Bay in Wisconsin's Door County, you will see fresh-caught whitefish strung from lines to dry before going into the smoker. Each little town has its favorite smoked whitefish, and this recipe welcomes them all. A relative of the British kedgeree and the Scottish cullen skink, this soup can take as much smoky flavor as you like, so vary the amount of smoked fish to suit your tastes.

SERVES 6 TO 8

1 tablespoon unsalted butter
2 leeks, white part only, cleaned
    well and sliced thin
1 medium yellow onion, chopped
2 large potatoes, peeled and
    chopped
2 cups chicken stock
1/2 to 1 cup chopped smoked
    whitefish
Pinch of dried marjoram
1 cup half-and-half
1/2 cup light cream
Salt and white pepper to taste

1. Melt the butter in a stockpot or large saucepan over medium-low heat. Add the leeks and onion, and sauté them until the onions are translucent and the leeks have softened, about 8 minutes.

2. Add the potatoes and stock and bring to a boil. Cover partially, and cook at a gentle boil for 15 minutes, or until the potatoes are tender. Reduce to a simmer, and add the whitefish, marjoram, half-and-half, cream, salt, and white pepper. Heat through for 2 to 3 minutes, taste, and adjust the seasonings. Serve hot.

THE PRAIRIE LIMNER

In 1930, the debut of Grant Wood's painting American Gothic caused a sensation with its minimalist style, much like that of the eighteenth-century New England naive artists called "limners," and with its stark emotional tone. The portrait of a dour farmer holding a pitchfork and his equally dour wife, the two of them standing soberly dressed in front of a Gothic-style farmhouse, would become the best known of all of Wood's work. One woman who viewed the painting when it was first displayed was quoted in the Des Moines Register as saying the farm wife's gaze "could positively curdle milk."

In the 1920s, Wood had visited the Eldon, Iowa, home depicted in the painting. What struck Wood was how the simplicity of the home on its lower floor contrasted with what he called the "pretentious" Gothic window on each gable end. He sketched the house on the back of an envelope and later used the sketch as the model for the backdrop to "American Gothic." As far as the dour couple is concerned, Wood used his own sister, Nan, and his dentist, Dr. B. H. McKeelby, as models. Although Wood intended the couple to represent a small-town farmer and his daughter, most people think of the pair as man and wife. The painting now hangs in the Art Institute of Chicago. The home in Eldon is still occupied.

B.B.'s BARBECUE GUMBO

On a visit to Kansas City, *Chicago Tribune* food columnist Bill Rice, a man who knows his barbecue, joined me for lunch at B.B.'s Lawnside Bar-B-Que. We grazed our way through small samplings of smoked ribs, sausage, and chicken, but when Bill took a bite of B.B.'s gumbo, he pronounced it "amazing" and proceeded to eat a big bowl full of the earthy brew. The smoked chicken and smoked sausage distinguish this gumbo from the Louisiana versions.

SERVES 6 TO 8

2 tablespoons canola oil or corn oil
1 medium yellow onion, chopped
2 celery ribs, sliced thin
2 garlic cloves, minced
1 green bell pepper, chopped
14 ounces canned tomatoes, chopped, with their juice
2 cups spicy tomato-based barbecue sauce

1 cup chopped smoked chicken
  breast (see Note)
1 cup 1-inch pieces smoked
  sausage (see Note)
12 ounces medium shrimp, peeled
  and deveined
2 cups 1-inch pieces fresh okra, or
  20 ounces canned cut okra,
  drained

1. Heat the oil in a stockpot or large saucepan over medium heat. Add the onion, celery, and garlic, and sauté them until the onion is translucent, 6 to 8 minutes.

2. Add the remaining ingredients, along with 1 cup of water. Bring to a boil over medium-high heat, reduce the heat, and simmer, partially covered, for 20 minutes. Stir occasionally as the gumbo cooks. Serve hot, over cooked rice if you like.

NOTE: You may use chicken and sausage that you have cooked in your own barbecue smoker, or you can use store-bought smoked meats.

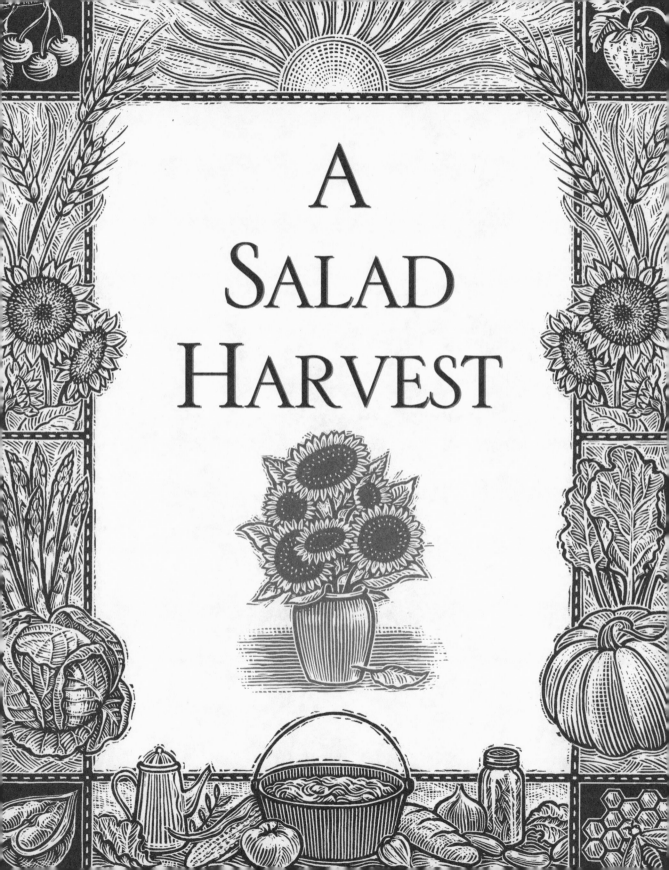

A
Salad
Harvest

A
SALAD HARVEST

WATERCRESS AND BRIE SALAD

Talking to a cheese expert about "midwestern Brie" is like talking to a wine aficionado about "California Bordeaux." Your interlocutor will not be impressed. In fact, there is good domestic Brie made in the United States, mainly in the dairy belt states of Illinois and Wisconsin. It may lack the ultra-richness of flavor of the French original, but, on the positive side, it also lacks the fat content and the big price tag. Make this salad in the spring when watercress is at its freshest and most peppery-tasting.

SERVES 4

3 bunches watercress, roots and
    dead leaves trimmed
6 ounces Brie, rind trimmed
1/4 cup fresh lemon juice
1/4 cup extra-virgin olive oil

1. Gently rinse the watercress and pat it dry. Separate the branches. Cut the Brie into bite-size cubes. Arrange the watercress and Brie on individual salad plates.

2. Whisk together the lemon juice and olive oil in a small bowl. Drizzle over each salad, and serve.

PEAR AND PECAN SALAD WITH WHEAT BEER VINAIGRETTE

Wheat beer of all kinds is a favorite, not surprisingly, in microbreweries in wheat country states like Kansas, Nebraska, and South Dakota. In a dressing, its mellow flavor needs a little jump start, from a tart wedge of lemon, a kick of raspberry, or, as in this recipe, balsamic vinegar.

SERVES 6 TO 8

FOR THE VINAIGRETTE:
    3/4 cup wheat beer
    2 garlic cloves, minced
    1 tablespoon wildflower or other
        medium-colored honey
    1 tablespoon Dijon mustard
    1/2 cup balsamic vinegar
    2/3 cup extra-virgin olive oil

FOR THE SALAD:
    4 cups mixed fresh greens, such as
        Bibb lettuce, redleaf lettuce,
        radicchio, baby spinach, and
        escarole
    3 to 4 ripe pears, peeled, cored, and
        sliced thin
    6 ounces fresh goat cheese
    1/2 cup toasted pecans

1. Bring the beer to a boil in a small saucepan. Boil until the volume is reduced to about 1/4 cup, about 10 minutes. Remove from the heat

and whisk in the garlic, honey, mustard, and vinegar. Slowly whisk in the oil. Taste, and adjust the seasonings.

2. Arrange the greens on 6 to 8 plates. Arrange the pear slices on top of the greens. Crumble the goat cheese on the pears and dress each salad with the vinaigrette. Sprinkle

the pecans over each salad, and serve. The vinaigrette will keep, covered, for several weeks in the refrigerator.

PEAR, BLUE CHEESE, AND TOASTED WALNUT MOLDS

S unday dinner at my grandmother's often meant a salad of canned pear halves on a lettuce leaf, with a cream cheese ball rolled in toasted walnuts nestled in the core of each pear. This recipe takes up that theme but is more savory in taste and opaque in appearance. It's still a refreshing counterpoint to a heavy meal.

SERVES 8

1 15-ounce can of pears in pear
    juice concentrate
2½ (¼-ounce) envelopes
    unflavored gelatin
Juice of 1 lemon
2 fresh pears, peeled, cored, and
    chopped fine
8 tablespoons crumbled blue
    cheese
8 large lettuce leaves
¼ cup mayonnaise, thinned with
    1 tablespoon milk
½ cup toasted walnuts or pecans,
    for garnish
Paprika, for garnish

THE ART OF GELATIN

T here are congealed salads, and there are congealed salads. An artificially flavored gelatin "salad," candy-colored and far too sweet, has long been the cliché of the family dinner and a staple of a not very good grocery store's salad bar. Many sophisticated cooks have scoffed at the gelatin salad. But done well, with natural ingredients, the molded salad can be a delicious palate cleanser or a light respite in a rich meal. The simple trick is to use natural unflavored gelatin, a liquid base of fruit juice or wine, and fresh fruits. Usually 1 tablespoon of gelatin will gel 2 cups of liquid. Because the gelatin will be served chilled, and chilling will dull the taste somewhat, the flavor of the liquid should be quite pronounced before the gelatin is refrigerated.

1. Lightly oil 8 ½-cup gelatin molds. Puree the pears and their juice in a food processor or blender. Strain the mixture through a fine-meshed sieve into a saucepan. Sprinkle the gelatin over the pear puree, and heat the mixture over low heat, stirring occasionally, until the gelatin has thoroughly melted, about 5 minutes. Stir in the lemon juice.

2. Distribute the chopped fresh pears among the 8 molds. Top with the blue cheese. Pour the gelatin mixture into each mold. Refrigerate, covered, for at least 2 hours until the gelatin has set.

3. Place the lettuce leaves on 8 individual salad plates. Turn each mold out onto a leaf. Drizzle each mold with a little of the thinned mayonnaise, sprinkle with the nuts, dust with paprika, and serve.

SMOKED GOAT CHEESE ON FIELD GREENS

If, like most people, you bought a smoker for cooking meats, smoked goat cheese is a terrific way to start branching out. It takes about an hour in the smoker; if you are smoking a brisket or chicken on one rack, you can simply add the cheese to another rack for the last hour. For me, this is the perfect spring-time salad, when the young greens are sassy and crisp and the goat cheese is mellow and smoky. For a true regional flavor, use a mid-western goat cheese like Capriole chèvre.

SERVES 4

FOR THE SALAD:
    ¼ cup olive oil
    ¼ teaspoon salt
    ¼ teaspoon fresh-ground black
        pepper
    ⅓ cup breadcrumbs, preferably
        fresh
    4 3-ounce logs or chunks fresh goat
        cheese
    Four handfuls of mixed fresh field
        greens, such as baby spinach,
        chicory, mizuna, garden cress,
        watercress, and arugula

FOR THE VINAIGRETTE:
    ¼ cup white wine vinegar
    ¾ cup olive oil
    Salt and fresh-ground black
        pepper to taste

1. Place soaked wood chunks in your smoker and bring the temperature to 225 degrees. Line a broiler pan or another pan with holes in the bottom with aluminum foil, and pierce holes in the foil to let the smoke through.

2. Combine the ¼ cup olive oil, ¼ teaspoon salt, and ¼ teaspoon pepper in a small bowl. Spread the breadcrumbs on a plate. Dip each log or chunk of cheese in the olive oil mixture and then in the breadcrumbs to coat. Transfer the cheese to the prepared pan. Place the pan on a rack in the smoker and smoke for 1 hour.

3. When the cheese is nearly done, whisk together the vinaigrette ingredients in a small bowl. Rinse the greens and pat or spin them dry. Gently toss the greens with the vinaigrette until each leaf is shiny and coated. Arrange the dressed greens on 4 individual salad plates, top each with a portion of goat cheese, and serve.

NOTE: There are other ways to use smoked goat cheese. Smoke it with the oil but without the breadcrumb coating, then spread, spoon, or pipe it onto endive leaves or cherry tomato halves for an appetizer. Or use it in just about any recipe that calls for goat cheese.

WILTED FIELD GREENS WITH COUNTRY HAM AND HICKORY NUTS

Indiana-born chef Susan Goss of Zinfandel in Chicago proudly revives classic midwestern dishes in her restaurant. If you make this salad, adapted from a recipe of hers, you might well be using greens picked on an Illinois farm, maple syrup from Wisconsin, and hickory nuts or native hardshell pecans from Missouri.

SERVES 8

8 cups mixed fresh field greens, such as spinach, arugula, chicory, kale, and mizuna
1/4 cup extra-virgin olive oil
1 cup thin-sliced red onion
1/2 cup hickory nuts or pecans
1/2 cup slivered country ham
2 tablespoons red wine vinegar
2 tablespoons maple syrup or sorghum
Salt and fresh-ground black pepper to taste

1. Rinse the greens and pat or spin them dry. Transfer them to a large salad bowl.

2. Heat the oil in a large skillet over medium-low heat. Add the onion, and sauté it until it is translucent, 6 to 8 minutes. Add the nuts and sauté, stirring occasionally, for 2 minutes more. Stir in the ham, vinegar, and maple syrup and cook, stirring, until the mixture is heated through, 3 to 4 minutes.

3. Pour the hot dressing over the field greens. Toss gently to blend and to wilt the greens. Season to taste with salt and pepper, and serve.

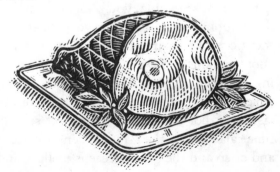

GREEN BEAN, WALNUT, AND FETA SALAD

Wisconsin cheesemakers now make just about every kind of Old World cheese, including Greek-style feta. Make this refreshing salad when your garden, or the farmers' market, offers up a surplus of crisp and fresh green beans.

SERVES 6 TO 8

FOR THE SALAD:

1½ pounds green beans, cut in half

1 cup chopped walnuts, toasted
1 cup diced red onion
1 cup crumbled feta cheese

FOR THE DRESSING:
½ cup extra-virgin olive oil
½ cup packed fresh mint leaves, chopped fine
¼ cup white wine vinegar or tarragon vinegar
1 small garlic clove, minced
½ teaspoon salt (see Note)
¼ teaspoon fresh-ground black pepper

1. Bring 2 quarts salted water to a boil in a saucepan over medium-high heat. Add the green beans, and cook them until they are crisp-tender, about 4 minutes. Drain the beans

GATHERING DANDELIONS

It took going to cooking school in Paris to change my mind about gathering "weeds" like dandelions. First I enjoyed a classic French dandelion and bacon salad at a bistro. Then, as I wandered along the Quai de Mégisserie, where the pet shops and seed stores are located, I noticed that several different kinds of dandelion, or pissenlit, seeds were for sale. That anyone would need to buy seeds for dandelions was a revelation to me, and I certainly was surprised that someone might prefer one variety over another. It turns out that the French grow dandelions in special raised beds just for dishes like the bistro salad.

Back in the U.S., there is no reason to plant dandelions when there are so many to gather in the wild. Just make sure the lawn or field has not been treated chemically. If you gather dandelion greens before the blossom heads have formed, you can eat them raw. However, if you gather them after the blossoms have begun to appear, you will need to boil them, to tenderize them and to remove some of the bitterness.

and plunge them immediately into ice water to stop their cooking. Drain them again and pat them dry.

2. Transfer the beans to a shallow serving bowl. Sprinkle with the walnuts, onion, and feta. Make the dressing: Combine the oil, mint, vinegar, garlic, salt, and pepper in a lidded jar and shake to blend. Pour the dressing over the bean mixture, toss thoroughly, and serve.

NOTE: If your feta cheese is particularly salty, reduce or omit the additional salt.

WARM ITALIAN GREEN BEAN SALAD

When green beans are in season, prepare this easy vegetable salad that goes with just about anything. Thin French filet beans or haricots verts make the best salad, but it is also fine with Blue Lake green beans, the variety most commonly grown.

SERVES 4

1 pound green beans
3 tablespoons extra-virgin olive oil
1 tablespoon red wine vinegar
1 garlic clove, minced
Salt and fresh-ground black
    pepper to taste

1. Bring 2 quarts salted water to a boil in a saucepan over medium-high heat. Add the green beans, and cook them until they are crisp-tender, about 2 minutes for filet beans or haricots verts and 4 minutes for larger beans. Drain the beans in a colander and plunge them immediately into ice water to stop their cooking. Drain them again, pat them dry, and transfer them to a serving bowl.

2. Make the dressing: Whisk together the oil, vinegar, garlic, salt, and pepper in a small bowl. Pour the dressing over the still-warm green beans, and toss to blend. Serve warm or at room temperature.

BABY BRUSSELS SPROUTS SALAD

Savvy gardeners will leave some baby brussels sprouts on the stalk to be touched by the first frosts of the fall, after which the sprouts' taste mellows and their flavor becomes nutty. Frozen baby brussels sprouts will do almost as well in this recipe. When the weather gets cold, serve this salad to accompany a hearty stew.

SERVES 4

FOR THE SALAD:
    2 cups fresh, preferably, or frozen
        and thawed baby brussels
        sprouts

4 cups mixed fresh greens, such as
Bibb lettuce, redleaf lettuce,
radicchio, baby spinach, and
escarole, larger leaves torn
1/4 cup chopped fresh parsley

FOR THE DRESSING:
1 teaspoon Dijon mustard
1/2 teaspoon Maggi seasoning,
preferably, or Worcestershire
sauce
1/2 teaspoon garlic salt
1/4 teaspoon bottled hot pepper
sauce
1/2 cup red wine vinegar
Juice of 1 lemon
1/2 cup extra-virgin olive oil

1. Steam the brussels sprouts until they are tender, about 12 minutes. Drain them and set them aside to cool to room temperature. Make the dressing: Whisk together the mustard, Maggi, garlic salt, hot pepper sauce, vinegar, lemon juice, and oil in a small bowl.

2. Transfer the brussels sprouts to a salad bowl. Add the greens and parsley, and toss gently. Drizzle the dressing over the salad, toss again, and serve.

RED CABBAGE, APPLE, AND BLUE CHEESE SALAD

This is an invigorating fall salad, red, white, and blue in color, to make when the apples are coming in and the summer vegetables are fading.

SERVES 6 TO 8

2 pounds red cabbage, cored and
shredded
1 Granny Smith apple, peeled,
cored, and chopped fine
1/4 cup chopped green onions,
white part and some green
part
8 ounces blue cheese, crumbled
1/4 cup cider vinegar
1/2 cup canola oil or corn oil
1/2 teaspoon fennel seeds
1 teaspoon sugar, or to taste
Salt and fresh-ground black
pepper to taste
1/2 cup pecans, toasted, for garnish

1. Toss together the cabbage, apple, green onions, and cheese in a large salad bowl. In a separate small bowl, whisk together the vinegar, oil, fennel seeds, and 1 teaspoon sugar. Taste, and add salt and pepper and, if you like, additional sugar.

2. Pour the dressing over the salad and toss to blend. Sprinkle the pecans on top, and serve.

CORN

"The sun shines, the rain falls, and the dry kernel becomes plump and sends forth a sprout, and lo, the first green leaf. The scent of a field of growing corn is honey-sweet and a trifle musky. You can hear the cornstalks grow. On a warm summer night the corn talks. It cracks its knuckles and seems to chuckle to itself."

—ELIZABETH LANDEWEER, KANSAS CITY, MISSOURI

LEMON-SWEET CUCUMBERS

Here is a pleasing way to serve garden-fresh cucumbers in the heat of summer. If you grow, or can find at a farmers' market, small, yellow cucumbers, use those.

SERVES 4 TO 6

2 cups thin-sliced cucumbers
1/4 cup sugar
1/4 teaspoon salt
1 tablespoon fresh dill, preferably, or 1/2 teaspoon dried dill
1/2 teaspoon lemon zest

1 teaspoon fresh lemon juice
1/2 teaspoon cider vinegar

1. Place the cucumber slices in a bowl of ice water and let them rest until crisp, about 30 minutes. Drain them well in a colander for at least 10 minutes.

2. Whisk together the sugar, salt, dill, lemon zest, lemon juice, and vinegar in a large non-reactive bowl. Add the cucumbers and stir to coat. Cover and refrigerate for at least 4 hours or overnight. Serve chilled.

SWEET AND SOUR CUCUMBER SALAD

Sweet onions used to show up in the super-market for just a week or two each year. Now you can find one variety or another, such as Vidalias, Mauis, and Texas 1015's, much of the year—or perhaps you grow your own.

SERVES 6 TO 8

2 large or 4 small cucumbers, sliced thin
1 medium sweet onion, sliced thin
1 teaspoon salt
1 teaspoon dry mustard
1 teaspoon celery seeds
2 tablespoons sugar
3/4 cup canola oil or corn oil
3/4 cup white wine vinegar

Toss together the cucumber and onion slices in a medium bowl. Whisk together the salt, mustard, celery seeds, sugar, oil, and vinegar in a small bowl, pour over the vegetables, and toss to blend. Cover and refrigerate for at least 4 hours to let the flavors blend. Serve chilled.

IOWA
PEA SALAD

You don't often see canned vegetables in cookbooks these days. You might want to debate the point, but I am of the view that a real midwestern cookbook ought to have a recipe or two in which the reader is licensed to use them. Here's one. Although this salad is commonly known by the Iowa name, it is just across the Iowa border in Minnesota where you find the Valley of the Green Giant, home of the town of Blue Earth—the birthplace of the ice cream sandwich and the site of the Green Giant/Seneca Foods Company, not to mention a towering statue of a green man—and also of the town of LeSueur, which has given its name to a brand of canned baby peas. Generous rainfall and cool summer temperatures make this a great pea-growing region. Sweet and tender fresh peas are fine in this salad, but the recipe does justice to the canned or frozen varieties, too.

SERVES 6

3 strips bacon, preferably
   apple-smoked
½ cup chopped green onions,
   white part and some green
   part
2 cups cooked fresh or frozen and
   thawed baby peas, or 2 cups
   canned baby peas
1 cup cooked macaroni
1 cup mayonnaise
½ cup shredded cheddar cheese

1. Fry the bacon until it is crisp in a skillet over medium-low heat. Remove from the heat and drain on absorbent paper. When it is cool enough to handle, crumble it.

2. Combine the green onions, peas, macaroni, and bacon in a bowl, and stir well to blend. Add the mayonnaise and stir well again. Transfer the salad to a serving bowl, cover, and refrigerate for at least 2 hours. Serve chilled, with the cheese sprinkled on top.

WINTER GARDEN
VEGETABLE SALAD

Former Cincinnatian Jim Gregory, now a chef and cooking instructor in Columbus, Indiana, gave me a recipe for a salad like this one many years ago, and my own version has evolved over time. The dressing works well with a variety of vegetables, so experiment, if you like. Bottled Maggi seasoning, a condiment with German origins that is popular in the midwest, is available at grocery stores and has a flavor like Worcestershire sauce.

SERVES 4 TO 6

FOR THE DRESSING:
    1 teaspoon Maggi seasoning
    1/4 teaspoon bottled hot pepper
        sauce
    2 tablespoons Dijon mustard
    3 tablespoons white wine vinegar
        or tarragon vinegar
    1/2 cup extra-virgin olive oil
    2 tablespoons chopped fresh
        parsley
    1/4 cup fresh-grated Parmesan
        cheese
    2 tablespoons drained capers

FOR THE SALAD:
    1/2 cup chopped green onions,
        white part and some green
        part
    1/2 cup chopped leeks
    1/2 cup small cauliflower florets
    1/2 cup chopped watercress
    3 small heads Bibb lettuce, leaves
        separated, or 3 cups assorted
        greens

1. Whisk together all of the dressing ingredients in a small bowl. Combine the green onions, leeks, cauliflower, and watercress in a medium bowl. Pour the dressing over the vegetables and stir to coat the vegetables well. Let the vegetables marinate in the dressing for 30 minutes.

2. Line a salad bowl with the lettuce leaves. Mound the marinated vegetables in the center, and serve.

SIMPLE TOMATO SALAD

Northwestern Ohio, from Toledo west toward the Indiana border, once was known as the Black Swamp. The moist, low-lying land, now drained and reclaimed, is ideal for tomato-growing, and people who live in the area say that when tomatoes are at their peak there's no reason to season them or dress them up at all. Still, it is hard to dispute that basil and balsamic vinegar bring out the flavor of a good tomato, as in this simple preparation. Reduce the amount of balsamic vinegar, if you like, if the vinegar you have on hand is particularly strong.

SERVES 4 TO 6

    1/4 cup balsamic vinegar
    1/2 cup olive oil
    Salt and fresh-ground black
        pepper to taste
    2 1/2 pounds ripe tomatoes, cut into
        wedges or sliced thin
    2 tablespoons torn fresh basil

Whisk together the vinegar and oil in a small bowl, and season with salt and pepper. Arrange the tomato slices decoratively on a plate. Drizzle with the vinaigrette, sprinkle with basil, and serve.

VARIATION:
If you grow, or find at a farmers' market, colorful heirloom tomatoes like Green Zebra, Big Rainbow, or Nebraska Wedding, use them in this recipe. The vinaigrette imparts a sheen that shows off their bright hues.

HEIRLOOM TOMATOES

After months of making do with pale substitutes from the hothouse, the first fresh tomato from the garden is reason to celebrate. That's especially true if your garden has heirloom tomatoes. Because they are old-time varieties bred for flavor and not for their ability to look perfect or to ward off plant diseases, heirlooms often taste better than their supermarket cousins. With their bright natural colors and odd shapes, they are pretty, too, making them the stars of any summer table.

Heirloom tomatoes do now make their way into better grocery stores, and they are widely available in farmers' markets. Among the more commonly seen heirlooms are:

❧ AMANA ORANGE. A huge beefsteak-style heirloom tomato from the Amana Colonies in Iowa, this is delicious marinated with cucumbers in a vinaigrette.

❧ BIG RAINBOW. Almost too beautiful to eat, with its striped and mottled salmon, gold, and red skin and flesh, the Big Rainbow has what growers call a true tomato flavor. I use it in tomato soups, tomato salads, and gratins.

❧ GREEN ZEBRA. The Green Zebra stays green even when ripe. Its stripes are a dark green and a lighter green. You can tell it is ripe when it gets to a beefsteak tomato size and turns a slightly yellower green. Makes a handsome tomato salad.

❧ NEBRASKA WEDDING. Developed in the late nineteenth century, this large beefsteak-style heirloom is dark orange and has a relatively tart and acidic flavor.

❧ OLD GERMAN. This large and beautiful tomato, yellow with red streaks, was brought to the prairie by the Mennonites. Luscious and sweet, this is a great tomato for slicing and serving on sandwiches. Some tomatoes weigh over a pound.

❧ YELLOW PEAR. Dating back to at least 1865 in Kansas, this small pear-shaped tomato, probably the most widely available heirloom, has a mild flavor and is great for eating straight up, with or without a little salt, or in green salads. These tomatoes volunteer every year in my Kansas garden, and I never have to resow.

FIREHOUSE TOMATOES

Perhaps not surprisingly, firefighters in small towns throughout the midwest turn out to be pretty good cooks. When they're not called out, they have time on their hands, and what better way to spend it than by cooking up something delicious, which this easy summertime dish certainly is? It also suits another criterion of a firefighter, or of a busy household—it can be prepared ahead and left to sit when other matters are more pressing. This is a version of a traditional recipe called Fire and Ice Tomatoes, said to be popular in firehouses.

SERVES 6

6 ripe tomatoes, sliced thin
1 red onion, sliced thin
1 green bell pepper, cut into strips
3/4 cup cider vinegar
1/2 teaspoon fresh-ground black
    pepper
1/4 teaspoon red pepper flakes
1 tablespoon sugar

Layer the tomatoes, onion, and green pepper in a nonreactive dish. Whisk together the vinegar, black pepper, red pepper flakes, and sugar with 1/4 cup water in a small bowl, and pour over the vegetables. Cover, and refrigerate for several hours or overnight. Serve chilled. Eat by the next day, because tomatoes do not do well if refrigerated for a long time.

TEARDROP TOMATO SALAD

Because they are often eaten right off the vine, "garden candy" is what the varieties of sweet and juicy little tomatoes that are used in this recipe are often called. Lower in acidity than larger tomatoes, they do well in the humid summers of the Ohio-to-Illinois tomato belt, but they can hold their own farther west on the prairie as well. They are easy to grow and often self-sow the next year; they are also becoming popular at farmers' markets. The Yellow Pear, an heirloom variety dating from the 1860s in Kansas, was rare a few years back but now is quite common. Good just as they are, these little tomato gems also benefit from this simple treatment, perfect for a summer brunch, a casual grilled supper, or a roasted chicken dinner.

SERVES 4

2 cups Red Teardrop or red cur-
    rant tomatoes
2 cups Yellow Pear tomatoes
1/4 cup chopped green onions,
    white part and some green
    part
2 tablespoons extra-virgin olive oil
Salt, preferably sea salt, to taste
Fresh-ground black pepper to taste
1/4 cup chopped fresh Italian
    parsley

1. Combine the tomatoes, green onions, and oil in a serving bowl. Season to taste with salt and pepper.

2. Heat a large skillet over medium-high heat. Add the tomato mixture and sauté, stirring several times, until the tomato skins begin to burst, about 3 minutes. Remove from the heat, pour back into the serving bowl, and sprinkle with parsley. Serve immediately.

FARMHOUSE TOMATO ASPIC WITH HERBED BUTTERMILK DRESSING

Before air conditioning, farm wives often made chilled congealed salads for summer-time suppers. Coming in from the heat of the field or garden, the family could enjoy something cool from the icebox. Because heat often zaps the appetite, this traditional salad had to have enough flavor to coax the taste buds into eating. (Note: The recipe may be doubled to make in a standard-size ring mold.)

SERVES 4

1²/₃ cups tomato juice
Juice of 1 lemon
¼ cup cider vinegar
⅛ teaspoon black pepper
¼ teaspoon paprika

1 tablespoon minced onion
1 (¼-ounce) envelope unflavored gelatin
Sugar to taste, optional
4 cups Bibb, butter, or oak-leaf lettuce leaves
2 cups Herbed Buttermilk Dressing (recipe follows)

1. Heat the tomato juice, lemon juice, vinegar, pepper, paprika, and onion in a saucepan over medium heat just until simmering. Sprinkle

"The first sight of Sophie Lundstrom's dinner table always made me gasp. It completely filled the long narrow dining room, whose south windows opened out on a sunporch beyond which one could see miles of snow-covered prairies reflecting the sun. Places were laid for fourteen with white china on a white damask tablecloth. There was no color on the table at all except a luscious ribbon of translucent jellies, relishes, and preserves that ran down the length of the table and caught up the sun—like a feast spread out in the snow. In the center was a glorious crown tomato aspic, and streaming down on either side were grape and chokecherry jellies, rhubarb jam and plum preserves, pickled beets, spiced crabapples, and watermelon pickles."

—CARRIE YOUNG,
Nothing to Do But Stay: My Pioneer Mother

the gelatin over the top of the mixture and stir to dissolve. Taste the mixture, and add sugar, if you like.

2. Pour into 4 individual molds and refrigerate for 1½ to 2 hours, or until set. Place the greens on 4 individual serving plates. Turn out the molded aspics onto the greens, and drizzle with the dressing.

HERBED BUTTERMILK DRESSING

MAKES ABOUT 2½ CUPS DRESSING

1 cup buttermilk
1 garlic clove, minced
1 tablespoon snipped fresh chives
1¼ cups sour cream
1 tablespoon sugar
2 tablespoons Dijon mustard
Juice of 1 lemon
Salt and fresh-ground black
*   pepper to taste*

Put all of the ingredients in a lidded jar. Shake to blend well. Refrigerated, the dressing will keep for up to 2 weeks.

SUMMERTIME GRILLED SUCCOTASH SALAD

If you grew up in the 1950s or '60s and view succotash rather dimly, give this revitalized version a shot. Fresh produce makes all the difference, as do the fresh herbs, and grilling turns what might be plain flavors into smoky and robust ones. This salad can be made and served immediately, or covered and refrigerated to take to a potluck gathering or summer picnic.

SERVES 4

½ pound green beans, haricots
*   verts, or wax beans*
1 tablespoon salt
2 cups uncooked fresh lima beans,
*   preferably, or 2 cups cooked*
*   frozen baby lima beans*
2 ears sweet corn, husked
¼ cup canola oil or corn oil
1 small yellow summer squash
1 small zucchini
1 tablespoon minced green onion,
*   white part and some green part*
Juice of 1½ lemons
2 tablespoons chopped fresh basil
2 tablespoons chopped fresh tarragon
¼ teaspoon fresh-ground black
*   pepper, or more to taste*
4 cups Bibb, butter, or oak-leaf
*   lettuce leaves*

1. Preheat a gas or charcoal grill to high. As the grill heats up, bring a large saucepan of water to a boil on the stove. Add the green beans and salt and cook until the beans are just crisp-tender, about 4 minutes. Remove the beans with a slotted spoon to a colander; do not drain the pot or turn off the heat. Refresh the beans under cold water.

2. If you are using fresh lima beans, add them to the pot and cook them until they are tender, 4 to 5 minutes. Remove the pot from the heat, drain the beans, and set them aside.

3. Brush the corn with a little of the oil and place the ears on the grill. Grill them, turning them occasionally with tongs as the kernels begin to brown, for 10 minutes. Once the corn is on the grill, cut the summer squash and zucchini in half lengthwise. Brush each side of the halves with a little of the oil. Grill the squash and zucchini 2 to 3 minutes on each side, or until fork-tender. Remove the corn and squashes from the grill and let cool. Slice the squashes into 1-inch-long pieces, and strip the kernels from the corn ears.

4. Combine the green beans, the cooked lima beans, corn, squash, zucchini, and green onion in a large bowl. Add the remaining oil, the lemon juice, the basil and tarragon, and the pepper, and toss the salad gently. Line 4 individual salad plates with lettuce leaves, spoon the succotash on top of the leaves, and serve.

MELTING POT BEAN SALAD

Each immigrant group that came to the midwest brought along their favorite dried beans to plant and eat in the New World. The French along the Mississippi brought navy beans and flageolets. The Swedish in the northern plains brought yellow-eye and brown beans (and also yellow peas; see page 127). Italians in the river cities brought fava beans, borlotti beans, and cannellini. Variety is the spice of life in this salad, and you can vary the kinds of beans you use every time; you might also try black, lima, or cranberry beans for different flavors and colors. Serve this salad as a vegetarian main course, if you like, or alongside grilled steak or fish.

SERVES 6 TO 8

1/4 cup olive oil
1/2 cup diced celery
1/2 cup diced red bell pepper
1/2 cup diced red onion
2 garlic cloves, minced
1 teaspoon dried thyme
1 cup cooked or canned and
    drained Swedish brown beans
    or kidney beans
1 cup cooked navy beans
1 cup cooked or canned and
    drained Swedish yellow-eye
    beans or pinto beans

1 cup cooked or canned and
   drained borlotti beans or
   cannellini beans
1/4 cup red wine vinegar
2 medium tomatoes, diced
1/2 cup chopped fresh Italian
   parsley
Salt and fresh-ground black
   pepper to taste

1. Heat the oil in a large saucepan over medium heat. Add the celery, bell pepper, and onion, and sauté until the onion is translucent, 6 to 8 minutes. Add the garlic, and sauté for 2 minutes more. Stir in the thyme and remove the pan from the heat. Let the contents of the pan cool to room temperature. (If you have recently cooked the beans, let them cool to room temperature, too.)

2. Place the beans in a large serving bowl and pour the sautéed vegetables and oil over all. Add the vinegar, tomatoes, and parsley, and toss gently to blend well. Season with salt and pepper, toss again, and serve.

"Everywhere, as far as the eye could reach, there was nothing but rough, shaggy grass, most of it as tall as I. . . . As I looked about me I felt the grass was the country, as the water is the sea. . . . And there was so much motion in it; the whole country seemed, somehow, to be running."
—WILLA CATHER, My Antonia

DILLED POTATO SALAD

The radishes and green peas add color, flavor, and texture to this traditional Scandinavian-style potato salad.

SERVES 6

6 new potatoes, skins on
1 medium red onion, sliced thin
8 radishes, sliced thin
1 1/2 cups cooked fresh or frozen
   and thawed green peas
2 hard-cooked eggs, sliced thin
2 cups mayonnaise
2 tablespoons chopped fresh dill
Salt and white pepper to taste
Sprigs of fresh parsley, for garnish,
   optional

1. Bring the potatoes to a boil in water to cover in a large saucepan. Cook them until they are tender, about 20 minutes. Drain them in a colander and let them cool slightly. When they are cool enough to handle, cut them in halves, if they are small, or wedges.

2. Transfer the potatoes to a large serving bowl. Add the remaining ingredients, and toss gently. Refrigerate, covered, for at least 1 hour. Serve chilled or at room temperature, garnished with parsley, if you like.

TRI-COLORED POTATO SALAD

A Sicilian version of the potato salad known as *insalata tricolore* became a popular dish with midwestern families who could grow the ingredients in their own gardens. The vivid red, white, and green colors salute the Italian flag.

SERVES 6

6 new potatoes, peeled and cut into
    ¾-inch cubes
1 pound green beans, cut in half
4 medium tomatoes, cut into
    wedges, or 12 cherry tomatoes,
    cut in half
¼ cup chopped red onion
Salt and fresh-ground black
    pepper to taste
½ cup olive oil
¼ cup white wine vinegar
¼ cup chopped fresh Italian
    parsley

1. Put the potatoes in a large saucepan with ample water to cover. Bring to a boil, and cook the potatoes until they are tender, about 15 minutes. About 5 minutes before the potatoes are done, add the green beans to the pot and cook them with the potatoes for the remaining time. Transfer the potatoes and beans to a colander, run them under cold water for 30 seconds, and let them drain.

2. Transfer the potatoes and green beans to a bowl, add the tomatoes and onion, and season with salt and pepper. Whisk together the oil, vinegar, and parsley in a separate small bowl, and pour over the vegetables. Toss gently, cover, and chill for at least 30 minutes. Toss again before serving.

PARSLEY PESTO POTATO SALAD

Make this colorful salad when there is a new crop of firm and shiny red potatoes in the market. Fine as a side dish with grilled meats or chicken, this one is substantial enough to serve as a main dish, too, if you have some vegetarian guests at a cookout.

SERVES 8

2 pounds red new potatoes, skins on
¾ cup chopped red onion
¼ cup chopped green onion, white
    part and some green part
¾ cup chopped red bell pepper
¾ cup chopped green bell pepper
¾ cup cooked fresh, preferably, or
    frozen corn kernels
1 cup Heartland Parsley Pesto
    (page 53)

1. Place the potatoes in a large saucepan with water to cover. Bring to a boil, and cook the potatoes until they are tender, about 20 minutes. Drain the potatoes and let them cool

slightly. When they are cool enough to handle, cut them into wedges and transfer the wedges to a large bowl.

2. Add the red and green onion, bell peppers, and corn. Pour the pesto over all, and toss gently to coat the vegetables well. Serve at room temperature. The salad will keep, covered in the refrigerator, for 3 to 4 days.

STRAWTOWN DUTCH LETTUCE

When eight hundred Dutch immigrants left their native province of Friesland for the rolling Iowa prairie in the nineteenth century, the grass-roofed sod dugouts they built gave their settlement its name, "Strawtown." Today, Strawtown is known as Pella, and the population is closer to eight thousand. Pella keeps its Dutch culinary heritage alive at the Jaarsma Bakery, the Strawtown Inn, and several local cafés, and in home kitchens and church suppers as well. This salad is a hearty and nourishing one-dish meal.

SERVES 6

1 tablespoon unsalted butter
1 tablespoon all-purpose flour
2 egg yolks, beaten
1/2 cup sugar
1/2 cup plus 1/3 cup cider vinegar
6 strips bacon, cut into small pieces

6 cups riced or mashed boiled
   potatoes, kept warm
6 cups coarsely cut iceberg or
   romaine lettuce, tossed with
   1/4 cup diced yellow onion
4 hard-cooked eggs, sliced thin

1. Melt the butter in a small saucepan over medium heat. Add the flour, and stir. When the flour is blended in well, add 1/2 cup water and bring to a boil, stirring constantly. Add the egg yolks, sugar, and 1/2 cup of the vinegar, and bring to a boil again, stirring constantly, until the dressing starts to thicken. Remove from the heat and set aside.

2. Fry the bacon in a large skillet over medium heat for about 5 minutes, or until it is browned and crisp. Drain the bacon fat and return the skillet to the heat. Stir in a scant 1/4 cup of the egg-and-flour mixture, along with the remaining 1/3 cup vinegar and another 1/2 cup water. Bring to a boil, reduce the heat, and keep at a simmer.

3. Spread out 1/2 of the potatoes in the bottom of a deep heatproof serving bowl. Layer 1/2 of the lettuce on top, and spread out 1/2 of the sliced hard-cooked eggs on top of the lettuce. Top with several tablespoons of the hot bacon dressing. Repeat the process. Drizzle the egg-and-flour dressing over all, and serve immediately.

TULIP TIME

If it's the second weekend in May, it's Tulip Time in Pella, a town in southern Iowa that first was settled by Dutch immigrants. Shops, bakeries, and restaurants make and sell Dutch foods.

On the day of the big parade, the Tulip Queen's procession down the main street is preceded by a band of "Street Scrubbers," dressed in traditional folk garb with aprons and lace hats, who bear long-handled brooms and have buckets of water hanging from wooden shoulder yokes. The Scrubbers keep alive a Dutch woman's reputation for a spotlessly clean environment.

Begun in 1935, Tulip Time is a celebration of local heritage–and a time to have a lot of fun, something the hard-working original immigrants might be shocked to know. Fleeing from Holland in 1847 to avoid persecution for having rebelled against the Dutch state church, some eight hundred settlers fashioned sod-covered dugouts on the Iowa prairie. Their community became known as "Strawtown."

If you go to Pella at Tulip Time, you can take home a frosted cake resembling a wooden shoe or a windmill. You can sip a bowl of homemade split pea soup and you can munch on Holland rusks or on spiced meat-filled saucijzebroodjes. And you almost certainly will dream of the tulips you'll plant next year.

GREAT PLAINS CRACKED WHEAT SALAD

Prairie cooks are always happy to discover new ways to make use of the abundant wheat harvest. When Middle Eastern *tabouli*, a dish you can both make and spell a hundred different ways, became popular across the country in the 1970s, the idea took hold in the Heartland, to the point where this salad is now a summertime staple.

SERVES 4

1/2 cup cracked wheat or bulgur
1/2 cup chopped green onions, white part and some green part
2 tomatoes, peeled, if you like, and chopped fine
1/2 cup chopped fresh parsley
1/4 cup chopped fresh mint
1/4 cup fresh lemon juice
1/4 cup extra-virgin olive oil
Salt and fresh-ground black pepper to taste
Romaine lettuce leaves

1. Soak the cracked wheat in warm water to cover until tender, 15 to 20 minutes. Drain any water that remains and wring the wheat in a tea towel until most of the moisture has been absorbed.

2. Place the wheat in a medium bowl. Add the green onions, tomatoes, parsley, and mint, and stir to mix well. Whisk together the lemon juice and olive oil in a small bowl, season with salt and pepper, and pour over the salad. Toss to blend. Line individual salad plates with lettuce leaves, mound the salad over the leaves, and serve.

APPLE-CARROT COLESLAW

Around the Great Lakes, this slaw is served alongside fresh-caught and pan-fried lake perch. It's made with an old-fashioned boiled dressing that binds all the ingredients together well and keeps the salad from becoming soggy.

SERVES 6 TO 8

FOR THE DRESSING:
   1 egg yolk
   2 tablespoons sugar
   2 teaspoons all-purpose flour
   1/4 teaspoon cayenne pepper
   1 teaspoon dry mustard
   1/2 teaspoon salt
   1/4 cup cider vinegar
   1/4 cup heavy cream
   1 tablespoon poppy seeds or celery
      seeds
   2 teaspoons finely grated
      horseradish

FOR THE SLAW:
   1 small head green cabbage, cored
      and shredded
   1 small head red cabbage, cored
      and shredded
   1/2 cup thin-sliced red onion
   1 carrot, peeled and shredded
   1 large Granny Smith apple, cored
      and chopped fine

1. Make the dressing: Bring the water in the bottom pan of a double boiler to a gentle simmer. In the top part of the double boiler, away from the heat, put the egg yolk, sugar, flour, cayenne, mustard, and salt, and stir to blend. Whisk in the vinegar until there are no lumps. Put the top of the double boiler over the simmering water and cook, stirring, for 1 minute. Whisk in the cream and cook, stirring constantly, for 3 to 4 minutes more, or until the mixture thickens. Remove from the heat and let cool to room temperature. Stir in the poppy seeds and horseradish, and set aside.

2. Toss together the cabbages, onion, carrot, and apple in a large salad bowl. Pour the dressing over the vegetables, and toss again to coat them well. Serve immediately.

ITALIAN OLIVE SALAD

When Felix Ricci left the Abruzzi region of Italy in 1910 and arrived at Ellis Island, he left behind the little village of Ateleta and all that was familiar to him. By 1934, after working his way across the country, he owned his own dairy farm in Comstock, Wisconsin. As other immigrants did, he kept alive his memories of the Old Country through stories and through food. Two of his daughters, Flora Ricci DeAngelo and Vera Ricci Kleiber, passed on the family's love of cooking to Felix's granddaughter, cookbook author Patricia Kleiber Wells. In her cookbook *Trattoria*, she offers her Aunt Flora's Olive Salad, made with sliced pimiento-stuffed olives, which the family ate with antipasti or with sausages and cheese. Here is another version of that salad, beloved of Italian families all through the Heartland.

SERVES 6 TO 8

1 pound large Italian-style green olives
2 tablespoons minced pimientos
1 small yellow onion, diced
2 small celery ribs, with leaves, diced
2 large garlic cloves, minced
1/4 teaspoon red pepper flakes
1/2 teaspoon dried oregano
1/4 cup red wine vinegar
1/4 cup extra-virgin olive oil

1. If the olives have not been pitted, crack them with a mallet to loosen the pits. Discard the pits. Chop the olives coarsely and transfer them to a medium bowl. Add the pimientos, onion, and celery, and toss to blend.

2. In a separate small bowl, whisk together the garlic, red pepper flakes, oregano, vinegar, and oil. Pour the dressing over the olive salad, and toss again to blend. Cover, and refrigerate for several hours or, preferably, overnight to allow the flavors to blend. Let the salad come to room temperature before serving. The salad keeps, covered in the refrigerator, for up to 3 weeks.

SMORGASBORD SILLSALAT

On Christmas Day, midwesterners of Scandinavian descent will set festive tables filled with all kinds of traditional foods for family and friends who drop by. Usually a baked ham is the centerpiece, surrounded by marinated vegetable salads, a creamy potato casserole, homemade breads, and rice pudding. Although I am not a fan of herring, I like this relish-like salad in which the herring provides a clean, salty flavor, much as anchovies do in Italian recipes. The ruby color of this salad, so brilliant at holiday time, deserves your prettiest glass bowl for serving.

SERVES 6 TO 8

½ cup chopped wine-marinated
   or wine-pickled herring fillets
   (see Note)
1 cup diced bottled or homemade
   pickled beets
1½ cups diced boiled peeled
   potatoes

1½ cups diced but not peeled
   Granny Smith apple
¼ cup diced yellow onion
⅓ cup diced bottled or homemade
   bread-and-butter pickles
¼ cup cider vinegar
¼ teaspoon white pepper

THE PRAIRIE

Of the original four hundred thousand square miles of prairie that once stretched from central Ohio westward to the foothills of the Colorado Rockies, and from Alberta, Manitoba, and Saskatchewan south to central Texas, less than one percent survives in its natural state. Nowadays most of the old prairie is productive farmland and small towns, cities, and suburbs. Chicago sprawls over the prairie, even though most Chicagoans do not give it much thought. Indianapolis, St. Louis, Des Moines, Kansas City, and Omaha are prairie cities, too.

If you visit the Z-Bar Ranch near Strong City, Kansas, you can experience the prairie as it once was. A sea of tall shaggy grasses bends in the wind and you can see for miles under the big sky. In August, the landscape is a brilliant yellow carpet of sunflowers. Struck with awe, you also can begin to understand why the prairie inspired fear.

For those hardy pioneers of the nineteenth century, the prairie was as alien as the sea. It is a landscape you have to get used to, as William Least-Heat Moon relates in PrairyErth: "It's not that I had to learn to think flat—the prairies rarely are—but I had to begin thinking open and lean, seeing without set points of obvious focus. . . . I came to understand that the prairies are nothing but grass as the sea is nothing but water."

Today, the prairie territories are rangeland for the cattle industry, the "fruited plain" that produces tons of farm-fresh food, and the nation's breadbasket. The eastern or shortgrass portions of the prairie in Ohio, Indiana, Illinois, and Iowa have become the Corn Belt. The western or tallgrass prairie in Kansas, Nebraska, the Dakotas and upwards into Canada has become the Wheat Belt. The hilly grasslands of the central mixed grass portion, now the Dairy Belt, run from southern Indiana northwestward through Illinois into Wisconsin. The three regions overlap, of course.

Place the chopped herring in a decorative serving bowl. Add the remaining ingredients and 2 tablespoons water. Stir gently to blend well. Cover, and let marinate and chill in the refrigerator for at least 1 hour before serving.

NOTE: Wine-marinated or wine-pickled herring fillets are sold in jars in the refrigerator section of most supermarkets. They are also available at a variety of ethnic delicatessens.

FLY-OVER COUNTRY DUCK OR GOOSE SALAD

Some Old World peasant dishes made of preserved foods still survive in the midwest for reasons of economy and, of course, taste. In many pockets of the midwest, it is not only produce from the garden that is "put up" by traditional methods. Game meats, birds, and fishes are also preserved. Lutefisk and duck or goose confit are examples of still-popular preserved foods that date from the days before refrigeration.

During the fall, when flocks of wild ducks and geese vee southward down the Mississippi Fly-over, waterfowl hunters take advantage of the brief weeks when hunting is permitted. So do the cooks in their lives. When freezers are full, these cooks turn to other methods, such as the long, slow braising that results in a confit. During one particularly cold and gray February, I was the happy recipient of a wild goose breast and goose fat that a friend's husband brought home from hunting on a Kansas lake. I tried making traditional French confit with untraditional ingredients and methods. It turned out well, and in this recipe I share the results with you.

Traditional confit is made entirely with goose fat or duck fat. From a game bird, however, as opposed to a domestic one, you will not have enough to make the traditional recipe. Fortunately, vegetable oils will take on the characteristic flavor of the fat and also lessen the cholesterol. You can make confit with an entire bird or just a few pieces; adjust the recipe accordingly. Savor pieces of silky and rich confit in this salad or in High Plains Hunter's Cassoulet (page 231), or serve the confit with homemade hash browns sautéed in some of the flavored confit oil and accompanied by a salad of bitter greens. Accompany this main-dish salad with a big-flavored red wine.

NOTE: A slow-cooker is required for this recipe.

SERVES 4

FOR THE CONFIT:
 1 whole wild duck or wild goose
 2 tablespoons sea salt
 3 to 4 bay leaves, torn into pieces
 2 teaspoons fresh thyme
 ½ to 1 cup mild vegetable oil, such as safflower or canola, or more if necessary

FOR THE SALAD:

4 cups mixed fresh greens, such as
    radicchio, endive, chicory,
    baby spinach, mizuna, and
    oak-leaf lettuce
1 orange, peeled, sliced, sectioned,
    and seeded
¼ cup chopped red onion
2 tablespoons balsamic vinegar

1. The night before you make the confit, cut the duck or goose into pieces, including the breast. Use a sharp knife to separate the fat from the pieces and the carcass. Place the fat in the bottom of a slow-cooker. Set the heat to low, cover, and let the fat render overnight. Place the meat pieces in a bowl, sprinkle the sea salt, bay leaves, and thyme leaves over the surface of the meat, cover, and refrigerate overnight.

2. In the morning, pour off the liquid that has drained from the duck or goose pieces. Remove and discard the cracklings from the fat that has rendered in the slow-cooker. Pour ½ cup of vegetable oil into the rendered drippings in the slow-cooker and stir to blend. Cut the breast into large chunks, and pack the duck or goose pieces in the slow-cooker. Top up with enough vegetable oil to cover the meat. Set the heat to low, cover, and cook for 6 to 8 hours, or until the meat is browned and tender. (The recipe may be made ahead to this point. Placed in a plastic container and kept covered with the oil, the confit will keep in the refrigerator for 3 to 4 weeks; it also freezes well.)

3. Make the salad: Arrange the greens on 4 individual salad plates. Top with the orange sections, and set the plates aside. Transfer 2 tablespoons of the confit oil to a large skillet over medium heat. When the oil has come to a sizzle, add 4 pieces of the confit and heat through until just warm, 4 to 6 minutes. Remove the confit pieces to a plate and add the red onion to the skillet. Sauté the onion until it is just softened, 3 to 4 minutes. Add the vinegar and deglaze the pan over medium-high heat. Remove from the heat and drizzle the skillet contents over the greens and oranges. Arrange a piece of confit on the top of each salad, and serve.

SPICED APPLE CIDER JELLY SALAD

A devoted reader of the late Laurie Colwin's books, I came across a recipe for a salad like this one in her *More Home Cooking.* I added a mulled apple wine to create my own version. The salad goes very well with fried chicken, roast turkey, roast pork loin, or a smoked brisket.

SERVES 8

5 (¼-ounce) envelopes unflavored
    gelatin
2 cups sugar
Grated zest of 1 lemon
Juice of 2 lemons
1 cup apple wine

1 quart apple cider

1 whole nutmeg

1 teaspoon whole cloves

1 cinnamon stick

BON VIEUX TEMPS

For a little less than a hundred years, from 1673, when Louis Joliet and Jacques Marquette charted the Mississippi River wilderness, to 1765, when the British took over Fort de Chartres after the French and Indian War, a vast tract of the Heartland served as a colonial outpost for the French Bourbon kings. The banks and floodplains of the Mississippi south of St. Louis were a center of French activity.

Twenty-five years after the voyage of Marquette and Joliet, Catholic missionaries from Quebec traveled down the river to establish a mission at Cahokia, in what is now southwestern Illinois, and convert the Native Americans. A few years later, they established another mission at Kaskaskia. In settlements like Prairie du Rocher and Ste. Genevieve, in what are now Illinois and Missouri, respectively, wheat was milled for pain de mie, holy days and saints' days were celebrated, minuets were danced, and long, low frame houses were built that would be familiar today in Normandy. Prairie du Rocher, or "Prairie of the Rock," settled in 1722, is the oldest town in Illinois. Settlers in the area took advantage of the fertile soil to raise grain,

which was shipped down the Mississippi to Louisiana and from there to the French islands of the Caribbean. They also grew melons, pumpkins, corn, cotton, and tobacco in strips of family-owned land, much as their ancestors in northwestern France did. In their gardens they grew fresh herbs and planted fruit trees.

The Pierre Menard home, which still stands in Ellis Grove, Illinois, about forty miles south of St. Louis, shows what a typical trader's or planter's house looked like. It is a clapboard home raised on stilts (because of the risk of floods), with a long, low balustraded porch, a hipped roof with gabled windows, and fireplaces on either end. Built by a Canadian trader in 1800, the home is one of the finest examples of French colonial architecture in the country.

The estimated French settlement of this area was only about a thousand inhabitants, but they have left their mark on the place names, foods, culture, and architecture of the region. Annual events like the Apple Fete in Prairie du Rocher or Cahokia's Le Fete du Bon Vieux Temps, a winter celebration of the French social season, keep alive French traditions and foods.

1. Place the gelatin, sugar, and lemon zest in a large heatproof bowl. Pour the lemon juice and apple wine over the gelatin mixture and stir to blend well.

2. Bring the cider, nutmeg, cloves, and cinnamon to a boil in a large saucepan. Reduce the heat, and simmer the cider for 15 to 20 minutes, skimming off any scum that forms as the mixture simmers. Remove the spices by pouring the mixture through a fine-mesh sieve into the gelatin mixture. Stir well to dissolve the gelatin and blend the ingredients. Let the mixture cool down slightly, but do not let it set.

3. While the gelatin mixture cools, lightly oil a 1-quart mold or 8 ½-cup molds. Pour the gelatin mixture into the mold or molds and refrigerate until set, about 3 hours for the larger mold and about 1 hour for the individual molds. Serve chilled.

RASPBERRIES AND RED CURRANTS IN HONEYSUCKLE JELLY

In the second half of June, the red currants in my garden are ruby-colored and as inviting for me as they are for the birds. My wild raspberries, trained to the side of the house, take real perseverance to pick, so vicious are the thorns on the canes. And every time I step outside, I notice that the warm summer air is fragrant with the honeysuckle tangled around my back fence. I wonder now why it took me so long to come up with this colorful gelatin salad that makes use of all three plants. The whim of the day decides whether this will be a fruit salad or a light dessert.

SERVES 4

1 (¼-ounce) envelope unflavored gelatin
½ cup sugar
Juice and grated zest of 1 large lemon
¾ cup Honeysuckle Syrup (page 61) or Honey Syrup (page 61)
1 cup red currants, stemmed and, if you like, seeded
1 cup fresh raspberries
Additional red currants and raspberries, for garnish
Fresh lemon balm leaves, for garnish

1. Sprinkle the gelatin over ¼ cup water in a small bowl. Set aside for 2 minutes until the gelatin has partially dissolved. Microwave the mixture on high for 40 seconds, or heat the mixture in the top of a double boiler over simmering water for 3 to 4 minutes, until the mixture is nearly clear and is very warm but not boiling.

2. Bring the sugar, lemon juice, lemon zest, and ¾ cup water to a boil in a large saucepan. Remove from the heat and whisk in the syrup and the warm gelatin mixture. Let cool

slightly, then refrigerate, covered, for 2 hours or until the mixture just barely begins to set. Gently stir in 1 cup each of the red currants and raspberries, and pour the mixture into four 4-ounce molds or a small loaf pan. Refrigerate, covered, for 2 hours more or overnight until set.

3. To serve, dip the molds or loaf pan into a pan of warm water to loosen the salad. Turn the salad out onto a serving plate or plates, and garnish with the additional fruits and the lemon balm.

VARIATIONS:

If you do not have red currants or raspberries, some fine replacement combinations are: whole blueberries and sliced strawberries; whole blackberries and diced peaches; or pomegranate seeds and sliced seedless green grapes. Use 1 cup of each, plus additional whole or sliced fruits for the garnish.

HONEYSUCKLE BERRIES

This simple fruit salad, which tastes, to me, like the essence of a summer afternoon, works nicely as a side dish for a warm-weather brunch or, for dessert, as an accompaniment to a homemade angel food cake.

SERVES 4

1½ cups Honeysuckle Syrup (page 61) or Honey Syrup (page 61)
6 cups mixed fresh berries, such as strawberries, blueberries, and raspberries
Fresh mint leaves or honeysuckle flowers, for garnish

Pour the syrup over the berries in a bowl and stir very gently to coat the fruits. Refrigerate, covered, for at least 1 hour. Serve chilled, garnished with mint or honeysuckle.

FRESH PARSLEY VINAIGRETTE

Sometimes the simplest things are best. When my garden yields up a wealth of zucchini or green beans, I steam them very briefly and pour this dressing over them. It will also liven up fresh tomato slices or wedges and just about any green salad.

MAKES ABOUT 4 CUPS VINAIGRETTE

1 cup minced fresh parsley
1 garlic clove, minced
3 cups extra-virgin olive oil
3 tablespoons fresh lemon juice
½ teaspoon Dijon mustard
½ teaspoon salt
¼ teaspoon fresh-ground black pepper

Place all of the ingredients in a blender or food processor. Blend for about 45 seconds, or until nearly smooth. Taste the vinaigrette and adjust the seasonings if you like. The dressing will keep, covered in the refrigerator, for 3 to 4 days if your parsley is at peak freshness, a day or two less if not.

MAYFAIR DRESSING

This venerable St. Louis salad dressing, named after a long-closed dining establishment, blends artichoke hearts with an herby Green Goddess–style dressing for a smooth and creamy foil for crisp, cold greens. Pureed in the blender or food processor, it's a salad dressing; stirred by hand, it's a great dip for raw vegetables.

MAKES 2 1/2 CUPS
DRESSING

3/4 cup mayonnaise
3/4 cup sour cream
1/4 cup fresh lemon juice
4 anchovy fillets, minced, or
    1 tablespoon anchovy paste
1/4 cup minced fresh Italian
    parsley
1 garlic clove, minced
2 tablespoons minced green onion,
    white part and some green
    part

RED RIVER RUSSETS

Russet potatoes, smooth-skinned and uniformly shaped, are the preferred potato for potato chips. The best russets grow in the Red River Valley that snakes through northwestern Minnesota and northeastern North Dakota, the third most productive potato-growing region in the United States. These "chipping potatoes" have less moisture than other varieties, which makes them perfect for a quick dip in hot oil to come out crunchy and delectable.

Many Heartland restaurants, from the Blackhawk Lodge in Chicago to J. Gilbert's in Kansas City, serve homemade potato chips with a blue cheese dip. You can make your own chips, too: Slice some russets very thin (a mandoline helps), and soak the slices in water to cover for 15 minutes. Drain, rinse, drain again, and pat very dry. Heat peanut oil to 350 degrees in a deep skillet and fry the chips in batches until crisp and browned. Drain on absorbent paper and sprinkle with salt. If you like, serve with Creamy Maytag Blue Cheese Dressing (page 173) as a dip.

2 tablespoons snipped fresh chives
2 tablespoons minced fresh
    tarragon
1/2 cup chopped canned or bottled
    artichoke hearts
Salt and fresh-ground black
    pepper to taste

1. To make as a dressing for greens or a salad: Place all of the ingredients in a blender or food processor, and puree until smooth. Taste the dressing and adjust the seasonings. Refrigerate, covered, until ready to serve.

2. To make as a dip: Stir together the mayonnaise, sour cream, and lemon juice in a bowl. Fold in the remaining ingredients, and stir to blend well. Taste the dip and adjust the seasonings. Refrigerate, covered, until ready to serve.

CREAMY MAYTAG BLUE CHEESE DRESSING

Jim Stevens, president and farm manager of Maytag Dairy Farms in Newton, Iowa, likes to recommend that you "add a little cheese to your life." Not a bad idea, especially when it's the mellow and creamy Maytag Blue Cheese. This is Jim's house dressing recipe, which he gracefully shares here.

MAKES ABOUT 4 CUPS DRESSING

2 cups regular, lowfat, or fat-free
    sour cream
6 ounces good-quality blue cheese,
    such as Maytag Blue
2/3 cup regular or lowfat
    mayonnaise
2 tablespoons apple cider vinegar
Onion salt, celery salt, and
    Worcestershire sauce to taste
3 drops bottled hot pepper sauce

Whisk together all of the ingredients in a bowl. For the best results, let the flavors combine, covered in the refrigerator, for 24 hours before serving. Serve chilled. The dressing will keep for about 1 week.

GOLDEN LAMB CELERY SEED DRESSING

The Golden Lamb in Lebanon, Ohio, was a stagecoach stop in the nineteenth century. Charles Dickens even slept there, on his notoriously ill-tempered speaking tour of post–Civil War America. Today, the Golden Lamb is an inn and restaurant serving Shaker-style food in the Heartland country tradition. When I was a child, a drive up to Lebanon for dinner was a favorite Sunday excursion. As a special treat during the summer, my mother, grandmother, sister, and I would travel up there for a ladies' lunch. I would always order the homemade cottage cheese salad topped with fresh summer fruit and this dressing over all. Today, when I serve my own Fresh Farmhouse Cheese (page 39), I make sure that nothing but this dressing goes on top. This is also delicious as a dressing for coleslaw.

MAKES ABOUT 1½ CUPS DRESSING

½ cup sugar
1 teaspoon dry mustard
1 teaspoon salt
1 teaspoon celery seeds
¼ teaspoon grated yellow onion
1 cup canola oil or safflower oil
⅓ cup white vinegar

Place the sugar, mustard, salt, and celery seeds in a food processor, and pulse to combine. Add the grated onion and 2 tablespoons of the oil and pulse for 4 to 5 seconds more. Add the vinegar and the remaining oil, in alternating tablespoons, through the feed tube and process until the dressing has emulsified. Covered and refrigerated, the dressing will keep indefinitely.

THE
MEAT
COURSE

THE MEAT COURSE

GARLIC RIBEYE

As a lot of midwesterners do, I normally prefer my steaks to be charcoal-grilled. But I'm always happy to make an exception for this pan-seared version. Perhaps because of the strong barbecue tradition, cooks in Missouri and Kansas, especially, make use of hearty rubs and marinades in their meat cookery, even when they are not barbecuing; the seasonings in this recipe are typical barbecue flavors. A green salad with blue cheese dressing, a fluffy baked potato, and fresh tomato slices are the perfect accompaniments.

SERVES 4

6 to 8 garlic cloves, minced
1/4 cup olive oil
1/4 cup paprika
1 teaspoon seasoned salt
1 teaspoon fresh-ground black pepper
4 boneless ribeye steaks, about 8 ounces each

1. Combine the garlic, oil, paprika, salt, and pepper in a shallow pan. Dredge both sides of each steak in the mixture. Marinate the steaks at room temperature for 30 minutes.

2. Heat a large cast-iron skillet or griddle over high heat. Sear the steaks about 3 minutes on each side for medium-rare, or to your taste. Serve immediately.

GRILLED FLANK STEAK MARINATED IN BEER, HERBS, AND MORELS

This is a hearty meal of prairie favorites: wheat beer, steak, and morels. I have adapted and simplified this recipe from one created by midwesterner-at-heart Larry Forgione of the American Place in New York. Accompany, if you like, with Blue Cheese Mashed Potatoes (page 313).

SERVES 4

1 cup wheat beer or amber ale
1 1/2 cups chicken stock
1 cup tomato juice
1 tablespoon Worcestershire sauce
1/2 teaspoon bottled hot pepper sauce
2 bay leaves
2 tablespoons chopped fresh oregano or 1 teaspoon dried oregano
2 tablespoons chopped fresh thyme or 1 teaspoon dried thyme
1/2 cup fresh morels or 1/4 cup dried morels
1 1/2 to 2 pounds flank steak
Salt and fresh-ground black pepper
2 tablespoons unsalted butter

2 tablespoons chopped green
 onions, white part and some
 green part
Chopped fresh Italian parsley, for
 garnish

1. Combine the beer, stock, tomato juice, Worcestershire sauce, hot pepper sauce, bay leaves, oregano, thyme, and morels in a large shallow dish. Place the steak in the marinade, and marinate for 1 hour at room temperature, turning the steak every 15 minutes. While the steak is marinating, preheat a gas or charcoal grill to high.

2. Remove the steak and reserve the marinade. Pat the steak dry, sprinkle it with salt and pepper, and set it aside. Bring the reserved marinade to a boil in a saucepan over high heat and reduce the marinade by half, about 8 minutes. Remove from the heat.

3. Melt the butter in a skillet over medium heat. Add the green onions and sauté them until they are tender, about 4 minutes. Add the reduced marinade and heat through. Reduce the heat to low, and keep warm until the steaks are done.

4. Grill the flank steak about 7 to 10 minutes per side for medium, or to your taste. Transfer the steak to a serving platter, slice the meat on the diagonal, pour the warm sauce over, garnish with parsley, and serve.

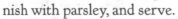

PRAIRIE-STYLE HAY-SMOKED GRILLED STEAK

Kansas Citian Ardie Davis, known in barbecue circles as Remus Powers, Ph.B., taught me how to cook a steak this way. One overcast Sunday afternoon, Ardie and I talked shop as our dinner literally rested on a bed of hay. The steaks will have a gentle, slightly sweet flavor and will be nicely aromatic. Ardie encourages you to "stick to the directions before you try variations." He gets his hay from a local farmer, and you can, too.

SERVES 4

1 large handful of prairie hay or
 wheat straw
4 strip steaks, cut 3 inches thick
1 tablespoon coarse sea salt or
 kosher salt
About 30 natural-hardwood
 charcoal briquets, preferably,
 or 30 standard bagged
 charcoal briquets
1 chunk of oak, about 12 inches
 long and 6 inches wide
1 tablespoon extra-virgin olive oil
Salt and fresh-ground black
 pepper to taste
Fresh lemon wedges, for garnish

1. Spread the hay on a platter and put the steaks on the hay. Sprinkle the steaks with

the salt and let them reach room temperature, about 2 hours if they have been in the refrigerator. About 20 minutes before you will grill the steaks, light the charcoal and oak in your charcoal grill.

2. When the grill temperature reaches medium-high, remove the steaks from the hay, and reserve the hay. Grill the steaks for 3 minutes on each side. Carefully remove the grill grate, with the steaks still on it, and set it aside. Drop the hay over the coals and oak and replace the grate on top of the grill. Grill the steaks for 15 to 20 minutes more, until the steaks are medium-rare to medium, turning them several times so that both sides absorb the smoky flavor. Remove the steaks to a platter or individual plates, drizzle them with olive oil, season to taste with salt and pepper, and serve, with lemon wedges alongside.

SANTA FE TRAIL SMOTHERED STEAK

The old-fashioned home cooking of Auntie Em meets the Santa Fe Trail in this flavorful update of Swiss steak, in which the steak is smothered in fresh vegetables seasoned with a spicy rub. Good accompaniments are mashed potatoes, for soaking up the sauce, and a salad or slaw topped with crumbled blue cheese.

SERVES 4

2 tablespoons canola oil or corn oil
1 boneless beef sirloin steak, about 2 pounds
1 medium yellow onion, chopped
3 celery ribs, chopped
1 cup chopped green bell pepper
2 teaspoons Fireworks Rub (page 56)
2 cups chopped canned and drained tomatoes

1. Heat the oil in a large skillet over medium-high heat. Brown the meat on both sides. Remove the steak to a plate, and set aside.

2. Reduce the heat to medium-low, and add the onion, celery, and bell pepper. Sauté the vegetables until the onion is just translucent and the celery has begun to soften, 5 to 7 minutes. Add the rub and stir to coat the vegetables. Add the tomatoes and 1 cup water, and stir to combine well. Return the steak to the skillet and cover it with the tomato mixture. Bring the mixture to a boil, reduce the heat, cover the skillet, and simmer gently for 45 minutes to 1 hour, or until the steak is quite tender. Transfer the steak to a platter, spoon the vegetables and cooking liquid over, and serve hot.

VARIATIONS:

A sirloin of venison or buffalo may be substituted.

ANXIETY AND JANE

Before 1880, an American steak meant a tough, stringy piece of beef from the rangy Texas longhorn, a breed descended from cattle abandoned by the Spanish in the southwest. On cattle drives on the Chisholm Trail from the southern tip of Texas up through Wichita to the rail lines in Abilene, a wily old longhorn usually led the way. The good news was that his life would be spared; the bad news was that he had to tramp back down the dusty trail to Texas and start all over again with another unruly herd.

About the time Americans had fully tired of chewing (and chewing and chewing) longhorn beef, a new culinary contender entered the scene—the Hereford breed from England. When Herefords were bred with the native longhorns, the result was bigger and hardier cattle. Consider Texas Jane, a sizable 1,260-pound heifer who was exhibited at the Kansas City Fat Stock Show in 1883. Her mother, a longhorn "scrub cow," had somehow wandered over into the meadow where a purebred Hereford bull was grazing, and you know what happened next. When Texas Jane was born, she quickly grew to be almost twice the size of her mother.

So cattlemen began to breed more scrub cows with purebred Herefords. A Hereford bull named Anxiety, raised in Illinois to breed more like him, produced many offspring before he died in 1879. When one of his sons, Anxiety IV, arrived in Independence, Missouri, in the early 1880s, he caused quite a stir. Cattlemen had known that the Hereford was an improvement on the longhorn, except for one characteristic. These early Herefords, so massive from the front, had skinny rear ends. These so-called "cat-hammed" hindquarters delved into cattlemen's profits—that is, until Anxiety IV came on the scene. "He had quite a hind end on him," remarked Thomas A. Simpson, who, with co-owner Charles Gudgell, kept Anxiety IV fat and happy. Through careful breeding practices, Simpson and Gudgell continued to improve the hindquarter situation. Today, nearly all American Herefords are descended from Anxiety IV. An oil painting of Anxiety IV, painted in 1890 and kept in the Jackson County (Missouri) Historical Society archives, still shows what all the fuss was about. A reproduction ought to be framed in every midwestern steakhouse.

North Country Pot Roast with Parsnips and Carrots

In the upper midwest, this pot roast finds favor in communities founded by Scandinavian or Dutch immigrants. Make this for fractious relatives or prickly friends; the aroma as the pot roast is cooking, and the taste once it is done, will ensure peace throughout your home. Serve with Homemade Egg Noodles (page 259), if you like, and a crisp-tender steamed green vegetable.

Serves 6 to 8

2 teaspoons ground allspice
3 pounds beef chuck roast
1/2 cup plus 1 tablespoon
     all-purpose flour
2 tablespoons canola oil or corn oil
1 1/2 cups beef stock, or more if
     necessary
2 tablespoons cider vinegar
2 tablespoons molasses or sorghum
1 teaspoon anchovy paste or
     2 canned anchovies, mashed
2 medium yellow onions, sliced
     thin
3 large parsnips, peeled and sliced
     diagonally
3 large carrots, peeled and sliced
     diagonally
1 cup pitted prunes

1 bay leaf
1 teaspoon salt
1/2 teaspoon fresh-ground black
     pepper

1. Preheat the oven to 350 degrees. Press or rub the allspice into all sides of the roast, then dredge the meat in 1/2 cup of the flour. Heat the oil in a large skillet over medium-high heat, and brown the meat on all sides. Transfer the meat to a covered roaster.

2. Add the stock, vinegar, molasses, and anchovy paste to the skillet, bring to a boil, and deglaze the pan. Pour the hot liquid over the roast and add the onions, parsnips, carrots, prunes, bay leaf, salt, and pepper. Cover, and braise in the oven for 2 1/2 to 3 hours, until the meat is quite tender. Remove the meat and vegetables to a serving platter.

3. Make a gravy: In the roaster or a skillet, bring the cooking juices to a boil; add more beef stock, or water, if necessary. Shake together the remaining 1 tablespoon of flour with 1 cup water in a lidded jar until all the lumps are gone. Pour this mixture into the hot cooking juices and whisk constantly until the gravy has thickened. Remove from the heat and let cool just a little. Taste the gravy, adjust the seasoning, and serve in a bowl or gravy boat alongside the roast.

VEGETABLE GARDEN POT ROAST

For a lazy summer Sunday or a picnic supper, this simple roast is a perfect entree. Vary the vegetables, if you wish, according to what is fresh and colorful in the garden.

SERVES 6 TO 8

3 tablespoons canola oil or corn oil
1 5-pound top or bottom round
    roast or rump roast
1½ cups dry red wine
1 green bell pepper, chopped
1 small summer squash or
    crookneck squash, chopped
2 cups cherry tomatoes, quartered
1 cup pitted black olives, sliced or
    quartered
1 bunch green onions, white part
    and some green part, chopped
2 garlic cloves, minced
2 tablespoons wine vinegar
¼ cup olive oil

1. Preheat the oven to 350 degrees. Heat the oil in a large skillet over medium-high heat. Add the meat, and brown it on all sides. Remove from the heat and transfer the meat to a roaster. Pour the wine on and around the meat, cover, and cook in the oven for 2½ to 3 hours, or until the roast is tender.

2. Meanwhile, combine the vegetables, garlic, vinegar, and olive oil in a bowl. Toss gently to distribute the liquid. Cover, and let marinate at room temperature until the meat is cooked.

3. Cut a piece of aluminum foil large enough to enclose the roast completely. On a work surface, place the cooked roast in the center of the foil. Using a serrated knife, cut the beef into ½-inch slices, cutting ¾ of the way through the roast but not all the way through. Spoon the marinated vegetable mixture between the slices, packing the vegetables in firmly. Wrap the foil around the roast and let the meat and vegetables rest for 15 minutes, so that the flavors blend. To serve, unwrap the roast and slice it all the way through, and transfer the meat and vegetables to individual plates.

VARIATION:

Although I prefer to roast the meat in the oven, if you want to keep your kitchen cooler, you can simmer the meat, covered, on the stovetop for 2½ to 3 hours.

SMOKED AND PEPPERED BEEF RIB ROAST WITH YORKSHIRE PUDDING

Across the barbecue belt in the southern midwest, it is not only traditional Bar-B-Q, like ribs and brisket, that gets cooked in a smoker. Here is a savory and memorable way to serve a holiday classic, with a once-a-year indulgence of decadent Yorkshire pudding. By using the smoker or covered grill for the meat, you also free up the oven to make the pudding. When you buy the roast, be sure it has enough fat for the pudding.

SERVES 8

FOR THE RIB ROAST:
Hickory or mesquite chunks, if you have a smoker, or hickory or mesquite chips, if you have a covered grill

POT ROASTS

Pot roasting, browning meat and then braising it in liquid, produces a tender, moist, flavor-rich result when done right. When I first set up my own household, I wrote down my mother's instructions for cooking roasts on an index card and put it in my recipe file. Now yellowed with age and splotched with a few spills, the advice on the card has not gone out of style and still produces delicious results.

"Beef Pot Roast. Use rump, chuck, or top round. Dredge the roast in seasoned flour, then brown it in hot oil on all sides. Put the meat in a covered roasting pan. Place onion slices on the top and add beef broth, red wine, or a combination of the two to reach halfway up the meat. Cover and roast 30 to 45 minutes per pound at 350 degrees."

"Pork Roast. Use loin end or center cut. Salt and pepper the top of the roast and sprinkle flour on the surface of the meat. Using a paring knife, cut small slits in the top of the meat and press in slivers of fresh garlic. Add chicken broth, dry white wine, or a combination of the two to reach halfway up the meat. Cover and roast 30 to 45 minutes per pound at 350 degrees."

Pot roast is good any time of year. It's a quintessential form of home cooking that never fell from favor in the Heartland. (As recently as five or ten years ago, midwesterners were teased for their affection for pot roasts. Lately, however, chic restaurants from New York to San Francisco have taken to serving pot roasts.) In the autumn, I prepare a pork roast with braised red cabbage, mashed potatoes with gravy made from the roast, a green salad with pears and blue cheese, and a Blitz Torte (page 405). I invite friends and family, and there's still enough for leftovers. For summer, I love Vegetable Garden Pot Roast (page 184), served either hot or at room temperature, with potato salad, Warm Italian Green Bean Salad (page 150), and a homemade pie.

1 4- to 6-pound standing rib roast,
  at room temperature
¼ cup extra-virgin olive oil
1 tablespoon garlic salt
½ cup cracked black peppercorns

FOR THE YORKSHIRE PUDDING:
  ¾ cup of white fat trimmed from
    the rib roast
  ¼ teaspoon fresh-ground black
    pepper
  ¾ teaspoon garlic salt
  2 eggs
  1 cup all-purpose flour
  1 cup milk
  ½ teaspoon salt
  2 tablespoons canola oil or
    safflower oil

1. Soak the wood chunks or chips for at least 30 minutes in water. If you have a smoker: Add the chunks to the smoker and bring the temperature to 225 degrees. If you have a grill, build an indirect fire and bring the temperature to 225 degrees. Wrap the soaked wood chips in aluminum foil, perforate the foil several times, and place the foil packet over the charcoal in the grill. Fill the water pan next to the indirect fire in the grill or in the lower part of the smoker.

2. Rub the roast with the olive oil, and press the garlic salt and cracked peppercorns into the surface of the meat. Insert a meat thermometer in the center of the roast. Place the roast, fat side up, on the food rack in the smoker or, in the covered grill, on a grill rack opposite the indirect fire. Smoke at 225 degrees for 3 to 3½ hours, or until the meat thermometer registers 140 degrees for medium-rare.

3. About 45 minutes before the roast will be done (including its resting time), preheat the oven to 450 degrees and prepare the Yorkshire pudding: Place the fat from the roast, the pepper, and the garlic salt in a heavy glass baking dish. Cover loosely with aluminum foil and place in the oven for 8 to 10 minutes, or until the fat has melted and browned slightly. Meanwhile, beat the eggs in a small bowl and stir in the flour, milk, and salt. Add the oil and whisk to a smooth batter. Remove the baking dish from the oven and carefully pour the batter over its contents. Return the baking dish to the oven and bake, uncovered, for 10 minutes. Reduce the temperature to 350 degrees and bake for 10 to 15 minutes more, or until the Yorkshire pudding is puffed and golden. Remove from the oven and cut into squares.

4. Remove the roast from the smoker or grill, wrap it tight in heavy aluminum foil, and let it rest for 15 to 20 minutes. Remove the foil and transfer the meat to a serving platter. Slice the roast, and serve with the Yorkshire pudding alongside.

NEW PRAGUE MEATLOAF

When John Schumacher was growing up on a Minnesota dairy farm, he watched his mother garden and preserve her fruits and vegetables. He helped with the milking and the butchering, and he hunted and fished. Today, as the owner of Schumacher's New Prague Hotel in the little town of New Prague, Minnesota, and as the chef in the hotel's kitchen, he brings all those skills to his job. He takes home-style basics and makes them exceptional. Dishes like this meatloaf and mashed potatoes are surprisingly flavorful; traditional Eastern European dishes like sauerbraten or braised red cabbage taste fresh and new. The tantalizing aroma of this meatloaf in the oven promises a lot—and the finished dish delivers.

SERVES 8 TO 10

2 eggs, beaten
1 cup minced yellow onion
1/4 cup rolled oats
3/4 cup homemade (page 55) or
    bottled chili sauce
1/4 cup Fresh Horseradish Sauce
    (page 46) or prepared
    horseradish
2 teaspoons Worcestershire sauce
    or Maggi seasoning
2 garlic cloves, minced
1 teaspoon salt
1 teaspoon fresh-ground black
    pepper
1 1/4 pounds ground beef, ground
    venison, or ground buffalo
1 1/4 pounds lean ground pork or
    ground veal

1. Preheat the oven to 350 degrees. Combine the eggs, onion, oats, 1/4 cup of the chili sauce, horseradish, Worcestershire, garlic, salt, and pepper in a large mixing bowl. Add the ground meats and mix well by hand. Pat the mixture into a large loaf pan.

2. Bake the meatloaf, uncovered, for 1 hour and 20 minutes, or until the loaf begins to pull away from the sides of the pan. Remove from the oven and carefully drain out the fat. Brush the remaining 1/2 cup of chili sauce on top of the meatloaf, and return the pan to the oven. Bake for 15 minutes more, or until a meat thermometer inserted in the center of the loaf registers 160 degrees. Let the meatloaf rest for 5 to 10 minutes before you slice and serve it.

BOILED BEEF WITH STAMPOTTEN

When my sister and I were kids, my mother used to serve us potatoes and carrots mashed together, a dish she learned from her father, who had eaten it growing up. Eventually I learned that my Dutch great-grandfather, Benjamin Vanderhorst, who had a restaurant in Maineville, Ohio, was the source of the dish. *Stampotten* (called *stappa* in Scandinavian cuisines) are simple purees of two or three root vegetables, usually potato plus carrot or parsnip or rutabaga, and they remain popular in old Dutch towns like Holland, Michigan, Pella, Iowa, and Minster, Ohio. The leftover beef and juices make a comforting, lightly sweet soup to serve the next day.

SERVES 8

1 large beef shin, about 4 pounds,
    or 4 pounds beef ribs
3 carrots, peeled and cut
    lengthwise into quarters
2 celery ribs with leaves
1 teaspoon salt
20 black peppercorns
2 rutabagas, peeled and sliced
    thick, or 2 large parsnips,
    peeled and cut lengthwise into
    quarters
3 large potatoes, peeled and
    quartered
1/2 teaspoon white pepper,
    preferably fresh-ground
1/8 teaspoon fresh-grated nutmeg
4 tablespoons unsalted butter

1. Place the beef, carrots, celery, salt, and pep-percorns in a large stockpot and add water to cover. Bring to a boil, reduce the heat, and simmer, partially covered, for 2 hours, skim-ming off foam from the surface occasionally. Add the rutabagas or parsnips and the pota-toes, and simmer for 30 minutes more, or until the vegetables are cooked through.

2. Remove the carrots, the potatoes, and the rutabagas or parsnips. Make the *stampotten* by mashing them with the white pepper, nutmeg, and butter. Remove the beef shin, place it on a serving platter with the *stampotten*, slice it, and serve.

GREAT LAKES GOULASH

Many cooks in Cleveland's and Toledo's large communities of Hungarian-Americans have their own favorite versions of this thick soup or stew, known as *gulyas* in the Old Country. Slowly simmered on the stove, goulash is a great dish to savor when cold winds blow down across Lake Erie from Canada and threaten to chill body, mind, and spirit. The tricks to making this dish are two: chopping the onion, garlic, and bell pepper as fine as possible (see Note), so that they melt into the sauce, and using sweet Hungarian paprika.

SERVES 6

1 large red onion, quartered
2 large garlic cloves
1 medium green bell pepper,
    quartered
1/2 cup all-purpose flour
2 1/2 pounds boneless beef chuck,
    cut into 2-inch cubes
4 tablespoons canola oil or corn oil
3 tablespoons sweet Hungarian
    paprika
1 tablespoon sea salt
1 teaspoon fresh-ground black pepper
2 bay leaves
3 medium baking potatoes, peeled
    and diced
4 carrots, peeled and cut
    diagonally into 2-inch pieces

1/2 pound green beans, cut
diagonally into 2-inch pieces
Sour cream, chopped fresh parsley,
and chopped pimiento, for
garnish

1. Put the onion, garlic, and bell pepper into the bowl of a food processor and pulse until they are chopped very fine. Set aside. Place the flour on a large plate and dredge the beef cubes on all sides.

2. Heat the oil in a deep lidded skillet or saucepan over medium-high heat. Brown the beef, in batches if necessary, on all sides. As the cubes brown, remove them with a slotted spoon to a bowl. Add more oil, if necessary, to the pan.

3. When all the beef is browned, add the onion mixture, and sauté, stirring often, until the onions are softened and translucent, about 3 minutes. Add the paprika, salt, pepper, and bay leaves, and stir to blend. Add 1 cup of water and deglaze the pan, stirring up any browned bits on the bottom of the pot. Add another 1 cup of water and stir. Return the beef to the pan, bring to a boil, reduce the heat, and simmer, covered, for 1 hour. Add the potatoes and simmer, covered, for 30 minutes more. Add the carrots and green beans and cook for 15 minutes more, or until the carrots are crisp-tender and the beans have softened.

4. Ladle the goulash into deep bowls. Garnish each bowl with a dollop of sour cream and a sprinkling of parsley and pimiento, and serve hot.

NOTE: To accomplish a very fine mince, the recipe uses a food processor, which is ideal. Alternatively, you can mince the vegetables very fine with a knife.

GERMAN BRESLAUER STEAKS WITH EGG NOODLES

Brought by northern German immigrants to Iowa and Nebraska, this dish is a cousin of Swedish meatballs; in both dishes, nutmeg flavors the meat, among other similarities. Serve with a steamed green vegetable or a simple green salad, either of which will provide a break from the heaviness of this dish.

SERVES 4 TO 6

1 recipe Homemade Egg Noodles
(page 259), or 12 ounces
packaged egg noodles
1 pound ground veal
1 pound ground pork
3 tablespoons snipped fresh chives
1/3 cup minced onion
1 teaspoon salt
1/8 teaspoon fresh-ground black
pepper
1/8 teaspoon fresh-grated nutmeg
2 tablespoons unsalted butter

½ pound mushrooms, sliced thin
¾ cup chicken stock
½ cup heavy cream
Chopped fresh parsley, for garnish

1. If you are using homemade noodles, prepare them up to the point at which they are ready to be cooked.

2. Mix together the veal, pork, chives, onion, salt, pepper, and nutmeg in a bowl. Shape the mixture into 4 large or 6 medium patties. Heat the butter in a large skillet over medium heat. Pan-fry the patties, in batches if necessary, for about 5 minutes on each side, or until they are cooked through (cut to the center of a patty with a knife to see that there is no pinkness left in the meat). Transfer the patties to a plate.

3. Pour off all but 3 tablespoons of the drippings left in the pan. Add the mushrooms, and sauté them until they begin to brown and give off their juices, about 5 minutes. Add the stock and cream, bring to a boil, reduce the heat to a simmer, transfer the steaks back to the pan, and simmer gently, uncovered, for 15 minutes.

4. Meanwhile, cook the egg noodles in a pot of boiling water, according either to the recipe for homemade noodles or to the package directions. Drain them in a colander, run them under cold water for a few seconds, and transfer them to individual plates. Top with the steaks, spoon the mushroom sauce over all, garnish with parsley, and serve.

VEAL T-BONES WITH LEMON-BUTTER SAUCE

Admittedly, veal T-bones are a luxury. This simple but elegant treatment does them justice, I believe. I prepare this dish in the spring, when I serve it with steamed asparagus and, for soaking up the sauce, herbed rice or a good bread.

SERVES 4

4 veal T-bone steaks, about
    ½ inch thick
1 teaspoon garlic salt
½ teaspoon fresh-ground black
    pepper
½ cup all-purpose flour
3 tablespoons extra-virgin olive oil
½ cup chicken stock
Juice of 1 large lemon
2 tablespoons unsalted butter
Chopped fresh Italian parsley, for
    garnish

1. Let the veal steaks come to room temperature. Season the steaks with the garlic salt and pepper and dredge them in the flour. Heat the oil in a large skillet over medium-high heat. Pan-fry the steaks, 2 at a time, for about 3 minutes on each side, until they are browned on the surface and just cooked through. Set the steaks aside and keep them warm.

2. Pour off the oil in the pan, reserving the browned bits. Pour in the chicken stock and bring to a boil over high heat, stirring occasionally to scrape up the browned bits from the bottom of the pan. Add the lemon juice, and cook for 1 minute more. Reduce the heat to a simmer, whisk in the butter and continue cooking, whisking constantly, until the sauce has thickened, 2 to 3 minutes more. Return the steaks to the skillet and cook for 2 to 3 minutes more.

3. Transfer the steaks to individual plates. Pour the sauce over the steaks, garnish with parsley, and serve.

BORDEAUX IN NEBRASKA

In the early nineteenth century, the Bordeaux Trading Post, near what is now the town of Chadron in northwest Nebraska, served as a way station for fur traders on their way out west to collect furs or on their way back to St. Louis to sell them. Today, the reconstructed post is part of Chadron's Museum of the Fur Trade, with extensive exhibits covering the entire fur-trading era from the sixteenth century to the twentieth. As you tour the museum, you step back in time and can almost hear the bartering among traders, trappers, and Native Americans. For more than two hundred years, the principal industry of what is now Wisconsin, Missouri, Iowa, and Nebraska was the fur trade. It offered incentives more powerful than those that inspired the missionary or the explorer.

The early French Canadian traders or voyageurs often were the first Europeans to contact Native Americans in the Heartland. They opened routes of travel and founded the first permanent white settlements in the prairies and woodlands. They bought and sold furs that later would be traded to the Hudson Bay Company, the North West Company, and other firms connected to European markets. By the mid-nineteenth century, new voyageurs were recruited not in Canada but from among teenage farm boys who lived near St. Louis and other trading cities.

The fur trade was the economic reason for venturing into the unknown lands west of the Mississippi. Along the way, the voyageurs learned to live off the land. They drank a refreshingly tart tea brewed from staghorn sumac berries in the summer. They ate pemmican made from dried buffalo meat pounded with marrow fat, and, in winter when meat was scarce, they ate dried and pounded chokecherries.

Herb-Crusted Grilled Loin of Veal

If you grill burgers or chicken for your family, here is an upscale—but still simple—grill recipe to prepare when company is coming. I like to serve it with Roasted Corn and Fava Bean Succotash (page 306); I spoon the succotash onto plates and put the veal right on top. I'm indebted to Steve Cole of Kansas City's Cafe Allegro for the idea for this recipe.

Serves 6

2 garlic cloves, minced
¼ cup extra-virgin olive oil
1 teaspoon salt
1 teaspoon fresh-ground black pepper
2 tablespoons Dijon mustard
1 2- to 3-pound boneless loin of veal, well trimmed
1 cup minced mixed fresh herbs, such as rosemary, oregano, Italian parsley, tarragon, or thyme

1. In a mortar and pestle, or in a bowl with a spoon, make a paste of the garlic, olive oil, salt, pepper, and mustard. Rub the paste all over the surface of the meat, then press the fresh herbs into the surface. Let the meat rest, covered in the refrigerator, for 1 hour.

Meanwhile, preheat a charcoal or gas grill to high.

2. Over high heat on the stovetop, brown the veal on all sides in a heavy skillet; no oil or butter will be needed. Grill the veal for about 15 minutes, for a doneness between rare and medium-rare. Transfer it to a serving platter, let it rest for 5 to 10 minutes, slice it, and serve.

Black Hills Bison Roulades with Wojapi

After nearing extinction in the late nineteenth century, the American buffalo or bison has made a comeback, especially in South Dakota. At the Nu 'Eta Corn and Buffalo Festival in South Dakota in August, corn and bison, ancestral foods of the native Sioux, are the featured items on the menu. This blue-plate special is a contemporary update of Sioux foodways—with a little help from German immigrants. Wojapi is a traditional Sioux fruit "pudding" usually made with chokecherries. It is a frequent accompaniment to buffalo on South Dakota tables, often with fry bread, too (see page 333), or with mashed potatoes or egg noodles.

Serves 6

3 pounds boneless buffalo sirloin, sliced very thin in pieces about 4 to 6 inches long and 4 inches wide
1/3 cup Dijon mustard
1/3 cup minced yellow onion
6 dill pickle quarter spears
2 tablespoons corn oil or canola oil
1 cup chicken stock
3 strips bacon, cut crosswise in half
1 1/2 cups Wojapi (recipe follows)

1. Preheat the oven to 300 degrees. Stack the sliced buffalo in 6 neat piles. Brush the top and sides of each pile with mustard and sprinkle with onion. Place a pickle quarter in the middle of each pile. Roll the meat tightly around the pickles and tie each roulade with kitchen string.

2. Heat the oil in a large skillet over medium heat. Add the roulades, and brown them on all sides, about 10 minutes total. Transfer the roulades to a casserole dish and pour the stock around them. Place a bacon piece on top of each roulade; the bacon will help keep the buffalo moist. Cover, and bake for 3 hours, or until the buffalo is tender.

3. Serve the roulades on top of or alongside bread, fry bread, mashed potatoes, or noodles, with wojapi drizzled over all.

Wojapi

Makes about 1 1/2 cups wojapi

1 1/2 cups fresh or frozen chokecherry juice or cranberry juice
2 tablespoons honey, or more to taste
1 teaspoon cornstarch, or more if necessary

Bring the fruit juice to a boil in a small saucepan. Stir in the 2 tablespoons honey. Spoon out a teaspoon or so of the syrup, let it cool, taste it, and add more honey if you like. Stir together the 1 teaspoon cornstarch and 1/4 cup of water until you have a smooth paste. Whisk the cornstarch mixture into the juice to thicken it. The wojapi should be a thick syrup; add more cornstarch mixture, if necessary, to thicken it. Serve immediately.

Grilled Pork Tenderloin with Three-Mustard Sauce

If you are a mustard aficionado, you need to make a pilgrimage to the Mt. Horeb Mustard Museum in Mt. Horeb, Wisconsin, just west of Madison. Continue your celebration of the condiment with this dish, experimenting, if you like, with your own favorite mustards.

SERVES 4

FOR THE TENDERLOIN:
  2 pork tenderloins, about
    1½ pounds each
  ¼ cup olive oil
  ¼ cup Fireworks Rub (page 56)
    or Aromatic Herb Rub
    (page 57)

FOR THE SAUCE:
  ½ cup heavy cream
  1 tablespoon whole-grain mustard
  1 tablespoon Dijon mustard

  1 teaspoon American-style
    mustard
  ½ teaspoon sugar
  1 teaspoon granulated onion
  ⅛ teaspoon white pepper
  ½ teaspoon Worcestershire sauce

1. Rub the surfaces of the tenderloins with the olive oil and then with the rub. Set aside for 30 minutes to let the flavors blend. Meanwhile, preheat a gas or charcoal grill to medium.

2. While the grill is heating up, make the sauce: Heat the cream in a small saucepan over medium heat. Stir in the 3 mustards and the rest of the ingredients. Bring the sauce to a simmer and cook until the flavors have blended and the mixture has thickened, about 10 minutes. Keep warm.

3. When the grill is hot, cook the tenderloins for 5 minutes per side for medium. Cut into a loin and make sure there is no pinkness left. Remove the tenderloins to a cutting board and slice them. Pour the sauce into a serving bowl. Transfer the grilled pork to a serving platter and serve, passing the sauce at the table.

IOWA CHOP

There are pork chops, and there are pork chops. None is so tender, juicy, and big as the Iowa chop. The definitive Iowa chop is a lean, center-cut loin chop or rib chop that is an inch to an inch and a half thick. It stays moist when it is grilled, and it's thick enough to be stuffed and braised. Iowans take their pork very seriously; farmers there produce twenty-five percent of the nation's supply. Cook Iowa chops and other pork to an internal temperature of 160 degrees on a meat thermometer.

IOWA BREADED PORK TENDERLOIN

In Iowa and in parts of Indiana and Missouri, this popular dish is served on a plate with mashed potatoes and a vegetable or on a sandwich with lettuce, tomato, and mayonnaise. Hand-cut tenderloins, rather than the machine-processed flattened, breaded, and frozen ones, are what set real country cafés apart from their city-slicker wannabes.

SERVES 4

2 whole pork tenderloins, about
*   1½ pounds each*
½ teaspoon salt
1 teaspoon white pepper
2 eggs, beaten
2 cups saltine cracker crumbs
6 tablespoons unsalted butter or
*   6 tablespoons shortening*

1. Make 3 lengthwise cuts in the pork tenderloins, cutting about ¾ of the way through the meat. Cut each tenderloin crosswise in half. Pound each tenderloin section to a ⅜-inch thickness with a meat mallet. Sprinkle the sections with the salt and white pepper and set aside.

2. Transfer the eggs to a plate. Place the cracker crumbs on a separate plate. Dip each tenderloin section in the eggs, then dredge it in the cracker crumbs. Let the tenderloins sit for 5 to 10 minutes so that the coating will set.

3. Melt the butter in a cast-iron skillet over medium-high heat. When the butter is hot, pan-fry the tenderloins until they are brown and crispy on each side, about 4 minutes per side. Serve hot.

ALMOND-CRUSTED ROAST PORK LOIN WITH SPICED PEAR STUFFING

Have the butcher butterfly the pork loin for you so you can spread the stuffing over the meat and roll it up in jelly-roll fashion. The delicious pear stuffing is also good with roast turkey or stuffed pork chops.

SERVES 10 TO 12

FOR THE STUFFING:
*   2 tablespoons unsalted butter*
*   1 medium yellow onion, diced*
*   4 celery ribs, diced*
*   3 sprigs fresh tarragon, chopped*
*   ½ teaspoon fresh-grated nutmeg*
*   ½ teaspoon ground cinnamon*
*   ½ teaspoon ground allspice*
*   4 fresh pears, peeled, cored, and diced*
*   ½ cup toasted chopped almonds*
*   4 slices homemade or good-quality*
*   store-bought bread, crumbed*

1 4-pound boneless pork loin,
*   butterflied*
½ teaspoon salt
½ teaspoon white pepper
1 cup dry white wine or 1 cup
*   chicken stock*
1 large yellow onion, cut in half
¼ cup wildflower or other
*   medium-colored honey*
¾ cup chopped almonds

1. Preheat the oven to 350 degrees. Prepare the stuffing: Melt the butter in a large skillet over medium heat. Add the onion, celery, tarragon, nutmeg, cinnamon, and allspice, and sauté, stirring often, until the onion is translucent, 6 to 8 minutes. Add the pears and sauté for 5 minutes more. Stir in the toasted almonds and enough of the breadcrumbs to bind the mixture together, and remove from the heat.

2. Lay the butterflied pork loin out on a work surface and season with the salt and white pepper. Spread the stuffing over the meat. Roll up the loin horizontally, starting with a long side. Tie the roll together at intervals with kitchen string. Place the tied and rolled pork loin in a roasting pan with the wine and onion. Roast, covered, for 1½ hours, or until the internal temperature of the meat is 140 degrees. Remove from the oven but leave the oven on.

3. Remove the pork loin from the roasting pan and pour the pan juices into a saucepan. Paint the surface of the pork loin with the honey and roll the loin in the chopped almonds. Return the loin to the roasting pan and cook, uncovered, for 20 to 30 minutes more, or until the internal temperature is 160 degrees. Meanwhile, bring the pan juices to a simmer.

4. To serve, remove the kitchen string, slice the meat into spirals, and nap with the simmering juices.

PRIZE-WINNING BARBECUED RIBS

People are passionate about slow-smoked barbecue in Kansas City. I am one of them. Growing up in Cincinnati, we simmered and then roasted our ribs, and finally we coated them with barbecue sauce. I had to give up my sacrilegious ways when I moved here and was converted to the idea that ribs had to be smoked to be good. Now I am part of an all-female barbecue team, the 'Que Queens. Once a year we compete with a men's team to see who can produce the best slow-smoked baby back ribs. To taste the ribs and vote, people who come to the Battle of the Sexes Barbecue Contest have to bring canned goods to stock a local food pantry. We rise early on a Saturday morning, get the smoker fired up by 6:30, prepare the ribs, and then smoke them for 3 hours before the final saucing. The men's team does the same, only they accompany their activities with bourbon-laced coffees and Bloody Marys, with a beer or two for dessert. Guess who usually wins?

SERVES 4 TO 6

2 whole slabs of baby back pork ribs, about 4 pounds total (see Note)
1 quart apple juice
3 to 4 chunks of hickory or apple wood, for a smoker, or 3 to 4 handfuls of hickory or apple wood chips, for a covered grill, soaked in water for 30 minutes

2 tablespoons brown sugar

1 tablespoon garlic salt

1 tablespoon fresh-ground black
   pepper

1 tablespoon paprika

1 tablespoon celery seeds

12 ounces beer

2 cups Smoky, Spicy Barbecue Sauce
   (page 57) or 2 cups homemade or
   bottled tomato-based barbecue
   sauce of your choice

1. The night before you cook the ribs, marinate the ribs in the apple juice overnight.

2. The next day, build a fire in a smoker, or an indirect fire in a covered grill, to a temperature of 225 to 250 degrees. Place a water pan next to the coals in a charcoal smoker or covered grill, or on the bottom rack of an electric smoker. When the smoker or grill has reached its cooking temperature, add the wood chunks (to the smoker) or the wood chips (to the grill). Remove the ribs from the marinade and pat them dry. Combine the brown sugar, garlic salt, pepper, paprika, and celery seeds in a small bowl. Rub this spice mixture onto the surface of the meat. Place the ribs in the smoker or covered grill and smoke them for 1½ hours.

3. Turn the ribs over, baste them with the beer, and cook for ½ hour more, basting every 10 minutes. Baste the ribs with about 1 cup of the barbecue sauce, wrap the sauced ribs in aluminum foil, and smoke for 30 minutes more. Serve hot, passing the remaining 1 cup sauce at the table.

HOMECOMING

Small towns throughout the Heartland hold annual homecoming festivities to welcome back families and friends who have moved away. Along with dinners shared in individual households, there are often town-wide feasts, featuring meats grilled or smoked outdoors and with side dishes and desserts brought, potluck-style, by the best cooks in town. In Missouri and Kansas, ribs are often the main course. Here is a menu for a summertime homecoming dinner, for a family or a whole town:

Prize-Winning Barbecued Ribs
   (page 196)

Dilled Potato Salad (page 160)

Smoked Baked Beans (page 299)

Baby Carrots with Zesty Lemon
   Dressing (page 305)

Grilled Corn and Red Pepper
   Relish (page 307)

Old-Fashioned Chocolate Cake
   with Boiled Frosting (page 407)

NOTE: One of the secrets to great ribs is to remove the bluish-white membrane on the back of each rib. Start at the narrow end and, using a paring knife, separate the membrane from the meat a little. Then use needlenose pliers to pull the rest of the membrane off. (Make sure your ribs are cold or the membrane will not come off easily.)

COTTAGE HAM AND GREEN BEANS

This is a one-dish meal you will find on many tables in areas of the midwest settled by German immigrants. Fresh horse-radish or an assertive mustard is the condiment of choice.

SERVES 6 TO 8

1 2-pound cottage ham or smoked
    pork butt (see Note), or
1 2-pound piece of Canadian
    bacon
1½ pounds green beans
1 medium yellow onion, quartered
1½ pounds new potatoes

1. Place the ham in a large stockpot with enough water to reach half way up the sides of the ham. Add the beans and onion. Bring to a boil, reduce the heat, and simmer gently, covered, for 2½ hours or until the cottage ham is just tender.

2. Add the potatoes and simmer, covered, for 30 minutes more. Remove the ham, slice it, and serve it hot, with the potatoes and green beans.

NOTE: A *cottage ham* is a cured and smoked pork shoulder. Some butchers and grocery stores sell it under that name, while others call it *smoked pork butt*. One way or the other,

it is available from good butchers, such as Avril and Son in Cincinnati or Lindy's Meat and Sausage in St. Louis, and by mail-order, from The Smoke House Market in St. Louis (see page 416). Alternatively, use Canadian bacon, which your butcher will sell you in a two-pound piece.

Cottage hams vary from butcher to butcher. If you buy yours without plastic wrap, just rinse it off briefly and put it into the pot. If you buy yours wrapped in plastic, rinse it off for at least 5 to 10 minutes, as it is likely to have more salt and sugar brine.

AMANA PORK SCHNITZEL

In German-American restaurants through-out the Heartland, Wiener schnitzel means pork schnitzel—not the original veal. It is a specialty at the Amana Colonies in Iowa, at a number of the restaurants there that serve hearty home-style cooking. Serve these chops, if you like, with mashed potatoes, seasoned green beans, braised red cabbage, a relish tray (see page 95), and homemade rolls. Note that while lard is the traditional oil for this recipe, a plain vegetable oil sub-stitutes fine.

SERVES 4 TO 6

½ cup all-purpose flour
1 teaspoon salt
1 teaspoon fresh-ground black
    pepper

1½ *cups breadcrumbs, preferably*
   homemade
2 *eggs, beaten*
⅓ *cup milk*
4 *to 6 butterflied pork chops*
½ *cup canola oil, corn oil, or lard*

1. Combine the flour with the salt and pepper on a plate. Spread out the breadcrumbs on a separate plate. Whisk the eggs with the milk in a shallow bowl. Dredge each pork chop in the seasoned flour, dip it in the egg mixture, and then dredge it in the breadcrumbs. Let the chops stand for 5 to 10 minutes to let the coating set.

2. Heat the oil in a heavy skillet over medium-high heat. Add the pork chops, and pan-fry them until they are crisp and golden, about 4 minutes per side. (Use a spatula or tongs to turn the chops so you don't pierce the meat.) Remove each chop with tongs and let it drain over the skillet for a few seconds, then place it on absorbent paper. Serve immediately.

HEARTLAND CHOUCROUTE GARNI

French and German culinary influences join together in this easy yet lavish one-pot meal. The legacy of German immigrants to the midwest remains alive in wonderful smoked meats and sausages available at local butcher shops; find the best smoked pork and sausages in your area to use in this hearty cold-weather dish. *Choucroute garni*, French for garnished sauerkraut, usually means pork, with or without other meats, cooked with sauerkraut, juniper berries, and wine. The meats are often but not always smoked. Served with mashed potatoes, a Blitz Torte (page 405), and a beer or a crisp Riesling wine, this *choucroute* will thaw out even the coldest night—and the leftovers are just as good the next day.

SERVES 8

2 *pounds store-bought or home-*
   made sauerkraut, drained
2 *tablespoons juniper berries*
2 *tablespoons caraway seeds*
1 *cup dry white wine*
1 *cup chicken stock*
8 *large (8-ounce or larger) smoked*
   pork chops or cooked regular
   pork chops
3 *smoked ham hocks*
4 *large or 8 small bratwursts*
1 *pound German- or Polish-style*
   sausage, such as kielbasa
Coarse-ground mustard
Fresh-grated horseradish

1. Preheat the oven to 350 degrees. Place the sauerkraut, juniper berries, caraway seeds, wine, and stock in a large covered roasting pan. Stir to blend. Arrange the pork chops, ham hocks, bratwursts, and sausages over the sauerkraut. Roast the *choucroute*, covered, for 1 hour. Check periodically, and add more

wine or stock if necessary to keep the *chou-croute* from drying out.

2. Remove from the oven. Remove the meats and sausages and set them aside. Mound the sauerkraut on a large serving platter and arrange the meats and sausages on the kraut. Serve the *choucroute* hot, with the mustard and horseradish in small serving bowls.

OMA'S SAUERKRAUT WITH WHITE BEANS AND PORK

*O*ma is the traditional term of endearment for a German grandmother. It's a term you still hear in the midwest—especially in the kitchen, where Oma is likely to be, putting together a dinner more or less like this one. This preparation is a more interesting German-American variation on the ubiquitous meat-plus-kraut "sauerkraut supper," but it is still rustic and simple. Serve with home-made noodles or buttery mashed potatoes.

SERVES 8

3 *strips bacon, cut into small pieces*
2 *medium yellow onions, chopped*
1 *pound store-bought or home-made sauerkraut, drained*
1 *large apple, peeled, cored, and sliced thin*
1 *bay leaf*

1 *tablespoon sugar*
1 *cup dry white wine*
1 *16-ounce can white northern beans, rinsed and drained*
Salt and fresh-ground black pepper to taste
4 *smoked pork chops or 2 pounds German- or Polish-style smoked sausage*

1. Fry the bacon in a skillet over medium heat until it is crisp, about 5 minutes. Remove the bacon with a slotted spoon and drain it on absorbent paper. Add the onions to the skillet, and sauté them until they are trans-lucent, about 6 minutes. Transfer the onions with a slotted spoon to a medium bowl. Add the cooked bacon and the sauerkraut to the bowl, and toss to blend well.

2. Transfer the sauerkraut mixture to a large saucepan. Add the apple, bay leaf, sugar, and wine. Bring to a boil, reduce the heat, and simmer, covered, for 30 minutes. Add a little water, or additional wine, if the mixture begins to dry out. Add the beans, salt, and pepper, cover, and simmer for 20 minutes more. Place the smoked pork chops or the sausages on top of the mixture, cover, and simmer for 20 minutes more, or until the meats have warmed through. Serve hot.

BRAISED RED CABBAGE, APPLES, AND SAUSAGE

If you wonder if a family is of German heritage, just look in their refrigerator for the cup of bacon fat. When these families have fried some bacon, they pour the hot fat into a cup, let it come to room temperature, and put it in the refrigerator. Used for frying hash browns or making gravy for biscuits, rendered bacon fat adds a rich, smoky taste, as in this cold-weather one-dish meal.

SERVES 4 TO 6

4 tablespoons rendered bacon fat
2 tablespoons sugar
1 small yellow onion, chopped
4 cups shredded red cabbage
2 tart red apples, such as Jonathan, cored and sliced thin but not peeled
2 tablespoons cider vinegar
1/2 teaspoon caraway seeds
1 to 1 1/2 pounds German- or Polish-style smoked sausage links, or bratwursts
1 pound new potatoes
Salt and fresh-ground black pepper to taste
1 cup beer

THE SMOKEHOUSE

German and Bohemian immigrants brought their knowledge of curing and smoking meats to the Heartland in the nineteenth century. In the Goosetown section of New Ulm, Minnesota, a typical house built by an immigrant family was surrounded by a vegetable garden, a chicken coop, a fenced hog yard, cow stalls, a toolshed, an outhouse, and a smokehouse. Built of brick, and rectangular in shape with a domed roof and a side chimney, the smokehouse was fired up in the fall after the hogs were butchered. When the embers from the logs were just right, the hams and sides of bacon, previously rubbed with salt and spices, were hung from the rafters on metal hooks and smoked for days. Sausages and cheeses also were smoked to help preserve them during the winter. The logs were typically hickory, but applewood was also used. Hickory- and apple-smoked hams, bacons, sausages, and other meats are widely available from midwestern purveyors to this day; see Resources, page 416.

1. Melt the bacon fat in a large skillet over medium heat. Add the sugar and cook, stirring often, until the sugar browns, about 4 minutes. Reduce the heat to medium-low, add the onion, and sauté it until it is golden, about 5 minutes. Add the cabbage, apples, vinegar, and caraway seeds, and stir to blend.

2. Place the sausage links and the potatoes on top of the cabbage mixture. Season with salt and pepper and pour the beer over all. Bring the mixture to a boil over medium-high heat, reduce the heat, and simmer, covered, for 45 minutes. Taste, adjust the seasonings, and serve hot.

BRATWURST WITH CARAMELIZED ONION AND APPLES

This is a fragrant and brothy one-dish meal that you serve in a deep plate or a shallow pasta bowl. Accompany the dish with good poppy seed bread and a nice medium-bodied beer, and you'll have a dressed up version of the classic beer and brats.

SERVES 4

2 tablespoons canola oil or corn oil
1 tablespoon unsalted butter
1 large yellow onion, sliced thin
1 teaspoon sugar

2 Granny Smith apples, peeled, cored and sliced thin
6 cups chicken stock
3/4 to 1 pound bratwurst, cut diagonally into 1/2-inch pieces
2 cups shredded green cabbage
Salt and fresh-ground black pepper to taste

1. Heat the oil and butter in a large saucepan over medium heat. Add the onion, and sauté it, stirring frequently, until it reaches a golden brown color, 10 to 12 minutes. Sprinkle the sugar over the onion and sauté for 5 minutes more. Add the apples and cook, stirring often, for 5 minutes more, or until the apples just begin to soften and brown.

2. Add the stock, bratwurst, and cabbage and cook, stirring frequently, for 10 minutes more, or until the bratwurst is cooked through and the apples are soft. Season with salt and pepper, and serve hot.

WISCONSIN DILLY BEER GRILLED BRATS

In Wisconsin, grilling a brat is an art form, much as smoking a slab of ribs is in Kansas City. If you want to witness something like a convention of brat grillers, visit the massive parking lot at Lambeau Field in Green Bay on the day of a Packers home game, where fans huddle around their fired up grills to keep warm and the aroma of seasoned bratwursts fills the air. Putting the brats in cold water before grilling assures a juicy sausage, and the beer pot serves two purposes: to add a last touch of flavor to the grilled brat and to keep it warm until it is served.

SERVES A HUNGRY DOZEN

1 large white onion, sliced thin
1/2 cup sugar
2 teaspoons salt
1 teaspoon dried dill
1/2 cup white vinegar
12 fresh bratwursts
36 ounces beer
12 hard rolls or kaiser rolls
Mustard, prepared horseradish,
    catsup, and bottled hot sauce,
    for garnish

1. Separate the onion slices into rings. Stir together the sugar, salt, dill, vinegar, and 1/4 cup of water in a large bowl. Add the onion rings and spoon the marinade over the onions. Cover, and refrigerate for at least 30 minutes, stirring gently once or twice during that time. One hour before grilling, put the brats in a large pan of cold water.

2. Preheat a gas or charcoal grill to very hot. Make a beer pot by pouring the beer into a clean 3-pound coffee can or similar container, and place the beer pot on the side of the grill grate, not directly over the fire, so that the beer will warm up. Remove the brats from the water, drain them briefly, and grill them,

turning frequently, about 4 minutes per side, or until they are cooked through completely; as each brat is done, transfer it to the beer pot. Slice the rolls nearly in half and toast them, cut side down, on the grill.

3. Remove the brats from their beer bath, split them lengthwise, and place them in the toasted rolls. Add the dilled onion rings to the sandwiches and serve hot, with mustard, horseradish, catsup, and hot sauce.

ROASTED ITALIAN SAUSAGE, PEPPERS, AND POTATOES

This is a simple and ancient *al forno* Italian dish that once would have been taken to the village baker to roast in his outdoor hive-shaped oven. Although this tastes great made in the kitchen oven, I think it tastes even better when made on the grill. (Both options are given here.) Use an old cast-iron baking pan or roaster on the grill.

SERVES 4

1 pound sweet or hot Italian
    sausage links
4 medium baking potatoes, peeled
    and quartered

EMANCIPATION DAYS

When you first see Nicodemus, an almost-ghost town in western Kansas, Promised Land is not what springs to mind. This small cluster of ramshackle buildings, across the road from wheat fields that stretch to the northern horizon, is home to a dwindling population of thirty. The school, post office, stores, and services have moved on to nearby Bogue and Hill City. The only things that move in the summer heat are pheasants taking wing over fields of golden wheat stubble or scissortail swallows catching insects. Sun-bleached and wind-blasted, Nicodemus seems like a place that time forgot.

But in 1877, to the several dozen ex-slaves who migrated here from Kentucky, Nicodemus really was The Promised Land. And once a year, as it has every year since 1878, the town comes back to life during the Emancipation Days festival in late July. Family members and friends come home to celebrate and remember the first settlers, called "Exodusters," who were lured by the prospect of owning their own land.

Once they got to the place they would call Nicodemus, named after the first slave to purchase his freedom, the Exodusters must have felt like the Israelites cast out into the desert rather than wanderers in the land of milk and honey. Without tools, money, or much of anything, they dug out homes on hillsides and on the banks of the Solomon River, roofed them with sod, and lived in them until they could work the local limestone into building materials. Gradually they made a life for themselves. Some sold buffalo bones to survive the first years. Others worked on the railroad and

2 green bell peppers, cut into
    eighths
2 large yellow onions, cut into
    eighths
1 pound mushrooms

1. Preheat the oven to 400 degrees, or preheat a covered gas or charcoal grill to medium-high. Place the sausages and potatoes in a large baking pan or roaster, and transfer to the oven or to the grill, the latter with

its cover on. Roast or grill the sausages and potatoes, turning them several times, for 30 minutes, or until they have just begun to brown.

2. Add the peppers, onions, and mushrooms to the pan or roaster. Roast or grill for 45 minutes more, turning occasionally, until the potatoes are browned on the outside and tender on the inside. Serve hot.

farmed on the side. Stores, hotels, schools, and a post office materialized during the next ten years. Nicodemus was a place where desperate hopes turned into modest dreams, and modest dreams became a hard-earned reality.

Today, the remaining inhabitants are primarily wheat farmers or retired wheat farmers. Their foodways reflect a southern heritage grafted onto a prairie landscape. Descendants of Henry Williams, the first child born in Nicodemus, still prepare foods for Emancipation Days crowds. For a recent festival, Ernestine Van Duvall, a queenly woman with a deeply melodic voice, prepared barbecued ribs, crispy summer pickles, peach cobbler, and mustard potato salad in the sweltering hundred-degree-plus heat. Charlesetta Bates, quiet and shy, made cinnamon rolls, while her husband, J.R. Bates, made his version of barbecued ribs. Small in stature but ample in size, Pearlena Moore fried chicken and baked several deep-dish peach cobblers flavored with cinnamon and nutmeg.

In the spring, women still gather wild prairie greens like pigweed, lamb's quarters, burdock, and wild mustard. By the time the wild greens are too tough to eat, the garden greens are in: Swiss chard, turnip, collard, and mustard. Slow-simmered with a smoked pork hock or hog jowl, greens are still a big part of Nicodemus meals. At the end of July, women go down to the creek banks to gather wild plums, which are destined for jelly. Returning relatives are sure to go back home with a jar or two.

As the oldest surviving African-American pioneer town west of the Mississippi, Nicodemus has recently been designated a National Historic Site. Despite the promise of new acclaim, however, the town's future is in doubt. For now at least, for many descendants of the original families, the last weekend in July still means "home to Nicodemus" for Emancipation Days.

EXODUSTER STEW

Although the roots of this one-pot meal run back to the coastal south, especially the islands off Georgia and the Carolinas, this dish is a favorite in African-American communities in river cities like Cincinnati, St. Louis, and Kansas City. When freed slaves—"Exodusters"—traveled up the Mississippi River after the Civil War to homestead in Kansas and Missouri, they brought the foodways of the south with them, and this stew has been passed down through the generations. Versions of it go by various names, like Soul Succotash, Low-Country Boil, and Frogmore Stew. The ingredients have been adapted to life away from the sea: Gone are the shrimp and the crab seasoning, replaced by the rich flavor of smoked turkey wings and lots of black pepper.

SERVES 6 TO 8

2 cups beer
1 pound smoked sausage, cut into
    2-inch pieces
1 pound smoked turkey wings
1 pound green beans
1 teaspoon black pepper, or more to
    taste
6 to 8 ears of fresh corn, husked
    and cut into 2-inch pieces
4 tablespoons butter, melted

1. Bring the beer and 2 cups of water to a boil in a large stockpot. Add the sausage, turkey wings, green beans, and pepper. Reduce the heat and simmer, covered, for 15 minutes. Add the corn and cook, covered, for 8 minutes more, or until the corn is tender. Taste, and add more pepper if you like.

2. Use a slotted spoon to transfer the sausage, turkey wings, green beans, and corn to a serving platter. Spoon a little of the cooking liquid over, and serve hot, with melted butter to pass at the table.

GRILLED BUTTERFLIED LEG OF LAMB WITH THYME AND GARLIC CREAM SAUCE

With lamb, it is often a good idea to seek out a good butcher or other supplier, even if you buy your other meats at the supermarket. At farmers' markets and better butchers in metropolitan areas of the Heartland, you can buy lamb fed only on rich native grasses and mother's milk. Served with steamed tiny green beans, such as French filet beans or haricots verts, and steamed new potatoes just dug up in the garden, a glass bowl of Gratin of Fresh Fennel (page 311) or Crabapples in Chambourcin (page 64), and Pear and Almond Upside-Down Cake (page 397), this gently seasoned grilled lamb will be the center of a simple but memorable meal.

SERVES 6 TO 8

1 4- to 5-pound leg of lamb, boned
    and butterflied
1 cup dry red wine
3/4 cup balsamic vinegar
6 garlic cloves, minced

FOR THE SAUCE:
2 cups heavy cream

12 sprigs fresh thyme
10 medium shallots
10 garlic cloves
3 tablespoons unsalted butter,
*   melted*
Salt and white pepper to taste
Squeeze of fresh lemon juice

1. Place the leg of lamb in a large glass dish or a sealable plastic bag. Whisk together the wine, vinegar, and minced garlic in a bowl. Pour the marinade over the lamb. Refrigerate the lamb, covered or sealed, for 6 hours or overnight.

2. Preheat the oven to 350 degrees. Bring the cream and the thyme to a gentle boil in a saucepan. Remove from the heat, cover, and let the mixture infuse at room temperature for 1 hour. Meanwhile, place the shallots and garlic cloves on a large sheet of aluminum foil and drizzle them with the melted butter. Fold the foil into a closed packet and bake the shallots and garlic in the oven for 1 hour, or until they are soft.

3. Once the shallots and garlic are in the oven, preheat a gas or charcoal grill to medium. Drain the marinated lamb and pat it dry. Grill the meat, turning it once, for 15 to 20 minutes per side for medium-rare. Let the meat rest off the heat while you finish the sauce.

4. Pour the cream into a food processor or blender; discard the thyme. Add the roasted shallots and garlic, discarding the butter or juices, and puree until smooth. Season the sauce with salt, white pepper, and lemon juice. Slice the lamb on the diagonal, nap with the sauce, and serve hot.

LAMB BRAISED IN CLARET

This slow-braised lamb can practically be eaten with a spoon. You might serve it with a green salad, Horseradish Mashed Potatoes (page 315), and Pear and Almond Upside-Down Cake (page 397).

SERVES 8

½ teaspoon salt
½ teaspoon fresh-ground black
*   pepper*
3 pounds lamb shoulder, cut into
*   ½-inch cubes*
3 tablespoons extra-virgin olive oil
1 carrot, peeled and diced fine
1 small celery rib, diced fine
2 shallots, diced
1 whole head of garlic, cloves
*   separated and peeled*
3 sprigs fresh thyme
2 tablespoons all-purpose flour
1 bottle (750ml) medium- to
*   full-bodied dry red wine*
1 teaspoon red-wine vinegar

1. Salt and pepper the lamb. Heat the olive oil over medium-high heat in a wide-bottomed pot with a tight-fitting lid. When the oil is very hot, add the lamb and brown the meat

THE AMERICAN ROYAL

During the first week of October each year, the air around Kansas City is hazy with the distinct aroma of barbecue smoke. The smoke is a signal that the American Royal Barbecue Contest is in full swing. Teams from as far away as Ireland and Thailand compete to see who can make the best smoked sausage, lamb, brisket, ribs, chicken, and pork butt, along with side dishes like potato salad and barbecued baked beans. For a $125 entry fee, each contestant submits an entry to be judged blind. In a separate hall, judges are presented with numbered food containers that they rate according to appearance, taste, texture, and evidence of a "smoke ring," a pinkish coloring of the outer part of the meat that indicates whether the meat was cooked at the right temperature for the right amount of time. "As a judge, if you eat only one ounce of all the barbecue you'll judge today, you'll have eaten six pounds of barbecue before you leave," Carolyn Wells warns the judges. As the Director of the Kansas City Barbeque Society, which runs the contest, she should know.

well on all sides, 8 to 10 minutes. Remove the meat and set it aside.

2. Reduce the heat to medium-low, and add the carrot, celery, shallots, garlic, and thyme. Add 2 tablespoons of water, and scrape up any brown crust on the bottom of the pan. Whisk in the flour and return the meat to the pot. Cook, stirring occasionally, for 5 minutes.

3. Add the wine to the pot and bring to a boil over high heat. Reduce the heat and simmer, covered, for 2 hours, stirring occasionally and adding water or more wine, if necessary, if the mixture gets too dry. Remove the meat with a slotted spoon to a serving platter and keep warm. Discard the thyme and transfer the remaining contents of the pot to a food processor or blender. Puree the sauce until it is nearly smooth. Stir the vinegar into the sauce and pour the sauce over the lamb. Serve immediately.

HERB-ROASTED RABBIT

Wild jackrabbit used to be the meat of choice for prairie cooks, who would fry it like chicken or would marinate it in a sweet-sour mixture then roast it for a Bohemian delicacy served with dumplings. Today, however, you usually need to go to a specialty butcher for rabbit, and often you have to order it ahead. Accompany this dish with Fresh Herb Noodles (page 259), if you like, with store-bought noodles, or with potatoes. Ask the butcher to bone the saddles for you, and to give you both the fillets and the chopped bones for the sauce.

SERVES 4

FOR THE SAUCE:
    1 tablespoon unsalted butter
    Chopped bones from the 3 rabbit
        saddles
    1 medium yellow onion, coarsely
        chopped
    1 carrot, coarsely chopped
    1 leek, cleaned well and coarsely
        chopped
    1/2 cup dry white wine
    2 cups chicken stock
    1 tablespoon tomato paste
    2 garlic cloves, minced
    10 whole black peppercorns

FOR THE RABBIT:
    2 tablespoons extra-virgin olive oil
    2 tablespoons chopped fresh basil
    2 tablespoons chopped fresh
        parsley
    2 tablespoons chopped fresh
        tarragon
    1 tablespoon chopped fresh
        rosemary
    1/2 teaspoon salt
    1/2 teaspoon fresh-ground black
        pepper

*3 saddles of rabbit, boned, with
    fillets and bones reserved*

1. Preheat the oven to 450 degrees. Make the sauce: Melt the butter over medium heat in a large saucepan. Brown the bones for 5 minutes, stirring often. Add the onion, carrot, and leek, and cook, stirring, for 5 minutes more. Add the rest of the sauce ingredients, bring to a boil, reduce the heat, and simmer, uncovered, for 20 minutes, or until the sauce has reduced to about 1 cup. Line a colander with cheesecloth and place over a bowl. Pour the contents of the saucepan into the lined strainer and strain the sauce. Keep the sauce warm while you cook the rabbit.

2. Make a paste, in a small bowl or a mortar and pestle, of the olive oil and chopped herbs. Salt and pepper the fillets, then rub the paste over the meat. Transfer the fillets to a heavy casserole and roast in the oven for 10 minutes for medium-rare. Remove from the heat, slice thin, transfer to a serving platter, and serve hot, with the sauce poured over the meat.

Chicken
and Other
Birds

CHICKEN AND OTHER BIRDS

ORCHARD CHICKEN WITH CIDER AND PRUNES

Early settlers in the Heartland often planted orchards. In pockets of the midwest, some of the rarer fruit varieties they planted still survive. In Indiana, for example, there are heirloom apples and crabapples. In Michigan, there are old varieties of grapes, plums, and cherries. I like to make this dish in the fall, when the fresh-fruit season is over, the plums have been sun-dried to make prunes, and apples are newly transformed into cider; however, you can make the dish any time of year. I serve it with Homemade Egg Noodles (page 259), mashed potatoes, Bohemian Spaetzle (page 268), or wild rice and a green salad.

SERVES 4

16 prunes, pitted
1½ cups apple cider, or more if necessary
16 whole pecans, toasted, optional
2 tablespoons canola oil or corn oil
1 3½- to 4-pound chicken, cut up, with breast cut in half on the bone
2 leeks, white part and a little green part, cleaned well and sliced thin
Salt and fresh-ground black pepper to taste

1. Place the prunes in a heatproof bowl. Heat the cider in a saucepan over medium-high heat. When it comes to a simmer, pour it over the prunes. Let the prunes steep for 15 minutes to soften. Drain the cider and reserve it. When the prunes are cool enough to handle, stuff each one, if you like, with a toasted pecan.

2. Heat the oil over medium-high heat in a heavy saucepan or casserole large enough to hold the chicken pieces. Brown the chicken pieces on all sides, about 10 minutes. Remove the chicken and set it aside. Reduce the heat to medium, add the leeks, and sauté them until they are browned and wilted, about 5 minutes.

3. Place the chicken on top of the leeks in the pan and season with salt and pepper. Arrange the prunes around the chicken. Pour in the reserved cider, cover, and bring to a simmer. Simmer gently for 50 minutes to 1 hour, or until the chicken is tender; add more cider, if necessary, if the pan becomes too dry. Serve hot.

ROAST CHICKEN AND POTATOES WITH LEMON, GARLIC, AND HERBS

Many of the Italian immigrants who settled in midwestern cities like

Columbus, Cleveland, St. Louis, and Chicago came from Abruzzi, in central Italy. Versions of this classic and succulent Abruzzi chicken dish are still prepared in family restaurants in those cities and, of course, in home kitchens, too.

SERVES 6

2 cups fresh lemon juice
1 cup extra-virgin olive oil
1 tablespoon red wine vinegar
2 garlic cloves, minced
1/2 teaspoon dried oregano
1 teaspoon salt
1/2 teaspoon fresh-ground black
    pepper
2 2 1/2- to 3-pound chickens, cut up,
    with breasts cut in half on the
    bone
6 medium potatoes, peeled and cut
    lengthwise into quarters
1/2 cup chopped fresh Italian parsley

1. Preheat the oven to 500 degrees. Whisk together the lemon juice, olive oil, vinegar, garlic, oregano, salt, and pepper in a medium bowl. Place the chicken pieces, skin side down, in a large roasting pan and surround with the potatoes. Drizzle the chicken and potatoes with 1/4 cup of the lemon juice mixture and roast, uncovered, for 20 minutes.

2. Remove the roasting pan from the oven, turn the chicken pieces skin side up, and flip the potato wedges. Drizzle with another 1/4 cup of the lemon mixture. Return the roasting pan to the oven and roast, uncovered, for

20 minutes more, or until the chicken is golden and juices from a thigh, when pricked, run clear.

3. Remove the chicken and potatoes to a serving platter and keep them warm. Drizzle the chicken and potatoes with another 1/2 cup of the lemon mixture. Combine the pan juices and the remaining lemon mixture in a saucepan, bring to a boil, and boil for 5 minutes, or until the mixture thickens somewhat. Remove from the heat and stir in the parsley. Nap the chicken and potatoes with some of the sauce and pass the rest at the table.

AMISH ROAST CHICKEN WITH TARRAGON

My great aunt Marie used to brine beef and chicken before roasting them. This method seemed eccentric and quaint to my family, much as her habit of wearing purple turbans did. It turns out, however, that Aunt Marie was on to something. According to food scientist Shirley Corriher, a soak in cold salted water before roasting ensures a cooked bird that will be moist and flavorful. Another lost art in chicken cookery is to start with a fresh bird. Happily, this art is making a comeback as well, with lots of free-range organic roasting birds available in the midwest and elsewhere. In much of the Heartland, Amish

CITY CHICKEN

In family-owned butcher shops in German-American towns and neighborhoods of the midwest, you will find for sale a curious thing called city chicken. Wooden skewers with alternating cubes of pork and veal are dredged in flour and in an egg wash and then rolled in cracker crumbs or breadcrumbs. Then the skewered meats are sautéed in oil or shortening. Some shops also will use the skillet drippings to make a gravy to serve with the chicken. Except that there is no chicken.

The reason for the name is lost in culinary history. The skewers do look a little like a fried chicken drumstick. Perhaps there was a time in some city or other when pork or veal was more plentiful than chicken, and there was a certain envy of the rural folk (and even early suburbanites) who had their own chicken coops. Iowa-born cookbook author Glenn Andrews has another theory. "It sounds," she says, "like part of an old joke that begins, 'Why, those city people are so dumb they think....'"

farms produce the best chickens, and I have named this dish in their honor. With the fragrant chicken roasting in the oven, make mashed potatoes or Bohemian Spaetzle (page 268) to accompany the delicious sauce. For other side dishes, try Ragout of Morels and Asparagus (page 295) in the spring, Zucchini with Summer Herbs (page 325) in hot weather, or Baby Carrots with Zesty Lemon Dressing (page 305) in fall and winter.

SERVES 4 TO 6

1/2 cup sour cream
1/2 cup heavy cream
1 5- to 6-pound roasting chicken,
    preferably free-range organic
1 cup salt
12 large sprigs fresh tarragon

1 lemon, cut in half
1/2 teaspoon fresh-ground black
    pepper
1/2 cup dry white wine

1. Whisk together the sour cream and heavy cream in a small bowl. Let the mixture sit, covered, at room temperature for several hours while you brine and roast the chicken.

2. Remove the giblets from the chicken and reserve them for another use or discard them. Rinse the chicken well inside and out, then place it in a large bowl. Sprinkle about 1/4 cup of the salt into the cavity of the chicken. Press the remaining salt onto the exterior of the chicken. Pour in enough ice water to cover the chicken and let it brine in the refrigerator for 3 hours.

3. Preheat the oven to 450 degrees. Remove the chicken from the brine and rinse it well, filling and draining the cavity at least 3 times to remove the salt. Place 6 of the tarragon sprigs and the 2 lemon halves in the cavity of the chicken. Place the chicken breast side up in a deep roasting pan and season with pepper. Roast the chicken for 1 hour and 20 minutes, or until the skin is puffed and golden brown and the thigh bone pulls away easily.

4. Remove the chicken from the oven and place it breast side down on a cutting board. Cover it with foil to keep it warm while you make the sauce.

5. Discard all but 2 tablespoons of the drippings in the roasting pan. Place the roasting pan over high heat, pour in the white wine, and bring to a boil, whisking to deglaze the pan. When the liquid is reduced by half, about 5 minutes, whisk in the sour cream and heavy cream mixture. Reduce the heat to medium, and cook for 5 minutes more. Using kitchen scissors, snip the leaves of the remaining 6 tarragon sprigs into the sauce and whisk to blend well. Taste the sauce, adjust the seasoning, and serve in a sauce boat. Turn the chicken breast side up, carve it, and serve it on a platter.

COMFORT FOOD CHICKEN AND NOODLES

When the dog bites or the bee stings, when you've had car trouble or lost the deal, when the baby has colic or the check wasn't in the mail, make this for dinner. Or, for the full measure of comfort, have someone else make it for you.

SERVES 4 TO 6

1 2- to 3-pound whole chicken
3 celery ribs, cut in half
1 large yellow onion, quartered
1 1/2 teaspoons salt
1/2 teaspoon fresh-ground black
     pepper
1 cube chicken bouillon, optional
1/2 teaspoon poultry seasoning
1/2 teaspoon dried sage
1 recipe uncooked Homemade
     Egg Noodles (page 259), or
     12 ounces uncooked packaged
     egg noodles
1/4 cup chopped fresh parsley

1. Remove the giblets from the chicken and reserve them for another use or discard them. Place the chicken in a large stockpot or kettle with a tight-fitting lid. Add water to cover the chicken, and add the celery, onion, salt, and pepper. Bring to a boil, reduce the heat, and simmer, covered, for 1 1/2 hours. Remove

the chicken and vegetables from the broth and pour the broth into a bowl or other container. Chill the broth in the refrigerator for at least 1 hour, then skim it to remove any excess fat. When the chicken is cool enough to handle, remove and discard the skin, gristle, and bone, and set the meat aside.

2. Pour the chilled and skimmed broth into a large saucepan; add water, if necessary, to total 8 cups. Add the bouillon, if you like, and the poultry seasoning and sage. Bring to a boil, and add the noodles, a few at a time, and cook until the noodles are tender, about 6 minutes for homemade noodles; follow the package directions for store-bought noodles. When the noodles are tender, reduce the heat, add the chicken, stir in the parsley, and simmer gently for 5 minutes to heat through. Ladle the chicken, vegetables, noodles, and broth into individual bowls, and serve hot.

TAKE-TO-THE-PICNIC FRIED CHICKEN

Just about every midwestern cook has a beloved recipe for fried chicken. I am indebted to Kansas City chef Peter Castillo for this one, a favorite of mine. Peter remembers his mother making this dish, with its tang of citrus and zip of garlic, to take to church gatherings and potlucks. He and his brothers always made a beeline for their mother's chicken, simply because "hers was the best."

SERVES 4 TO 6

1 3- to 4-pound chicken, cut up, with
    breast cut in half on the bone
Juice of 2 lemons
10 garlic cloves, minced
1 tablespoon salt
1 teaspoon black pepper
1½ quarts vegetable oil, for frying

FOR THE BREADING:
    3 cups all-purpose flour
    ¼ cup granulated garlic
    2 tablespoons salt
    ½ tablespoon black pepper

1. Rinse the chicken pieces well, pat them dry, and place them in a large stainless steel or porcelain bowl. In a mortar and pestle or in a small bowl, make a paste of the lemon juice, minced garlic, salt, and pepper, and rub the paste over the chicken. Cover, and refrigerate for at least 2 hours.

2. Bread the chicken: Combine the flour, granulated garlic, salt, and pepper in a paper or plastic bag. Shake the bag to distribute the flavors evenly. Place 1 or 2 pieces of chicken in the bag and shake until the chicken is coated well with the breading. Repeat the process until all the chicken is breaded.

3. Heat the oil to a temperature of 350 degrees in a large pan or pot. Fry the chicken pieces, in batches, turning frequently, until the pieces begin to float. Remove the chicken with a slotted spoon and drain it on absorbent paper. Serve hot or at room temperature.

FRIED CHICKEN
DINNER

Southerners may lay claim to creating the ritual of the fried chicken dinner, but midwesterners raised it to an art form. For many in the Heartland, home-cooked Sunday supper simply is fried chicken with mashed potatoes and creamy chicken gravy, slow-cooked green beans seasoned with ham and onion, a gelatin salad, and homemade cinnamon rolls. Venerable home cooks swear by fresh free-range chicken, flour well seasoned with salt and lots of pepper, a cast-iron skillet, lard or a mixture of lard and shortening, and patience. Frying chicken is not something you do in a hurry.

When the automobile made people more mobile, from the 1920s onward, fried chicken restaurants became destination spots. In Kansas and Missouri, fried chicken emporiums abound. People around these parts know their fried chicken. National writers Calvin Trillin and Jane and Michael Stern are on record as having judged Stroud's fried chicken, in Kansas City, among the best anywhere. Further west, in Kansas, the Brookville Hotel, outside Salina, makes the chicken dinner its claim to fame, with homemade cottage cheese, a real relish tray, and other goodies that pay homage to the Sunday dinner of yesteryear. Heading south towards Wichita, you enter the chicken dinner war zone, where Chicken Annie's and Chicken Betty's have faced off for years. If you don't think great fried chicken is something worth fighting for, then you need to taste theirs.

When you want to make peace in your family, tempt your college kids to come home for something other than laundry, or show international visitors what true midwestern cooking is all about, then a fried chicken dinner is your menu:

Old-Fashioned Pan-Fried Chicken
    with Gravy (page 221)

Fresh Farmhouse Cheese (page 39),
    flavored with diced cucumber and
    chopped green onion

Farmhouse Tomato Aspic with
    Herbed Buttermilk Dressing
    (page 157)

Mashed potatoes

Seasoned Green Beans (page 311)

Sour Cream Cinnamon Rolls
    (page 344)

OLD-FASHIONED PAN-FRIED CHICKEN WITH GRAVY

A lot of cooks on the prairie will swear that a buttermilk marinade and frying in lard are the two keys to the most golden brown, moist, and tender fried chicken. Try it yourself with this recipe, a good one to serve with traditional accompaniments like homemade vegetable relishes and preserves to start, then mashed potatoes, seasoned green beans, and hot yeast rolls. Old homesteaders used to fry jackrabbit this way.

SERVES 4 TO 6

FOR THE CHICKEN:
1 pint buttermilk
1 2½- to 3-pound chicken, cut up,
    with the breast cut in half on
    the bone, or 6 chicken breast
    halves
1 cup all-purpose flour
2 teaspoons salt
2 teaspoons black pepper
½ cup lard or vegetable oil

FOR THE GRAVY:
¼ to ½ cup all-purpose flour
½ cup milk
Salt and black pepper to taste

1. Pour the buttermilk into a bowl, add the chicken pieces, and toss gently to coat. Marinate the chicken, covered in the refrigerator, for 1 hour or overnight.

2. Preheat the oven to 200 degrees. Combine the flour, salt, and pepper in a paper or plastic bag. Pat the chicken pieces dry and place them, 1 or 2 at a time, in the bag. Shake the bag to coat the pieces. Transfer the pieces to a rack for 5 to 10 minutes to let the coating set. Repeat with the remaining pieces.

3. Heat the lard or oil in a lidded cast-iron skillet over medium heat. When the oil is hot, put the chicken pieces, 3 or 4 at a time, in the skillet. Cover the skillet (to keep the grease from spattering), and pan-fry the pieces, turning them occasionally, for 15 to 20 minutes, until they are brown on all sides and cooked through. Transfer the cooked pieces to a heat-proof plate and keep them warm in the oven. Continue until all of the pieces are cooked.

4. Make the gravy: Drain all but ¼ cup of the drippings in the skillet through a sieve into a bowl. Return the browned bits in the sieve back to the skillet and return the skillet to medium heat. Whisk in ¼ cup of the flour, or more if necessary, to make a paste. Cook the mixture, whisking frequently, until it browns. When it reaches a medium brown, pour in 1 cup of water and whisk constantly until the mixture becomes smooth and thick. Whisk in the milk and cook for about 2 minutes more, or until the gravy is heated through. Season with salt and pepper to taste. Transfer the gravy to a gravy boat and the chicken pieces to a serving platter, and serve.

Church Supper Chicken and Wild Rice Hot Dish

Hot dish means casserole in the language of Minnesotans. Often it is something of a joke, the sort of meal a harried mother or disinterested cook might throw together. In its worst form, it contains ground beef and one or another—or even several—kinds of canned soup, stirred together with some frozen potatoes and then baked. But not all hot dishes are created equal. Here is one that does Minnesota proud. Take this to a potluck supper and you will get lots of requests for the recipe.

Serves 8

1/4 cup unsalted butter
1/2 cup chopped yellow onion
1/4 cup all-purpose flour
1 1/2 cups chicken stock
1 1/2 cups half-and-half
1 teaspoon salt
1/2 teaspoon fresh-ground black
    pepper
1/4 teaspoon fresh-grated nutmeg
1/4 cup dried mushrooms, such as
    morels or porcini
3 cups diced cooked chicken
2 tablespoons chopped fresh
    parsley
3 cups cooked wild rice

1 cup grated brick, Muenster, or
    other mild white cheese

1. Preheat the oven to 350 degrees. Heat the butter in a large skillet over medium heat. Add the onion, and sauté it until it is translucent, 5 to 7 minutes. Sprinkle on the flour and stir to blend it in. Pour in the stock and half-and-half, and bring just to a simmer, whisking frequently. Simmer gently for 5 minutes, whisking often, then add the salt, pepper, and nutmeg. Stir in the dried mushrooms, chicken, and parsley.

2. Lightly oil, or spray with cooking spray, a 2-quart casserole. Spread the wild rice in the bottom of the casserole. Spoon in the chicken mixture, then sprinkle the cheese over the top. Bake for 30 minutes, or until the casserole is hot and bubbling. Serve hot.

Smoked Herbed Chicken

If you do not eat both of these succulent chickens for dinner, use one of them for Heartland Smoked Chicken and Corn Chowder (page 137), or for a chicken salad or sandwiches.

Serves 4 to 6

2 2- to 3-pound whole chickens
2 lemons, cut in half

*6 tablespoons Aromatic Herb Rub
(page 57)*

*Oak, pecan, or apple wood chunks,
if you have a smoker, or oak,
pecan, or apple wood chips, if
you have a covered grill*

1. Remove the giblets and necks from the chickens and reserve them for another use or discard them. Rinse the chickens thoroughly and pat them dry. Sprinkle each chicken inside and out with the juice of 1 lemon, then place the lemon halves in the cavities of the chickens. Sprinkle 1 tablespoon of the herb rub inside each cavity, then press 2 tablespoons of the rub on the outside of each bird. Refrigerate the chickens for 1 hour or until you are ready to smoke them.

2. Soak the wood chunks or chips for at least 30 minutes in water. If you have a smoker:

WILD RICE

Wild rice, an aquatic grass and not a true rice, was a staple food of the Sioux and Chippewa peoples. It is the only edible grain native to North America. True wild rice still grows in the lakes and rivers of Minnesota, where four-fifths of the world supply originates, and also in northern Michigan, northern Wisconsin, and lower central Canada. French voyageurs called it folle avoine, crazy oats. Around Tower, Minnesota, the Chippewa still harvest wild rice from murky-bottomed Big Rice Lake and Lost Lake. With two people to a canoe, one paddles to the plants while the other uses a cedar stick to flail the ripened grains from the stalks so that the grains fall into the canoe. When they get to shore, the harvesters spread out the rice on a tarp over an open fire to dry the rice. Then it is winnowed, husked, and packaged.

Today, wild rice is also grown in manmade paddies. Connoisseurs can tell the difference, although the average consumer cannot. Ecologists like the development of new paddies because they provide excellent habitats for waterfowl and other wildlife.

Wild rice is a staple of the midwestern pantry. It can be stored indefinitely in tightly sealed containers. One cup of raw wild rice makes 3 to 4 cups cooked wild rice. Because the cooking process takes about 45 minutes, many cooks keep cooked wild rice in the freezer for convenience.

In Minnesota, wild rice is popular in pancakes, pilafs, muffins, fritters, and "glorified rice," a kind of rice pudding in which cooked wild rice is blended with cherry or pineapple syrup and heavy cream.

Add the chunks to the smoker and bring the temperature to 200 degrees. If you have a covered grill, build an indirect fire and bring the temperature to 200 degrees. Wrap the soaked wood chips in aluminum foil, perforate the foil several times, and place the foil packet over the charcoal in the grill. Fill a water pan and place it next to the indirect fire in the grill or in the lower part of the smoker.

3. Place the chickens, skin side up, in the smoker or grill. Smoke the chickens for 2½ hours, or until the juices run clear from a pierced thigh and the leg joint moves easily. Transfer to a platter and serve hot.

GRILLED CHICKEN SPIEDINI WITH AMOGIO AND MODIGA

During the late nineteenth and early twentieth centuries, many immigrants from poverty-stricken Sicily started new lives in the midwest. Because they were from an area that grew winter wheat, pastas and breads were a main part of their diet, along with citrus fruits, eggplant, cauliflower, pine nuts, and fava beans. In the midwest, meat and chicken were more plentiful and affordable, so dishes like this one were prepared in homes and restaurants on the Hill in St. Louis or in the River Market area of Kansas City. Spiedini are made with boneless chicken breast or veal. Amogio is a marinade composed of lemon juice, white wine, olive oil, garlic, and herbs; the exact recipe varies from household to household. Modiga is a seasoned breadcrumb mixture. Wonderful hot or cold, spiedini make great tailgate or picnic food.

SERVES 6

6 skinless, boneless chicken breasts, about 3 pounds total
Wooden skewers, soaked in water for 30 minutes, or metal skewers

FOR THE AMOGIO:
½ cup extra-virgin olive oil
½ cup dry white wine
½ cup fresh lemon juice
3 tablespoons minced garlic
¼ cup chopped fresh Italian parsley
1 tablespoon chopped fresh mint
¼ teaspoon red pepper flakes

FOR THE MODIGA:
2 cups breadcrumbs, preferably homemade
1 teaspoon dried oregano
1 teaspoon dried basil

1. Cut the chicken breasts into bite-size pieces and transfer the pieces to a nonreactive bowl. Make the amogio marinade by whisking together all of the ingredients in a separate bowl. Reserve ½ cup of the marinade and set it aside. Pour the remaining amogio over the chicken and marinate, covered in the refrigerator, for at least 1 hour or overnight.

2. Preheat a charcoal or gas grill to medium-high. Make the modiga by stirring together the breadcrumbs and herbs on a large plate. Drain the chicken, roll each piece in the modiga to coat, and thread the skewers with the chicken. Grill the spiedini, turning them once, for 6 to 8 minutes, or until they are cooked through. Drizzle a little of the reserved amogio on each skewer, and serve hot.

VARIATION:

The spiedini may be broiled instead of grilled. Broil them for about 6 minutes, turning them once.

CHICKEN WITH MORELS

The first cooking class I ever took was taught by Jim Gregory, a chef who had consulted with fellow Cincinnatian Marion Rombauer Becker on later editions of *The Joy of Cooking*. On the top floor of the carriage house behind his Victorian home, Chef Gregory would hold forth on the importance of the "four friends" in seasoning food: 1 teaspoon garlic salt, 1 teaspoon liquid Maggi seasoning, 1 teaspoon monosodium glutamate, and 1 dash of Tabasco sauce. Whether the credit goes to Jim's genius or to the four friends, every recipe of his I have tried has been outstanding. Here is an adaptation, without the MSG and with a few other changes, of one of Chef Gregory's best dishes.

SERVES 4

1 cup fresh morels or ½ cup dried morels
4 skinless, boneless chicken breasts
½ cup all-purpose flour
4 tablespoons unsalted butter
1 medium yellow onion, chopped
½ teaspoon garlic salt
½ teaspoon Maggi seasoning
1 dash bottled hot pepper sauce
½ teaspoon dried thyme
¼ cup canned tomato puree
1 cup chicken stock
Fresh-ground black pepper to taste
Juice of ½ lemon
Chopped fresh parsley, for garnish

1. If you have fresh morels, soak them in salted water to cover for 30 minutes to remove any debris. Rinse with cold water, pat dry, and cut in half lengthwise. If you have dried morels, pour 1 cup boiling water over the morels in a bowl and let steep for 30 minutes. Remove the morels, discarding the liquid, rinse them and pat them dry, and cut them in half lengthwise.

2. Flatten the chicken breasts slightly with a meat mallet or the bottom of a saucer. Dredge them in the flour and set them aside.

3. Heat the butter in a large skillet over medium heat. Add the onion, and sauté it until it is translucent, 6 to 8 minutes. Add

the chicken breasts, and sauté them until they are lightly browned, about 3 minutes on each side.

4. Stir in the morels and the garlic salt, Maggi, hot pepper sauce, thyme, tomato puree, and chicken stock. Bring to a boil over medium-high heat, reduce the heat, and simmer, uncovered, for 20 minutes, or until the sauce has thickened slightly. Season to taste with pepper, stir in the lemon juice, garnish with parsley, and serve.

THE SHADED PRAIRIE

"*The most surprising thing about these places is the growth of the trees. I left bare prairie; I returned to find a score of miniature forests in sight from any point of view. The wheat and cornfields were unfenced, of course, but several acres around every house were set in hedges, orchards, lanes, and alleys of trees—trees in lines, trees in groups, and trees all alone. In many cases the houses were hardly visible from the road, and in a few years will be entirely hidden in the cool shade.*"

—NOBLE L. PRENTIS,
From the Steppes to the Prairies

SPRING CHICKEN

Two hundred years after the Louisiana Purchase, it is easy to forget, despite the many rivers, towns, and counties that still bear French names, that much of the prairie and the midwest once was French territory. Historians tell us that when the French had forts along the Mississippi and Missouri rivers, the officers' quarters had elaborate kitchens and dining rooms, with poultry houses, ice houses, well-stocked kitchen gardens, and the like surrounding the quarters. The French have always eaten well. I like to think, when I cook this elegant but homey French-style dish, that the typically French vegetables in it—sorrel, baby peas and carrots, and leeks—are descendants of the stock the French first planted here. A loaf of fresh-baked crusty bread or a bowl of Parsley-and-Chive Rice (page 318) to help sop up the sauce, steamed asparagus, and Lemon-Zested Mulberry and Rhubarb Crisp (page 396) round out a springtime meal.

SERVES 4

4 skinless, boneless chicken breasts
1/2 teaspoon white pepper
Juice of 1 lemon
4 tablespoons unsalted butter
1 leek, white part only, cleaned
    well and chopped
1/4 cup chicken stock
1/4 cup dry white wine
1 cup heavy cream
1/2 cup baby carrots

*½ cup fresh or frozen and thawed
    baby peas*
*6 to 8 fresh sorrel leaves, cut into
    thin strips, or 1 cup loosely
    packed spinach leaves, cut into
    thin strips*
*Salt and additional white pepper
    to taste*
Chopped fresh parsley, for garnish

1. Preheat the oven to 400 degrees. Cut a circle of parchment or waxed paper that is the circumference of your flameproof casserole dish and set it aside. Season the chicken with the ½ teaspoon white pepper, and sprinkle the chicken with half of the lemon juice.

2. Heat the butter over medium heat in a heavy flameproof casserole dish. Add the leeks and chicken. After 30 seconds, turn the chicken over. Place the parchment or waxed paper circle on top of the chicken, cover the casserole, and transfer it to the oven. Bake for 6 minutes, or until the chicken just feels springy to the touch.

3. Discard the parchment or waxed paper circle, remove the chicken to a warm dish, and cover while making the sauce. Pour the stock and wine into the cooking juices in the casserole and bring to a boil over high heat. Reduce the liquid until it begins to have a syrupy consistency, 4 to 5 minutes. Whisk in the cream and continue to boil, whisking frequently, until the sauce thickens somewhat. Whisk in the remaining lemon juice. Return the chicken to the pan and add the

carrots, peas, and sorrel. Reduce the heat to medium-high, cover, and cook for 4 to 5 minutes, or until the sorrel has wilted, the carrots are heated through, and the peas are soft. Season to taste with salt and additional white pepper. Transfer the chicken to individual plates, spoon the sauce and vegetables over and around it, garnish with parsley, and serve.

CHICKEN AND CORN PUDDING

This fragrant dish might just be the very essence of midwestern home cooking. In the 1930s or 1940s, it would have been made with a poached whole chicken, but today we use readily available chicken breasts. When you smell and taste this dish, you think of zinc-topped tables, cherry-print tablecloths, pale green enamelware utensils, and milk in glass bottles. Homemade breadcrumbs and fresh shoepeg or sweet corn make all the difference.

SERVES 4 TO 6

4 skinless, boneless chicken breasts
1 bay leaf
1 celery rib, chopped
1 small yellow onion, chopped
¼ cup chopped fresh parsley
2 cups chicken stock
2 cups milk, scalded
3 eggs, lightly beaten
4 cups corn kernels, preferably fresh
1 teaspoon dried tarragon

$^{1}/_{8}$ *teaspoon cayenne pepper*
$^{1}/_{2}$ *teaspoon salt*
$^{1}/_{2}$ *teaspoon white pepper*
2 *tablespoons unsalted butter*
1 *cup fresh breadcrumbs*

1. Preheat the oven to 350 degrees. Place the chicken, bay leaf, celery, onion, parsley, and stock in a large saucepan. Bring to a boil, reduce the heat, and simmer, covered, for 10 minutes to poach the chicken. The chicken should feel firm to the touch. Remove from the heat. Transfer the chicken to a cutting board and cut it into bite-size pieces. Drain and discard the broth and discard the bay leaf.

2. Lightly butter a 1-quart baking dish. Place the cooked chicken, vegetables, and parsley in the dish. Beat together the milk and eggs in a bowl, and stir in the corn, tarragon, cayenne, salt, and white pepper. Pour over the chicken, and stir once or twice to distribute evenly. Melt the butter in a small skillet and stir in the breadcrumbs. Spoon the buttered breadcrumbs over the pudding. Bake for 20 to 25 minutes, or until the pudding is bubbling and golden brown. Serve hot.

GRILLED TURKEY BREAST WITH PEANUT SAUCE

In this dish, the peanut butter marinade keeps the turkey moist and flavorful as it is grilled. Serve this juicy dish, if you like, with Summertime Grilled Succotash Salad (page 158), Herbed Buttermilk Spoonbread (page 336), and Blackberry Ice Cream (page 408).

SERVES 6 TO 8

1 *cup chunky peanut butter*
$^{1}/_{2}$ *cup soy sauce*
$^{1}/_{2}$ *cup dark sesame oil*
2 *large garlic cloves, minced*
1 *tablespoon brown sugar*
$^{1}/_{2}$ *cup cider vinegar*
1 *teaspoon red pepper flakes*
2 *cups sour cream*
1 *turkey breast, about 6 pounds*

1. Combine the peanut butter, soy sauce, sesame oil, garlic, brown sugar, vinegar, red pepper flakes, and sour cream in a bowl. Spoon out half of the marinade to a separate bowl, cover, and refrigerate. Coat the turkey with the remaining marinade. Place the turkey in a large sealable plastic bag or a covered bowl, and marinate in the refrigerator for several hours or overnight.

2. Preheat a charcoal or gas grill to medium-high. Grill the turkey breast for 45 to 60 minutes, turning it every 10 to 15 minutes, until the meat reaches an internal temperature of 170 degrees. After the first 20 minutes, baste the turkey with a little of the reserved marinade, if necessary. Slice the turkey and serve it hot, with the remaining reserved marinade on the side.

PEANUT BUTTER

Peanuts may have traveled from Africa to the American South, but they became a household commodity because of a midwestern physician. Peanut butter was developed around 1890 by a now-unknown St. Louis doctor who had wanted a soft health food to give his patients. He had been hand-cranking the peanuts in a meat grinder until he contacted George A. Bayle, the owner of a food products company, and asked him to process and package the ground peanut paste. Bayle mechanized the process and began selling peanut butter out of barrels in the St. Louis area. Around the same time, in Battle Creek, Michigan, Dr. John Harvey Kellogg began experimenting with peanut butter as a vegetarian source of protein for his patients. John Harvey and his brother, W.K. Kellogg, received a patent for the "Process of Preparing Nut Meal" in 1895. Their nut meal, which they described as "a pasty adhesive substance," did not catch on, perhaps because they steamed rather than roasted their peanuts first. The Kellogg brothers refocused their attention on the cereals that would make them famous.

Peanut butter finally went mainstream at the St. Louis World's Fair in 1904, when a vendor named C.H. Sumner sold $705.11 worth of the gooey treat at his concession stand. By 1908, the Krema Products Company of Columbus, Ohio, was selling peanut butter; today the company is the oldest peanut butter maker still in operation. In the early years Krema's founder, Benton Black, used the slogan "I refuse to sell outside of Ohio," because peanut butter packed in barrels and without preservatives spoiled quickly and did not travel well.

In the Iowa P.E.O. Cookbook, first published in 1910, several recipes give directions for making your own peanut butter, which at the time was considered a kind of condiment like catsup or mustard. Since then, after a few misses like the peanut butter and mayonnaise or peanut butter and lettuce sandwiches, the favored combination came to be peanut butter and jelly. By the 1930s, peanut butter was homogenized, and stirring the separated oil back into the peanut paste became a lost art. Eventually, peanut butter made its way from sandwich filling to cookies, pies, and candy, too. Today, 85 percent of American households buy peanut butter, and by the time the average child finishes high school he or she will have eaten over fifteen hundred peanut butter and jelly sandwiches.

Herb-Roasted Duckling

The midwest, especially Indiana and Illinois, is a great source for both wild and farm-raised ducks. The three top farm-raised duck breeds—white Pekin, Muscovy, and moulard (the latter is the sterile offspring of the first two)—provide birds that are tender and meaty. This is a festive and succulent dish to make in celebration of a hunter's successful return or, perhaps, your discovery that the local grocer now stocks a fine farm-raised bird. Serve with a salad of bitter greens, a crusty bread, and a fruity dessert.

Serves 4

1 4- to 5-pound duckling
2 tablespoons Aromatic Herb Rub
   (page 57)
1 orange, cut in half
4 to 5 garlic cloves
1 cup orange juice
1/4 cup dry red wine
2 cups chicken stock
16 ounces plain or black-pepper fresh
   or dried fettuccine noodles

1. Preheat the oven to 400 degrees. Press the herb rub all over the duckling inside and out. Stuff the duckling with the orange halves and garlic cloves. Place the duckling in a roasting pan or on a deep baking sheet and roast it for 1 hour, checking every 15 minutes to remove excess duck fat from the roaster with a bulb baster or a spoon. After the first 30 minutes of roasting, prick the duckling skin all over with a fork or paring knife to help release the fat.

2. After the duck has roasted for 1 hour, reduce the oven temperature to 325 degrees. Continue to roast the duck and remove its fat. When all the fat has run out and the juices from the duck start to run, after about 1/2 hour, baste the duck with some of the orange juice. Continue roasting and basting until the duck reaches an internal temperature of 180 degrees and is very tender, about 1 hour more.

3. Remove the duckling from the oven to a plate and cover it with aluminum foil to keep it warm. Deglaze the roasting pan and make a sauce: Pour the wine into the cooking juices in the pan and bring to a boil over high heat. Scrape up any bits that are stuck to the bottom of the pan. When the liquid is reduced by 1/3, whisk in the stock, reduce the heat, and simmer, uncovered, for 10 minutes. Remove from the heat and pour the sauce through a fine-meshed sieve into a saucepan. Keep the sauce warm over low heat.

4. Bring a pot of salted water to a boil. Meanwhile, slice the warm duck breast and its crisp skin and set aside to keep warm. Shred the rest of the duck meat and add it to the sauce in the pan. When the water is boiling, add the fettuccine and cook until tender, about 5 minutes for fresh noodles and 8 to 10 minutes for dried. Drain the fettuccine and transfer the noodles to individual plates. Top with the

sauce and with pieces of duck breast and crispy skin, and serve.

HIGH PLAINS HUNTER'S CASSOULET

This is a savory and robust dish, especially fine with the uniquely wonderful flavor of a duck or goose confit but still very good if you do not use the confit. When the temperature plummets and there is a blizzard howling outdoors, make this hearty dish and enjoy it in front of the fire. Accompany the cassoulet with a young red wine and a green salad.

SERVES 8 TO 10

1 cup wheatberries
1 cup navy beans or flageolet
   beans
2 cups chicken stock
2 tablespoons confit fat from the
   confit in Fly-Over Country
   Duck or Goose Salad (page
   167) or any duck or goose fat,
   or 2 tablespoons canola oil or
   safflower oil
1 large yellow onion, chopped
4 garlic cloves, minced
1 cup chopped fresh or canned
   tomatoes
2 sprigs fresh thyme

2 pounds garlic-flavored sausage
2 pieces, such as 2 thighs or
   1 thigh and 1 leg, of confit
   from Fly-Over Country Duck
   or Goose Salad (page 167) or
   2 pieces roasted duck
1 cup breadcrumbs, preferably
   homemade

1. Soak the wheatberries and beans in water to cover for several hours or overnight. Drain the wheatberries and beans and put them in a saucepan with the stock. Bring to a boil, reduce the heat, and simmer gently, uncovered, for 35 to 40 minutes, or until the wheatberries and beans are plumped and softened.

2. Melt the confit fat in a heatproof casserole dish over medium heat. Add the onion and garlic, and sauté them until the onion is translucent, 6 to 8 minutes. Add the wheatberries and beans, including any liquid that remains in their pan. Stir in the tomatoes. Place the thyme and sausage on top and bring the mixture to a simmer. Simmer gently, covered, for 1 hour.

3. Preheat the oven to 350 degrees. Shred the meat from the 2 confit pieces. Remove the sausage and cut it into 2-inch lengths. Stir the confit meat and sausage pieces into the cassoulet and sprinkle the top with the breadcrumbs. Bake, uncovered, for 15 to 20 minutes, or until the breadcrumbs have browned. Remove and discard the thyme. Serve hot.

> *The prairie sings to me in the*
> *   forenoon*
> *And I know in the night*
> *I rest easy in the prairie arms, on*
> *   the prairie heart.*
> — CARL SANDBURG, "Prairie"

PHEASANT BAKED WITH CREAM

On the semiarid western prairie from the middle of Kansas northward through Nebraska and the Dakotas, September means the start of pheasant season. It seems as if everyone has at least a few pheasant recipes; this tasty one is from Marllys Yelton, who lives in the tiny central Kansas town of Palco. Serve with noodles or potatoes and, if you like, braised green cabbage.

SERVES 4

1/2 cup all-purpose flour
1 teaspoon salt
1 teaspoon white pepper
1 21/2- to 3-pound whole pheasant, dressed
1/4 cup canola oil or corn oil
1 cup heavy cream
1 large yellow onion, quartered
4 garlic cloves
1 teaspoon dried thyme

1. Preheat the oven to 300 degrees. Shake together the flour, salt, and white pepper in a large paper bag. Put the pheasant in the bag, and shake well to coat it with the seasoned flour.

2. Heat the oil in a large skillet over medium-high heat. Add the pheasant and brown it on all sides. Transfer the bird to a roasting pan and pour the cream over the pheasant. Add the onion, garlic, and thyme to the roaster. Bake, covered, for 2 hours. The pheasant is done when the juices run clear from a pierced thigh. Transfer the pheasant to a carving board, and carve the breast and separate the other pieces. Arrange the pheasant on a platter, pour any remaining pan juices over, and serve.

APPLE ORCHARD PHEASANT

The first generation of homesteaders in Kansas and Iowa busted the tough prairie sod and planted their cash crops, mainly wheat and corn. They also planted gardens and orchards to make their households self-sufficient. By the second generation of homesteaders, around 1900, the ring-necked pheasant had been imported to the prairie, where it has thrived in Iowa, Kansas, Nebraska, the Dakotas, Illinois, and Indiana ever since. Because pheasant hunted in the wild is often skinned as it is dressed, using a moist-heat method of cooking, as in this recipe, is essential for a tender, juicy result.

SERVES 6 TO 8

2 tablespoons unsalted butter, or
   more if necessary
2 young whole pheasants, about
   2½ pounds each, dressed
18 to 20 small pearl onions
1 teaspoon salt
½ teaspoon fresh-ground black
   pepper
1 cup chicken stock
½ pound mushrooms
2 tart apples, peeled, cored, and
   sliced thin
½ cup dry white wine
½ cup cream

1. Preheat the oven to 375 degrees. Melt the butter in a large skillet over medium-high heat. Add the pheasants and brown them on all sides. Transfer the pheasants to a deep flameproof casserole dish and set them aside. Add more butter, if necessary, to the skillet, and add the onions. Sauté the onions, stirring often, until they begin to brown, 4 to 5 minutes. Remove from the heat.

2. Season the pheasants with salt and pepper. Pour the stock in the bottom of the casserole, cover, and roast for 25 minutes. Remove the

casserole from the oven and add the browned onions and the mushrooms and apples. Cover, and roast for 20 to 25 minutes more.

3. Transfer the pheasants to a carving board and cover them with aluminum foil to keep them warm. Remove the vegetables and apples from the casserole with a slotted spoon and place them in a bowl; cover the bowl to keep warm. Pour the wine into the casserole and bring to a boil over high heat. Scrape the bottom to remove any browned bits, and reduce the liquid until about ½ cup remains. Reduce the heat to a simmer, add the cream, and stir well to blend. Add the vegetables back to the sauce and remove from the heat. Carve the pheasant, nap the bird with the sauce, and serve.

BROILED QUAIL WITH RED CURRANT SAUCE

In November, when the prairie skies are etched with vees of wildfowl flying south, the bare corn fields and wheat fields teem with upland game birds like pheasant and quail.

SERVES 8

8 quail or Cornish game hens

1/4 pound (1 stick) unsalted butter,
  melted
1 teaspoon garlic salt
1 teaspoon Maggi seasoning
1/4 teaspoon bottled hot pepper sauce
1 large yellow onion, minced
1/2 cup dry red wine
3/4 cup jelly made from a tart fruit,
  such as Old World Red
  Currant Jelly (page 72),
  Wild Plum Jelly (page 74),
  Chokecherry and Buffalo
  Berry Jelly (page 73), or other
  homemade or store-bought

jelly
Juice of 1 lemon
8 large Homemade Croutons
  (page 41)

1. Rinse the quail and pat them dry. Transfer the quail to a broiler pan. Preheat the broiler.

2. Stir together the butter, garlic salt, Maggi, and hot pepper sauce in a small bowl. Brush each bird with this mixture. Sprinkle the onion over the quail. Broil the quail, about 3 inches from the heat, for 10 to 15 minutes, turning the birds 2 to 3 times as they brown. When the quail are browned on all sides, remove them from the broiler pan and place them in a large casserole dish. Cover with aluminum foil to keep warm. Pour the juices from the broiler pan into a saucepan.

3. Bring the juices in the saucepan to a boil and add the wine. Whisking constantly, add the jelly and boil the sauce until it has thickened enough to coat the back of a spoon, about 8 minutes. Stir in the lemon juice and remove from the heat. Place a large crouton on each of 8 plates and top with a quail. Pour a little of the sauce on each bird, and serve.

GAME BIRDS

Most farm-raised game birds are on the young side, but if your game comes from a hunter, the age of the bird will be more of a mystery. The bird's age has an effect on the choice of a cooking method. A young bird will cook more quickly and need little tenderizing treatment. Grilling, broiling, and pan-frying are good methods. Older birds benefit from a longer, slower, and moister treatment, such as braising.

To test whether a hunted game bird is young or old, look at its claws. Older birds have blunt claws. The younger the bird, the sharper its claws will be.

ROASTED QUAIL ON A BED OF LEEKS

If there is an autumn hunter in the family or the neighborhood, here is a very fine way to enjoy the bounty.

SERVES 6

6 quail or 6 Cornish game hens
1 teaspoon salt
1 teaspoon fresh-ground black
    pepper
6 tablespoons unsalted butter
2 leeks, white part and some green
    part, cleaned well and sliced
    thin
1/2 pound mushrooms, chopped
4 ounces prosciutto, chopped
1/2 teaspoon dried oregano
1 cup dry white wine
2 tablespoons lemon juice
2 teaspoons cornstarch stirred into
    1/2 cup chicken stock

1. Preheat the oven to 350 degrees. Rinse the quail and pat them dry. Rub the quail well with the salt and pepper.

2. Heat 4 tablespoons of the butter in a large skillet over medium-high heat. Add the quail, and brown them on both sides. Set them aside and cover them with aluminum foil to keep warm. Melt the remaining 2 tablespoons of butter in the skillet. Add the leeks, and sauté them for 2 minutes. Add the mushrooms, prosciutto, and oregano and sauté, stirring, for 2 minutes more. Transfer the mixture to a casserole dish large enough to hold the quail.

3. Place the quail over the leek mixture. Combine the wine and lemon juice and pour over the quail. Roast the quail, uncovered, for 45 minutes, or until the quail are tender and cooked through. Remove the quail to a plate, and transfer the leek mixture with a slotted spoon to a serving platter. Pour the liquid that remains in the casserole into a small saucepan and bring to a boil. Whisk in the cornstarch mixture and continue boiling, whisking frequently, until the sauce begins to thicken, about 5 minutes. Place the quail on top of the leeks, pour the sauce over the quail, and serve hot.

Fresh
Fish

FRESH FISH

RICH AND CREAMY OYSTER STEW

My father loved to have oyster stew on Christmas Eve. The creamy pepper-flecked broth, with butter floating on the top, held hard little oysters boiled to a rubbery consistency. Needless to say, my sister and I turned thumbs down on this dish and never made it when we became adults. Then we were served a sublime version at the American Restaurant in Kansas City, with fresh oysters poached just enough to be tender and floated at the last minute in a flavorful cream enriched with chicken broth and bay leaf. I begged chefs Debbie Gold and Michael Smith for the recipe. Here it is, adapted for the home kitchen.

SERVES 4 TO 6

*5 dozen fresh oysters, shucked and
    liquid reserved*
2 tablespoons unsalted butter
*1 cup finely chopped leeks, white
    part and some green part*
1 cup finely chopped yellow onion
*4 cups peeled and diced baking
    potato*
4 cups chicken stock
1 bay leaf
1 sprig fresh summer savory
4 cups heavy cream
*Salt and fresh-ground black
    pepper to taste*

*Homemade Croutons (page 41)
and snipped fresh chives,
for garnish*

1. Set the oysters and their liquid aside in a cool place. Heat the butter in a large stock-pot over medium heat. Add the leeks, onion, and 3 cups of the potatoes, and sauté them until the onion is translucent, 6 to 8 minutes. Add the stock, the reserved oyster liquid, the bay leaf, and the savory. Bring to a boil over high heat, reduce the heat, and simmer, un-covered, until the potatoes are tender, about 15 minutes. Add the cream and bring to a boil again. Remove from the heat, and let the soup cool for 30 minutes.

2. Puree the soup in a blender or food proces-sor. Return the soup to the pot, add the re-maining 1 cup of potatoes, bring to a boil, reduce the heat, and simmer, uncovered, until the newly added potatoes are just soft, about 15 minutes. Season to taste with salt and pepper. Add the oysters and simmer for 3 to 4 minutes, or until they are just firm. Ladle the stew into bowls, garnish with croutons and chives, and serve.

SCALLOPED OYSTERS

Midwesterners have been cooking oysters for a long time, as this updated version of a recipe from an 1875 Dayton, Ohio, church cookbook attests. When oysters were cheap and plentiful, arriving in barrels of brine at the railroad depot, dishes like this one were everyday fare.

SERVES 4

1½ cups coarse saltine cracker
    crumbs (see Note)
1 pint fresh oysters, shucked
½ teaspoon salt
½ teaspoon white pepper,
    preferably fresh-ground
6 tablespoons cream
¼ pound (1 stick) unsalted butter,
    melted
2 tablespoons chopped fresh
    parsley, for garnish

1. Preheat the oven to 400 degrees. Lightly butter a 1-quart baking dish.

2. Sprinkle ⅓ of the cracker crumbs on the bottom of the baking dish. Arrange half the oysters over the cracker crumbs and season the oysters with the salt and white pepper. Pour half of the cream over the oysters.

3. Repeat the process, beginning with another ⅓ of the cracker crumbs, the remaining oysters, and the remaining cream, but do not add more salt and white pepper. Sprinkle the remaining ⅓ of the cracker crumbs on top and drizzle the melted butter over all.

4. Bake for 30 minutes, or until the dish is bubbling and the top has browned. Serve hot, garnished with parsley.

NOTE: To make crumbs with the right consistency, place the saltine crackers between 2 tea towels and crush the crackers with a rolling pin.

BAKED WALLEYE PIKE

Lake trout, cisco, lake perch, pickerel, and walleye pike keep Great Lakes fishermen busy in the warmer months. In much of the lake country of the upper midwest, Memorial Day ushers in fishing season, when the lake waters have warmed up just a little but before the mosquitoes and black flies have gotten too bad. With fresh-caught fish, the simplest preparation is the best. Fix your catch of the day in this classic manner that has been a Heartland favorite for a very long while.

SERVES 4

1 cup milk
1½ to 2 pounds walleye pike fillets,
    preferably, or whitefish or
    pickerel fillets
½ cup breadcrumbs, preferably
    homemade

½ teaspoon salt

½ teaspoon fresh-ground black
   pepper

1 tablespoon chopped fresh parsley

¼ pound (1 stick) unsalted butter,
   melted

Lemon wedges, for garnish

1. Pour the milk over the fish fillets in a bowl, and let the fillets soak for 30 minutes. Preheat the oven to 350 degrees. Lightly butter a baking dish.

2. Combine the breadcrumbs, salt, pepper, and parsley on a plate. Drain the milk from the fish and dredge each fillet in the seasoned

OYSTERS IN KANSAS

The town of Sigel is no more. It is seventy feet below the water at Clinton Dam, near Lawrence, Kansas. But there still are people around Lawrence who keep alive the memory of Sigel's annual wintertime Oyster Feed.

Once the railroads crisscrossed the prairie in the latter years of the nineteenth century, it was possible to get oysters packed in barrels full of brine. Little House readers will remember the Ingalls family's joy at finally being able to open the barrel of oysters intended for their Christmas dinner—in May, after the snow had cleared and the train at last could get through. Oysters were plentiful and cheap at that time and became part of the Heartland cook's repertoire.

Before the folks in Sigel could enjoy their oyster dinner, a few preliminaries were in order. On a freezing day before Christmas, two teams of men and boys would go out into the surrounding prairie to hunt jackrabbits. As they

hunted, runners would bring back the game for the women and girls to tally and then to skin and dress. Once dressed, the rabbits were wrapped and set outside to freeze. (The skins were cleaned and destined to be sold to furriers.) At sundown, the contest ended. The losing team—the one with the fewest rabbits—was given responsibility for the Oyster Feed.

The day before the Feed, the losing team hitched a wagon to pick up the oyster barrels at the railroad station. The women relatives of the team members began to bake homemade bread and mincemeat pie. The day of the event, the men brought to the local schoolhouse big washing cauldrons, gallons of milk and cream, large quantities of fresh-churned butter, and, of course, the oysters. That night, everyone from miles around came to town for a bowl of piping hot oyster stew, plenty of fresh bread and butter, a big slice of pie, and a steaming cup of coffee.

breadcrumbs. Place the fillets in the baking dish and drizzle with the melted butter. Bake the fillets, uncovered, for 20 to 25 minutes, or until the fish flakes easily with a fork. Garnish with lemon wedges, and serve.

WALLEYE PIKE WITH FENNEL AND HERBS

Of both land and lake, this dish is perfect to enjoy in June, after the fishing season has begun and the herb garden has begun to yield. Open the packets right at the table, if possible, to get the full experience of this fragrant preparation.

SERVES 4

4 8-ounce walleye pike fillets,
    preferably, or whitefish or
    pickerel fillets
1/2 teaspoon salt
1/2 teaspoon white pepper,
    preferably fresh-ground
2 fennel bulbs, trimmed and sliced
    thin vertically
2 lemons, sliced thin
1/4 pound (1 stick) unsalted butter,
    cut into dots
4 fresh sage leaves
4 sprigs fresh parsley
1/4 cup snipped fresh chives

1. Preheat the oven to 375 degrees. Tear off 4 pieces of aluminum foil large enough to wrap up the fish fillets. Place each fillet on a piece of foil and season the fish with salt and white pepper. Arrange the fennel and lemon slices on top of the fish. Dot each fillet with butter, place a sage leaf and a parsley sprig on top of each, and sprinkle with chives. Close each packet up tight and transfer to a baking sheet.

2. Bake the fish packets for 20 minutes. To test if the fish is done, carefully unwrap a packet; if the fish flakes easily with a fork, it is done. Transfer the packets to individual plates, and serve.

GRILLED WALLEYE PIKE WITH TOMATO-BASIL SAUCE

Here is a sprightly midsummer dish that celebrates the bounty of the lake and the garden.

SERVES 4

2 tablespoons unsalted butter
1 large tomato, peeled, seeded, and
    chopped fine
2 tablespoons chopped fresh basil
White pepper, preferably
    fresh-ground, to taste
Fresh lemon juice to taste

4 8-ounce walleye pike fillets,
    preferably, or whitefish or
    pickerel fillets
1 tablespoon canola oil or
    safflower oil

1. Preheat a charcoal or gas grill to medium heat.

2. Make the sauce: Whisk together the butter and tomato in a small saucepan over medium-low heat until the butter is just melted. Whisk in 1/4 cup water, then taste. Season with the basil, white pepper, and lemon juice, taste, and adjust the seasonings. Reduce the heat to low and keep the sauce warm as the fish is grilled.

3. Brush the fish fillets on both sides with the oil. Place the fillets in a fish basket, preferably, or on a well-oiled grill grate, and grill them for 3 minutes on each side, or until the fish is opaque and flakes easily with a fork. Transfer the fillets to individual plates, top with the sauce, and serve.

GRILLED CATFISH WITH GREEN ONION-HORSERADISH SAUCE

Bewhiskered catfish troll along the bottoms of many midwestern rivers. Whether you catch your own or buy milder-tasting farm-raised catfish, grilling them brings out their flavor well. You can use this sauce, which midwesterners often serve instead of tartar sauce, on grilled fish of all kinds. Serve the catfish, if you like, with corn on the cob and with potato kebabs, both of which you can put on the grill about 10 minutes before the fish.

SERVES 6

1/2 cup chopped green onions, white
    part and some green part
1/2 cup sour cream
1/2 cup prepared horseradish
6 6- to 8-ounce catfish fillets
2 tablespoons Fireworks Rub
    (page 56)

1. Stir together the green onions, sour cream, and horseradish in a small bowl. Cover and refrigerate until the catfish are grilled. Preheat a charcoal or gas grill to medium-high heat.

2. Sprinkle the fillets on both sides with the rub. Place the fillets in a fish basket, preferably, or on a well-oiled grill grate. Grill the fillets for about 3 minutes per side, or until they flake easily with a fork. Transfer the fillets to individual plates, top with a dollop of the sauce, and serve.

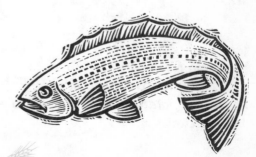

BRANDADE WITH OVEN-DRIED TOMATOES AND THYME

Dried salt cod, a centuries-old winter peasant food, still appears in many midwestern kitchens hundreds of miles from the sea. Because it kept without refrigeration, dried salt cod could be purchased once a year, then kept in the pantry or cellar until needed. Norwegian families turn it into lutefisk, after soaking it in a lye solution. Italian families soak and cook the fish and then flavor it with olive oil, parsley, garlic, lemon juice, and pepper. The late-nineteenth-century *Buckeye Cookery and Practical Housekeeping* recommends serving salt cod in a white sauce enriched with egg yolks, accompanied by beets and carrots. My grandmother's old *The Presbyterian Cookbook*, from Dayton, Ohio, tells how to make salt cod fritters. A brandade is a traditional Provençal mixture of soaked and cooked salt cod pureed with cooked potato and olive oil. This version gets a contemporary twist with preserved tomatoes and thyme, and the option of using fresh fish.

SERVES 8

¾ pound fresh whitefish fillets or
¾ pound dried salt cod
1 medium potato, baked and peeled
4 garlic cloves, minced

4 tablespoons fresh thyme or
2 teaspoons dried thyme
¼ cup Oven-Dried Tomatoes (page 42) or ¼ cup dry-packed sun-dried tomatoes, soaked in hot water for 15 minutes and drained
1 cup extra-virgin olive oil
Salt and fresh-ground black pepper to taste
8 large Homemade Croutons (page 41), for garnish

1. If you are using salt cod, rinse the fish well, transfer it to a bowl, add water to cover, and refrigerate for at least 24 and preferably 48 hours, changing the water once or twice a day. Drain, rinse, and pat dry.

2. Preheat the oven to 350 degrees. Put the whitefish or salt cod and the potato, garlic, thyme, and tomatoes in a food processor. Pulse 10 to 15 times to make a nearly smooth puree. With the machine running, pour in the olive oil in a steady stream until all of it has been incorporated. Taste, and add the salt and pepper.

3. Transfer the brandade into 8 8-ounce ramekins or 1 large soufflé dish. Bake for 25 minutes for the ramekins, 1 hour for the large soufflé dish. Serve hot or warm, topped with the croutons.

NOTE: The brandade can be made ahead to the end of step 2 and kept, covered in the refrigerator, for up to 2 days before serving. If you do so, there is no need to preheat the oven until step 3.

CHRISTMAS EVE BACCALA

Brigida Maria Marasco, now Brigid Burgett, grew up with her family on the same street in Des Moines, Iowa, as her father's four brothers and their families. Brigid's mother had emigrated to the United States from Calabria in 1939; her marriage to Brigid's father had been arranged, in the traditional Calabrian practice. Brigid remembers big Sunday dinners, with her father and uncles playing *bocce* afterward and drinking wine her father had made. Her father also made sausages at home and hung them in the cellar to cure. Her mother seasoned and canned vegetables from their extensive garden; later these would come to the table

A POLISH WIGILIA

Fish in horseradish sauce usually is the first dish served in the traditional Polish Christmas Eve meal, which is eaten shortly after sundown. The Polish word for Christmas Eve is Wigilia, pronounced vi-GEE-lee-ah. It is related to the English word vigil, and it signifies, as you would expect, the wait for Christ to be born. At the end of the Wigilia meal the family goes off to midnight mass at church.

The traditional Wigilia dinner has twelve dishes, in honor of the twelve apostles. Some families serve thirteen, because they include Christ in their count. There is no red meat in the meal, because Advent, a season of penance, continues until midnight. The meal starts when the first star can be seen; this star is said to symbolize the star of Bethlehem.

The tradition of Wigilia, though centuries old, still is celebrated in many Polish-American households in Chicago, Detroit (and Hamtramck), Cleveland, and other midwestern cities. There is no fixed set of rules for what the dishes must be—they vary by location and by the availability of ingredients. Some of the dishes you might be served for Wigilia include almond soup, pickled beets or pickled herring, sauerkraut with dried wild mushrooms, apples poached in red wine, and a Christmas pudding called kutia, flavored with poppy seeds, lemon peel, and dried fruit. There are many traditions for the serving of the meal, too. For example, some families place straw under the tablecloth to symbolize the manger in which Christ was born, and most families set an extra place for the stranger who might be passing by.

as antipasto dishes. The highlight of the culinary year came on Christmas Eve, when the traditional *baccala*, or salted dried cod, was prepared for a buffet. Brigid continues the tradition today with her own family, and I am indebted to her for sharing her family's recipe.

SERVES 4

1 pound dried salt cod
1/4 cup olive oil, plus more for the
    baking dish
2 small yellow onions, sliced thin
2 teaspoons dried oregano
1/2 cup red wine vinegar
1/4 cup chopped fresh Italian
    parsley, for garnish

1. Rinse the salt cod well, transfer it to a bowl, add water to cover, and refrigerate for at least 24 and preferably 48 hours, changing the water once or twice a day. Drain, rinse, and pat dry.

2. Preheat the oven to 325 degrees. Lightly oil a baking dish with olive oil. Brush the salt cod on both sides with the 1/4 cup olive oil and transfer to the baking dish. Arrange the onion slices over the fish. Bake the fish for 30 minutes.

3. Meanwhile, combine the oregano and vinegar in a small bowl. Remove the fish from the oven, and pour the vinegar mixture over the fish. Bake the fish for 15 minutes more. Remove from the oven again, let rest for 5 to 10 minutes, and serve warm, garnished with the parsley.

PLATED PERCH

As little girls, my sister and I caught our first perch in the icy waters of Lake Superior. The event was a tribute to the patience of our father and grandfather. When we came back to shore, we watched—fascinated and somewhat disgusted—as our dad gutted and scaled the fish. When my mother and grandmother sautéed the fishes for dinner, we were both a little surprised that they tasted so good. (Until then, our only experience with fish was the dreaded tuna casserole on Friday nights.) This recipe uses a rustic and primitive cooking method that is fun to try in a cabin, a fishing lodge, or a galley kitchen on a boat as well as at home. Serve with a good crusty bread, if you like, for mopping up the buttery cooking juices.

SERVES 2

2 8-ounce fresh lake perch fillets
    (see Note)
2 tablespoons unsalted butter
1/2 teaspoon salt, preferably
    sea salt
1/2 teaspoon white pepper
2 tablespoons dry white wine
Juice of 1/2 lemon
Lemon wedges and watercress
    sprigs, for garnish

1. Select 4 large heatproof dinner plates. Trim the fish fillets to make sure they fit within the circumference of the dinner plates. Select 2 saucepans that are smaller in circumference

than the dinner plates. Fill the saucepans nearly full with water, bring to a boil over high heat, then reduce the heat to a simmer.

2. Generously butter the center of each dinner plate. Arrange the fish fillets on 2 of the plates. Sprinkle the fillets with the salt and white pepper, then drizzle them with the wine and lemon juice. Invert 1 of the remaining plates over 1 of the plates with the fish so that the fish is sandwiched between 2 plates. Repeat the process with the remaining plates.

3. Place each "sandwich" directly on top of a pan of simmering water and cook for 8 to 10 minutes. Using oven mitts to protect your hands, remove the "sandwich" from the pan and the top plate from the bottom plate. The fish is done when it is opaque and flakes with a fork. Garnish with lemon wedges and watercress, and serve.

NOTE: If you live away from a supply of perch, the dish may be made with another thin white fish, such as sole.

SUNFLOWER-CRUSTED TROUT

After the snow has melted in spring, anglers try to lure the elusive brown trout, which like to lay low around submerged tree stumps in midwestern streams. After all the hard work of reeling them in, the cook and fly-fisherman alike can celebrate with a fish that is crunchy and crisp on the outside, tender and flavorful on the inside. If there is no angler in your household, there is plenty of trout in the marketplace, too, of course.

SERVES 4 TO 8

8 fresh trout fillets
1/4 cup salted sunflower seeds
1/4 cup cornmeal
1/4 cup all-purpose flour
1/2 teaspoon fresh-ground black pepper
1/2 cup sunflower oil or canola oil

1. Rinse the fish fillets and pat them dry. In the bowl of a food processor, chop the sunflower seeds to a fine meal. Scrape the sunflower seed meal onto a plate and combine with the cornmeal, flour, and pepper. Dredge both sides of each fillet with the flour mixture.

2. Heat the oil in a cast-iron skillet over medium-high heat. Add the fillets and pan-fry them, turning them once, for about 3 minutes on each side, until they are browned and crisp but not overcooked. Serve hot.

SHAKER POACHED LAKE FISH WITH TARRAGON CREAM SAUCE

The North Union community of Shakers, in what is now Cleveland, Ohio, was established in 1822 and disbanded in 1889. At one time, the community numbered three "families" totaling over two hundred people who lived in typical Shaker fashion—men on one side of the house, women on the other, with strict laws of celibacy in between. Their energies were spent in farming, in growing and selling medicinal herbs, and in setting a fine table.

One of the members of the North Union community wrote in a journal: "Last evening a number of the brethren went fishing in Lake Erie. Toward noon today they brought home their catch, except the small ones which they always cast into their mill-pond on the way

PLANKED WHITEFISH

Juilleret's of Harbor Springs, Michigan, has been serving planked whitefish and planked prime rib for more than sixty years. This method of cooking was a favorite in midwestern cookbooks from the early twentieth century. The presentation at Juilleret's looks almost too beautiful to eat. A beautiful border of duchesse potatoes is piped around the outer edge of the plank, with the whitefish or prime rib, a stuffed tomato, and bouquets of beans, peas, or mushrooms in the middle. All the juices stay within the boundaries of the potato "dike."

If you want to cook a planked whitefish at home, you will need solid, kiln-dried oak planks about 12 inches long. A new plank has to be seasoned, much like a cast-iron skillet. Rub the board with vegetable oil and put it in a 225 degree oven for 1 hour, then set it aside to cool.

To make the planked whitefish, broil the whitefish fillets until almost done and place them in the center of the plank. Make up the duchesse potatoes by mixing 4 cups of mashed potatoes with 2 egg yolks and 2 tablespoons of softened butter; do so when the potatoes are hot enough to cook the yolks. Pipe a potato border around the plank. Fill in the gaps with cherry tomatoes, sautéed mushrooms, or steamed green beans. Run the plank under the broiler briefly until the potatoes start to brown, and serve immediately.

home. They had enough fish for all three families. There were several muskies, a fine haul of white fish, a number of pike along with a lot of catfish and yet other kinds. They are all splendid eating. This evening we had a good supper of boiled catfish with herb sauce, fried potatoes, boiled greens, pickled peppers, hot bread, and lemon pie and tea." This dish, which I have adapted from an original North Union recipe, remains a fine way to serve fresh lake fish.

SERVES 6

1/2 cup white wine vinegar or dry
*   white wine*
1/2 teaspoon black peppercorns,
*   crushed*
1 large yellow onion, chopped
2 teaspoons dried tarragon
3 pounds whitefish fillets or other
*   fresh lake fish fillets, cut into*
*   pieces about 3 inches square*
2 eggs
1 tablespoon unsalted butter
1 tablespoon all-purpose flour
1/2 cup heavy cream
Salt and fresh-ground black
*   pepper to taste*
Fresh lemon juice and additional
*   dried tarragon to taste,*
*   optional*

1. Bring 1 quart of water to a boil in a large saucepan. Add the vinegar, peppercorns, onion, and 2 teaspoons tarragon. Reduce the heat and simmer the broth, uncovered, for 15 minutes to blend the flavors well.

2. Add the fish to the broth and simmer gently, uncovered, to poach the fish until it is tender but not soft, about 20 minutes. Remove the fish to a platter and keep the fish warm while you make the sauce.

3. Pour the poaching liquid through a strainer; reserve the liquid and discard the solids. Beat the eggs in a medium bowl. Pour the strained poaching liquid over the eggs, and whisk until the mixture is blended. Set aside.

4. Melt the butter in a saucepan over medium-low heat. Whisk in the flour and cook, whisking, for 2 minutes. Reduce the heat to low, and add the egg mixture, whisking constantly. Continue cooking, whisking frequently, until the sauce begins to thicken, 4 to 5 minutes. Stir in the cream and cook for about 2 minutes more, to heat through. Season with salt and pepper and, if you like, lemon juice and additional tarragon. Pour the sauce over the fish, and serve.

FISH SCHNITZEL

In this recipe, the delicate, sweet, and buttery flavor of the freshwater fish is accentuated, not overpowered, by a method more commonly used to prepare an Eastern European Wiener schnitzel. I have adapted this delicious recipe, and borrowed its offbeat title, from one created by John

Schumacher, chef and owner of the New Prague Hotel in New Prague, Minnesota.

SERVES 4

1½ pounds freshwater fish fillets, such as lake perch, whitefish, pickerel, or pike
¼ cup all-purpose flour
4 eggs, beaten
1 cup fresh breadcrumbs
4 tablespoons unsalted butter
Juice of 1 lemon

2 tablespoons chopped fresh parsley, for garnish
Lemon wedges, for garnish

1. Preheat the oven to 350 degrees.

2. Cut the fish fillets into pieces about 3 inches square. Dredge each piece of fish in the flour, then dip it in the beaten eggs and roll it in the breadcrumbs.

3. Melt the butter over medium heat on the stovetop in an ovenproof skillet that has a lid. Brown the fish, uncovered, on one side for 2 to 3 minutes. Turn the fish, splash with the lemon juice, cover the skillet, and transfer to the oven. Bake for 20 minutes, or until the fish flakes easily with a fork. Transfer to individual plates, top with the parsley, and serve, with lemon wedges on the side.

DOOR COUNTY FISH BOIL

In Door County, Wisconsin, summer visitors are often entertained by the antics of the Fish Boil, a dramatic way to cook fish. As a cauldron filled to the brim with water boils over an outdoor fire, first the potatoes and onions are lowered into the kettle. After several minutes, the fish are lowered in and—whoosh!—clouds of steam, drifts of wood smoke, and a good time is had by all. Aside from the drama, the method actually does a good job of removing fish oils, which rise to the surface of the water then spill out of the cauldron. The traditional dessert is a slice of Sour Cherry Pie (see page 390 for a recipe).

MEXICAN FISH STEW

One cold spring evening in Kansas City, I went out with a group of volunteers and a van full of warm soup, fresh fruit, homemade desserts, and hot coffee to feed homeless people where they live—on river banks, under overpasses and bridges, along railroad tracks, and in other "invisible" places. That night, we fed two men who had stowed away on a freight train all the way from Mexico. Soon, they would blend into the fabric of midwestern life, as had many earlier

Mexican immigrants who came to the midwest to work on the railroads or, later, to pick produce in the fields. This soup is from Mexico, too, where catfish teem in the rivers and small gardens yield corn, squash, and peppers. Today it is served in cafés and restaurants along Southwest Boulevard in Kansas City. (One of the best-kept secrets of the midwest is that you do not need to go to the southwest or the West Coast for great Mexican food.) The soup is traditionally served with warm corn tortillas.

SERVES 6

1 7-ounce can chipotle peppers in adobo sauce
2 tablespoons lard or corn oil
1 large yellow onion, diced
1½ cups tomatoes, diced
5 potatoes, peeled and cut into cubes
6 carrots, peeled and sliced thin
½ head of green cabbage, coarsely chopped
3 ears fresh corn, cut into 3-inch lengths
4 small zucchini, sliced thin
1½ pounds fresh catfish fillets or trout fillets, cut into pieces about 3 inches square
Lemon wedges, for garnish

1. Puree the chipotles with their sauce in a blender or food processor. Set aside.

2. Heat the lard or oil in a large stockpot over medium heat. Add the onion and tomatoes and sauté them until the onion is translucent, 6 to 8 minutes. Add the pureed chipotles, the potatoes, the carrots, and 8 cups of water, and bring to a boil over high heat. Reduce the heat and simmer, uncovered, for 10 minutes, or until the potatoes have begun to soften.

3. Add the cabbage, corn, and zucchini and cook for 10 minutes more, or until the vegetables are tender. Add the catfish and cook for 5 to 7 minutes more, or until the fish is cooked through but not falling apart. Spoon the vegetables and fish into large, deep bowls, top up with the broth, and serve, with lemon wedges alongside.

Noodles, Dumplings, and Savory Pies

NOODLES,
DUMPLINGS,
AND SAVORY PIES

HOMEMADE EGG NOODLES

The process of rolling out homemade noodle dough by hand gave generations of midwestern farm wives their weekly upper-body workout. It is a rewarding but not an easy task. The job is much easier if you have a manual or electric pasta machine.

MAKES ABOUT 12 OUNCES NOODLES

2 large eggs
2 cups all-purpose flour, sifted

1. Beat the eggs well with a fork in a medium bowl. Gradually beat in the flour, 1/4 cup at a time, mixing well with each addition. When all of the flour has been incorporated, mix with a fork until the dough starts to form a ball.

2. Turn out the noodle dough onto a lightly floured board. Knead the dough until it is smooth, about 6 to 8 minutes. Alternatively, knead the dough in a pasta machine or in a heavy-duty electric mixer fitted with a dough hook. Cover the dough with plastic wrap and let it rest at room temperature for 15 minutes.

3. Divide the dough into 2 equal portions. Roll out 1 portion on a floured board until the dough is quite thin, or roll the portion through the pasta machine until quite thin. Repeat with the second portion. Let the sheets of dough stand, uncovered, for 20 minutes, or until they are just dry enough to cut. In the pasta machine, or by hand with a paring knife, cut the sheets into fettuccine-width strips. Cook the noodles; or dry them by hanging them over the backs of chairs and store them at room temperature in an airtight container (they will keep indefinitely).

4. To cook the noodles, bring a large pot of salted water to a boil. Add the noodles and cook them until they are al dente, about 3 to 4 minutes for fresh noodles and 8 to 10 minutes for dry noodles. (The time depends on the thickness and width of the noodles.) Drain, toss with a little butter, and serve.

FRESH HERB NOODLES

These are fresh tasting and beautifully patterned noodles that you can serve alongside meats, fowl, or fish. With the food processor and a pasta machine, the work goes quickly. The noodles are also delicious cooked in chicken broth for a simple soup.

MAKES ABOUT 16 OUNCES NOODLES

3 cups all-purpose flour
3 eggs, beaten
1 tablespoon extra-virgin olive oil
16 fresh basil leaves
16 fresh tarragon leaves

1. In a mixing bowl or in a food processor, blend the flour, eggs, olive oil, and 1 tablespoon water until the dough holds together. Turn out the noodle dough onto a lightly floured board. Knead the dough until it is smooth, about 6 to 8 minutes. Alternatively, knead the dough in a pasta machine or in a heavy-duty electric mixer fitted with a dough hook. Form the dough into a ball, cover it with plastic wrap, and let it rest for 1 hour at room temperature.

2. When the dough has rested, cut the dough into 4 equal portions and roll each portion through the pasta machine until it is very thin. Lay out each rectangle of thin dough on a lightly floured surface and place 4 basil leaves and 4 tarragon leaves on each rectangle. Fold up the dough in thirds as you would fold a business letter and run each portion through the pasta machine again until it is very thin. Finally, run each portion through the machine to cut it into fettuccine. Cook the noodles, or transfer them to zippered plastic bags and freeze them to use later.

3. To cook the noodles, bring a large pot of salted water to a boil. Add the noodles and cook them until they are al dente, 3 to 4 minutes. Drain, toss with a little butter, and serve.

ROSY BEET NOODLES WITH POPPY SEEDS AND BROWN BUTTER

I created this dish not with one particular midwestern-immigrant culinary tradition in mind, but to honor the range of Eastern European peoples—Hungarian, Polish, Bohemian, Czech, and German—who like to cook with beets and poppy seeds. I make this dish in late summer or early fall, when beets are fresh from the garden.

SERVES 4

4 medium red beets or Chioggia
*   beets with their greens*
2 cups all-purpose flour
2 large eggs, beaten
1/4 pound (1 stick) unsalted butter
1 teaspoon poppy seeds
Juice of 1 lemon
1/2 teaspoon salt
1/2 teaspoon fresh-ground black
*   pepper*

1. Trim the greens off the beets. Rinse, pat dry, and reserve 1 packed cup of the best greens, and discard (or reserve for another use) the remaining greens. Set the cup of greens aside. Bring the beets in water to cover to a boil in a saucepan. Cook the beets for 10 to 15 minutes, or until they are tender when pierced with a knife. Drain the beets

and let them cool slightly. When they are cool enough to handle, peel them and chop them coarsely. Puree 1 of the chopped beets in a food processor. Set the pureed beet and the chopped beets aside.

2. Make the noodles: Put the flour in the bowl of a food processor fitted with a steel blade. With the machine running, add the eggs and the pureed beet through the feed tube until the dough starts to form a ball. Turn out the noodle dough onto a floured board. Knead the dough until it is smooth, about 6 to 8 minutes. Alternatively, knead the dough in a pasta machine or in a heavy-duty electric mixer fitted with a dough hook. Cover the dough with plastic wrap and let it rest for 15 minutes at room temperature.

3. Divide the dough into 2 equal portions. Roll out 1 portion on a floured board until the dough is quite thin, or roll the portion through a pasta machine until quite thin. Repeat with the second portion. Let the sheets stand, uncovered, for 20 to 30 minutes, or until they are just dry enough to cut. In the pasta machine, or by hand with a paring knife, cut the sheets into the shape you like. Cook the noodles; or, to reserve them for later use, dry them by hanging them over the backs of chairs and store them at room temperature in an airtight container (they will keep indefinitely).

4. To cook the noodles, bring a large pot of salted water to a boil. While the water is heating, begin making the sauce: Melt the butter in a large saucepan over medium-low heat. Continue cooking the butter, stirring occasionally, until the butter starts to brown, about 5 minutes. Add the poppy seeds, the chopped beets, and the beet greens and sauté, stirring occasionally, until the beets are warmed through and the greens are wilted, about 3 minutes more. Stir in the lemon juice, salt, and pepper. Reduce the heat to low and keep warm as you cook the noodles.

5. Add the noodles to the boiling water and cook them until they are al dente, 3 to 4 minutes. Drain the noodles and transfer them to a heatproof serving bowl. Toss the noodles with the sauce, and serve hot.

NOODLES WITH CHARD AND CARAMELIZED ONION

I particularly like this dish with rainbow chard, for its color, but you can also use green chard or red rhubarb chard as well. A big and hearty red wine, some crusty bread, a plate of the season's last ripe tomatoes, and a dish of baked pears drizzled with honey make for an easygoing and very tasty late summer or early fall dinner.

SERVES 4

1 tablespoon canola oil or safflower oil

2 tablespoons unsalted butter
3 large yellow onions, sliced thin
1 teaspoon sugar
2 tablespoons port
2 cups chicken stock
1 cup chard stems, chopped fine
½ teaspoon salt
½ teaspoon fresh-ground black
   pepper
12 ounces Homemade Egg
   Noodles (page 259) or dried
   fettuccine
2 cups packed torn chard leaves

1. Heat the oil and butter together in a large skillet over medium heat. Add the onions and sauté them for 5 minutes. Sprinkle the onions with the sugar, reduce the heat to medium-low, and sauté the onions, stirring occasionally, until they are translucent in the center

and browned at the edges, about 15 minutes more. Pour the port over the onions and stir. Remove the skillet from the heat. Remove the onions with a slotted spoon to a plate and set aside. Do not rinse or wash the skillet.

2. Bring a large pot of water (for cooking the noodles) to a boil. When the water is nearly boiling, return the skillet in which the onions were cooked to the stove. Add the stock and the chard stems to the skillet, bring to a boil over high heat, reduce the heat, and simmer, uncovered, for 5 minutes, or until the chard stems are tender. Stir in the salt and pepper and keep warm over low heat.

3. When the pot of water boils, add the noodles and cook them until they are al dente, about 4 minutes for fresh noodles. (Follow the package directions for dried noodles.) Drain the noodles and add them to the skillet with the stock and the chard stems. Add the chard leaves and the reserved caramelized onions and cook over medium heat for 5 minutes, or until the chard leaves have wilted and the pasta is heated through. Transfer to individual pasta bowls, and serve hot.

VARIATIONS:

Although the flavor will be different according to the green you choose, kale, chicory, arugula, or mustard greens also work fine in place of the chard in this preparation.

SEEING RED

To preserve, during cooking, the red color in beets, red cabbage, ruby chard, rhubarb chard, and other red vegetables, make sure you have added an acid like lemon juice or vinegar to the cooking liquid. Adding an acid keeps the red coloring stable. In recipes like braised red cabbage, a tart apple provides both a complementary flavor and enough acidity to keep the cabbage red.

PASTA WITH CAULIFLOWER, RAISINS, AND PINE NUTS

Each year on March 19, Sicilian Catholic churches throughout the midwest mark St. Joseph's Day with the St. Joseph's Table, an elaborate feast that honors the life of the humble carpenter. One reason the celebration has survived into the present is that St. Joseph was seen by Sicilian immigrants as a man who worked hard with his hands, and therefore as someone with whom they could identify. Because the event takes place during Lent, church suppers feature meatless pasta dishes, like this one, and many kinds of Italian pastries, all for a donation to the church's fund to feed the poor.

SERVES 4

1 small to medium head of
   cauliflower, cut into florets
3/4 cup olive oil
1/2 cup chopped yellow onion
1 1/2 tablespoons anchovy paste or
   mashed anchovies
1/4 teaspoon crushed or powdered
   saffron
1 cup dark or golden raisins,
   plumped in hot water for 10
   minutes and drained
1/4 cup pine nuts, toasted
1/2 teaspoon salt
1/2 teaspoon fresh-ground black
   pepper
16 ounces dried bucatini,
   spaghetti, or linguine, broken
   in half
3/4 cup breadcrumbs, toasted

1. Bring a large pot of salted water to a boil. Add the cauliflower and cook, uncovered, for 5 minutes. With a slotted spoon, transfer the cauliflower to a bowl and set aside. Reserve 3 cups of the cooking water and discard the rest.

2. Heat the olive oil in a large saucepan over medium heat. Add the onion and anchovy and cook, stirring occasionally, for 5 minutes. Add the 3 cups reserved cooking liquid and stir in the saffron, raisins, pine nuts, salt, and pepper. Bring to a boil, reduce the heat, and simmer, uncovered, for 10 minutes, stirring occasionally. Add the reserved cauliflower, and simmer for 5 minutes more. While the sauce is simmering, cook the pasta according to the package directions until al dente.

3. Drain the pasta, add it to the saucepan, and toss gently to coat the noodles with the sauce. Remove the saucepan from the heat and let the mixture rest for 5 minutes. Toss again, transfer to individual pasta bowls, top with the toasted breadcrumbs, and serve.

BAKED MACARONI AND CHEDDAR

With minor variations, this is the traditional way to cook macaroni and cheese in the Heartland. What makes a decent mac and cheese a great one is, of course, the cheese you pick out. Use your best dairy-land cheddar, sharp but not biting, mellow but not bland, in this dish.

SERVES 4 TO 6

1 cup dried macaroni
1 tablespoon unsalted butter
1 tablespoon all-purpose flour
1 cup milk
1 teaspoon salt
1/4 teaspoon black pepper
1/4 teaspoon paprika
2 cups grated cheddar cheese, such
    as Mound View from
    Wisconsin

1. Preheat the oven to 400 degrees. Lightly butter a 1-quart baking dish. Bring a saucepan of salted water to a boil, add the macaroni, and cook according to the package directions until al dente. Drain the macaroni and set aside.

2. Melt the butter in a separate saucepan over medium-low heat. Whisk in the flour and cook, whisking constantly, for 2 minutes.

Whisk in the milk and continue cooking, whisking constantly, until the sauce thickens, about 5 minutes. Stir in the salt, pepper, and paprika, and remove the pan from the heat.

3. Layer half of the cooked macaroni in the bottom of the baking dish and top with half of the cheese. Top with the remaining macaroni and pour the sauce over all. Top with the remaining cheese, and bake for 20 minutes, or until the casserole is bubbling. Remove from the oven, let the casserole rest and set for 5 to 10 minutes, and serve hot.

PASTA WITH TOMATO SAUCE SIMMERED WITH PORK

When I lived in Columbus, Ohio, our neighbors, the Monte family, used to make this pasta on Sundays. Sometimes we were the happy beneficiaries of leftover sauce brought over to us in a cottage cheese container. The Montes first would bake the spare ribs in the oven to brown the meat and to release some of the fat, and then would add the pork to a large pot of marinara sauce to simmer for hours. Here is my version of the dish I remember. When you serve this as the pasta course in a traditional Italian meal, you use very little sauce on the noodles. To serve as a more robustly flavored main dish, reduce the amount of pasta by half.

THE CURD BELT

Not everyone favors the sharp bite of an aged cheddar. In Wisconsin, especially, and also west into Minnesota and south into Illinois and Missouri, a lot of folks like their cheddar in the toddler stage, as cheese curds. In Wisconsin, a pub or bar that does not serve cheese curds probably will not be in business for long.

In making cheddar, after the milk is heated and the rennet is added to make the curds, the whey is poured off and the curds remain. Next the curds are pressed into a mold to eliminate more moisture, and then they are aged into cheese.

But you can interrupt the process and eat the curds. A curd that is a stringy, squeaky blob with a texture about like that of a rubber band is a fresh curd, not an old refrigerated one, an important distinction for aficionados. Cheese curds are made for snacking, accompanied by a glass of beer and a good dough pretzel.

SERVES 8 AS A FIRST COURSE OR PASTA COURSE OR 4 AS A MAIN DISH

1 2-pound slab pork spareribs
About ¾ teaspoon garlic salt
About ½ teaspoon black pepper
2 tablespoons olive oil
2 garlic cloves, minced
1 medium yellow onion, chopped
2 (22-ounce) cans Italian plum
    tomatoes, with their juice
6 ounces canned tomato paste
1 teaspoon dried basil
32 ounces dried spaghetti,
    bucatini, or penne

1. Preheat the oven to 375 degrees. Sprinkle the ribs all over with garlic salt and pepper. Place the ribs on a baking sheet and roast them in the oven for 30 minutes, or until they are browned and crisp.

2. About 10 minutes before the ribs are done, begin making the sauce: Heat the olive oil in a stockpot or large saucepan over medium heat. Add the garlic and onion, and sauté them until the onion is just softened, about 5 minutes. Do not let the garlic brown. Add the tomatoes, tomato paste, and basil. Pour in 1½ cups water and stir gently to blend.

3. When the ribs are ready, remove them from the oven and cut them into individual ribs. Add the ribs to the sauce and stir. Bring to a boil, reduce the heat, and simmer, covered, for 1½ to 2 hours, or until the sauce has thickened and the meat falls off the bones. Remove the ribs from the sauce and set aside

to cool slightly. When they are cool enough to handle, pick off the meat and return the meat to the sauce. Discard the bones. Keep the sauce warm over low heat.

4. Bring a large pot of salted water to a boil and cook the pasta according to the package directions until al dente. Drain the pasta and transfer it to a serving bowl. Pour the sauce over the pasta, toss to coat the noodles, and serve hot. Leftover sauce will keep, covered in the refrigerator, for 1 week; it also freezes well.

VERENICKE WITH SMOKED HAM GRAVY

Verenicke is a still-popular traditional dish in Russian Mennonite wheat-farming communities from Kansas up through the prairie provinces of Canada. Huge numbers of these cheese-filled "prairie ravioli" disappear at Mennonite community events. Some cooks make their verenicke round, as in this recipe, while others make them crescent-shaped. Some people enjoy them with gravy, as here, while others prefer them served with jelly or a fruit syrup.

MAKES ABOUT 40 VERENICKE

FOR THE VERENICKE:
2½ cups sifted all-purpose flour
1½ teaspoons salt
3 eggs, separated
½ cup milk
½ cup half-and-half
2½ cups Fresh Farmhouse Cheese (page 39), drained, or dry curd cottage cheese
1 teaspoon minced yellow onion

FOR THE GRAVY:
3 tablespoons unsalted butter
3 tablespoons all-purpose flour
1 cup half-and-half
1 cup sour cream
1 cup finely chopped smoked ham
½ teaspoon salt
½ teaspoon black pepper

1. Make the verenicke: Combine the flour and 1 teaspoon of the salt in a deep bowl. Blend together the egg whites, milk, and half-and-half in a separate bowl or in a food processor. Make a well in the center of the flour mixture and pour in the egg white mixture. Knead the dough until it holds together well, then turn it out onto a floured board. Knead the dough further until it is smooth and elastic, about 5 minutes. Return the dough to the bowl, cover, and refrigerate for at least 1 hour.

2. Meanwhile, prepare the filling: Stir together the cheese, the onion, the egg yolks, and the remaining ½ teaspoon salt in a medium bowl.

3. Turn out the chilled dough onto a floured board. Divide the dough into 4 equal

portions. Roll out 1 of the portions to a sheet ⅛ inch thick. Cut out circles 3 inches in diameter with a cookie cutter, biscuit cutter, or drinking glass. Place a generous teaspoonful of filling in the centers of half of the circles. Moisten the edges of the circles with a little water, and place an unfilled circle on top of each of the filled circles. Pinch the edges of the verenicke together to make a secure seal. Repeat with the remaining 3 portions of dough.

4. Bring a large pot of salted water to a boil. Add the verenicke, a few at a time. When they float to the top, after about 3 minutes, cook them for 1 more minute. Transfer them with a slotted spoon to a colander to drain, and continue until all of the verenicke have been cooked. Cover the colander with aluminum foil to keep the verenicke warm as you make the gravy.

5. Make the gravy: Melt the butter in a skillet over medium heat. Whisk in the flour to make a roux. Whisk in the half-and-half and sour cream, increase the heat to medium-high, and cook, whisking constantly, until the mixture thickens and comes to a boil. Reduce the heat to low, stir in the smoked ham and the salt and pepper, and heat through for 1 minute.

6. Transfer the verenicke to individual plates, spoon the gravy over them, and serve.

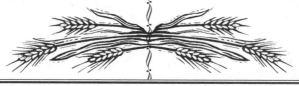

WHEAT

*W*heat is an ancient cereal crop, gathered in the wild during prehistoric times and first cultivated domestically about nine thousand years ago. Wheat first came to America with colonists in the seventeenth century. In 1875, Russian Mennonite immigrants brought to the prairie Turkey red hard winter wheat, from which most hard red winter wheat grown today in the United States is descended. Forty percent of the U.S. wheat crop is hard red winter wheat, and nearly half of that crop is grown in Kansas. Most American breads are made with flour from hard red winter wheat. The prairie states, particularly Kansas, Minnesota, and the Dakotas, also produce much of the U.S. crop in durum wheat, used for pasta and couscous, in hard red spring wheat, used in high-gluten bread flours, and in soft red winter wheat, from which cake flours and pastry flours are made.

BOHEMIAN SPAETZLE

Bohemian immigrants and their descendants serve spaetzle, delicate noodles that are dropped from a colander or *hobl* into boiling water to cook, with stews and roasted meats. (A *hobl* is an Eastern European colander-like utensil with relatively large holes; if you do not have one, use a colander or sieve with large holes.) Traditional spaetzle are left unseasoned or are just lightly seasoned with nutmeg—their role is to soak up the juices, sauces, or gravies of meat dishes.

SERVES 4 AS A SIDE DISH

1½ *cups all-purpose flour*
2 *eggs, beaten*
⅔ *cup heavy cream*
½ *teaspoon salt*
⅛ *teaspoon fresh-grated nutmeg*
2 *tablespoons unsalted butter*

1. Bring a large pot of salted water to a boil. Whisk together all of the ingredients except the butter in a bowl until you have a fairly stiff batter.

2. When the water is boiling, set a colander or *hobl* over the pot. Pour in the spaetzle batter and, working quickly so that the spaetzle cook evenly, press the batter through the holes with a wooden spoon. When all the batter has been used, remove the colander and let the spaetzle boil, uncovered, until they are tender, about 5 minutes. Drain the spaetzle, toss with the butter, and serve.

VARIATION:

For more robustly flavored spaetzle, I add roasted garlic to the batter. To roast garlic, preheat the oven to 350 degrees and cut off about ½ inch from the stem end of the garlic. Place the garlic cut side down in a roasting pan, drizzle with olive oil, and roast until soft, 45 minutes to 1 hour. Squeeze all of the cloves into a bowl, mash with a fork, and add to the spaetzle batter.

CZECH POTATO DUMPLINGS

Czech-American families in the Heartland love dumplings every which way—made with potato, bread, flour, or a combination; boiled or baked; plain or filled. Show up for dinner in a Nebraska or Iowa town and dumplings like these may well be on the menu. Serve these with a pot roast or a beef or chicken stew.

SERVES 4 TO 6 AS A SIDE DISH

2 *cups packed riced boiled*
    potatoes, at room temperature
1 *cup all-purpose flour*
1 *heaping teaspoon uncooked*
    farina or cream of wheat
1 *egg, beaten*

1 teaspoon salt
4 tablespoons unsalted butter
2 slices white bread, crumbed

1. By hand on a lightly floured board, or in the bowl of a food processor, mix the potatoes, flour, farina, egg, and salt together to form a stiff dough. Pinch off ½ cup of the dough and shape it into a ball. Continue until all of the dough has been used.

2. Bring a large pot of salted water or, if you like, beef stock or chicken stock, to a boil. Drop in the dumplings and cook them, partially covered, for 12 minutes.

3. While the dumplings are cooking, melt the butter in a skillet and sauté the breadcrumbs until they are golden brown. When the dumplings are done, transfer them to plates, top with the breadcrumbs, and serve hot.

Variations:

Press a small pitted prune, a dried cherry, or a dried apricot into the dough as you make the balls. Seal the fruit in the dough. The cooking time will be the same.

Pierogi

These plump and tender half-moons, made from a noodle dough, represent one of the glories of the Polish kitchen. As with Russian Mennonite verenicke or Italian ravioli, great pierogi depend on homemade dough and fillings. At the Red Apple on Milwaukee Avenue in Chicago, a plate of savory filled pierogi and a big bowl of hearty soup provide a welcome escape from the chilly winds off the lake. For the home cook, a batch of pierogi that is not entirely consumed at dinner can be frozen for later use.

MAKES ABOUT 48 PIEROGI,
TO SERVE 8 TO 12 AS A MAIN DISH

4½ cups all-purpose flour
2 cups sour cream
2 tablespoons butter, melted
2 tablespoons canola oil or
safflower oil
2 eggs plus 1 egg yolk, lightly
beaten together
2 teaspoons salt

1. Prepare and have ready the filling of your choice; recipes follow.

2. Make the pierogi: Mix all of the ingredients (except the filling) in a large bowl. Turn out the dough onto a lightly floured surface and knead it until it is soft and pliable, about 5 minutes. Divide the dough in half and let it rest, covered with plastic wrap, for 10 minutes. Roll out each half into a circle about ¼ inch thick. Using a drinking glass or a 2-inch biscuit cutter, cut the dough into circles.

3. Place a scant tablespoon of filling in the center of each circle. Wet the edges of the circle with water and fold them over to create a half-moon shape. Press the edges together to seal in the filling.

4. Bring a large pot of salted water to a boil. Add the pierogi in batches, and cook them for 10 minutes. Drain the pierogi in a colander and serve hot.

CHEESE PIEROGI FILLING

1 cup dry curd cottage cheese or
    Fresh Farmhouse Cheese
    (page 39), drained
1 teaspoon unsalted butter, melted
1 egg, beaten
2 tablespoons sugar
1 tablespoon fresh lemon juice

Rice the cheese or push it through a medium sieve. Stir together the cheese and the remaining ingredients in a bowl.

SAUERKRAUT AND WILD MUSHROOM PIEROGI FILLING

1 ounce dried mushrooms, such as
    morels or porcini, soaked for
    30 minutes in warm water
    and drained
2 tablespoons unsalted butter
1 small yellow onion, chopped fine
2 cups rinsed and drained
    sauerkraut, chopped fine
1/2 teaspoon salt
1/2 teaspoon fresh-ground black
    pepper

Chop the mushrooms fine. Heat the butter in a skillet over medium-low heat, add the mushrooms and onion, and sauté them until the onion is translucent, 6 to 8 minutes. Reduce the heat to low, add the sauerkraut, salt, and pepper, and cook the mixture, stirring occasionally, for 15 minutes. Remove from the heat and set aside to cool slightly. For a variation on this filling, use 2 cups finely shredded cabbage instead of the sauerkraut.

MEAT PIEROGI FILLING

1 pound ground beef, veal, pork,
    turkey, or a combination, cooked
1 egg, beaten
1/4 cup minced fresh parsley or
    snipped fresh chives
1/2 teaspoon salt
1/2 teaspoon fresh-ground black
    pepper

Combine all of the ingredients in a bowl and pack together firmly with your hands.

BIEROCKS

What's in a name? Variations on these savory pies, which consist of a meat filling enclosed in a sweetened yeast dough, are called krautanzas, runzas, and bierocks in various Heartland communities. At Dave's

Deli in Newton, Kansas, they are called bierocks and are flavored with shredded American cheese and yellow mustard. The bierocks are a favorite of the wheatcutter teams who help harvest the winter wheat in June. At Gwen's Diner in the tiny town of Bogue in western Kansas, the bierocks are made with sauerkraut and beef. At the chain of Runza restaurants in Nebraska, the filling is heavy on the ground beef and light on the cabbage. In tiny St. Donatius in northeastern Iowa, the descendants of the Luxembourgians who settled there in the mid-1800s add caraway seeds and garlic powder to the filling. Whatever you call them and however you make them, bierocks are great for lunchboxes, casual suppers, or picnics. I serve them in the summer with a marinated cucumber salad and in the winter with pickled beets. They also freeze well.

MAKES 24 BIEROCKS,
TO SERVE 12 AS A MAIN DISH

2 (1/4-ounce) packages quick-rising
    active dry yeast
3 cups milk
1/2 pound (2 sticks) unsalted butter
3/4 cup sugar
1 teaspoon salt
4 eggs, beaten
6 to 8 cups all-purpose flour
2 pounds ground beef
1 medium head of green cabbage,
    cored and chopped fine
2 medium yellow onions, chopped
    fine

1. Sprinkle the yeast over 1/4 cup lukewarm water in a small bowl. Set aside at room temperature for 5 minutes to proof to a foamy consistency.

2. Scald the milk in a saucepan, add the butter, cook over low heat until the butter melts, and pour into a large bowl. Set aside for 15 minutes, or until lukewarm. Blend in the sugar, salt, and eggs. Stir in the yeast mixture. Beat in the flour, 1 cup at a time, until you have a soft dough. Turn out the dough onto a lightly floured board and knead it until it is smooth and elastic, 5 to 10 minutes. Return the dough to the bowl and let the dough rise, covered with a tea towel, at room temperature for 30 minutes. Punch down the dough and let it rise again, covered, for 20 minutes more.

3. While the dough rises the second time, make the filling by browning the beef in a skillet over medium heat. Drain the fat, add the cabbage and onion, and sauté until the cabbage has wilted, about 5 minutes. Remove from the heat and set aside.

4. Turn out the dough onto a lightly oiled surface. Divide the dough into 4 equal portions, then divide the portions into 6 pieces each. Take each piece of dough in 1 hand, make a fist, and squeeze the dough upward between your palm and your clenched fingers. Twist off the dough ball with your other hand and set the ball on the oiled surface. Repeat the process until all the dough is used.

5. Preheat the oven to 350 degrees and lightly oil 2 baking sheets. Using your palm, flatten

each dough ball to a circle about 6 inches round and about 1 inch thick. Place a scant ½ cup of filling in the center of each round and fold the edges up to meet in the center. Pinch the edges together. Put the filled bierocks seam side down on the baking sheets

LEWIS AND CLARK

What moment in history would today's historians most like to have witnessed? The signing of the Declaration of Independence? Washington crossing the Delaware? The Battle of Gettysburg? When American Heritage magazine posed this question, the answer was: traveling with Meriwether Lewis and William Clark as they explored the Louisiana Purchase from 1804 to 1806. After President Thomas Jefferson had bought the millions of acres from Napoleon, sight unseen, he sent Lewis and Clark to look into what he had acquired.

Lewis and Clark set out from St. Louis and followed a northerly course along the Missouri River through what is now Missouri, Kansas, Nebraska, Iowa, South Dakota, and North Dakota. From there they turned westward and made their way to the mouth of the Columbia River. If you read the journals these two men meticulously kept, especially the horticultural entries by Clark, you get an early glimpse of prairie foods and foodways.

"We observed black walnut and oak, among the timber; also honeysuckle and the buck's eye with the nuts on it," they wrote in July of 1804 as they traveled along the Kansas River. Later that year, they spent part of the winter at a Mandan Indian village in what now is Mercer County, North Dakota. An entry from December of 1804 reads, in part, "Kagohami or Little Raven brought his wife and son loaded with corn, and she entertained us with a favorite Mandan dish, a mixture of pumpkins, beans, corn, and chokecherries." After Lewis and Clark spent the next winter along the Columbia River eating nothing but moose meat, they probably looked back on the Mandan dishes as college students marooned at a foreign university remember pizza.

When the weather broke, the party journeyed back from the Pacific Northwest, separating for hundreds of miles in Montana and miraculously reuniting just across the North Dakota border. "The prairies here approach the river and contain many fruits, such as plums, raspberries, wild apples, and, nearer the river, vast quantities of mulberries," they wrote as they returned through present-day Jackson County, Missouri, where Kansas City now lies.

and let rise, uncovered, for 15 minutes. Bake the bierocks until they are golden brown, 15 to 18 minutes. Serve hot.

VARIATION:

For Salmon and Wild Rice Bierocks, gently combine in a bowl 1 pound poached or grilled salmon, broken into small pieces, 1 cup cooked wild rice, 1 pound fresh spinach, steamed and chopped fine, 1 cup sour cream, 2 tablespoons chopped fresh dill, and ½ teaspoon each of salt and black pepper. Use this as the filling instead of the ground beef mixture.

PORK EMPANADAS

Eastern European immigrants to the midwest established and have kept up the regional taste for savory filled pastries. Newer immigrants from Latin America, who have settled both in large cities and in farming communities, have added to the tradition.

MAKES 32 EMPANADAS,
TO SERVE 8 AS A MAIN DISH

2 cups shredded cooked pork
½ cup Smoky, Spicy Barbecue
    Sauce (page 57) or bottled
    tomato-based barbecue sauce
2 tablespoons chopped fresh
    cilantro
½ teaspoon salt
½ teaspoon pepper

1 (17¼-ounce) package frozen
    puff pastry sheets, thawed
2 eggs beaten with 2 tablespoons
    water

1. Preheat the oven to 400 degrees. Line a baking sheet with parchment paper or lightly oiled aluminum foil. Prepare the filling by mixing together the pork, barbecue sauce, cilantro, salt, and pepper in a medium bowl.

2. Place a sheet of puff pastry on a lightly floured board. Roll out the pastry to a 12-inch square. Cut the dough into 3-inch circles using a biscuit cutter or a drinking glass. Place a generous tablespoon of the filling in the center of each circle and fold the circle into a half-moon shape. Brush the edges and top with the egg mixture, then press the edges with a fork to seal. Transfer the empanadas to the baking sheet. Repeat the process with a second pastry sheet. Bake the empanadas for 10 minutes, or until they are golden brown. Serve hot.

IRON COUNTRY PASTIES

When Cornish immigrants came to the Iron Country of northeastern Wisconsin and the Upper Peninsula of Michigan to work in the mines, they brought their love of pasties with them. Local bakeries still specialize in these portable savory pastries that are well suited for a tailgate lunch or a casual dinner. Across Lake Superior in Ontario, similar meat pies feature a blend of beef and pork.

SERVES 6

3 cups all-purpose flour, sifted
1 cup shortening
1 teaspoon salt
About 1/2 cup ice water
3 tablespoons unsalted butter
1 cup diced peeled potato
1 cup diced peeled rutabaga
3/4 cup diced peeled carrot
1/2 cup diced chopped yellow onion
1 tablespoon chopped fresh parsley
1 1/2 teaspoons dried thyme
1 large garlic clove, minced
1 pound boneless beef top sirloin,
    diced
1/2 teaspoon salt
1/2 teaspoon black pepper
2 eggs, beaten

1. Make the pastry dough: Blend the flour, shortening, and salt in a mixing bowl with a pastry blender, or in the food processor fitted with a steel blade, until you have a crumbly dough. Blend in the water a little at a time until the dough is not sticky. Remove the dough, wrap it in plastic wrap, and refrigerate it for at least 30 minutes until ready to use.

2. Prepare the filling: Melt the butter in a large heavy skillet over medium-low heat. Add the potato, rutabaga, carrot, onion, parsley, thyme, and garlic. Sauté the vegetables until they are just tender, about 12 minutes.

Add the beef, and sauté the mixture until the meat is browned and cooked through, about 10 minutes more. Stir in the salt and pepper. Remove from the heat and let cool to room temperature. (The filling may be prepared up to 1 day ahead and kept covered in the refrigerator.)

3. Preheat the oven to 425 degrees. Have the beaten eggs ready in a small bowl. Divide the chilled pastry dough into six equal pieces. Roll out 1 of the pieces on a lightly floured surface to a circle 8 inches in diameter and about 1/4 inch thick. Spoon 1/6 of the filling onto half of the circle, leaving a perimeter of about 1/2 inch. Brush the perimeter of the circle with beaten egg. Fold the other half of the circle over the filling to make a half-moon. Press the edges with a fork to seal the pasty and brush the top with beaten egg. Repeat the process with the remaining dough and filling. Transfer the pasties to an ungreased baking sheet and bake them for 30 minutes, or until golden brown. Serve hot.

WATERCRESS, BACON, AND GOAT CHEESE STRUDEL

You could take a six-month strudel tour of the midwest, with stops at bakeries, bake sales, restaurants, cafés, and home kitchens, and there still would be strudels you had not yet sampled. Most strudels are sweet, flavored with apple, cherry, plum, poppy seed, and so on. But there are savory strudels, too, and here is one I particularly like. Sliced and served in spirals, a strudel was a wrap long before there were wraps.

MAKES 2 STRUDELS, TO SERVE 8 TO 12

FOR THE FILLING:
> 1½ cups loosely packed chopped watercress
> 16 ounces fresh spinach, stems removed
> ½ cup chopped green onions, white part and some green part
> 3 tablespoons unsalted butter
> 1 medium yellow onion, chopped
> ¼ cup all-purpose flour
> 1 cup milk
> 2 eggs, beaten
> ⅛ teaspoon fresh-grated nutmeg
> ½ teaspoon salt
> ½ teaspoon fresh-ground black pepper
> 5 strips bacon, cooked crisp and crumbled
> 6 ounces goat cheese, cut into small pieces or crumbled

FOR THE STRUDEL:
> 8 16-by-11-inch sheets frozen phyllo pastry, thawed according to package directions
> About ⅜ pound (1½ sticks) unsalted butter, melted
> ½ cup breadcrumbs

1. Steam the watercress, spinach, and green onions in a large pot for 3 minutes or until the spinach is just wilted. Remove from the heat and set aside.

2. Heat the butter in a large saucepan over medium heat. Add the onion and sauté it until it is translucent, 6 to 8 minutes. Stir in the flour and cook, stirring, for 1 minute. Whisk in the milk, increase the heat to medium-high, and cook the sauce, whisking constantly, until it boils and thickens, about 5 minutes. Beat 1 tablespoon of the hot sauce into the eggs, then whisk the eggs back into the sauce. Stir in the nutmeg, salt, and pepper, and remove from the heat. Fold in the steamed vegetables.

3. Preheat the oven to 425 degrees and lightly oil a baking sheet. Spread out a sheet of phyllo dough on a floured surface so that the 16-inch side is perpendicular to you. Brush the surface with melted butter, sprinkle with 1 tablespoon of breadcrumbs, and top with another sheet. Repeat the process until you have a stack of 4 sheets; do not butter or crumb the top sheet. Spread half of the filling over the pastry, leaving a 2-inch border on all sides. Sprinkle half of the bacon and half of the goat cheese over the filling. Fold the top and bottom borders over the filling. Then, starting with the right or left side, roll the pastry and filling together in jelly-roll fashion. Place the strudel seam side down on the baking sheet and brush the top with melted butter. Repeat the process with the remaining 4 phyllo sheets and the other half of the filling, bacon, and goat cheese.

4. Bake the strudels for 15 to 18 minutes or until they are browned. Cut the strudels with a serrated knife, and serve hot.

FLY-OVER COUNTRY DUCK STRUDEL

Right before the first frost in late October, the big prairie skies are crosshatched with vees of wildfowl flying south. When there is a nip in the air and you reach for a warm woolen sweater, this is the dish to make for company. Herb-Roasted Duckling (page 230) is especially delicious in this dish, but any roasted duck will do fine. The cooked strudel freezes well, if you would like to get your holiday larder off to an early start.

MAKES 2 STRUDELS, TO SERVE 8 TO 12

FOR THE FILLING:
  4 tablespoons unsalted butter
  1 pound mushrooms, sliced
  2 leeks, cleaned well and sliced
    thin
  1/4 cup all-purpose flour
  1 tablespoon minced fresh
    tarragon
  1 tablespoon minced fresh thyme
  1 tablespoon minced fresh parsley
  2 cups heavy cream
  8 ounces herb-and-garlic soft
    cheese, such as Boursin, cut
    into pieces
  4 cups chopped roasted duck meat

  1/2 teaspoon salt
  1/2 teaspoon fresh-ground black
    pepper

FOR THE STRUDEL:
  12 16-by-11-inch sheets
    frozen phyllo pastry,
    thawed according to
    package directions
  About 1/2 pound (2 sticks) unsalted
    butter, melted

1. Prepare the filling: Heat the butter in a large skillet over medium heat. Add the mushrooms and leeks and sauté them until they are softened, about 7 minutes. Sprinkle the flour over the vegetables and cook, stirring constantly, for 1 minute. Stir in the herbs and cream and continue cooking, stirring frequently, until the sauce thickens, about 5 minutes. Add the cheese and cook, stirring occasionally, until the cheese melts into the sauce, about 5 minutes more. Fold in the duck and cook for 3 to 4 minutes more to blend the flavors. Stir in the salt and pepper, and remove from the heat. Let cool to room temperature.

2. Preheat the oven to 425 degrees and lightly oil a baking sheet. Spread out a sheet of phyllo dough on a floured surface so that the 16-inch side is perpendicular to you. Brush the surface with melted butter. Place a second sheet on top of the first one and brush the surface of the second sheet with melted butter. Continue until you have a stack of six sheets; do not butter the top sheet. Spread half of the duck filling over the pastry, leaving

a 2-inch border on on all sides. Fold the top and bottom borders over the filling. Then, starting with the right or left side, roll the pastry and filling together in jelly-roll fashion. Place the strudel seam side down on the baking sheet and brush the top with melted butter. Repeat the process with the remaining 6 phyllo sheets and the other half of the filling.

3. Bake the strudels for 18 to 20 minutes or until they are browned. Cut the strudels with a serrated knife, and serve hot.

SOUR CREAM AND ONION KUCHEN

Somewhere between a savory shortcake and a quiche, this main-dish bread smells wonderful as it bakes. Serve in wedges with a soup or a salad, or cut into smaller pieces for appetizers or finger food.

SERVES 6 TO 8 AS A MAIN DISH

FOR THE PASTRY:
   2 cups all-purpose flour
   4 teaspoons baking powder
   1 teaspoon salt
   6 tablespoons chilled unsalted
      butter, cut into small pieces
   1/2 cup cold buttermilk, or more if
      necessary

FOR THE FILLING:
   6 tablespoons unsalted butter
   6 large yellow onions, sliced thin
   1 cup sour cream
   2 eggs, beaten
   1 teaspoon salt
   1/2 teaspoon white pepper

1. Make the pastry: Put the flour, baking powder, and salt in a mixing bowl or in the bowl of a food processor. With a pastry blender (in the mixing bowl) or with the steel blade of the food processor, work the butter into the dry ingredients until the mixture resembles coarse meal. Add enough buttermilk to make a sticky dough. Turn out the dough onto a floured board and knead it until it is smooth, about 5 minutes. Roll out the dough to a circle about 15 inches in diameter and pat the circle into the bottom and up the sides of an ungreased 9-inch springform pan. Refrigerate, covered with plastic wrap, for at least 30 minutes until ready to use.

2. Preheat the oven to 450 degrees. Heat the butter for the filling in a large skillet over medium heat. Add the onions and sauté them until they are translucent, 6 to 8 minutes. Spread the onions over the pastry in the pan. Stir together the sour cream, eggs, salt, and white pepper in a bowl and pour the mixture over the onions.

3. Place the springform pan on a baking sheet and transfer both to the oven. Bake the kuchen for 10 minutes, reduce the heat to 350 degrees, and bake for 45 minutes more, or until the top is browned and the kuchen

has pulled away from the sides of the pan. Remove from the oven, release from the pan, cut into wedges or smaller pieces, and serve hot.

WILD MUSHROOM POT PIES WITH AN HERB CRUST

I serve these pies as a main course for lunch or a light dinner in the spring or fall. Use whatever wild mushrooms are available, such as chanterelles, morels, or cèpes, or use a combination of wild mushrooms along with cultivated mushrooms like portobellos, shiitakes, oyster mushrooms, and standard white button mushrooms.

SERVES 6

FOR THE HERB CRUST:
  1/2 cup white breadcrumbs
  1/2 cup fresh-grated Parmesan cheese
  1/2 cup fresh-grated Gruyère cheese
  3 tablespoons chopped fresh parsley
  1 tablespoon chopped fresh basil
  1 teaspoon chopped fresh thyme

FOR THE PIES:
  2 tablespoons unsalted butter
  1/2 cup chopped green onions, white part and some green part
  2 garlic cloves, minced
  4 1/2 cups wild mushrooms or mixed wild and cultivated mushrooms, cleaned well, patted dry, and coarsely chopped
  1 1/2 cups heavy cream
  1/2 cup port
  1/2 teaspoon salt
  1/2 teaspoon white pepper

1. Stir together all of the crust ingredients in a bowl and set aside.

2. Heat the butter in a large skillet over medium heat. Add the green onions and garlic and sauté them until the onions have softened, 4 to 5 minutes. Add the mushrooms and sauté them, stirring frequently, until they have released much of their liquid, 5 to 7 minutes. With a slotted spoon, remove the mushrooms to a bowl and set aside. Whisk the cream and port into the contents of the skillet. Continue to cook, stirring occasionally, until the mixture has thickened enough to coat the back of a spoon, about 5 minutes.

3. Preheat the broiler. Return the mushrooms to the skillet, and stir in the salt and white pepper. Spoon the mushroom mixture into 6 ovenproof 6- to 8-ounce ramekins. Sprinkle the crust mixture over the filling in each ramekin and heat the pies under the broiler until the crust has browned, about 4 minutes. Serve hot.

VEGETABLE TARTLETS IN SAVORY PASTRY

These tartlets are a hearty vegetarian main dish that looks sophisticated but is easy to make. Make the pastry, if you like, before you go out to pick from the garden or shop at the market. I make the tartlets with squash in the summer and with cabbage in the winter.

SERVES 4

FOR THE SAVORY PASTRY:
  2½ cups all-purpose flour
  1 teaspoon salt
  ½ teaspoon white pepper
  1 tablespoon fresh thyme or
      ½ teaspoon dried thyme
  ½ pound (2 sticks) chilled unsalted
      butter, cut into cubes
  ¼ to ½ cup ice water

FOR THE FILLING:
  2 tablespoons extra-virgin olive oil
  2 medium red onions, sliced ¼
      inch thick
  4 small zucchini or yellow
      crookneck squash, or a
      combination, sliced thin,
      or ¼ head of green or red
      cabbage, cored and shredded
  2 tablespoons fresh thyme or
      1 teaspoon dried thyme
  2 tablespoons red wine vinegar
  1 teaspoon sugar
  ¼ pound Asiago cheese, shredded

1. Make the pastry dough: Combine the flour, salt, white pepper, and thyme in the bowl of a food processor fitted with the steel blade. Add the butter a cube at a time and process until the mixture resembles coarse meal. With the motor running, slowly pour in ice water until the dough forms a ball. Remove the dough, wrap it in plastic wrap, and refrigerate it until firm, about 30 minutes. (The dough may be made up to 1 day ahead and stored in the refrigerator.)

2. Preheat the oven to 400 degrees. Heat the oil for the filling in a large skillet over medium heat. Add the onions and sauté them until they have just softened, about 5 minutes. Add the squash or cabbage and the thyme, vinegar, and sugar. Reduce the heat to medium-low, cover the skillet, and cook for 5 minutes more, or until the squash have softened or the cabbage has wilted. Remove the skillet from the heat.

3. Turn out the dough onto a lightly floured board. Divide the chilled dough into 4 equal portions. Roll out each portion to a 6- to 7-inch round. Drape each round in the bottom and up the sides of a 4-inch tartlet pan. Spoon the filling over the dough and sprinkle with the cheese. Gently fold over the excess pastry to enclose some of the filling.

4. Bake the tartlets for 15 to 20 minutes, or until the pastry is browned and the filling is bubbling. Remove the tartlets from the oven and let them rest for 10 minutes. Serve warm.

Potato and Bacon Tourtière

French Canadians traveled through the Great Lakes and down the waterways of the Heartland to establish fortifications and settlements from the mid-eighteenth century onwards. St. Louis and Kansas City, the latter known long ago as Chez les Canses, were early trading posts. One of the dishes that the French Canadians brought with them was the *tourtière*, a savory pie. The name comes from the cast-iron covered pot on legs in which the pies were baked over the coals of the hearth. Needless to say, you do not need to own such a pot for this updated version.

Serves 8

FOR THE PASTRY:
2½ cups all-purpose flour
1 teaspoon salt
½ teaspoon white pepper
1 tablespoon fresh thyme or
    ½ teaspoon dried thyme
½ pound (2 sticks) chilled unsalted
    butter, cut into cubes
¼ to ½ cup ice water

FOR THE FILLING:
5 medium potatoes, peeled and
    sliced thin
3 strips bacon, cooked crisp and
    crumbled
¼ cup chopped fresh parsley
¼ cup chopped green onions, white
    part and some green part
½ teaspoon salt
½ teaspoon fresh-ground black
    pepper

1 egg, beaten
1 cup sour cream or lowfat sour
    cream
2 tablespoons milk
1 tablespoon snipped fresh chives

1. Make the pastry dough: Combine the flour, salt, white pepper, and thyme in the bowl of a food processor fitted with the steel blade. Add the butter a cube at a time and process until the mixture resembles coarse meal. With the motor running, slowly pour in ice water until the dough forms a ball. Remove the dough, wrap it in plastic wrap, and refrigerate it until firm, about 30 minutes. (The dough may be made up to 1 day ahead and stored in the refrigerator.) Meanwhile, place the potatoes in a bowl with salted water to cover and let stand at room temperature for at least 1 hour.

2. Divide the chilled dough in half and roll out 1 half on a lightly floured board to a ¼-inch thickness. Trim the pastry to a circle 10 inches in diameter. Place the pastry circle on an ungreased baking sheet and set aside.

3. Preheat the oven to 375 degrees. Drain and rinse the potatoes and pat them dry. Put the potatoes, bacon, parsley, green onions, salt, and pepper in a large bowl and toss gently to blend. Arrange the potato mixture on the

pastry circle, leaving a 1-inch border around the perimeter.

4. Roll out the second half of the dough to a ¼-inch thickness. Trim this pastry to a circle 13 inches in diameter, and place the circle on top of the tourtière. Gently crimp together the borders of the top and bottom crusts to seal the pie. Brush the beaten egg over the top crust. With a paring knife, cut evenly spaced ½-inch-long vents, parallel to the edge of the pie, around a 4-inch circle in the center of the pie. Bake the pie for 55 minutes, or until the crust is browned.

5. Stir together the sour cream, milk, and chives in a small bowl. When the tourtière is done, cut out and remove the center circle of pastry outlined by the vents. Pour in the sour cream mixture. Let the tourtière rest for 5 minutes. Cut into wedges and serve warm.

CANADIAN PRAIRIE TOURTIÈRE

In the prairie province of Saskatchewan, this hearty cold-weather meat pie is a festive dish for Sunday supper or, on Christmas Eve, after midnight mass. The breadcrumbs bind the spiced meats together, much as in a cassoulet.

SERVES 6 TO 8

FOR THE FILLING:
½ pound lean ground beef
½ pound lean ground pork
1 small yellow onion, chopped fine
1 garlic clove, minced
½ teaspoon salt
½ teaspoon dried summer savory
¼ teaspoon celery salt
¼ teaspoon ground cloves
½ teaspoon dried oregano
About ½ cup breadcrumbs

FOR THE PASTRY:
3 cups all-purpose flour, sifted
1 cup shortening
1 teaspoon salt
½ cup ice water

1. Make the filling: Put all of the filling ingredients except the breadcrumbs in a large pot. Add ½ cup water, bring the water to a boil, reduce the heat, and simmer partially covered, stirring occasionally, for 20 minutes or until the meats are cooked through. Remove the pot from the heat and stir in enough breadcrumbs to absorb the juices. Set aside.

2. Preheat the oven to 375 degrees. Make the pastry: Blend the flour, shortening, and salt in a mixing bowl with a pastry blender or in a food processor fitted with a steel blade until the mixture is crumbly. Add the ice water, 1 tablespoon at a time, and blend until the dough is not sticky. Turn out the dough onto a lightly floured board. Cut the dough in half and roll out 1 half to fit a 9-inch pie pan. Line the pie pan with the dough and spoon in the filling. Roll out the top crust and place this

"SPARING-PIE"

In 1870, twelve-year-old Percy G. Ebbutt, his father, and his ten-year-old brother set out from the village of Blanxton, England, to seek their fortunes in Kansas. The three lived in a dugout for a while and homesteaded. Then the two brothers went to work for another farm family to make more income. Finally, the Ebbutts went back to England. In 1886, Percy published Emigrant Life in Kansas, a lively account of his experiences that is much-used today by historians. In the book he writes, "Game was very plentiful, and we used to bring home lots for the landlady at the Empire Hotel, to make 'sparing-pie' as she called it."

Ebbutt does not say what sparing pie is. I searched through a number of midwestern cookbooks from the mid- to late-1800s in search of a recipe. I found none. But I did find recipes for "Spare Rib Pot Pie," an economical boarding-house dish of spareribs simmered until tender, layered with slices of potato in a large pan, topped with a biscuit crust, and baked in the oven. I now believe that the young Percy, new to Kansas, to American English, and to spareribs, misheard his landlady, and that I'll never find a recipe for sparing pie.

over the filling. Trim the edges of the crusts and flute the edges of the pie. Cut steam vents in the top of the pastry.

3. Place the pie plate on a baking sheet and transfer both to the oven. Bake the tourtière for 25 to 30 minutes, or until the pastry has browned. Remove from the oven and let rest for 5 to 10 minutes. Cut into wedges and serve hot.

RANCHHAND'S PIE

When cowboys—and, yes, there still are plenty of cowboys in the prairie states—saddle up (or hop in the pickup) to go back to the ranch after an afternoon in far-flung pastures, they're hungry. They don't want hors d'oeuvres, sushi, consommé served in thin china cups, or an airy soufflé. They want food with an aroma that will hit them as soon as they walk in the door and with a robustness that will fill them up shortly thereafter. The ranchhands' cook is happy to oblige, especially if the dish doesn't require much fuss in the kitchen. This pie pleases everyone, especially if the cook can use leftovers from last night's pot roast. Even little cowpokes will be happy with a green salad and, for dessert, Honey Custards with Warm Spiced Berries (page 377).

SERVES 4 TO 6

4 cups chopped cooked beef pot roast
    meat, with up to 1/4 cup pan
    juices or gravy from the roast
2 tablespoons unsalted butter
1 cup julienned or shredded yellow
    onion
1 cup julienned or shredded celery
1 cup julienned or shredded peeled
    carrot
2 cups cooked mashed potatoes or
    Horseradish Mashed Potatoes
    (page 315), hot or at room
    temperature

1. Lightly oil a 9-by-13-inch baking dish and place the beef and pan juices in the bottom of the dish. Set the dish aside.

2. Heat 1 tablespoon of the butter in a large lidded saucepan or skillet over very low heat and add the onion, celery, and carrot. Cover the top of the vegetables snugly with a sheet of aluminum foil. Put the lid on the pan and cook the vegetables for 15 to 20 minutes, or until the vegetables have steamed through. Meanwhile, preheat the oven to 350 degrees.

3. Spread the cooked vegetables over the beef in the baking dish. Spread the mashed potatoes over the filling and dot the surface

with the remaining tablespoon of butter. Bake the pie for 25 to 30 minutes, or until the top has browned and the filling is bubbling. Remove from the oven and let rest for 10 minutes. Cut into pieces, and serve.

SHAKER BACON AND EGG PIE

The Heartland Shakers were making this dish before anyone stateside ever had heard of quiche. For a simple picnic or porch supper, a plate of sliced tomatoes and a juicy peach for dessert is all you will need.

SERVES 4 TO 6

1/2 recipe Flaky Pie Crust (page 384)
    or other pastry for 1 9-inch pie
    crust
6 strips bacon, cooked crisp
3 eggs, beaten
1 cup light cream
1 tablespoon all-purpose flour
1/2 teaspoon salt
1/2 teaspoon fresh-ground pepper
1/8 teaspoon fresh-grated nutmeg

1. Preheat the oven to 400 degrees. Roll out the pie crust and place it in a 9-inch pie pan. Crumble the bacon over the crust.

2. Whisk together the rest of the ingredients in a bowl and pour the mixture over the bacon. Bake the pie for 15 minutes, reduce

the heat to 325 degrees, and bake for 30 minutes more, or until a knife inserted in the center comes out clean. Remove from the oven and set aside for 5 to 10 minutes. Cut into wedges, and serve.

POLENTA-CRUSTED ITALIAN SAUSAGE PIES

Northern Italian immigrants to Chicago and Milwaukee brought a taste for polenta and for spicy stews. The two ideas are combined in this savory pie.

SERVES 4

4 cups chicken stock
1 cup fine-ground yellow
    cornmeal
2 tablespoons unsalted butter
1 pound hot Italian-style sausage
    links, cut into 1-inch pieces
1 green bell pepper, diced
1 yellow onion, chopped
1 large tomato, peeled and
    chopped
1/4 cup fresh-grated Parmesan
    cheese

1. Bring the stock to a gentle boil in a large saucepan. Sprinkle the cornmeal into the stock and whisk constantly for 5 minutes. Reduce the heat and simmer, uncovered, for 10 to 15 minutes, until the polenta has bubbled into a fairly thick mass. Stir in the butter thoroughly. Remove the pan from the heat and set it aside.

2. Sauté the sausage, green pepper, and onion together in a skillet over medium heat until the sausage is cooked through and the vegetables have softened, 8 to 10 minutes. Add the tomato and cook for 5 minutes more.

3. Preheat the oven to 350 degrees. Spoon 1/4 of the sausage mixture into each of 4 ramekins or other individual baking dishes. Spoon out 1/4 of the polenta onto the sausage mixture in each bowl and press down to make a crust. Sprinkle the crust with the cheese and bake for 25 to 30 minutes, or until the filling is bubbly and the crust has browned. Remove from the oven, let rest for 5 to 10 minutes, and serve.

LAP OF LUXURY CHICKEN POT PIE

When I was in graduate school at Ohio State, I used to get tiny chicken pot pies from a bakery in Columbus. Now that I have a little more time and a little more money, this is the version I prefer. Make this when a huge project you have been working on is complete and you need to make amends to friends and family for your distraction. A good green salad and poached pears round out the meal.

SERVES 6

FOR THE FILLING:

   3 pounds bone-in chicken breasts,
     skins removed
   1 large yellow onion, cut in half
   1 carrot, peeled
   1 cup dry white wine
   2 sprigs fresh thyme
   1/2 teaspoon whole black
     peppercorns
   1/2 bunch fresh parsley
   3 tablespoons unsalted butter
   1/2 pound mushrooms, sliced
   1 tablespoon all-purpose flour
   1/2 cup heavy cream
   1/4 teaspoon fresh-grated nutmeg
   1/2 teaspoon salt
   1/2 teaspoon white pepper

FOR THE PASTRY:

   1 1/2 cups unbleached all-purpose
     flour
   1/3 cup cake flour
   1/4 teaspoon salt
   10 tablespoons chilled unsalted
     butter, cut into small pieces
   1/3 to 1/2 cup ice water
   5 tablespoons unsalted butter,
     softened

1. Prepare the filling: Put the chicken, onion, carrot, wine, thyme, peppercorns, and 2 cups of water in a stockpot and bring to a boil. Cut the stalks off the parsley and set the leaves aside. Bruise the stalks with a mallet or a knife and add them to the pot. Reduce the heat and simmer, uncovered, for 35 to 45 minutes, or until the chicken is cooked through and tender. Remove the chicken to a plate to cool slightly and remove the pot from the heat. When the chicken is cool enough to handle, shred the meat from the bones and set it aside; discard the bones. Pour the cooking liquid through a sieve into a bowl and reserve 1 cup of the liquid.

2. Heat 2 tablespoons of the butter in a skillet over medium-low heat. Add the mushrooms and sauté them for 7 to 10 minutes, or until they have browned and softened. Remove them to a plate and set aside. Add the remaining tablespoon of butter to the skillet, increase the heat to medium, and whisk in the tablespoon of flour. Cook, whisking constantly, for 2 minutes, then add the 1 cup reserved cooking liquid and whisk until smooth. Continue cooking, whisking frequently, until the sauce has thickened, about 5 minutes. Whisk in the cream, nutmeg, salt, and white pepper. Reduce the heat to very low, stir in the chicken and mushrooms, and keep the filling warm as you make the pastry.

3. Preheat the oven to 425 degrees. Make the pastry: Put the 2 flours and the salt in a mixing bowl or in a food processor fitted with a steel blade. Work in the chilled butter with a pastry blender (in the mixing bowl) or by pulsing (in the food processor) until the mixture resembles coarse meal. Add the ice water, 1 tablespoon at a time, until the dough forms a ball. Turn out the dough onto a floured board and roll the dough into a 9-by-18-inch rectangle with the 18-inch side perpendicular to you. Spread the top or bottom (not the left or right) 2/3 of the surface with 2 tablespoons of the softened butter.

TRAY BIEN

Ready-made comfort food is the beacon that draws crowds to cafeterias in the Heartland as nowhere else in the country. Pick up a tray and a colorful array of timeless dishes tempt you: dinner rolls, banana bread, baked fish, liver and onions, stewed tomatoes, real mashed potatoes, seasoned green beans, sugar cream pie, lemon meringue pie, and more. Such venerable institutions as Luby's Cafeteria in Topeka, Kansas, and Kansas City, Missouri, the Jerre Anne in St. Joseph, Missouri, Miss Hulling's in St. Louis, and the Laughner Cafeteria in Indianapolis serve up loads of these uncomplicated and tasty foods.

Cafeterias blossomed in the early twentieth century. Their clientele consisted of office workers, shop girls, railroad men, and other big-city laborers of modest means. Decent working folk wanted a clean and safe place to get well-made food. Many of these urban workers had lunch hours that fell short of an hour, so the fact that the food was ready was a big plus. When "free-lunch saloons" closed during Prohibition, cafeterias thrived even more.

In no other state is the cafeteria as revered as it is in Indiana, where a number of families have been in the business for a long while. Jonathan Laughner, who had gotten his start in the candy and confection trade, estab-lished Indianapolis's first cafeteria around 1890. A century later, Jane and Michael Stern declared in the New Yorker that Laughner's fried chicken is "the best in the midwest." Today, Laughner's and MCL, started by a branch of the Laughner family in 1950, operate twenty-eight cafeterias in Indiana and neighboring states.

In 1970, brothers Lawrence and Kenneth Gray decided that bigger was better and moved their father's Mooresville Café, in Mooresville, just southwest of Indianapolis, to a more prominent location on a state highway. Gray Brothers Cafeteria was an immediate hit, and it is, as one food writer put it, the quintessential "Little Cafeteria on the Prairie." If you're smart, you'll avoid the after-church rush, when the line snakes out the front door. Each year at Thanksgiving, more than a thousand people get in the Gray Brothers takeout line to bring home one of the cafeteria's famous strawberry pies.

The most recent arrival on the Indiana cafeteria scene is Jonathan Byrd's Cafeteria, in Greenwood in suburban Indianapolis, which opened in 1988 and seats a whopping five hundred hungry diners. If you run into someone who tells you about their splendid sugar cream pie, you'll want to squeeze your way in to be the five hundred and first.

Fold the rectangle in thirds, first folding the unbuttered third over half of the buttered portion, then bringing the uncovered buttered third up over the top. Turn the pastry a quarter turn and roll it out again into a 9-by-18-inch rectangle. Spread the remaining 3 tablespoons of softened butter on 2/3 of the pastry and fold, turn, and roll as before. Repeat the folding, turning, and rolling 2 more times. Finally, roll the pastry into a 10-by-14-inch rectangle.

4. Lightly oil a 9-by-13-inch baking dish. Chop the reserved parsley leaves and fold them into the chicken and mushroom filling. Pour the filling into the baking dish. Place the pastry over the filling and flute the edges. Bake the pie for 25 to 35 minutes, or until the crust has puffed and browned and the filling is bubbling. Remove from the oven and let rest for 5 to 10 minutes. Cut into squares and serve.

SAFFRON-CRUSTED WHITEFISH POT PIES

This is a sublime way to make use of leftover cooked fresh fish. If you do not live in the midwest and do not have access to freshwater whitefish, substitute cod, orange roughy, or a similar mild and firm fish.

SERVES 4

2 cups flaked cooked whitefish or
other firm-fleshed white fish
8 ounces cream cheese, softened
2 tablespoons milk
1 teaspoon Worcestershire sauce
1 tablespoon chopped fresh dill or
* 1 teaspoon dried dill*
1 cup breadcrumbs from Saffron
* Bread (page 355) or 1 cup*
* white breadcrumbs sautéed*
* with 2 tablespoons butter and*
* 1/4 teaspoon crushed saffron*

1. Preheat the oven to 350 degrees. Put the fish in a medium bowl and set aside. Puree the cream cheese with the milk, Worcestershire sauce, and dill in a food processor or blender. Fold the cream cheese mixture gently into the fish. Spoon the mixture into 4 8-ounce ramekins and top each with 1/4 cup of the breadcrumbs.

2. Bake the pies for 20 to 25 minutes, or until the filling is bubbly and the crumbs have browned. Serve immediately.

EAGLE RIVER VENISON AND CRANBERRY DEEP DISH PIE

In Wisconsin, where cranberries ripen in marshes in the Eagle River Valley and deer wander in the woodlands, homey dishes like this one satisfy appetites made keen by the cold. Tuck into this flaky deep dish pie on a weekend night in front of the fire, with a big glass of your favorite midwestern micro-brewed beer nearby.

SERVES 4

FOR THE PASTRY:
 2½ cups all-purpose flour
 1 teaspoon salt
 ½ teaspoon white pepper
 1 tablespoon fresh thyme or
   ½ teaspoon dried thyme
 ½ pound (2 sticks) chilled unsalted
   butter, cut into cubes
 ¼ to ½ cup ice water

FOR THE FILLING:
 ½ cup all-purpose flour
 ½ teaspoon salt, plus more to taste
 ½ teaspoon black pepper, plus
   more to taste
 1 pound venison, cut into small
   cubes
 2 tablespoons canola oil or corn oil
 1 pound small mushrooms, stems
   trimmed
 2 leeks, white part and some green
   part, cleaned well and sliced
 ½ cup red wine
 ½ cup beef stock
 ½ cup Chokecherry and Buffalo
   Berry Jelly (page 73), Old World
   Red Currant Jelly (page 72), or
   store-bought chokecherry or
   red currant jelly
 1 tablespoon Dijon mustard
 2 sprigs fresh thyme or

 ½ teaspoon dried thyme
 1 cup fresh cranberries

1. Make the pastry dough: Combine the flour, salt, white pepper, and thyme in the bowl of a food processor fitted with a steel blade. Add the butter a cube at a time and process until the mixture resembles coarse meal. With the motor running, slowly pour in ice water until the dough forms a ball. Remove the dough, wrap it in plastic wrap, and re-frigerate it until firm, about 30 minutes. (The dough may be made up to 1 day ahead and stored in the refrigerator.)

2. Preheat the oven to 350 degrees. Prepare the filling: Combine the flour, salt, and pepper on a plate. Dredge the venison in the flour mixture and set aside. Heat 1 tablespoon of the oil in a large casserole over medium-high heat. Add the mushrooms, and sauté them until they begin to soften, 2 to 3 minutes. Transfer the mushrooms with a slotted spoon to a plate, add 1 more tablespoon of oil to the

casserole, add the venison and leeks, and cook until the meat is browned on all sides, about 7 minutes. Add the wine, stock, jelly, mustard, and thyme and bring to a boil, stirring frequently. Return the mushrooms to the casserole, stir, and remove from the heat.

3. Cover the casserole and bake for 1 hour, or until the venison is quite tender. Remove from the oven and season to taste with salt and pepper. Stir in the cranberries. Portion out the venison mixture into 4 individual deep dish ovenproof bowls.

4. Increase the heat to 400 degrees. Divide the chilled pastry dough into 4 equal portions. Roll out each portion on a floured board to the diameter of the deep dish bowl. Place the pastry on top of the venison filling. Bake for 25 to 30 minutes, or until the pastry is browned and the filling is bubbly. Remove from the oven and serve immediately.

COUNTRY
SIDES

COUNTRY SIDES

GOLDEN POACHED APPLES WITH LINGONBERRIES

These apples make a fragrant accompaniment to roast turkey, duck, goose, or pork. The natural sweetness of Golden Delicious apples contrasts with the sharper flavor of the filling. Tart and sweet, lingonberry preserves are often used in Scandinavian cooking in the upper midwest; other preserves, or a holiday-style cranberry relish, do fine in this dish as well.

SERVES 6

*6 Golden Delicious apples, cored
    and left whole but not peeled
3/4 cup dry white wine
1/4 cup honey
Juice of 1 lemon
1 1/2 cups lingonberry preserves
    or other tart preserves, or
    cranberry relish*

1. Peel away a 1-inch width of skin around the stem end of each apple, but leave the rest of the skin on. In a saucepan just large enough to hold all the apples, bring the apples, wine, honey, and lemon juice to a boil. Remove the saucepan from the heat, cover tightly, and let steep for 5 minutes.

2. Drain the apples and spoon the preserves into the cavity of each apple. (The dish can be made up to 24 hours ahead, covered, and refrigerated until ready to serve.) Let the apples come to room temperature, and serve.

RAGOUT OF MORELS AND ASPARAGUS

Sixty or seventy years ago, according to my mother, my Ohio grandmother used to buy fresh mushrooms and asparagus in the late spring from a market gardener who brought his produce around on a horsedrawn cart. She would serve creamed asparagus with mushrooms on toasted homemade bread for supper on those nights. Here is my version.

SERVES 4

*1 tablespoon unsalted butter
1/4 pound fresh morels, rinsed well
1 tablespoon minced green onion,
    white part and some green
    part
2 tablespoons dry white wine or
    vermouth
1/3 cup heavy cream
16 thin asparagus spears, tough
    ends removed
Salt and white pepper to taste
4 slices of good-quality bread,
    toasted, or 4 prebaked puff
    pastry shells
Chopped fresh parsley, for garnish*

1. Heat the butter in a large skillet over medium heat. Add the morels and green onion, and sauté them until the onion is softened, about 5 minutes. Increase the heat to high, add the wine, and deglaze the pan, stirring up any browned bits from the bottom. Add the cream, bring to a boil, reduce the heat, and simmer, uncovered, for 5 minutes.

Hunting for Morels

Pale to dark brown in color and with a honeycomb-like surface, wild morel mushrooms push through the moist, chalky soil of the midwest in the spring, from late March in Kansas to late April and early May in Minnesota and Michigan. In deep woodlands or in patchy stands of trees dotted across the eastern prairie, morels hide under dead leaves or at the base of trees, sometimes under a blanket of snow. Foragers know where to find them and have their favorite haunts. Armed with sharp knives and collecting bags, morel hunters harvest the specimens they want from two main varieties: Morchella esculenta, with its cream-colored stem, dark brown cap, and spongy texture, and Morchella elata, with its white stem, pale brown cap, and firmer texture. The very best specimens end up in the kitchens of restaurant chefs, at farmers' markets, or on the forager's own table. Some go on display at gatherings like the Harrison Mushroom Festival, in Harrison, Michigan, or the National Mushroom Hunting Championship and Festival in Boyne City, Michigan.

Morel hunting also is popular in southern Illinois, along the banks of the Illinois River and on its many small islands. From mid-April through early May, morel hunters bring their prizes to market in the Illinois towns of Hardin, Brussels, Kampsville, Hamburg, and Grafton, where the mushrooms sell for eight to fifteen dollars a pound, depending on the size of the year's crop.

Dried morels are now available in grocery stores and supermarkets. They can be revived by soaking them in hot water for 10 to 15 minutes. Fresh morels, on the other hand, should not sit in water for any length of time; they begin to deteriorate. They should, however, be rinsed well to rid them of insects. Their flavor is best if they are cooked as soon as possible after they are gathered, but they can be stored for a few days in the refrigerator. Too dense and chewy to be eaten raw, morels, which are relatives of truffles, add a smoky, salty, earthy flavor to chicken, asparagus, and potato dishes and to cream sauces for pastas and meats.

2. Cut off the tip of each asparagus spear and set the tips aside. Chop the rest of the spear into 1-inch pieces, add them to the morel mixture, and simmer for 5 minutes more. Add the asparagus tips and simmer for 5 minutes more, or until the asparagus is tender. Season to taste with salt and white pepper. Spoon the ragout over the toast, garnish with parsley, and serve.

CZECH BAKED BARLEY WITH MUSHROOMS

Barley was a favorite grain among the Czech immigrants who settled in the midwest, especially Illinois and Iowa. In Iowa, versions of this dish are sometimes made with fresh morels gathered in the spring. This hearty side dish goes well with pork chops, game, or beef.

SERVES 4

2 cups beef stock
1/2 cup pearl barley
1 tablespoon unsalted butter
1/2 pound white mushrooms, sliced thin, or 1/4 pound fresh morels
1/2 cup minced green onions, white part and some green part
1/2 cup minced celery
1 garlic clove, minced
1/2 teaspoon dried thyme

Salt and fresh-ground black pepper to taste

1. Preheat the oven to 350 degrees. Lightly butter or oil a 1-quart casserole dish. Bring the stock to a boil in a large saucepan. Sprinkle the barley on top and stir to blend. Reduce the heat and simmer, covered, for 45 to 60 minutes, or until the barley is tender. Drain the barley, if necessary.

2. Heat the 1 tablespoon butter in a large skillet over medium-low heat. Add the mushrooms, green onions, and celery, and sauté them for 2 minutes. Add the garlic and thyme, and sauté for 2 minutes more. Stir in the cooked barley and the salt and pepper. Pour the mixture into the casserole dish. Bake for 30 minutes, or until the liquid at the perimeter is bubbling and the barley is heated through. Serve hot.

CALICO BLACK BEANS AND CORN

Serve this flavor-packed side dish, an easy recipe that you can make in minutes, with grilled meats, barbecued ribs, or as a vegetarian taco filling.

SERVES 4 TO 6

2 tablespoons canola oil or corn oil

1 medium red onion, chopped

2 garlic cloves, minced

1 jalapeño pepper, seeded and minced

3 cups cooked or canned and drained black beans

2 cups fresh or frozen and thawed corn kernels, preferably shoepeg corn

1/2 bunch fresh cilantro, chopped

1. Heat the oil in a large skillet over medium heat. Add the onion, garlic, and jalapeño, and sauté them until the onion is translucent, 6 to 8 minutes.

2. Stir in the black beans and corn. Reduce the heat to medium-low, and cook, stirring occasionally, until the corn is tender, 8 to 10 minutes. Stir in the cilantro, and serve.

HEIRLOOM BEAN RAGOUT

Just about every immigrant family that came to the Heartland brought its own stock of dried beans. Some of the beans have been in continuous use, while others fell into disuse. A number of the latter ones, like Swedish Brown or Yellow Eye beans, Chestnut Limas, and Checker Beans, are undergoing a revival as heirlooms and are again available in bulk in midwestern stores. An early convenience food that did not need refrigeration or special treatment, dried beans made the trek across the country and became a staple not only of European immigrant cooking but also of Native American cuisine. In this recipe, they come together for an elegant yet homey stew.

SERVES 4

2 tablespoons canola oil or corn oil

6 garlic cloves, minced

2 carrots, peeled and cut into 1-inch pieces

1 medium yellow onion, quartered

2 celery ribs, cut into 1-inch pieces

1/4 cup each of 4 different heirloom beans (see Note), picked over and rinsed well

2 quarts chicken stock

4 sprigs fresh thyme

4 bay leaves

Salt and fresh-ground black pepper to taste

Pinch of sugar, optional

2 green onions, white part and some green part, chopped

1/2 cup diced prosciutto

1. Heat the oil in a stockpot or large saucepan over medium heat. Add the garlic, carrots, onion, and celery, and sauté them until the onion is translucent, 6 to 8 minutes. Do not let the garlic brown, or the beans will have a bitter taste.

2. Add the beans, stock, thyme, and bay leaves. Bring to a boil over high heat, reduce the heat, and simmer, covered, for 20 to 25

minutes, or until the beans are tender. Season to taste with salt and pepper, and add a pinch of sugar, if you like. Add the green onions and prosciutto, and stir to heat through for 1 to 2 minutes. Spoon onto plates or into bowls, and serve.

NOTE: If heirloom beans are hard to find in your area, substitute for some or all of them more common beans like navy, pinto, black, or cannellini.

SMOKED BAKED BEANS

This dish starts with a humble midwestern staple, canned pork and beans, and makes them a whole lot better. Barbecuers cook these beans in the smoker right alongside a slab of ribs or a brisket; you can use a smoker (or covered grill), too, or the oven. The oven version will be slightly milder in flavor.

SERVES 4 TO 6

4 cups canned pork and beans
1/2 cup packed brown sugar
1 medium yellow onion, diced
1 1/2 cups bottled smoke-flavored
    tomato-based barbecue sauce
    or Smoky, Spicy Barbecue
    Sauce (page 57)
1/4 cup Dijon mustard
2 cups diced smoked meat, such as
    beef, pork, chicken, or turkey,
    preferably, or 2 cups diced
    cooked bacon

1. To cook in the oven, preheat the oven to 350 degrees. To cook in a smoker or covered grill, build a fire to a temperature of 200 to 225 degrees.

2. Combine all of the ingredients in a large cast-iron or other heavy pot. Add the pot, uncovered, to the oven, smoker, or covered grill. In the oven, cook the beans for 1 1/2 hours, stirring the beans 2 to 3 times during that time. Or smoke the beans in the smoker or covered grill for 3 hours, stirring occasionally. Serve hot.

BRAISED WHITE BEANS WITH BACON AND PEARS

Here is an old German-American spin on baked beans. The pears sweeten the beans in a more interesting way, I think, than the usual brown sugar.

SERVES 4

1 pound white navy beans, picked
    over and soaked overnight in
    water to cover
1 pound uncooked smoked bacon,
    diced
4 pears, peeled, cored, and diced
1 teaspoon salt

½ teaspoon fresh-ground black
 pepper
¼ cup chopped fresh parsley,
 for garnish

1. Drain the beans, rinse them well, and set them aside. Cook the bacon in a skillet over medium-low heat until just brown, about 5 minutes. Remove from the skillet and drain on absorbent paper.

2. Place the beans in a large saucepan. Add the cooked bacon and the pears, salt, and pepper. Pour in 3 cups of water, bring to a boil over medium-high heat, reduce the heat, and simmer, covered, for 1¼ to 1½ hours, or until the beans are tender. Stir the beans 2 or 3 times as they cook, adding some water if they are too dry. Spoon onto plates or into bowls, garnish with parsley, and serve.

HAM AND BEANS

Whether main dish, side dish, or soup, a pot of beans baked or simmered with ham is a nearly universal staple of the Heartland kitchen. Versions vary from place to place. Around Cincinnati, the cured and smoked pork butt known as cottage ham is simmered with green beans and an onion and served with boiled or mashed potatoes and a dollop of horseradish. In German-American kitchens in the midwest, a favorite savory side dish is white beans cooked with pears and bacon. In community festivals and celebrations in southern Indiana and Illinois, white beans are simmered with ham in blackened kettles over a wood fire and served with cornbread on the side. In Italian communities like The Hill in St. Louis, when fresh fava beans are available, they are cooked with pancetta, onion, and olive oil. In Kansas City, hickory-smoked ham and sparerib meat, plus a spicy tomato-based barbecue sauce, go into baked beans meant to be eaten with down-home barbecue. In the Dakotas and Minnesota, Norwegian-American households like their white beans simmered with pickled pigs' feet and bay leaves.

At the Norske Nook in Osseo, Wisconsin, one of the beloved roadside cafe's most requested dishes is a bowl of white beans simmered with cream and topped with crumbled crisp bacon. In Milwaukee households, white beans share the plate with sauerkraut and smoked pork chops or smoked sausages. Out on the Great Plains in central Kansas, folks cook up a pot of baby lima beans seasoned with watermelon syrup from the homemaker's pantry and a good ham from the local meat locker.

SWEDISH BROWN BEANS WITH PEARS

Bruna bonor, brown beans, have a mild flavor that lends itself to a sweeter treatment than do navy or pinto beans. This dish is delicious with pork chops, a baked ham, or Swedish Potato Sausages (page 30).

SERVES 4 TO 6

1½ cups Swedish brown beans,
    preferably, or pinto beans,
    picked over and rinsed well
1 cinnamon stick
2 teaspoons salt
¾ cup brown sugar
¼ cup cider vinegar
¾ cup dark corn syrup, molasses, or
    Watermelon Syrup (page 61)
2 large pears, peeled, cored and
    chopped

1. Place the beans in a large bowl with water to cover, and soak overnight; the next day, drain and transfer to a stockpot or saucepan and add water again to cover. Or use the quick soak method: Bring the beans in water to cover to a boil, boil for 2 minutes, and let stand for 1 hour.

2. Add the cinnamon stick to the beans and bring to a boil. Reduce the heat, and simmer, covered, for 45 minutes. Add the salt, brown sugar, vinegar, corn syrup, and pears and simmer, covered, for 2 to 2½ hours more, or until the beans are tender. Transfer to a serving bowl, and serve.

OLD-FASHIONED HAM AND BABY LIMAS

As you go west from Michigan, Ohio, and Indiana toward Iowa, Nebraska, and Kansas, butcher shops gradually come to be called meat lockers. Both generally make their own sausages and, sometimes, lunch meats, but meat lockers often cure and smoke their own hams. A salt-cured country ham is dark pink, somewhat dry, and a little pungent; commercially produced smoked hams are often injected with liquid to stay light pink, plump, mild-tasting, and tender. A ham sold as "old-fashioned ham," typical of the hams sold by midwestern meat lockers, is somewhere in between: a medium pink, not as dry as a country ham but not as moist or as "pretty" as a commercial ham. A locally cured and smoked ham is worth seeking out on your travels, and makes a big difference in this dish; in a pinch, use a good-quality commercial ham.

SERVES 4

4 ounces old-fashioned cured ham,
    chopped
1 cup fresh or frozen and thawed
    baby lima beans
3 tablespoons brown sugar
1/4 teaspoon salt
1 teaspoon dry mustard
3 tablespoons Watermelon Syrup
    (page 61), sorghum, or molasses

Combine all of the ingredients and 2 cups of water in a saucepan and bring to a boil. Reduce the heat and simmer, uncovered, for 1 to 1½ hours if you are using fresh lima beans, or ½ to 1 hour if you are using frozen ones, or until the beans are tender and the flavors have blended quite thoroughly. Stir the beans 2 or 3 times as they cook, adding some water if they are too dry. Serve hot or at room temperature.

BRAISED PRAIRIE GREENS

In Kansas in the spring, rural women still gather wild greens such as burdock, lamb's quarters, wild mustard, and pig weed along river banks and hedgerows. Some also grow mustard, Swiss chard, turnip, and collard greens in their gardens. This recipe works with either wild or garden greens, and with a mixture of greens or with just one kind.

SERVES 4

1 pound washed and torn wild
    or domestic greens, such as
    burdock, lamb's quarters,
    Swiss chard, and collard
1 smoked ham hock or hog jowl
Salt and fresh-ground black
    pepper to taste
Cider vinegar or balsamic vinegar

1. Place the greens, ham hock, and 2 cups of water in a large stockpot. Bring to a boil, reduce the heat, and simmer gently, covered, until all the greens are tender. Young spring greens will need only 15 minutes, while tougher greens like Swiss chard and pig weed need to cook slowly for 1 hour or more. (If you have a mix of greens, it is fine to leave the quick-cooking ones in the pot as the slow-cooking ones cook.)

2. When the greens are tender, season them with salt and pepper. Serve them warm, with a cruet of vinegar to pass at the table.

FRESH BEET GREENS WITH LEMON AND OLIVE OIL

A decade ago you were lucky if you found a fresh beet in the grocery store. Then they started showing up, but often without their greens. Happily, most stores now sell the greens, too. Here is a simple preparation for them, which works nicely with spinach as well.

SERVES 4

1 pound beet greens, rinsed well
   but not dried
3 tablespoons extra-virgin olive oil
Juice of 1 small lemon
Salt and fresh-ground black
   pepper to taste

1. Place the greens in a large saucepan (but not on a steamer rack). Steam the greens over high heat, covered, in just the water that clings to their leaves after rinsing, for 1 minute. Remove from the heat.

2. Pour the olive oil and lemon juice over the greens. Toss gently in the pan, season with salt and pepper, and serve.

AFTER-CHURCH SUPPER

After the service in many African-American churches across the Heartland, from large ones like Metropolitan Mission Baptist Church on Chicago's West Side to tiny ones like the Baptist church in the rural hamlet of Nicodemus, Kansas, everyone heads downstairs or across the hall for Sunday dinner. Sometimes, before the sermon has finished, the delicious aromas of what the church ladies have cooked up or what families have brought can seem like the devil's work, tempting stray thoughts of heaven on earth rather than heaven above. Children wiggle in the pews and adults struggle mightily to pay attention to the preacher.

Communal after-church dining was a tradition brought to the midwest from the south. There, the mild weather and the long distance home from church prompted mothers to pack large meals for family—and friends—to spread out on quilts on the grass, picnic-style. According to Joyce White, a writer from Alabama who has chronicled the history of church dinners, "The churches were our restaurants. We didn't have to worry about segregation or not feeling welcome."

For your own home-style after-church dinner, you might try Apple-Carrot Coleslaw (page 164), Old-Fashioned Pan-Fried Chicken with Gravy (page 221), Braised Prairie Greens (page 302), Herbed Buttermilk Spoonbread (page 336), and Summertime Deep Dish Peach Cobbler (page 395).

BRAISED GREEN CABBAGE

"Serve it forthwith, and you'll have one of the finest vegetable dishes known to man," said the venerable James Beard about cabbage. Cut into quarters or thin slices, cooked briefly in salted water until just barely wilted, drained, and drenched in butter liberally seasoned with salt and pepper, this peasant vegetable can be fit for a king. The generally mild flavor of cabbage—keep to the leaves and avoid the stronger tasting core and ribs—makes it a welcoming host for almost any flavor addition. Even in the depths of wintery, blizzard-blasted North Dakota, you can still find cabbage to cook with. Here, it goes uptown.

SERVES 6 TO 8

8 tablespoons unsalted butter
1 large yellow onion, sliced thin
2 cups dry white wine
5 bay leaves
1 tablespoon salt
1 teaspoon white pepper,
    preferably fresh-ground
1 head of green cabbage, cored
    and sliced thin

1. Preheat the oven to 450 degrees. Heat 2 tablespoons of the butter over medium-low heat in a heavy casserole that has a tight-fitting lid. Add the onion, and sauté it until it is translucent, 6 to 8 minutes.

2. Increase the heat to high and add the wine, bay leaves, salt, and white pepper. When the mixture comes to a simmer, add the cabbage and cook, stirring, until the cabbage begins to wilt, 4 to 5 minutes. Cover tightly, transfer to the oven, and let the cabbage braise for 40 minutes. Remove from the oven and stir in the remaining 6 tablespoons of butter. Taste, adjust the seasonings, transfer to a serving bowl or platter, and serve.

CABBAGE AND BACON BOXTY CAKES

When the Irish started emigrating to this country in great numbers during the potato famines of the 1840s, many were unskilled laborers who competed with freed slaves for jobs no one else wanted. In Illinois, Irish immigrants dug the canals, using only hand shovels, that link the Great Lakes with the Ohio River. Back in Ireland, these immigrants might, if they were lucky, have had a piece of bread fried in lard accompanied by a mug of sweet tea for their dinner. In Illinois, they at least could enjoy an Irish peasant dish—with real meat, a humble vegetable, and butter—like this one. These boxty cakes (the name is a traditional Irish one for a variety of sautéed or pan-fried potato cakes) are also good served over a bed of greens and topped with a warm bacon dressing for a main-course salad.

SERVES 4

2 baking potatoes, peeled and
    chopped fine
1/2 small head of green cabbage,
    shredded
4 slices Canadian bacon, diced
1/2 teaspoon salt
1/2 teaspoon fresh-ground black
    pepper
4 tablespoons unsalted butter
4 green onions, white part and
    some green part, chopped fine
1 tablespoon canola oil or corn oil

1. Cook the potatoes in boiling salted water for 12 to 15 minutes, or until the pieces can be pierced with a knife. Drain them and set them aside. Meanwhile, cook the cabbage in boiling salted water until wilted, but still green, about 5 minutes. Drain the cabbage, rinse well with cold water, and drain again. Pat the cabbage dry.

2. Sauté the bacon pieces until they are browned, about 5 minutes, in a large skillet over medium heat. Add the cabbage and cook, stirring often, for 8 to 10 minutes, or until the cabbage begins to brown. Add the potatoes, season with the salt and pepper, and stir. Remove from the heat and add 3 tablespoons of the butter and the green onions. When the butter is melted, use 2 wooden spoons to form the mixture into a mass. Set the mixture aside to cool down. When it is cool enough to handle, form the mixture into four cakes about 3 inches in diameter. Chill the cakes, covered in the refrigerator, for 1 hour.

3. Heat the remaining 1 tablespoon of butter with the oil in a large skillet over medium heat. Sauté each boxty cake on both sides until crisp and browned on the outside, 4 to 5 minutes per side. Serve warm.

BABY CARROTS WITH ZESTY LEMON DRESSING

This is a vibrantly colored garden-fresh dish that is the perfect side for grilled chicken or fish, barbecued brisket, or meat-loaf. You can assemble the dish up to 2 hours ahead, so it is a nice choice for a summer picnic or potluck.

SERVES 4

1 pound baby carrots
2 tablespoons fresh lemon juice
2 tablespoons extra-virgin olive oil
1 tablespoon ground cumin
1 garlic clove, minced
2 tablespoons minced fresh
    cilantro

1. Steam the carrots over boiling water in a covered saucepan for 5 to 7 minutes, until the carrots are crisp-tender. Remove from the heat and transfer the carrots to a bowl.

2. Add the lemon juice, oil, cumin, garlic, and cilantro. Toss to blend. Cover the bowl and let the flavors blend at room temperature for 15 minutes. Serve warm or at room temperature.

GOLDEN CARROT RING

Here is a stylish and venerable old workhorse from Sunday dinners of the 1940s and '50s. Its heartwarming flavors still merit a place on our tables.

SERVES 6 TO 8

1/4 pound (1 stick) unsalted butter, softened
3/4 cup brown sugar
1 egg, beaten
1 cup shredded peeled carrots
1 cup all-purpose flour
1 teaspoon baking powder
1/2 teaspoon baking soda
Juice of 1 lemon
Juice of 1 orange
1/4 cup breadcrumbs

CORN SYRUP

"Moonlight butters the whole Iowa night. Clover and corn smells are thick as syrup."
—W.P. KINSELLA, Shoeless Joe

1. Preheat the oven to 350 degrees. Lightly oil a 4-cup ring mold. Cream together the butter and brown sugar. Add the egg and beat the mixture well with an electric mixer. Fold in the carrots, flour, baking powder, and baking soda. Add the lemon juice and orange juice and stir to blend well.

2. Sprinkle the bottom and sides of the ring mold with the breadcrumbs. Pour the carrot mixture into the mold. Bake for 25 to 30 minutes, or until a toothpick inserted in the center comes out clean. Serve hot in the mold, or turn out onto a platter and serve warm.

ROASTED CORN AND FAVA BEAN SUCCOTASH

When Sicilians first came to the Midwest, they left behind a mainly vegetarian diet in which fava beans, both fresh and dried, played a large role. For years in this country, fava beans were hard to come by unless you grew them yourself. Now they are common at farmers' markets and in grocery stores, and they are certainly easy to find in Italian neighborhoods. In this recipe, fava beans replace the classic lima beans. This is a wonderful accompaniment to Herb-Crusted Grilled Loin of Veal (page 192).

SERVES 6

2½ cups fresh corn kernels (from
   about 4 large ears), preferably,
   or 2½ cups frozen and
   thawed corn kernels
4 tablespoons unsalted butter
1 red bell pepper, diced
1 leek, white part and a little green
   part, cleaned well and sliced
   thin
2 cups fresh hulled, blanched, and
   peeled fava beans
1 teaspoon curry powder
¼ cup heavy cream
Salt and fresh-ground black
   pepper to taste
2 tablespoons minced fresh
   cilantro

1. Place the corn kernels in a cast-iron skillet over medium-high heat. Stirring frequently, scorch the kernels on all sides, about 5 minutes. Remove from the heat and set aside.

2. Melt the butter in a large skillet over medium heat. Add the corn, bell pepper, and leek, and sauté for 2 minutes. Add the fava beans and the curry powder, and sauté for 2 minutes more. Stir in the cream, and season with salt and pepper. Reduce the heat to medium-low, and cook, stirring occasionally, until the mixture reduces and thickens a little, about 5 minutes. Stir in the cilantro, and serve hot.

GRILLED CORN AND RED PEPPER RELISH

A good corn relish was a cornerstone of the traditional farmstead pantry. In addition to selling her surplus butter and eggs, a farm wife would make corn relish at the end of the harvest to sell to city folk. The old recipes, which were made to be canned and preserved, have celery and celery seeds as dominant flavors. This one, made to be served fresh, relies on caramelized flavors from the grill for a smoky, robust taste.

SERVES 4

4 ears fresh corn, husked
4 garlic cloves
1 medium red onion, cut in half
   horizontally
1 medium yellow onion, cut in half
   horizontally
1 large red bell pepper, cut in half
   vertically
¼ cup corn oil
¼ cup white wine vinegar
2 tablespoons minced fresh basil or
   fresh parsley
Salt, fresh-ground black pepper,
   and sugar to taste

1. Preheat a charcoal or gas grill to medium. Brush the corn, garlic cloves, red and yellow onion, and bell pepper with the corn oil. Place

the vegetables in a grill basket or grill wok and grill them until they are browned on all sides; do not blacken them. As each vegetable browns, remove it and set it aside. The total grilling time will be about 10 minutes.

2. Using a paring knife, cut the corn kernels from the cobs into a large bowl. Mince the garlic and chop the onions and bell pepper, and add these vegetables to the bowl. Add the vinegar and basil, and toss the relish well. Season with salt, pepper, and sugar to taste, and toss again. Serve hot, at room temperature, or chilled.

SCALLOPED PEACHES-AND-CREAM CORN

This is a warm and comforting side dish from the Amish community in Harmony, Minnesota. I make it with Peaches and Cream corn, a midwestern variety that has very sweet golden yellow and white kernels on each ear. You can use any sweet corn you have; the results will be less colorful but just as good.

SERVES 4 TO 6

3 eggs, beaten
1 cup milk
1/2 cup heavy cream
1 tablespoon sugar

2 cups corn kernels, preferably fresh
1 teaspoon salt
1/2 teaspoon white pepper, preferably fresh-ground
1/2 cup saltine cracker crumbs
1 tablespoon unsalted butter, melted

1. Preheat the oven to 350 degrees. Lightly oil or butter a 1-quart baking dish.

2. Beat together the eggs, milk, cream, and sugar until smooth. Fold in the corn, salt, and white pepper. Pour the mixture into the baking dish, sprinkle the cracker crumbs on top, and drizzle with the melted butter. Bake, uncovered, for 1 hour, or until the top is golden brown and a knife inserted in the center comes out clean. Remove from the oven, let rest for 5 to 10 minutes, and serve hot.

CORNHUSKER CORN CASSEROLE

As a side dish or brunch dish, this savory yet mellow quiche features both sweet corn and hominy.

SERVES 6 TO 8

2 cups canned yellow or white hominy, drained and patted dry

2 cups fresh corn kernels,
preferably, or 2 cups frozen
and thawed corn kernels
1 garlic clove, minced
8 ounces sharp cheddar cheese,
shredded
2 cups milk
4 eggs, beaten
1 teaspoon salt
1/4 teaspoon cayenne pepper

1. Preheat the oven to 350 degrees. Lightly oil or butter a baking dish or casserole.

2. Stir together the hominy and corn in the baking dish and level off the top of the mixture with a rubber spatula. Top with the garlic and cheddar. Whisk together the milk, eggs, salt, and cayenne in a medium bowl, and pour this mixture over the top. Bake for 50 to 60 minutes, or until the casserole is set and the top is bubbling. Remove from the oven, let rest for 5 to 10 minutes, and serve hot.

CODDLED CRABAPPLES

From eating preserved spiced crabapples as a child, I always thought that crabapples had a strong flavor. Not so. When cooked, they taste just like apples, only with a softer texture. When orchard crabapples appear on grocers' shelves around Thanksgiving, snatch them up to make this dish. In vintage midwestern cookbooks from the early twentieth century, coddling or poaching fruit in a sugar syrup was a common cooking method for autumn produce. Serve this updated version as an accompaniment to roast pork or, if you like, as a breakfast or brunch dish in place of a compote or fruit salad. The coddling or gentle poaching is necessary so that the crabapple skins will not crack. Even if they do, the fruit is still delicious, and it looks wonderful piled in a glass or earthenware bowl.

SERVES 6 TO 8

2 pounds fresh crabapples, with
skins and stems intact
2 cups light- to medium-bodied
dry red wine
1 cup sugar
1 vanilla bean
1 cinnamon stick

1. Prick the crabapples all over with a fork or paring knife to keep the skins from bursting. Transfer the crabapples to a nonreactive saucepan.

2. In a separate saucepan, bring to a boil the wine, sugar, vanilla, and cinnamon. Pour the boiling liquid over the crabapples and bring to a simmer. Simmer, covered, for 5 minutes, or until the crabapples are cooked through and tender. Remove from the heat and let cool slightly. Discard the vanilla bean and cinnamon stick. Spoon the whole crabapples into a serving bowl, pour the poaching liquid over them, and serve.

EVERYDAY THINGS

When I imagine bounteous Sunday dinners or harvest tables in small Heartland towns of a century ago, I picture dishes like Coddled Crabapples (page 309) or Seasoned Green Beans (page 311) presented in yellowware bowls. Simple and plain, yellowware pottery was as common in nineteenth-century midwestern kitchens as Corningware is today. Yellowware gets its name from the color of the clay used to make it, ranging from a buttery yellow to a light tan. Because it was fired at a high temperature and coated with an alkaline glaze, yellowware would withstand high heat and often would go straight from the stove to the table. The bowls, in a variety of sizes, were sometimes banded around the top rim in blue, white, brown, or brick red. Later examples from the twentieth century were imprinted with basket-weave designs in the clay. Although yellowware was first created in England, by the 1830s it was being made in New Jersey. By the 1860s, production sites had moved to Ohio, first in East Liverpool and Cincinnati, then in Crooksville and Roseville. English potters emigrated to Ohio to help make the bowls, which are widely sought collectibles today.

TAKE-TO-THE-PICNIC DEVILED EGGS

These classic accompaniments to a casual meal, whether served indoors or out, have never fallen out of fashion in the midwest. The vinegar combats the egginess of the eggs and makes this version lighter in taste than others.

SERVES 6 TO 12

12 eggs
1 heaping tablespoon mayonnaise
3 tablespoons distilled white vinegar
3 tablespoons sugar
1/2 teaspoon salt
1/4 teaspoon fresh-ground black pepper
Paprika and minced fresh parsley, for garnish

1. Gently place the eggs in a large saucepan, cover them with cold water, and bring to a boil. Cover tightly with a lid, remove from the heat, and let stand 30 minutes.

2. Drain the eggs, peel them, and cut them in half lengthwise. Put the yolks in a bowl and

add the mayonnaise, vinegar, sugar, salt, and pepper. Blend with an electric mixer until smooth and creamy. Fill the whites with the mixture. Cover the eggs carefully with plastic wrap and refrigerate for at least 1 hour. Garnish with paprika and parsley, and serve chilled.

GRATIN OF FRESH FENNEL

A long with the rhubarb, the spring onions, and the early greens, fennel is part of the late-spring harvest from my Kansas garden. Its licorice-like flavor is a welcome tonic, and the smell of this dish baking in the oven is heavenly. I serve it alongside a roasted chicken.

SERVES 4

2 medium fennel bulbs
2 tablespoons unsalted butter, cut
    into dots
2 tablespoons breadcrumbs
1/2 teaspoon salt
1/4 teaspoon fresh-ground black
    pepper

1. Preheat the oven to 400 degrees. Lightly oil a shallow baking dish. Bring a pot of salted water to a boil. Trim off the hard base and the top stalks of the fennel, cut each bulb in half lengthwise, and transfer to the boiling water. Cook the fennel for 10 minutes, then drain it and set it aside to cool down.

2. When the fennel is cool enough to handle, cut it into thin slices. Place the slices, in an overlapping pattern, in the baking dish. Dot with the butter, sprinkle with the breadcrumbs, and season with salt and pepper. Bake for 15 to 20 minutes, or until the top and edges are browned and crispy. Serve hot.

SEASONED GREEN BEANS

I t was not so long ago that most vegetables were served completely unadorned, and so you really were making a point when you announced that they were *seasoned*. That has changed, but the expression lives on in the title of this humble dish, a hands-down essential for an authentic midwestern fried chicken dinner. The character of the dish rests simply in the quality of the ham. In many midwestern towns, "country ham seasoning" is available in meat departments at local grocery stores; if you can find some, add it to the dish. If you use a country ham, omit the extra salt.

SERVES 4 TO 6

1/2 to 3/4 pound country ham or
    smoked ham, cut into cubes
1 pound fresh green beans, ends
    trimmed

1 large yellow onion, quartered
Salt to taste, optional
Fresh-ground black pepper to taste

1. Brown the ham cubes on all sides in the bottom of a large saucepan over medium-high heat. Add the green beans, onion, and water to cover, and bring to a boil over high heat. Reduce the heat and simmer very gently, covered, for 2 to 3 hours or until the beans and ham are quite tender and the flavors are very well blended.

2. Just before serving, season with salt (if you did not use a country ham) and pepper to taste. Transfer the contents of the saucepan to a serving bowl, and serve hot.

CREAMED GARDEN PEAS AND NEW POTATOES

I hate to cook fresh baby peas. It does not seem right to turn all that sugary goodness into a bland starch. In this spring recipe, however, the peas go in at the last possible moment just to warm them through. Find the tiniest new potatoes and the freshest peas; in a pinch, use frozen baby peas.

SERVES 4

1 pound small new potatoes,
   skins on
1 tablespoon unsalted butter
1 tablespoon all-purpose flour
1 cup half-and-half
1/2 teaspoon fresh-grated nutmeg
Salt to taste
1 cup shelled fresh baby peas

1. Steam the new potatoes over boiling water in a covered pan until just tender, about 10 minutes. Remove from the heat and set aside.

2. Heat the butter in a large saucepan over medium heat. When it is hot, whisk in the flour and cook, whisking constantly, for 2 minutes. Whisk in the half-and-half and continue cooking, whisking constantly, until the mixture thickens, 3 to 4 minutes. Reduce the heat to low, and stir in the nutmeg and salt. Fold in the potatoes and peas and cook, stirring several times, just to heat through, 3 to 4 minutes. Serve hot.

BLUE CHEESE MASHED POTATOES

Creamy and pungent, mellow and smooth, these potatoes are a terrific accompaniment to a grilled steak.

SERVES 4

6 large baking potatoes, peeled and
    diced
1/2 to 3/4 cup milk
8 ounces blue cheese, such as
    Maytag Blue from Iowa,
    crumbled
1 tablespoon unsalted butter
Salt to taste, optional
White pepper, preferably
    fresh-ground, to taste

1. Bring the potatoes in water to cover to a boil in a large saucepan. Cook at a gentle boil for about 15 minutes, or until the potatoes are tender. Remove from the heat, drain, and pour in 1/2 cup of the milk. Mash the potatoes until they are smooth, adding more milk if necessary.

2. Add the blue cheese and butter to the potatoes and mash until well blended. Season with salt (you may not need any if your blue cheese is quite salty) and white pepper, transfer to a serving bowl, and serve hot.

TWICE-BAKED MOREL-STUFFED POTATOES

Dried morels now are available year-round. A lot of them come from midwestern suppliers, and they are sold at farmers' markets, as well as supermarkets, throughout the Heartland. The morels give the filling a smoky and rich flavor.

SERVES 4

1/2 cup heavy cream, half-and-
    half, or evaporated skim milk
2 tablespoons dried morels
4 potatoes, baked
Salt and fresh-ground black
    pepper to taste
1/2 cup fresh-grated Parmesan
    cheese

1. Preheat the oven to 350 degrees. Pour the cream over the morels in a small saucepan and place over medium-high heat until the cream is hot, about 2 minutes. Remove from the heat and let the mushrooms steep for 15 minutes.

2. Meanwhile, cut each baked potato in half lengthwise and scoop the pulp into a medium bowl; reserve the skins intact. Mash the pulp. With a slotted spoon, remove the morels from the cream and chop them fine. Stir the chopped morels back into the cream, and

BLUE CHEESE HEAVEN

A couple of miles north of Interstate 80, which runs east-west across the rolling cornfields of Iowa, and about twenty-five miles east of Des Moines, is the small city of Newton. If you exit the highway here and follow the signs for Maytag Blue Cheese, you will pass herds of black and white Holsteins and will come eventually to a large 1970s-vintage building that looks slightly Mediterranean. Inside, some of the best blue cheese on earth is made.

How this came to be is a story of serendipity. The name Maytag is the same one you associate with washing machines, dryers, and other appliances. Elmer Maytag, a son of the appliance company founder, had assembled a herd of Holsteins during the 1920s and 1930s. Upon his death in 1940, his sons wondered what to do with all those cows. By coincidence, nearby Iowa State University had just patented a process for making blue cheese, and the milk from the Maytag champion herd was just the right flavor. The rest is cheese history.

More mellow and less pungent than French Roquefort, smoother in texture than the crumbly Danish bleu, Maytag Blue Cheese is among the most widely praised cheeses made in the United States. Regardless of the acco-

lades, the people at Maytag Blue Cheese do not take themselves too seriously. "Our truck is newer and our cheesemakers are older," reads their brochure. If you ask nicely, you can even get to talk to their CEO, Jim Stevens, in person, and he is a delight. He will show you a photo of himself in the 1940s when he came to work here as a teenager. "I thought they had put me down there and forgotten about me," he says about his first day on the job, when he was assigned to scrubbing the mold off the cheeses. Fifty years later, with a penchant for wild Holstein-patterned ties, Jim relies on his dry sense of humor to keep him—and the company—from "getting a big head." With worldwide acclaim from food critics and customers alike for the three hundred thousand pounds of cheese they produce each year, the folks here could be excused for being a little vain. But Jim won't have it. "We know we do a good job, but we just let other people blab on about it," he says.

Jim will even give you the blue cheese dressing recipe (see page 173) that he and his wife make at home. When you spoon it over a salad of crisp lettuce and fresh tomatoes and then take a bite, all will be right with the world.

pour the mixture into the potato pulp. Mash well and season with salt and pepper. Spoon the filling into the potato skins, sprinkle Parmesan on each potato half, and bake for 20 to 25 minutes, or until the cheese and pulp have browned. Serve hot.

HORSERADISH MASHED POTATOES

Serve these punchy potatoes alongside grilled bratwursts, game meats, or any number of sauerkraut dishes.

SERVES 8

8 medium to large potatoes, peeled
    and cut into quarters
1 cup sour cream
4 tablespoons unsalted butter
1 tablespoon fresh-grated
    horseradish or prepared
    horseradish, or more to taste
1/2 teaspoon salt, or more to taste
1/2 teaspoon fresh-ground black
    pepper, or more to taste
Chopped fresh parsley, for garnish

1. Bring the potatoes to a boil in a large pot of salted water. Boil them for 15 minutes, or until a sharp knife will pass through them. Drain the potatoes and transfer them to a large bowl.

2. Add the sour cream and butter and mash until the potatoes are smooth. Stir in the horseradish, salt, and pepper, taste, and adjust the seasonings. Garnish with parsley, and serve hot.

SWEDISH POTATO GRATIN

In families of Swedish descent, this potato dish is among the offerings in a traditional Christmas smorgasbord. The saltiness of the anchovies cuts through the richness of the dish. If you are not putting together your own smorgasbord, the gratin stands up nicely alongside North Country Pot Roast (page 183), Smoked Herbed Chicken (page 222), a holiday ham, or any other robust meat dish.

SERVES 4

18 anchovy fillets in a can or
    1 2-ounce can Swedish anchovies
4 cups thin-sliced peeled potatoes
5 tablespoons unsalted butter
1 medium yellow onion, sliced thin
1 cup half-and-half
1/2 teaspoon white pepper

1. Preheat the oven to 400 degrees. Drain the anchovies, reserving 1 tablespoon of their liquid. Lightly oil or butter a 1-quart baking dish. Rinse the potato slices in cold water, then drain them and pat them dry. Layer

half of the potatoes in the bottom of the baking dish.

2. Heat 2 tablespoons of the butter in a skillet over medium heat. Add the onion, and sauté it until it is translucent, 6 to 8 minutes. Spread out the onion and the anchovies over the potatoes in the baking dish. Top with the remaining potatoes. Drizzle the anchovy liquid over the potatoes, and then the half-and-half. Sprinkle with the white pepper, and dot with the remaining 3 tablespoons of butter. Cover with foil and bake for 30 minutes. Remove the foil, and bake uncovered for 20 to 25 minutes longer, or until the potatoes are browned

and have softened but are not falling apart. Serve hot.

BLUE CHEESE POTATO GRATIN

This sublimely simple side goes handsomely with grilled steaks, burgers, or sirloin tips. For a variation on this classic dish from the midwestern repertoire, use 2 tablespoons of chopped morels instead of the blue cheese.

HORSERADISH

In addition to perking up the flavor of foods, horseradish also has a practical function in midwestern kitchens. When it is added to vinegared preserved vegetables, it keeps scum from forming on top. Maliner Kren, a Bohemian horseradish variety sold in the Heartland since 1904, is the standard variety for this use and also for horseradish condiments. In the garden, it comes back every year like rhubarb and is ready for harvest after the first year. You simply dig up a root, clean it and scrape it as you would a carrot, and then grate it or shred it by hand or in the food processor.

If you are used to prepared horseradish but have never had fresh horseradish, give it a try. Grating the root right before your meal is best, but grated horseradish also can be kept in a lidded jar, filled with cider vinegar or distilled white vinegar to cover, and refrigerated. The deli departments in many midwestern grocery stores offer fresh-grated horseradish, too.

The area around Collinsville, Illinois, just inland across the Mississippi River from St. Louis, is dubbed the Horseradish Capital of the World. The soil here is sandy and full of potash, a nutrient that allows the horseradish plant to thrive. Over ten million pounds of horseradish root are grown annually in this region, nearly 85 percent of the world's supply.

SERVES 6

2 to 3 large russet potatoes, peeled
and sliced as thin as possible
1/2 cup crumbled blue cheese, such
as Maytag Blue from Iowa
1 cup heavy cream
1/2 teaspoon sea salt
1/2 teaspoon fresh-ground black
pepper

1. Preheat the oven to 350 degrees. Lightly oil or butter a 9-by-13-inch baking pan.

2. Rinse the potato slices in cold water, then drain them and pat them dry. Layer 1/3 of the potatoes in the bottom of the pan, and top with 1/3 of the blue cheese followed by 1/3 of the cream and 1/3 of the salt and pepper. Repeat the process with 2 more layers.

3. Bake the gratin, uncovered, for 45 to 55 minutes, or until the potatoes are tender and the top is browned and bubbling. Serve hot.

ROASTED ROOT VEGETABLES

As you reach into the vegetable bin in the refrigerator and the potato bin in the kitchen cupboard, imagine yourself making a trip to the root cellar through drifts of snow in the farmyard. The sugars in the root vegetables caramelize while roasting, giving them a wonderful flavor that goes well with a roasted or grilled beef tenderloin, a pork roast, or veal T-bones. Use two or more varieties of potatoes, such as Red Creamer, Yellow Finn, or Yukon Gold, in this dish, if you like.

SERVES 6

12 small potatoes, quartered
2 carrots, peeled and cut into
2-inch lengths
1 parsnip, peeled and cut into
2-inch lengths
3 tablespoons extra-virgin olive oil
1 tablespoon fresh thyme or
1 teaspoon dried thyme
1 1/2 teaspoons sea salt
3/4 teaspoon fresh-ground black
pepper

1. Preheat the oven to 400 degrees. Distribute the potatoes, carrots, and parsnip in a roasting pan, drizzle them with the olive oil, and sprinkle with the thyme, salt, and pepper. Toss well to coat.

2. Roast the vegetables, uncovered, for 35 to 45 minutes, stirring occasionally, until the vegetables are tender and browned. Transfer to a platter or bowl, and serve hot.

PARSLEY-AND-CHIVE RICE

In the midwest, everyone calls this old-time recipe "green rice." It is especially good with a roast chicken or a barbecued brisket.

SERVES 4

2 tablespoons unsalted butter
1/4 cup chopped green onions,
    white part and some green
    part
3/4 cup uncooked white rice
1 1/2 cups chicken stock
1/2 teaspoon Maggi seasoning or
    Worcestershire sauce
1/2 teaspoon garlic salt
1/4 cup chopped fresh parsley
1/4 cup snipped fresh chives

1. Heat the butter in a large saucepan over medium heat. Add the green onions, and sauté them until the white part is translucent, about 4 minutes. Add the rice and stir to coat with the butter and green onions. Pour in the chicken stock, Maggi, and garlic salt, bring the mixture to a boil over high heat, reduce the heat, and simmer gently, covered, for 15 minutes, or until the rice is fluffy and tender.

2. Remove from the heat and let rest, covered, for 5 minutes more. Stir in the parsley and chives and serve hot.

STUFFED RED PEPPERS WITH FARMHOUSE CHEESE AND HERBS

These are traditional stuffed peppers freshened up for the contemporary palate. Any sweet bell pepper—yellow, purple, orange, or red—works well in this recipe. (I avoid green peppers, which have a little bite to their taste.) Dried basil will not have the flavor in this dish that fresh basil does. You might also serve these peppers as a summer main dish for lunch or a light dinner.

SERVES 6

3 red bell peppers, cut crosswise in
    half
1 1/2 cups Fresh Farmhouse Cheese
    (page 39), drained, or 1 1/2 cups
    cottage cheese, drained
2 eggs, beaten
1/2 cup minced fresh basil
1/2 cup chopped fresh Italian parsley
1/2 teaspoon salt
1/2 teaspoon fresh-ground black
    pepper

1. Preheat the oven to 350 degrees. Lightly oil a baking sheet. Trim each pepper half so that it will sit squarely on the baking sheet; do not cut all the way through the skin. Transfer the peppers to the baking sheet.

2. Stir together the cheese, eggs, basil, parsley, salt, and pepper in a bowl. Spoon the filling into the peppers to a level about 1/2 inch from the top. Bake the peppers, uncovered, for 20 minutes, or until the filling is browned on top. Remove from the oven, carefully transfer with a spatula to a serving platter or individual plates, and serve hot.

SALSIFY WITH BACON AND PEARL ONIONS

Salsify is an old-fashioned cold-weather root vegetable perfect for the holiday table. To keep salsify from darkening, wrap it in plastic once you have picked it or bought it and do not peel it until just before you make the recipe. In this dish, the mild oyster-like flavor of salsify goes well with the smoky richness of bacon and the sweetness of the pearl onions.

SERVES 6 TO 8

6 medium salsify roots, peeled
Juice of 1 lemon
2 cups chicken stock
18 pearl onions
4 garlic cloves
2 sprigs fresh thyme
1/4 pound bacon, preferably
    apple-smoked, diced
Salt and fresh-ground black
    pepper to taste

Chopped fresh thyme, for garnish,
    optional

1. Cut the salsify roots into 2-inch lengths and transfer them to a medium bowl. Sprinkle them with the lemon juice and add cold water to cover.

2. Pour the chicken stock into a medium saucepan. Add the pearl onions, the garlic cloves, and the 2 sprigs of thyme, and bring to a boil over high heat. Reduce the heat and simmer, uncovered, for 5 minutes. Drain the salsify and add it to the saucepan. Cover and simmer for 7 to 8 minutes more, or until the salsify and onions are just tender.

ON THE DAKOTA PRAIRIE

"Our horses picked their way along the edge of a prairie-dog town whose residents had disappeared down their holes, and all there was to see were earthen mounds and short clumps of buffalo grass. As we approached the valley, which was only a dozen miles from my home, I noticed taller grasses, stalks of bluestem and wheatgrass. The sun emerged from behind the clouds, and the landscape burst into color, dotted with sunflowers, bluebells, blazing stars, and purple sage."
—SUSAN POWER, *The Grass Dancer*

3. Meanwhile, fry the bacon in a skillet over medium heat until browned, about 5 minutes. Drain the salsify and onions, discarding the garlic and thyme, and add them to the skillet. Sauté the mixture, stirring occasionally, until the salsify and onions are browned, 4 to 5 minutes more. Season with salt and pepper. Transfer with a slotted spoon to a serving platter or bowl, and serve hot, garnished with chopped thyme, if you like.

SPINACH SUPREME

Baked spinach casseroles topped with buttered breadcrumbs were part of every good midwestern cook's repertoire for much of the twentieth century. The tradition gets revived in our family once a year, at Thanksgiving. I have tried making this dish without the canned mushroom soup, but, well, it just isn't the same—and, I suppose, a book about prairie home cooking really ought to grant at least a token appearance to this time-honored ingredient. Do not add any salt as you cook the dish; there is plenty in the soup. For holiday cooking, make this dish a day ahead and reheat it in the microwave, with no loss of flavor, and thereby save the oven for the turkey, for other side dishes, and for desserts.

SERVES 6

2 pounds fresh spinach, stemmed
    and rinsed but not spun or
    patted dry
6 tablespoons unsalted butter
3 celery ribs, chopped fine
1 large yellow onion, chopped fine
1 15½-ounce can cream of
    mushroom soup
½ cup breadcrumbs, preferably
    homemade

1. Preheat the oven to 375 degrees. Lightly oil, or spray with cooking spray, a 1-quart baking dish. Steam the spinach, covered, over medium-high heat in a saucepan in just the amount of water that clings to the leaves from rinsing. When the spinach is wilted, after about 4 minutes, drain it and pat it dry between tea towels. Chop the spinach fine, transfer it to a bowl, and set it aside.

2. Heat 2 tablespoons of the butter over medium heat in a large skillet. Add the celery and onion, and sauté them until the onion is just translucent, about 5 minutes. Add the celery, onion, and mushroom soup to the spinach and stir to blend well. Pour the spinach mixture into the prepared baking dish and set aside.

3. Melt the remaining 4 tablespoons of butter over medium heat in the same skillet and brown the breadcrumbs, stirring frequently, for about 4 minutes. When the buttered breadcrumbs are golden brown, spoon them over the spinach casserole. Bake for 30 minutes, or until the casserole is hot and bubbling. Serve hot.

Yellow Velvet Corn and Squash

By the first decade of the nineteenth century, the Shakers had established settlements in a half dozen communities in Ohio and Indiana. This dish, adapted from the traditional Shaker repertoire, does look like yellow velvet and tastes like a golden summer day in corn country. Use the smallest, tenderest yellow squash and the freshest sweet corn for the best flavor.

Serves 4 to 6

2 cups finely chopped yellow
   summer squash
2 cups corn kernels, preferably
   fresh
1 cup heavy cream, half-and-half,
   or evaporated skim milk
Salt and white pepper to taste

1. Place the squash and corn in 2 separate saucepans and add water just to cover. Bring each to a boil, reduce the heat, and simmer, uncovered, until just tender, about 4 minutes for each. Remove from the heat and drain.

2. Puree the cooked corn kernels in the bowl of a food processor. Combine the corn puree and the cooked squash in a saucepan and stir in the cream. Heat gently over medium-low heat, stirring occasionally, until just warmed

through, 4 to 5 minutes. Season with salt and white pepper, transfer to a bowl, and serve.

Scalloped Summer Squash

Everyone used to do so, but midwesterners *still* like their vegetables scalloped and smothered. If this preparation feels a little heavy to you, promote it from side dish to a meatless main dish and you'll be just fine.

Serves 6 as a side dish or 4 as a main dish

3 tablespoons unsalted butter
1 pound yellow summer squash,
   chopped fine
1 medium yellow onion, chopped
   fine
2 eggs, beaten
1/2 cup shredded cheddar cheese
1 cup milk
1 cup cracker crumbs
1 teaspoon salt
Dash of fresh-ground black
   pepper

1. Preheat the oven to 375 degrees. Lightly oil a casserole dish.

2. Heat the butter over medium heat in a saucepan or skillet. Add the squash and onion and sauté them, stirring occasionally, until the

THE HOOSIER CABINET

In the early twentieth century, the Hoosier cabinet was what every home cook wanted in her kitchen. For women who had to turn out three hearty meals a day, it was the ultimate kitchen organizer. It had a bread drawer, a cutting board, storage areas for flour, sugar, and spices, and compartments for pots and pans. A shallow work surface in the front of the cabinet allowed the cook to measure out ingredients without having to move around the kitchen. In the words of one advertisement, the Hoosier cabinet, at a cost of $12.50, promised to save "time and strength and health by saving steps."

The Hoosier Manufacturing Company of Albany, Indiana, introduced this efficient kitchen device to the American market in 1898. By 1910, they had sold three hundred thousand of them. Ten years later, the company boasted that over two million American women had a Hoosier cabinet. During the heyday of the Hoosier cabinet, from 1910 to 1925, more than forty different companies made them. The trend towards built-in kitchen cabinets eventually led to the Hoosier cabinet's demise. But what goes around comes around, and today's cooks who are tired of the same old thing are scouring antique stores, farm auctions, and flea markets for this unique, and still useful, piece of Americana.

squash is tender, about 6 to 7 minutes. Transfer the contents to a bowl and mash the mixture coarsely with a fork. Stir in the remaining ingredients, and pour into the casserole dish.

3. Bake the casserole for 45 minutes, or until a knife inserted near the center comes out clean. Remove from the oven and let rest for 5 to 10 minutes. Serve hot.

GOLDEN NUGGET CUSTARD

I first cooked up this recipe on a mellow and sunny October afternoon, when the sky was a brilliant blue and a shower of leaves—yellow redbud, bronze pin oak, salmon and maroon Bradford pear, and scarlet maple—was falling outside. The day was made perfect and complete when this fragrant and comforting dish emerged from the oven.

6 Golden Nugget winter squashes
   or 6 acorn squashes
2 eggs, beaten
1 cup half-and-half
2 teaspoons fresh thyme leaves,
   preferably, or 1 teaspoon dried
   thyme
6 tablespoons fresh-grated
   Parmesan cheese
12 sprigs fresh thyme, optional,
   for garnish

1. Preheat the oven to 400 degrees. Lightly oil a baking sheet. Cut the squashes crosswise in half and scoop out and discard the seeds and stringy fibers. Trim the bottom of each squash half so it will stand up on the baking sheet. Transfer the squash halves, cut side up, to the baking sheet, and cover each with aluminum foil.

2. Bake the squash halves for 20 to 25 minutes to soften them. Remove from the oven and set aside. Keep the oven on.

3. Whisk together the eggs and half-and-half in a bowl. Add the thyme and whisk to blend it in. Spoon the egg mixture into the cavities of the squash, and sprinkle with Parmesan. Bake for 20 to 25 minutes more, or until the squash is tender when pierced with a small knife and the custard is softly set. Serve hot, garnished, if you like, with thyme sprigs.

SWEDISH TURNIP AND CARROT CHARLOTTE

Immigrants from northern Europe brought with them a variety of ways to make delicious use of root vegetables during the winter months. This colorful and fancy dish, for Sunday or company or both, might have been served when the pastor came to dinner or for another formal occasion.

1½ pounds small turnips, about
   2 to 3 inches in diameter and
   roughly uniform in size,
   peeled and cut into ¼-inch
   slices
2 large carrots, about 2 inches in
   diameter, peeled and cut
   crosswise into ¼-inch slices
1 cup heavy cream
½ teaspoon salt
½ teaspoon fresh-ground black
   pepper
⅛ teaspoon fresh-grated nutmeg
2 egg whites

1. Place the carrots and turnips in separate saucepans with water to cover. Bring both to a boil, and boil gently until tender, 15 to 20 minutes for each. Meanwhile, preheat the oven to 350 degrees and butter a 1-quart soufflé dish or charlotte mold. When the

vegetables are done, drain them.

2. Reserve ¾ cup of the cooked turnips and ⅓ cup of the cooked carrots. Arrange the remaining carrot and turnip slices in a decorative pattern on the bottom and sides of the buttered dish or mold. Puree the reserved ¾ cup turnips in a food processor. Add the cream, salt, pepper, and nutmeg, and puree again.

3. Whip the egg whites in a bowl until they form stiff peaks. Fold the pureed turnips into the egg whites until well blended. Pour the mixture into the vegetable-lined dish or mold. Arrange the reserved ⅓ cup carrots on the top (which will become the bottom). Place the dish or mold in a larger deep pan with enough water to reach 3 to 4 inches up the sides of the dish or mold. Bake the charlotte for 30 minutes, or until a knife inserted in the center comes out clean.

4. Remove the charlotte from the oven and from the water pan and let the charlotte cool and set for 10 minutes. Loosen the sides with a paring knife and invert onto a serving platter. Slice and serve hot or warm.

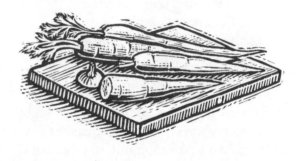

WILD HARVEST

The first waves of European pioneers in the midwest soon learned how to prepare foods that grew in the wild. Foods like huckleberries, chokecherries, native persimmons, fox grapes, native pecans and black walnuts, wild rice, and prickly pear were gathered from midsummer to early fall. In the spring, morels were delicious additions to the larder. Later in the fall, the banana-like paw-paw added variety. But because many settlers thought of gathering foods from the wild as a sign of desper-ation—what you had to do if you did not have a good garden or a productive farm—the practice often did not survive into the second generation of immigrant families.

Native Americans, from whom many of the settlers learned to forage, still do collect wild foods. In Ojibwa and Sioux communities in Minnesota and the Dakotas, for example, folks still gather juneberries and chokecherries to make into pies and jellies.

ZUCCHINI WITH SUMMER HERBS

If you have ever grown zucchini in your garden, you know what's coming. Zucchini are like toddlers—you have to watch them every minute. If you take your eyes off them, even for just a few hours of sleep, they get way too big and nearly inedible. Make this dish, a fine accompaniment for grilled chicken or fish, when these summer vegetables are small, tender, and flavorful.

SERVES 4

10 to 12 small zucchini, scrubbed
    but not peeled
1 tablespoon Dijon mustard
1 cup heavy cream or evaporated
    skim milk

2 tablespoons unsalted butter
2 tablespoons chopped fresh
    tarragon or 1 tablespoon dried
    tarragon
1 tablespoon minced fresh parsley
Salt and fresh-ground black
    pepper to taste

1. Grate the zucchini in a food processor or with a hand grater. You should have about 2 cups grated. Whisk together the mustard and cream in a small bowl.

2. Heat the butter in a heavy skillet over medium heat. Add the zucchini, and sauté it, stirring often, for 5 minutes. Add the mustard-cream mixture. Bring to a gentle simmer and simmer, uncovered, for 5 minutes, stirring occasionally, until the zucchini has absorbed much of the sauce and the mixture has thickened. Add the tarragon, parsley, salt, and pepper, and stir to blend. Transfer to a serving bowl, and serve hot.

FROM THE BREADBASKET

FROM THE BREADBASKET

Swedish Knackebrod

Homemade knackebrod, the original of which packaged rye crisp is a later imitation, gets snapped up fast at bake sales in Swedish communities throughout the northern Midwest. Once you have tasted the homemade variety, and once you know how easy it is to make, you will not want to go back to the packaged kind. Knackebrod is a wonderful accompaniment to homemade cheese spreads or a good, thick soup.

Makes about 24 pieces knackebrod

1⅓ *cups rye flour*
¾ *teaspoon sugar*
¼ *teaspoon salt*
4 *tablespoons unsalted butter*
⅓ *cup plus 1 tablespoon milk*

1. Preheat the oven to 300 degrees. Lightly oil a baking sheet. Combine the flour, sugar, and salt in a mixing bowl or in the food processor. Cut in the butter with a pastry blender, if you have a mixing bowl, or by processing in the food processor. Add the milk, a little at a time, by stirring with a spoon or by pulsing in the food processor, until you have a stiff dough.

2. Roll out the dough as thin as possible on a floured board. Cut the dough into 2-by-3-inch strips. Pierce small holes in the strips with the point of a small knife or with the tines of a fork. Bake the strips for 10 minutes, or until they are golden brown. Remove the knackebrod from the oven and let cool on racks. Serve warm or at room temperature. Stored in a plastic bag or other airtight container, knackebrod will keep well for 1 week.

Buttermilk Bannock

This is a simple bread of the dispossessed. Brought to Canada by Scots who were displaced from their lands during the infamous "clearances" of the late 1700s, bannock eventually would become one of the first breads that Native Americans learned to make when they were confined to reservations in the prairie states. Easy to prepare, bannock is a lowfat bread that is good for breakfast with a sweet or tart berry jelly.

Makes 1 round loaf

1½ *cups whole wheat flour or bread flour*
½ *teaspoon baking soda*
1 *teaspoon salt*
¼ *cup plus 2 tablespoons buttermilk*

1. Preheat the oven to 425 degrees. Lightly flour a baking sheet. Sift the flour, soda, and salt together into a mixing bowl, then invert the sifter and shake it so that the bran that

remains in it falls into the dry ingredients. Stir in the buttermilk with a wooden spoon to make a soft dough.

2. Shape the dough into a round and place the round on the baking sheet. Mark the top of the round in quarters with a sharp serrated knife. Lightly oil, or spray with cooking spray, a sheet of aluminum foil and cover the dough with the foil. Bake the bannock for 30 minutes, then remove the foil and bake for 10 minutes more, or until the crust has just browned. Remove from the oven to cool on a rack. Serve warm or at room temperature.

WASNA

In community cookbooks from Native American reservations in the prairie states, recipes range from ancient ones, handed down from the days before European contact, to modern ones, like tuna salad.

Sioux reservation cookbooks offer ways to make wasna, the high-energy fruitcake-like trail food that the Dakota Sioux have enjoyed for centuries, waskuya, a Sioux corn soup, and wojapi, a wild fruit sauce (see page 193). These dishes still turn up at potluck dinners after pow-wows or church. Reservation recipes like bannock and fry bread, from the early 1900s, recall the days when the government provided basic staples like flour, salt, soda, and bacon to Native Americans lately forced to give up their nomadic lifestyles.

In the community cookbook from Enemy Swim Lake in Waubay, South Dakota, is this Sioux recipe for corn wasna: "Use white flint corn. Grind to a fine texture. Brown over low heat in a heavy skillet. Add melted tallow and brown or maple sugar. Make into round balls and wrap in wax paper to preserve." Other versions of this dish call for 2½ pounds corn meal, 1 box of raisins or dried wild fruit, and 1 cup of melted beef suet or tallow.

Louise Erdrich, in her novel The Bingo Palace, tells of the Chippewa (Ojibwa) version of wasna. A character named Lipsha describes another woman, Zelda, who "draws out a foil-wrapped brick and presses it toward me. The thing is heavy as a doorstop. I don't need to ask—it is Zelda's old-time holiday fruitcake, made with traditional hand-gathered ingredients, chokecherries pounded with the pits still in them, dried buffalo meat, molasses, raisins, prunes, and anything else that carries weight. Winter traction, I think as I heft it."

sunflower seeds in a separate bowl. Stir the dry ingredients into the egg mixture until you have a rough batter; do not overmix.

2. Pour the batter into the baking pan. Bake the cornbread for 20 to 25 minutes, or until a toothpick inserted in the center comes out clean. Remove from the oven and serve hot or at room temperature.

IRISH POTATO GRIDDLE SCONES

My great-great-grandmother, Catherine McGriffin, emigrated to Ohio from Ireland in 1861, when she was twelve years old. Catherine married Dennis O'Neil, originally from Limerick, and one of their children was my great-grandmother, Anna O'Neil Mooney. My grandmother, Agnes Mooney, married a second-generation German immigrant whose family had a butcher shop in Lockland, Ohio. Agnes had a weak heart and died when the youngest of her four sons, my father, was only four years old. When she passed away, gone was the domestic and emotional comfort in the household—and any of the Old Country foodways she might have passed along to future granddaughters like me. I like to explore old Irish recipes as a way to open the door, if just a crack, to my immigrant past. Here is one I like.

MAKES 16 SCONES

1 large baking potato, peeled and coarsely chopped
4 tablespoons unsalted butter, melted
1 large egg, beaten
1/4 cup minced fresh parsley
3/4 cup unbleached all-purpose flour
Vegetable oil

1. Place the chopped potato in water to cover in a small saucepan. Bring to a boil, and cook for 10 minutes, or until the potato is just tender. Pour off the water and return the pan briefly to medium-high heat to evaporate any extra water. Mash the potato coarsely. Measure 1 cup of potato into a mixing bowl. Stir in the butter, egg, and parsley until the mixture is evenly blended. Stir in half of the flour, mix well, add the remaining flour, and stir well again.

2. Turn out the dough onto a floured board. Knead the dough for 3 to 4 minutes, until it is smooth and elastic. Cut the dough in half. Roll out one half on a floured board into a circle about 6 inches in diameter. Cut the circle into 8 wedges. Repeat the process with the remaining half of the dough.

3. Heat a cast-iron skillet or griddle and brush the surface with vegetable oil. Cook the scones, 6 to 8 at a time, for about 5 minutes on each side, or until they are puffed and lightly browned. Transfer to a plate and cover with a tea towel to keep warm as you cook the remaining batches. Serve hot or at room temperature.

HERBED BUTTERMILK SPOONBREAD

A southern dish that traveled up the Mississippi River and took root in Missouri, Iowa, and beyond, spoonbread is a lighter and more delicate version of baked grits. It's perfect paired with fried chicken, fried fish, or even with rabbit.

SERVES 4 TO 6

2 cups buttermilk
1½ cups yellow or white cornmeal, preferably stone-ground
1 teaspoon salt
1 tablespoon sugar
4 tablespoons unsalted butter

YEAST OF THE NEW EDEN

Yeast is the essence of homemade bread, what makes it aromatic and delicious. Each package of yeast contains thousands of tiny microorganisms. When nurtured by a warm liquid, such as water, and by sugar and starch, yeast molecules begin to bubble, releasing carbon dioxide gas. This process is what makes bread rise and beer foam.

Before packaged yeasts, homemakers had to make a leaven of flour mixed with water and leave it exposed to the air to ferment naturally. Austro-Hungarian immigrants to Missouri changed all of that. In 1868, brothers Charles and Maximillian Fleischmann transformed their yearning for the softer-textured breads of the Old World into a new yeast technology. In Europe, Charles had worked on new methods of commercial yeast production, and he helped introduce the technology in America. Along with American businessman Charles Graff, the Fleischmanns developed and patented a way to make cakes of compressed fresh yeast. They built a plant in Cincinnati to produce this revolutionary new way to leaven bread reliably.

During World War II, the company invented a way to dry yeast for the armed forces. Because fresh compressed yeast cakes require refrigeration, packets of dry yeast were better suited to wartime conditions. (A living organism, yeast goes into a dormant phase but is not killed when it is dried.) It is mainly professional bakers and serious hobbyists who now still use fresh yeast. Dry yeast is now the standard for home cooks.

2 tablespoons fresh thyme or
   1 teaspoon dried thyme
5 eggs
1 tablespoon baking powder
1 teaspoon fresh-ground black
   pepper

1. Preheat the oven to 425 degrees. Butter a 2-quart casserole dish or lightly oil a cast-iron skillet. Bring the buttermilk and 1½ cups water to a boil in a saucepan. Sprinkle the cornmeal, salt, and sugar into the liquid and whisk for 2 to 3 minutes until the mixture thickens. Remove from the heat, whisk in the butter and thyme, and set aside.

2. Whisk the eggs, baking powder, and pepper together in a large bowl until the mixture is frothy. Whisk in the cornmeal mixture until the batter is evenly blended. Pour the batter into the casserole dish or skillet. Bake the spoonbread for 30 minutes, or until it is puffed and golden brown. Remove from the oven, spoon onto individual plates, and serve hot.

Norwegian Potato Doughnuts

Make extra mashed potatoes the night before so that you can make these delectable treats the next morning. The doughnuts freeze well and may be reheated in the microwave or the oven.

Makes about 24 doughnuts

1½ cups hot mashed potatoes
⅓ cup shortening or unsalted
   butter
3 eggs
2 cups sugar
1 cup buttermilk
1 teaspoon vanilla extract
5½ cups all-purpose flour
4 teaspoons baking powder
1½ teaspoons baking soda
1 teaspoon salt
1 teaspoon fresh-grated nutmeg
Vegetable oil, for frying

1. If you have made the mashed potatoes the day before, reheat them. Stir the shortening into the potatoes in a small bowl. With an electric mixer, beat the eggs and sugar together in a separate large bowl for 3 to 4 minutes, or until the eggs are a pale yellow. Stir in the buttermilk and vanilla, then stir in the potatoes. Stir in the flour, baking powder, baking soda, salt, and nutmeg, and refrigerate, covered, for at least 1 hour.

2. Turn out the dough onto a floured surface, roll it to about a ½-inch thickness, and cut it with a doughnut cutter. Add the oil to a depth of 2 inches in a deep skillet, and heat the oil to a temperature of about 350 degrees. Fry the doughnuts in batches, turning them once, until both sides are browned, 2 to 3 minutes on each side. Transfer with a slotted

spoon to absorbent paper to drain. Serve warm or at room temperature.

FEATHERWEIGHT YEAST ROLLS

These light and yeasty dinner rolls require no kneading. They are even easier (but it is not required that you do so) if you make the dough in a bread machine and then finish the rolls by hand. The dough for these rolls is looser and more batter-like than traditional roll dough. When you go to the trouble of making homemade rolls, enjoy some, give some away, and freeze the rest.

MAKES ABOUT 48 ROLLS

1 cup lukewarm water
2 (1/4-ounce) packages active dry
    yeast
1 cup sugar
2 eggs, beaten
1/2 pound (2 sticks) plus 4
    tablespoons unsalted butter,
    softened
2 cups warm milk
2 teaspoons salt
7 cups all-purpose flour

1. *To make the dough by hand:* Pour the lukewarm water into a large bowl and sprinkle in the yeast and sugar; do not stir. Set aside to proof, uncovered, for 5 minutes. Add the eggs, 2 sticks of the butter, and the milk and mix together well with an electric mixer. Mix in the salt and then the flour, 1 cup at a time, until you have a smooth dough. Cover the bowl with a tea towel and let the dough rise in a warm place until it is doubled in bulk, about 1½ hours.

To make the dough in a bread machine: Pour the lukewarm water into the bread pan, and add the sugar, the eggs, 2 sticks of the butter, and the milk. Add the salt and flour, and then add the yeast. Select the dough cycle. When the dough is ready, lightly oil a large bowl, transfer the dough to the bowl, cover with a tea towel, and let the dough rise in a warm place until it is doubled in bulk, about 1½ hours.

2. Butter or oil 4 9-inch round cake pans. Dust your hands with a little flour, pinch off about ¼ cup of dough, and form the dough into a round. Place the round in a prepared cake pan, and continue until all the dough is used. You will have about 12 rolls in each pan. Cover each pan with a tea towel, and let the rolls rise in a warm place for 45 minutes. Meanwhile, preheat the oven to 425 degrees.

3. Bake the rolls for 20 minutes, or until they are lightly browned. While they are baking, melt the remaining 4 tablespoons of butter. Remove the rolls from the oven. While the rolls are still hot in the pan, brush the tops with the melted butter. Serve hot, warm, or at room temperature.

NEVER-FAIL REFRIGERATOR ROLLS

These traditional Sunday supper rolls are easy enough for a beginner but good enough for a gourmet. They get their name because the dough can be made well in advance and refrigerated. The finished rolls freeze well, too.

MAKES ABOUT 30 ROLLS

2 cups milk
1/2 cup sugar
1/2 cup shortening or unsalted butter
2 (1/4-ounce) packages active dry
    yeast
1 teaspoon salt
5 to 6 cups sifted all-purpose flour

1. Combine the milk, sugar, and shortening in a saucepan over medium-high heat and scald, but do not boil, the milk. Remove from the heat and let cool to lukewarm, about 90 degrees. Sprinkle the yeast on top (do not stir), and let stand for at least 5 minutes to proof to a foamy consistency. Stir the mixture to dissolve the yeast and add the salt. Pour the mixture into a large bowl. With an electric mixer, beat in the flour, 1 cup at a time, until the dough is firm.

2. Lightly oil a separate large bowl. Turn out the dough onto a floured board. Knead the dough gently until it is smooth and elastic. Transfer the dough to the oiled bowl, cover with a tea towel, and let the dough rise in a warm place until it is doubled in bulk, about 1 hour. (The dough may be made ahead to this point and refrigerated, covered, for up to 5 days.)

3. Punch the dough down and divide it in half. Lightly oil a large baking sheet. From each half of the dough, portion off 15 or 16 pieces and roll the pieces into round balls. Transfer the balls to the baking sheet. Cover the balls with tea towels and let the dough rise in a warm place until it is again doubled in bulk, about 45 minutes. Meanwhile, preheat the oven to 400 degrees.

4. Bake the rolls for 15 minutes, or until they are lightly browned. Transfer to a rack to cool slightly, and serve warm or at room temperature.

CARAWAY HORNS

Long a staple in the breadbaskets of up-scale midwestern restaurants, these stylish crescent rolls are easy to make at home.

MAKES 16 ROLLS

3 teaspoons sugar
1/2 cup lukewarm water
1 (1/4-ounce) package active dry
    yeast

1 tablespoon shortening or
    unsalted butter
1 egg, beaten
1/4 cup caraway seeds
3/4 teaspoon salt
1/2 cup milk
3 cups all-purpose flour
4 tablespoons unsalted butter,
    melted
1/4 cup coarse sea salt, kosher salt,
    or pretzel salt

1. Stir the sugar into the lukewarm water in a small bowl. Sprinkle the yeast over the surface; do not stir. Set aside for about 5 minutes to proof to a foamy consistency. With an electric mixer, cream together the shortening and egg in a large bowl. Mix in the caraway seeds, salt, and milk, and then mix in the yeast mixture. Mix in the flour, 1 cup at a time, until you have a stiff dough. Turn out the dough onto a floured board, and knead the dough until it is smooth and elastic. Lightly oil a large bowl, transfer the dough to the bowl, cover with a tea towel, and let the dough rise in a warm place until it is doubled in bulk, about 1 hour.

2. Lightly oil a baking sheet. Divide the dough into two roughly equal portions. Roll out one portion into a circle on a floured board, and cut the dough into 8 wedges. Roll up each wedge, starting with the wide end and ending with the point, and transfer the wedges, point side up, to the baking sheet. Bend each wedge slightly into a crescent shape. Repeat

POLISH EASTER

Carole Cottrill, a Cincinnatian, grew up in a Polish neighborhood and remembers going to church on Easter Saturday for the blessing of the food. "We would bring all of our Easter baked goods in baskets to be blessed, just like everyone else in the church," she told me. "When it came time for the priest to bless the food, everyone would carefully unfold the napkins that enclosed the food. The aromas that filled the church were indescribable."

Many such traditions are still alive. In the Polish neighborhoods along Milwaukee Avenue in Chicago, small groceries sell butter formed into the traditional lamb shape. Bakeries sell mazurek, the Polish Easter cake that is made with dried fruit and nuts, chruscik, which are fried pastries dusted with powdered sugar, almond babkas, and poppy seed coffeecakes.

A typical Polish Easter feast is like an all-day breakfast buffet. Dishes with eggs and ham, the butter lamb, and special breads and pastries underscore the theme of rebirth, of the spirit and of the landscape.

the process with the other half of the dough. Brush each of the crescents with a little of the melted butter and sprinkle with a little of the sea salt. Cover with a tea towel and let the dough rise in a warm place until it is again doubled in bulk, about 1 hour. Meanwhile, preheat the oven to 425 degrees.

3. Bake the rolls for 10 minutes, or until they are lightly browned. Transfer to a rack to cool down. Serve warm or at room temperature.

WILD RICE STALKS

These breadsticks are a decorative and tasty way to make use of one of Minnesota's best-known crops.

MAKES 16 BREADSTICKS

1 cup cooked wild rice, at room temperature
2 teaspoons salt
1½ cups hot (105 to 115 degrees) water
1 tablespoon sugar
2 (¼-ounce) packages active dry yeast
¼ cup canola oil or safflower oil
1½ teaspoons fennel seeds
½ cup rye flour, preferably dark rye flour, or pumpernickel flour

3½ cups bread flour
4 tablespoons unsalted butter, melted
1 egg beaten with 1 tablespoon water
3 tablespoons coarse salt, preferably sea salt

1. Preheat the oven to 375 degrees. Stir together the cooked wild rice, 2 teaspoons salt, hot water, and sugar in a large bowl. Sprinkle the yeast over the top of the mixture; do not stir. Let the mixture stand for 5 minutes, or until the yeast proofs to a foamy consistency. Stir in the ¼ cup of oil, fennel seeds, and rye flour. Stir in the bread flour, ½ cup at a time, until you have a stiff dough. Let the dough rest, uncovered, for 15 minutes.

2. Turn out the dough onto a floured board and cut it into 4 sections; then divide each section into 4 pieces to make 16 pieces in all. Lightly oil 2 baking sheets. Using your hands, roll each piece of dough to make a stalk 16 to 20 inches long, or the length of your baking sheets. Transfer the rolled stalks to the baking sheets, and brush the top and sides of the stalks with the melted butter. Using kitchen shears, snip diagonally into the top third of each stalk at random intervals to resemble the seed head of a grain stalk. Brush the stalks with the egg mixture and sprinkle with the coarse salt.

3. Bake the breadsticks for 20 to 25 minutes, or until they are browned and crisp. Remove from the heat and transfer to racks to cool. Serve warm or at room temperature.

HONEY-WHEAT HAMBURGER BUNS

Driving down to Wichita from Kansas City, you might stop for lunch in a small-town café. The menu may be limited—mostly sandwiches, burgers, soups, and pies—and it may or may not be the best food you have ever tasted. But if you order a burger chances are you will get an unexpected treat: a fresh-baked hamburger bun. Little extras like home-made buns can turn an everyday backyard barbecue into something special. Sliced and toasted on the grill, these buns are a fitting tribute to the first warm-weather grilled hamburger you have been hungering for all winter. This recipe freezes well; if you like, you can make a larger batch and freeze some for later.

MAKES ABOUT 36 HAMBURGER BUNS

1/2 pound (2 sticks) unsalted butter
1/2 cup wildflower, clover, or other
    medium-colored honey
2 cups boiling water
2 (1/4-ounce) packages active dry
    yeast
1/3 cup lukewarm water
1 teaspoon baking powder
2 teaspoons salt
2 eggs, beaten
3 1/2 cups whole wheat flour
3 1/2 cups white or unbleached
    all-purpose flour

1. Place the butter and honey in a large heat-proof bowl and pour the 2 cups boiling water over all. Stir the mixture and set it aside to cool. Meanwhile, sprinkle the yeast over the 1/3 cup lukewarm water in a separate bowl (do not stir), and set aside for 5 minutes to proof to a foamy consistency.

2. When the butter-honey mixture is cool enough to touch, use an electric mixer to beat in the baking powder, salt, and eggs. Add the yeast mixture, and blend it in well with the electric mixer. Mix in the whole wheat and all-purpose flours, about 1 cup at a time, alternating between the 2 flours. Turn out the dough onto a floured board and knead it for 10 minutes, or more if necessary, until the dough is elastic and shiny. Lightly oil a large bowl and transfer the dough to the bowl. Cover the bowl with a tea towel, and let the dough rise in a warm place until it is doubled in bulk, about 50 minutes.

3. Lightly oil 2 large or 3 medium baking sheets. Punch down the dough and turn it out onto a floured board. Pinch off pieces of dough, about 1/2 cup at a time, and shape each one into a round about 3 inches in diameter. Transfer the rounds, with ample space between them, to the baking sheets; you will have about three dozen buns. Cover with tea towels, and let the dough rise until it is again doubled in bulk, about 30 minutes. Meanwhile, preheat the oven to 400 degrees.

4. Bake the buns for 15 to 18 minutes, or until they are lightly browned. Serve warm, perhaps toasted, or at room temperature.

VARIATION:

The same recipe may be used to make dinner rolls. It will make about 50 of them. In step 3, break off smaller pieces of the dough and form them into rounds about 2 inches in diameter. Transfer them, fitting them snugly together, to 2 to 3 lightly oiled cake pans. Bake at 400 degrees for 10 to 12 minutes, or until lightly browned.

SAFFRON BUNS FOR ST. LUCIA DAY

These buns are the signature Swedish sweet rolls, well known and beloved throughout the upper midwest. Swedish-American families make them in a variety of shapes, including spirals, coxcombs, and in the form of a Lucia cat, with a small circle placed atop a larger circle. They are traditionally served on December 13, St. Lucia Day.

MAKES 20 SMALL BUNS OR
1 LARGE TEA RING

1 (1/4-ounce) package active dry yeast
1/4 cup lukewarm water
1/4 pound (1 stick) unsalted butter
1 cup half-and-half
1/2 cup sugar
1/2 teaspoon salt
1/2 teaspoon crushed saffron

1 egg, beaten
4 cups sifted all-purpose flour
Additional 1 egg, beaten
Additional 1/4 cup sugar, preferably coarse large-granule sugar
40 dark raisins

1. Sprinkle the yeast over the lukewarm water in a large bowl; do not stir. Set aside for 5 minutes to proof to a foamy consistency. Melt the butter in a small saucepan over low heat and add the half-and-half. When the mixture is just warmed through, pour it into the bowl with the yeast. Stir in the sugar, salt, saffron, and 1 egg. Beat in the flour with a wooden spoon until you have a smooth and spongy dough. Lightly oil a second large bowl, and transfer the dough to it. Cover with a tea towel, and let the dough rise in a warm place for 30 minutes or until it is doubled in bulk.

2. Turn out the dough onto a lightly floured board. Knead the dough until it is smooth and shiny, about 5 minutes. Lightly oil a large baking sheet.

3. *To make the buns:* Pinch off small pieces of dough and shape them into strips about 1/2 inch wide and 5 inches long. Transfer the strips, with ample room between them, to the baking sheet and shape each strip into an S figure (or another shape of your choice). Cover with tea towels and let the dough rise at room temperature until it is again doubled in bulk, about 1 hour. Meanwhile, preheat the oven to 400 degrees.

To make a tea ring: Roll the dough into a round about 2 inches thick. Cut the dough into 16 wedges. Place a 2½-inch-diameter glass tumbler on the baking sheet and arrange the dough wedges in a circle around the glass, with the point of each wedge touching the glass and the wide end of the wedge at the periphery, like the petals of a daisy. The wedges should just touch each other. Remove the glass, cover with a tea towel, and let the dough rise at room temperature until it is again doubled in bulk, about 1 hour. Meanwhile, preheat the oven to 400 degrees.

4. Brush the buns or the tea ring with the beaten egg and sprinkle with the additional ¼ cup sugar. Place a raisin in each loop of the S or distribute the raisins on top of the tea ring. Bake the buns for 10 to 12 minutes or the tea ring for 20 minutes, or until lightly browned. Transfer to a rack to cool slightly, and serve warm or at room temperature.

SOUR CREAM CINNAMON ROLLS

Midwesterners love their cinnamon rolls. Far from having the sweet, fragrant treats only at breakfast or for a coffee break, they will serve them and eat them just about anytime. Homestyle chicken dinner emporiums throughout the Heartland serve the rolls warm and tender in a basket to accompany your feast. The rolls are a must at school and church suppers, potlucks, and "chili feeds." A friend or family member in need of a little TLC will perk up immediately when you bring homemade cinnamon rolls and say, "Let's put on the coffee." Make extra batches, if you like, and freeze them after they are baked.

MAKES ABOUT 24 ROLLS

FOR THE DOUGH:
    1 (¼-ounce) package active dry yeast
    ¼ cup lukewarm water
    1 cup sour cream
    2 tablespoons unsalted butter
    3 tablespoons granulated sugar
    ⅛ teaspoon baking soda
    1 teaspoon salt
    1 large egg
    3 cups all-purpose flour

FOR THE FILLING:
    ¾ cup packed dark or light brown sugar
    1½ teaspoons ground cinnamon
    4 tablespoons unsalted butter, melted

FOR THE GLAZE:
    ¾ cup confectioners' sugar
    2 tablespoons milk or light cream
    ½ teaspoon vanilla extract

1. Prepare the dough: Sprinkle the yeast over the lukewarm water in a small bowl; do not stir. Set aside to proof to a foamy consistency. Heat the sour cream in a saucepan over low heat, stirring occasionally, until the sour

cream is lukewarm, about 4 minutes. Add the butter, sugar, baking soda, and salt, and cook, stirring occasionally, until the butter is melted, about 5 minutes more. Transfer the mixture to a mixing bowl, and, using an electric mixer, blend in the egg and the yeast mixture. Mix in the flour, ½ cup at a time; you will have a sticky and somewhat thick dough. Turn out the dough onto a floured board and knead it for 3 to 4 minutes, or until the dough is elastic and no longer sticky. Return the dough to the bowl, cover with a damp tea towel, and let the dough rise for 10 minutes.

2. Prepare the filling: Combine the sugar and the cinnamon in a bowl and set aside. Divide the dough in half, and transfer one of the halves to a floured board. Roll out the dough into a 13-by-10-inch rectangle that is about ¼ inch thick. Brush half of the melted butter over the surface of the dough and sprinkle it with half of the cinnamon-sugar mixture. Roll up the dough in jelly-roll fashion, starting with the long side that is least even; you will end up with a roll about 13 inches long. Lightly oil a baking sheet. Cut the roll into 1-inch lengths and place each piece, with a spiral side facing up, on the baking sheet. Repeat the process with the other half of the dough. Cover the cinnamon rolls with a tea towel, and let them rise for 1 hour, or until they have about doubled in bulk. Meanwhile, preheat the oven to 375 degrees.

3. Bake the cinnamon rolls for 15 minutes, or until they are puffed and browned. While the rolls bake, make the glaze: Whisk together the confectioners' sugar and the milk in a bowl. When the mixture is smooth, whisk in the vanilla.

4. Remove the rolls from the oven, and, while they are still hot, drizzle them with the glaze. Let them cool slightly on their sheet or on racks. Serve warm or at room temperature.

VARIATION:

To make sticky buns, omit the glaze and replace it in the following manner. Melt 4 tablespoons unsalted butter in a saucepan, add ¾ cup packed brown sugar (and, if you like, ½ cup chopped pecans), stir until the mixture is evenly blended, and spread on the baking sheet before you roll out the dough. Place the cinnamon rolls directly on this mixture, then let rise and bake as above. When you remove the baked cinnamon rolls from the oven, immediately invert the baking sheet on aluminum foil and let the cinnamon rolls cool with the sticky glaze on top.

WHEAT COUNTRY ZWIEBACK

At Vern and Janice Demel's Country Kitchen restaurant in Moundridge, Kansas, about an hour north of Wichita, platters of zwieback—small yeast rolls with the shape of a brioche—are served as part of weekend buffets that feature traditional homestyle Russian Mennonite dishes. During the long journey from the Ukraine to central

Kansas in the 1870s, Mennonite families packed large sacks of toasted zwieback to eat along the way. Bakeries in mid-Kansas still sell fresh zwieback as well as bags of toasted zwieback. Zwieback are typically served and eaten as dinner rolls. They are also delicious sliced and toasted in a slow oven.

MAKES 4 DOZEN ZWIEBACK

1½ tablespoons quick-rising
   active dry yeast
½ cup plus 1 tablespoon sugar
1 cup lukewarm water
2 cups scalded milk
2½ teaspoons salt
2 eggs, beaten
12 tablespoons unsalted butter,
   melted, or 12 tablespoons
   shortening, melted
8 to 10 cups all-purpose flour

1. Sprinkle the yeast and the 1 tablespoon sugar over the lukewarm water in a bowl; do not stir. Set aside for at least 5 minutes to proof to a foamy consistency. With an electric mixer, blend together the ½ cup sugar and the milk, salt, eggs, and butter in a large bowl. Add the yeast mixture and blend evenly.

2. Mix in the flour, 1 cup at a time, until you have a soft and pliant dough. Cover the bowl with a tea towel and let the dough rise in a warm place until it is doubled in bulk, about 30 minutes. Punch down the dough, cover it, and let it rise until it is again doubled, about 30 minutes more.

3. Lightly oil 2 large baking sheets. Turn out the dough onto a floured surface. Cut out and set aside one-fourth of the dough. Divide the remaining three-fourths of the dough into 4 equal portions. Form 12 balls of dough from each of the 4 portions; the balls will be about 3 inches in diameter. Place the balls 2 inches apart on the baking sheets. With the reserved one-fourth of the dough, make 48 smaller balls of dough. Using your thumb, make an indentation in the center of each of the larger balls. Place a smaller ball in each indentation, and press down gently.

4. Cover the zwieback with a tea towel and let them rise until they are again doubled in bulk, about 30 minutes more. Meanwhile, preheat the oven to 400 degrees. Bake the zwieback for 15 to 17 minutes, or until they are lightly browned. Remove from the oven and transfer to racks to cool.

VARIATION:

Zwieback that have been sliced and then toasted in the oven may be iced. Combine 2 tablespoons cream or milk, ¼ teaspoon vanilla extract, and ½ cup confectioners' sugar in a saucepan over medium-low heat. When the mixture is heated through, drizzle it over the zwieback after they have come out of the oven but while they are still hot.

MA'S SOURDOUGH STARTER

The Little House *series is perhaps the best chronicle of early pioneer food on the prairie. In* By the Shores of Silver Lake, *which takes place in the Dakota Territory, Laura Ingalls Wilder tells how Ma made her sourdough starter. Ma would put some flour and warm water in a jar and let it stand, uncovered, until it captured yeast from the air and soured. From this, she would make a sponge that would become the basis for breads, biscuits, and pancakes. Every few days, she would feed the starter with flour and liquid.*

Before packaged yeast and factory-milled flours were available, these sourdough breads made from a sponge starter were the norm. They required a long rising time and had a spongy, chewy texture from the hand-milled grain and the natural yeast. Today, such breads are making a comeback as artisan breads. After a century or so, the time- and labor-intensive everyday breads of Great Plains settlers are back in fashion.

AMISH FRIENDSHIP STARTER

A couple of years ago, my good friend Vicki Johnson, a professional food stylist (someone who prepares food for photography) and a great home cook, gave me a batch of this starter, which she has had for more than twenty years and which is said to have originated in an Amish community. I use it to make sourdough pancakes, scones, biscuits, and bread. I have not always followed precisely the directions for feeding it (see step 5 below), but the sourdough is very forgiving. Ideally, you get a sweetened starter like this from a friend. When you have accumulated more starter than you can use, you pass along a cup of the treasure to another friend. In the absence of such a generous friend, here is how you can start your own starter. If the feed-and-bake, feed-and-bake cycle gets to be too much, or if you are going to be away from home for a few weeks, simply use the 1 cup you remove in step 5 and freeze the rest. Bring the frozen starter to room temperature, and begin with step 5 again.

MAKES ABOUT 8 CUPS STARTER

4 cups all-purpose flour
2 cups lukewarm (90 degrees) water
1 (¼-ounce) package active dry yeast
2 cups milk
2 cups sugar

1. On Day 1: With a whisk or a wooden spoon, mix 2 cups of the flour, the lukewarm water, and the yeast thoroughly in a glass or ceramic bowl. Let the mixture sit, uncovered, on a kitchen counter; do not refrigerate.

2. On Day 5: Stir the yeast-flour mixture with a wooden spoon. Stir in 1 cup of the flour, 1 cup of the milk, and 1 cup of the sugar. Stir well. This step is called "feeding the starter." Let the mixture sit, uncovered, on a kitchen counter; do not refrigerate.

3. On Day 9: Stir the mixture and add the remaining 1 cup flour, 1 cup milk, and 1 cup sugar. Stir well. Let the mixture sit, uncovered, on a kitchen counter; do not refrigerate.

4. On Day 12: Ladle 1 cup starter into a plastic container with a lid. Freeze for safe-keeping (in case you forget to feed your starter and it expires). Ladle the rest of the starter (you should have about 7 cups) into a larger plastic container with a lid and refrigerate, covered, until you wish to use it.

5. Ten days later, feed your refrigerated starter again. Begin by removing 1 cup starter; reserve this cup to use in a recipe or to give to a friend, or discard it. Add ¼ cup sugar, 1 cup flour, and 1 cup milk to the remaining starter in the container. Stir well to blend and return, covered, to the refrigerator. (The starter will be ready to use again—that is, it will have reached the "sourdough point"— after 4 more days.) Repeat step 5 every 10 days.

NOTE: If bacteria take over the starter and it takes on a pink color and an offensive smell, discard it.

AMISH FRIENDSHIP SCONES

The flavorings for these scones may be chosen according to what is in season or in your larder. Raisins soaked in rum, dried cranberries or dried cherries, chopped ripe apple or pear, fresh blueberries tossed in flour spiced with ground cinnamon (so that the berries will not bleed into the batter), or grated cheddar cheese are all attractive options. Using the Friendship Starter (see the previous recipe) is as easy as using a mix, but the finished product will be twice as good.

MAKES 12 SCONES

1 cup Amish Friendship Starter or
　　other prepared sourdough
　　starter
1 cup self-rising flour
1 egg yolk, beaten
¼ cup plus 2 tablespoons unsalted
　　butter, melted
1 teaspoon vanilla extract
¾ cup fresh fruit, such as chopped
　　apple or pear, or dried fruit,
　　such as raisins, cranberries,
　　or cherries, mixed with 2
　　tablespoons sugar, optional
¾ cup grated cheddar cheese,
　　optional

1. Preheat the oven to 400 degrees. With a wooden spoon, stir together the starter, flour, egg yolk, ¼ cup of the butter, vanilla, and, if

you are using it, the fruit or the cheese together in a mixing bowl. Turn out the dough onto a floured board. Knead the dough until it is elastic, 3 to 4 minutes. Pat the dough into a circle and cut it into biscuit shapes with a 2-inch biscuit cutter, or into wedges. Brush the scones with the remaining 2 tablespoons of butter.

2. Lightly oil a baking sheet. Transfer the scones to the sheet, and bake them for 12 to 15 minutes, or until they are lightly browned. Transfer to racks to cool slightly, and serve warm or at room temperature.

GOLDEN BUFFALO BREAD

This is a simple and very fine bread with a yeasty flavor, a soft crumb, and wonderful keeping qualities. I have named it after one of my favorite products from my home state, Golden Buffalo organic bread flour, which is produced in Marienthal, in western Kansas. The bread makes delicious toast.

MAKES 2 LOAVES

1/2 cup plus 3 tablespoons sugar
4 cups lukewarm water
2 (1/4-ounce) packages active dry yeast
6 cups good-quality bread flour, such as Golden Buffalo
7 tablespoons powdered whole milk
2 teaspoons salt
2 eggs, beaten
6 tablespoons canola oil or safflower oil
1/2 cup honey
1 1/2 to 2 cups all-purpose flour

1. Stir the 3 tablespoons of sugar into 2 1/2 cups of the lukewarm water in a small bowl. Sprinkle the yeast over the top; do not stir. Set aside for at least 5 minutes to proof to a bubbling consistency.

2. Stir together 3 cups of the bread flour, the powdered milk, the salt, and the remaining 1/2 cup sugar in a large bowl. With an electric mixer, blend in the yeast mixture and then the eggs, oil, and 1 cup of the lukewarm water. Mix well, then add the remaining 3 cups of the bread flour, 1 cup at a time. Add the remaining 1/2 cup of lukewarm water and the honey.

3. Sprinkle 1/2 cup of the all-purpose flour on a board, turn out the bread dough onto the floured board, and sprinkle the dough with another 1/2 cup of the all-purpose flour. With a dough scraper, scrape the top half of the dough over and down to fold the dough in half. Give the dough a quarter turn and repeat, dusting with more all-purpose flour if the dough is sticky. Keep folding over and turning until the dough is pliable and not sticky. Scrape the top half of the dough over and down 1 more time, then knead the dough from the bottom upwards. Knead 15 times.

4. Lightly oil a large bowl. Transfer the dough to the bowl, cover with a tea towel, and let the dough rise in a warm place until it is doubled in bulk, about 2 hours.

5. Preheat the oven to 350 degrees. Oil 2 9-by-5-by-3-inch loaf pans. Turn out the dough onto a floured board, cut the dough evenly in half, and transfer each half to a loaf pan. Set the loaves aside, uncovered, to rise for 15 minutes. Bake the loaves for 30 minutes, or until the loaf pulls away from the sides of the pan and a thump with your fingers yields a hollow sound. Remove from the oven and transfer to a rack to cool.

HOW WARM IS LUKEWARM?

Dry yeast must be proofed in a lukewarm liquid. (By becoming foamy or bubbly, and giving off carbon dioxide, the yeast "proves" that it is still alive and active, ready to go to work.) With practice, an experienced baker can tell by feel when a liquid is lukewarm. Because yeast is killed at temperatures over 130 degrees, beginning bread bakers would be wise to use an instant-read thermometer for recipes that call for starting yeast in lukewarm water. Ninety to 120 degrees is the range within which water is lukewarm for proofing; the middle part of the range is considered ideal.

BUTTERMILK-OATMEAL BREAD

The traditional three-year crop rotation in the midwest has been corn the first year, wheat or oats the second year, and hay in the third year. One of the largest oat-processing centers in the United States is Cedar Rapids, Iowa. This oat-rich bread has become our household favorite for everyday eating.

MAKES 1 1½-POUND LOAF

2 teaspoons quick-rising active
    dry yeast
1¼ cups lukewarm water
3½ cups bread flour
¼ cup rolled oats
2 tablespoons sugar
1 teaspoon salt
2 tablespoons unsalted butter,
    melted
½ cup buttermilk

1. Sprinkle the yeast over the lukewarm water in a small bowl; do not stir. Set aside for at least 5 minutes to proof to a foamy consistency. Stir together the flour, oats, sugar, and salt in a large bowl. Add the butter, buttermilk, and yeast mixture and beat with an electric mixer until the ingredients are well blended. Turn out the dough onto a floured board and knead for about 5 minutes, until the dough is smooth and elastic. Lightly oil a large bowl, and transfer the dough to the bowl. Cover with a tea towel, and let the

dough rise in a warm place until it is doubled in bulk, about 1 hour.

2. Punch the dough down and let it rise again, covered with a tea towel, for 45 minutes. Meanwhile, preheat the oven to 350 degrees and oil a 9-by-5-by-3-inch loaf pan.

3. Punch the dough down again and place it in the loaf pan. Bake for 35 to 40 minutes, or until the loaf pulls away from the sides of the pan and a thump with your fingers yields a hollow sound.

VARIATION:

To make in a bread machine, add the ingredients to the machine's bread pan in the order suggested by the manufacturer. Use the regular white cycle and the medium crust setting.

MENNONITE OATMEAL-WHOLE WHEAT BREAD

This hearty bread, perfect for sandwiches, has a full but still delicate flavor and, for a whole wheat bread, a surprisingly soft crumb. The recipe is a common one in wheat-farming Mennonite communities in Kansas, the Dakotas, Saskatchewan, and Manitoba. The secret to this bread is measuring the all-purpose flour by weight, not by volume.

MAKES 1 1½-POUND LOAF

1½ teaspoons quick-rising active dry yeast
¾ cup lukewarm water
15¾ ounces all-purpose flour
⅜ cup whole wheat flour
⅜ cup quick-cooking rolled oats
1½ teaspoons salt
3 tablespoons dark or light brown sugar
3 tablespoons canola oil or safflower oil
¾ cup milk

1. Sprinkle the yeast over the lukewarm water in a small bowl; do not stir. Set aside for at least 5 minutes to proof to a foamy consistency. Stir together the all-purpose flour, whole wheat flour, oats, salt, and brown sugar in a large bowl. Stir in the yeast mixture, oil, and milk, and continue stirring until the dough forms a soft ball. Lightly oil a large bowl, and transfer the dough to the bowl. Cover with a tea towel, and let the dough rise in a warm place until it is doubled in bulk, about 1 hour.

2. Punch down the dough and let it rise, covered with a tea towel, until it is again doubled in bulk, about 1 hour more. Meanwhile, preheat the oven to 350 degrees and lightly oil a 9-by-5-by-3-inch loaf pan. Transfer the dough to the loaf pan, and bake the bread for 30 minutes, or until it is browned and a thump with your fingers yields a hollow sound. Remove from the oven and transfer to a rack to cool.

VARIATION:

To make in a bread machine, add the ingredients to the machine's bread pan in the order suggested by the manufacturer. Use the white cycle. After 5 minutes into the knead cycle, check the dough: It should form a soft ball around the kneading paddle. If too dry, add water 1/2 tablespoon at a time. If too wet, add more all-purpose flour.

POLISH POPPY SEED BREAD

This is a festive and complex bread that is typically served, in Polish-American homes, at Easter or for a Wigilia (see page 247) buffet. Although it has an Old Country taste and feel, it can be made in the bread machine; see the Variation.

MAKES 1 1½-POUND LOAF

2¼ teaspoons active dry yeast
1 cup plus 1 tablespoon lukewarm
    water
3 cups bread flour
3 tablespoons powdered whole milk
1½ teaspoons salt

3 tablespoons poppy seeds
1½ tablespoons grated orange zest
¼ cup honey
3 tablespoons unsalted butter,
    melted
1 egg, beaten
1 egg yolk, beaten
⅓ cup dark or golden raisins
⅓ cup slivered almonds

1. Sprinkle the yeast over the lukewarm water in a small bowl; do not stir. Set aside for at least 5 minutes to proof to a foamy consistency. With a wooden spoon, mix together the flour, powdered milk, salt, and poppy seeds in a large bowl. Add the yeast mixture and mix evenly with an electric mixer. Add the orange zest, honey, butter, egg, and egg yolk, and mix until you have a firm dough. Mix in the raisins and almonds. Turn out the dough onto a floured board and knead for 5 minutes, or until the dough is elastic and not sticky. Lightly oil a large bowl, and transfer the dough to the bowl. Cover with a tea towel, and let the dough rise in a warm place until it is doubled in bulk, 1¼ to 1½ hours.

2. Punch the dough down and let it rise again, covered with a tea towel, until it is again doubled in bulk, 45 minutes to 1 hour. Meanwhile, preheat the oven to 375 degrees and lightly oil a 9-by-5-by-3-inch loaf pan.

3. Transfer the dough to the loaf pan and let it rise, covered with a tea towel, for 15 minutes. Bake the loaf for 35 to 45 minutes, or until the loaf pulls away from the sides of the pan and a thump with your fingers yields

a hollow sound. Remove from the oven and transfer to a rack to cool.

VARIATION:

To make in a bread machine, add all of the ingredients except the raisins and almonds in the order suggested by the manufacturer for sweet breads. Use the sweet bread cycle. At the beep, add the raisins and almonds.

SAUERKRAUT RYE BREAD

This is a great Old World bread for sandwiches of grilled bratwursts and horseradish or of shaved ham and mayonnaise. Cocoa powder, the surprising ingredient here, deepens both the color and the flavor of the bread.

MAKES 1 1½-POUND LOAF

½ cup lukewarm water
2 tablespoons light unsulphured molasses
2 teaspoons quick-rising active dry yeast
1¼ cups bread flour, or more if necessary
1 cup whole wheat bread flour
1¼ cups rye flour or pumpernickel flour
2 tablespoons cocoa powder
3 tablespoons caraway seeds
1¼ teaspoons salt

¾ cup chopped sauerkraut, drained with ½ cup of the sauerkraut liquid reserved
½ cup buttermilk
3 tablespoons canola oil or safflower oil
2 tablespoons Dijon mustard

1. Stir together the lukewarm water and molasses in a small bowl. Sprinkle the yeast over the top; do not stir. Set aside for at least 5 minutes to proof to a foamy consistency.

2. Stir together the 1¼ cups bread flour and the whole wheat bread flour, rye flour, cocoa, caraway seeds, and salt in a large bowl. With an electric mixer, mix in the sauerkraut and its reserved liquid, buttermilk, oil, and mustard. Add the yeast mixture and mix well to form a stiff dough, adding more bread flour if necessary. Turn out the dough onto a floured board and knead for 5 minutes, or until the dough becomes soft and elastic. Lightly oil a large bowl, and transfer the dough to the bowl. Cover with a tea towel, and let the dough rise in a warm place until it is doubled in bulk, about 1 hour. Punch the dough down and let it rise, covered with a tea towel, until it is again doubled in bulk, about 45 minutes. Meanwhile, preheat the oven to 350 degrees and lightly oil a 9-by-5-by-3-inch loaf pan.

3. Transfer the dough to the loaf pan. Bake the bread for 30 to 35 minutes, or until a thump with your fingers yields a hollow sound. Remove from the oven and transfer to a rack to cool.

VARIATION:

To make with a bread machine, add all of the ingredients to the machine's bread pan in the order suggested by the manufacturer. Use the whole wheat cycle with the medium crust setting. Because the moisture content of the sauerkraut may vary, you might have to add a bit more bread flour if the sauerkraut is on the wet side. Check the dough after 5 minutes on the knead cycle and, if it is sticky and has not formed into a ball, sprinkle in more bread flour, 1 tablespoon at a time, until the dough is firm enough.

DOUBLE TROUBLE

Many bread recipes, and some pastry recipes, tell you to let the dough rise until it has doubled in bulk. How do you know when it has? It certainly is not easy to measure the volume of such an unevenly shaped mass. You are left to trust what your eyes tell you and to rely on the suggested timing in the recipe. (The time it takes for the dough to double in bulk depends on the temperature and on the amounts and types of ingredients in the recipe.) Another way to test: Press two fingers about 1/2 inch into the top of the dough. If the dough feels light and spongy, and the depressions in the dough remain, then the dough has risen sufficiently.

SLAVIC POTATO BREAD

Here is a moist, slightly savory bread that is good served with smoked sausages and chunks of a hearty cheese.

MAKES 1 1-POUND LOAF

3/4 cup Fresh Farmhouse Cheese
    (page 39) or ricotta cheese
2 teaspoons active dry yeast
1/3 cup lukewarm water
2 2/3 cups bread flour
3/4 teaspoon fresh-grated nutmeg
3/4 teaspoon salt
1/4 teaspoon cayenne pepper
3/4 cup cooked mashed potatoes,
    at room temperature
1 egg, beaten
1 egg yolk, beaten

1. Drain the cheese in a sieve lined with cheesecloth for 30 minutes.

2. Sprinkle the yeast over the lukewarm water in a small bowl. Set aside for at least 5 minutes to proof to a foamy consistency. Stir together the flour, nutmeg, salt, and cayenne in a mixing bowl.

3. With an electric mixer or a wooden spoon, combine the cheese and the potatoes in a large bowl. Blend in the egg and the egg yolk. Mix in the seasoned flour mixture, 1/2 cup at a time, until you have a stiff dough. Turn out

the dough onto a floured board and knead for about 5 minutes, until the dough is smooth. Lightly oil a large bowl, and transfer the dough to the bowl. Cover with a tea towel, and let the dough rise in a warm place until it is doubled in bulk, about 1 hour. Meanwhile, lightly oil a 9-by-5-by-3-inch loaf pan.

4. Punch the dough down and transfer it to the loaf pan. Let it rise, covered with a tea towel, for 1 hour more. Meanwhile, preheat the oven to 350 degrees.

5. Bake the bread for 40 to 45 minutes, or until a thump with your fingers yields a hollow sound and the bread pulls away from the side of the pan. Remove from the oven and transfer to a rack to cool.

VARIATION:

To make in a bread machine, drain the cheese in a sieve lined with cheesecloth for 30 minutes. Add all of the ingredients in the order suggested by the manufacturer. Use the white cycle.

SAFFRON BREAD

Scandinavian-American families cook a lot of breads and pastries with saffron (also see Saffron Buns, page 343). The dough needs to sit overnight before baking so that the saffron flavor will develop. The bread makes a good toast, and I also use its crumbs to top vegetable dishes and fish dishes.

MAKES 1 LOAF

2 (1/4-ounce) packages active dry yeast
1/2 cup lukewarm water
1/4 pound (1 stick) unsalted butter, melted, brought to room temperature
1 cup milk
1/2 cup sugar
2 eggs, lightly beaten
1/4 teaspoon crushed saffron
4 cups all-purpose flour

1. The night before you will bake the bread, sprinkle the yeast over the lukewarm water in a large bowl; do not stir. Set aside for at least 5 minutes to proof to a foamy consistency. Mix together the butter and milk in a small bowl and stir this mixture into the yeast mixture. Stir in the sugar, 1 of the eggs, and the saffron. Using an electric mixer, beat in the flour, 1 cup at a time, until the dough is smooth. Cover the bowl and refrigerate the dough overnight.

2. The next day, turn out the dough onto a lightly floured surface. Knead the dough until it is smooth and shiny, about 5 minutes. Lightly oil a 9-by-5-by-3-inch loaf pan and transfer the dough to the loaf pan. Cover with a tea towel, and let rise in a warm place until doubled in bulk, about 2 hours. Meanwhile, preheat the oven to 350 degrees.

3. Brush the top of the loaf with the remaining egg. Bake the bread for 25 minutes, or until a thump with your fingers yields a hollow sound and the bread pulls away from the side of the pan. Remove from the oven and transfer to a rack to cool.

WHEN IS BREAD DONE?

For novice bakers and even for experienced ones, telling when a loaf of bread is done can be a challenge. You can look for a toasty color in the crust, you can check to see when the loaf pulls away from the side of the pan, and you can listen for a hollow sound when you tap the loaf with your fingertips. These time-tested indicators usually work. If you have an instant-read thermometer, you can tell more precisely when your loaf is done. Insert the thermometer into the center of the loaf; the bread is done if the internal temperature is 200 degrees. Some breads are done at slightly different temperatures, but the range for most loaves falls within 5 or 10 degrees of 200, so it is a good figure to keep in mind.

BLUE CHEESE BREAD

This is a savory bread, actually bluish in color, that I like to serve alongside a tomato salad for a light summer lunch. The bread makes terrific croutons, too, for salads and soups.

MAKES 1 1½-POUND LOAF

1 (¼-ounce) package active dry
    yeast
¼ cup lukewarm water
3 cups bread flour
1 tablespoon sugar
1 teaspoon baking powder
1 teaspoon salt
1 cup lukewarm buttermilk
8 ounces crumbled blue cheese,
    such as Maytag Blue from
    Iowa, at room temperature

1. Sprinkle the yeast over the lukewarm water in a small bowl. Set aside for at least 5 minutes to proof to a foamy consistency. With a wooden spoon, combine the flour, sugar, baking powder, and salt in a large bowl. Using an electric mixer, mix in the buttermilk and the yeast mixture. Add the cheese and mix well.

2. Turn out the dough onto a floured board and knead until the dough is elastic and not sticky, about 5 minutes. Lightly oil a large bowl, and transfer the dough to the bowl.

Cover with a tea towel, and let the dough rise in a warm place until it is doubled in bulk, about 1 hour. Punch the dough down, cover with a tea towel, and let rise again for 45 minutes. Meanwhile, preheat the oven to 350 degrees and oil a 9-by-5-by-3-inch loaf pan.

3. Transfer the dough to the loaf pan. Bake the bread for about 45 minutes, or until a thump with your fingers yields a hollow sound and the bread pulls away from the side of the pan. Remove from the oven and transfer to a rack to cool.

VARIATION:

To make in a bread machine, place all of the ingredients in the machine's bread pan in the order suggested by the manufacturer. Use the white cycle.

BRAIDED CHEDDAR-ALE BREAD

Cheese and beer, great go-togethers, give this bread a robust and heartwarming flavor. I serve it as part of an appetizer spread, along with a selection of midwestern sausages, and I use it for sandwiches as well.

MAKES 1 1-POUND LOAF

*1/2 cup ale or other medium-
bodied beer*

3/4 teaspoon sugar
1/2 cup lukewarm water
*1 (1/4-ounce) package active dry
yeast*
1/4 cup canola oil or safflower oil
1 egg, beaten
*1/4 cup packed dark or light brown
sugar*
1 teaspoon salt
1 cup whole wheat flour
*2 cups all-purpose flour, or more if
necessary*
*2 1/4 cups shredded aged cheddar
cheese*
*1 egg yolk, beaten with 1
tablespoon water*

1. Bring the ale to a boil in a small saucepan. Remove immediately from the heat and stir briefly to reduce the foam. Set aside to cool to lukewarm. Meanwhile, dissolve the sugar in the lukewarm water in a small bowl. Sprinkle the yeast over the top and let stand for 10 minutes to proof to a frothy consistency.

2. With an electric mixer, combine the lukewarm ale with the oil, egg, brown sugar, salt, whole wheat flour, and 2 cups all-purpose flour in a large bowl. Pour in the yeast mixture, and beat until smooth. Mix in additional all-purpose flour, if necessary, to make a soft dough. Add 2 cups of the cheese, and mix well.

3. Turn out the dough onto a lightly floured surface. Knead for 8 to 10 minutes, adding more all-purpose flour, if necessary, to make a dough that is smooth and elastic. Generously

oil a large bowl, transfer the dough to the bowl, and turn the dough mass several times to coat it with oil. Cover with plastic wrap, and let the dough rise in a warm place until it is doubled in bulk, about 1½ hours.

4. Oil a large baking sheet. Punch down the dough, turn it out onto a lightly floured surface, and divide it into 3 equal portions. Gently roll each portion into a rope about 12 inches long. Place the 3 ropes side by side on the baking sheet. Loosely braid together the 3 sections. At the 2 ends of the loaf, pinch the ropes together, and tuck them under the loaf slightly, to form a smooth surface. Brush the top of the loaf with the egg yolk mixture. Sprinkle the loaf with the remaining ¼ cup cheese. Cover the loaf with tea towels and let rise in a warm place until again doubled in bulk, about 1¼ hours. Meanwhile, preheat the oven to 350 degrees.

5. Bake the bread for 40 to 45 minutes, or until a thump from your fingers yields a hollow sound. Remove from the oven and let cool.

FRENCH PEAR BREAD

When my two Kieffer pear trees are ready to harvest in late August or early September, I know I am in for a glut of pears. Because these pears are better for cooking than for eating raw, I look for recipes to make with my bounty. One of my favorites is to drizzle pear slices with a good honey and bake them until they are softened and browned; I usually make extra so that I can use the baked pears in this bread. A pretty pale yellow, and with a soft and spongy texture, the bread is especially good toasted and spread with Gingered Pear Butter (page 66) or a store-bought pear butter.

MAKES 1 1½-POUND LOAF

1 tablespoon honey
¼ cup lukewarm water
1 teaspoon quick-rising active
    dry yeast
3 cups bread flour, or more if
    necessary
¾ teaspoon salt
¼ teaspoon fresh-grated nutmeg
¾ cup mashed Honey-Baked
    Pears (page 374, step 1 only),
    mashed canned and drained
    pears, or Gingered Pear
    Butter (page 66)
1 egg, beaten

1. Stir the honey into the lukewarm water in a small bowl. Sprinkle the yeast over the top and set aside for at least 5 minutes to proof to a foamy consistency.

2. Stir together the 3 cups flour and the salt and nutmeg in a medium bowl. With an electric mixer or a wooden spoon, combine the pears and the egg in a large bowl. Add the yeast mixture to the pear mixture and mix

GRIST FOR THE MILL

Many midwesterners have fond memories of their mothers or grandmothers grinding grain to bake loaves of homemade bread. After falling out of use for a generation or so, home grain mills, both electric and hand-cranked, are coming back.

Grinding your own flour at home is easy. You can get enough flour for a loaf of bread in seconds from an electric mill and in a few minutes from a hand mill. The result is a dough that will rise higher and a loaf with a fresher flavor and a softer, fuller texture.

Because the wheat germ, the inner seed of the wheat kernel or berry, con-tains oil, true whole wheat flour can go rancid very quickly. It must be used quickly or frozen. Most whole wheat flour available commercially has only part of the bran, and not the germ, and therefore is not true whole wheat flour. To get true whole wheat flour with its good taste and all of its nutritional benefits, grinding grain at home is the first choice.

Grain mills of all kinds are available at health-food stores and through mail-order baking catalogs. For whole wheat flour, you start with hard red winter wheatberries, available from the same sources.

well. Beat in the flour mixture, 1 cup at a time, until you have a stiff dough; add more flour if necessary. Turn out the dough onto a floured board, and knead for 5 minutes, or until the dough is soft and elastic. Lightly oil a large bowl, and transfer the dough to the bowl. Cover with tea towels, and let the dough rise in a warm place until it is doubled in bulk, about 1 hour. Punch the dough down and let it rise, covered with a tea towel, until it is again doubled in bulk, about 45 minutes. Meanwhile, preheat the oven to 350 degrees and lightly oil a 9-by-5-by-3-inch loaf pan.

3. Transfer the dough to the loaf pan. Bake the bread for 40 to 45 minutes, or until the bread pulls away from the side of the pan and a thump from your fingers yields a hollow sound. Remove from the oven and transfer to a rack to cool.

VARIATION:

To make in a bread machine, add all of the ingredients to the machine's bread pan in the order suggested by the manufacturer. Use the white cycle.

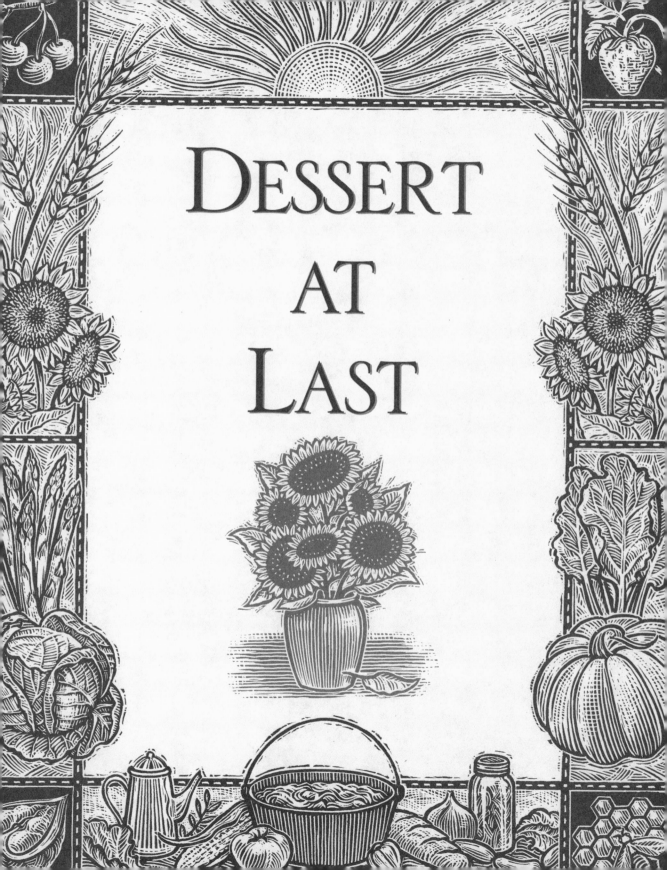

DESSERT

AT

LAST

DESSERT AT LAST

CRINKLE-TOP SPICE COOKIES

Growing up on a hilltop in hilly Cincinnati, my sister and I looked forward to the one day of the week when my mother would get the car all to herself. That was a day of frenetic activity. We would head down the steep hill to the shopping area of downtown Reading, Ohio, to do our grocery shopping at Gus Koehl's, to pick up our order at Schmidt's Meats, and to pop into the Osterhues Bakery. If we were lucky, we left the bakery clutching warm crinkle-top spice cookies. This dough keeps indefinitely wrapped in plastic in the refrigerator, so you can pinch off enough to make fresh batches of cookies every few days.

MAKES ABOUT 48 COOKIES

1 cup granulated sugar
1 cup shortening
1 cup dark molasses
2 eggs, beaten
4 cups all-purpose flour
1 teaspoon baking soda
1 teaspoon salt
2 teaspoons ground cinnamon
1 teaspoon ground dried ginger
½ cup confectioners' sugar

1. Preheat the oven to 350 degrees. Lightly oil a baking sheet. With an electric mixer, cream together the granulated sugar and shortening in a large bowl. Add the molasses and eggs and mix well. Sift the flour, baking soda, salt, cinnamon, and ginger into the bowl and mix well.

2. Sift the confectioners' sugar onto a plate. Pinch off about 1 heaping tablespoon of dough and roll the dough into a ball. Dip one half of the ball into the sugar. Place the ball, sugar side up, on the baking sheet and flatten with the bottom of a drinking glass. Repeat with the remaining dough, spacing the cookies about 3 inches apart on the baking sheet. Bake the cookies for 12 to 15 minutes, or until they are just browned.

PEPPARKAKOR

These holiday ginger cookies traditionally were cut out in the shape of the *julgalt*, or fat Christmas pig, in Swedish-American communities throughout the Heartland. When early settlers could not get saffron for St. Lucia buns (see page 343), these spice cookies filled in. Today, both saffron buns and pepparkakor are served during St. Lucia festivities in the upper midwest. Make enough so that some are left over to have with a cup of hot tea on a wintry afternoon.

MAKES ABOUT 60 COOKIES

¾ pound (3 sticks) unsalted butter, softened
2 cups sugar, plus additional sugar for rolling the cookies

2 eggs, beaten
1/2 cup molasses or sorghum
4 cups all-purpose flour
1 1/2 teaspoons ground cinnamon
1 1/2 teaspoons ground cloves
3 teaspoons ground dried ginger
2 teaspoons baking soda
1/2 teaspoon salt

1. Preheat the oven to 350 degrees. Lightly oil a baking sheet. With an electric mixer, cream together the butter and sugar in a large bowl. Add the eggs and molasses and mix well. Sift in the flour, spices, baking soda, and salt, and beat well after each 1/2 cup or so is added. You will have a stiff dough.

2. Roll out the dough thin on a sugared board. Cut with cookie cutters and transfer the cookies sugar side up to the baking sheet. Bake the cookies for 5 to 6 minutes, or until they are lightly browned.

VARIATION:

You can make the pepparkakor as round balls instead of flat cookies. Instead of rolling out the dough, pinch it off in teaspoon-size pieces, roll the pieces into balls, and roll the balls in the sugar. Bake the balls for 8 to 10 minutes.

CZECH POPPY SEED COOKIES

Bohemians and Czechs settled in large numbers in Nebraska, Iowa, Illinois, and Wisconsin in the late nineteenth century. Many of the immigrants' baked goods were flavored with poppy seed and lemon, including these traditional cookies, still popular today. If you cannot find ground poppy seeds, grind your own in the food processor, blender, or spice grinder.

MAKES ABOUT 24 COOKIES

FOR THE DOUGH:
    1/4 pound (1 stick) unsalted butter, softened
    1/3 cup sugar
    1 egg
    2 tablespoons sour cream
    2 cups all-purpose flour
    1/2 teaspoon salt
    1 teaspoon grated lemon zest

FOR THE FILLING:
    1/2 cup milk
    1 tablespoon honey
    1 cup ground poppy seeds
    2 tablespoons sugar
    1 teaspoon ground allspice

1. Make the dough: With an electric mixer, beat together the butter, sugar, egg, and sour cream in a large bowl. Mix in the flour, salt, and lemon zest to make a stiff dough. (The

POPPIES

A little band of very famous Kansans—Dorothy, Toto, Scarecrow, Tin Man, and Friendly Lion—once fell asleep in a field of poppies. Had Frank L. Baum, the South Dakota native who created them, recently eaten a cake filled with unripe poppy seeds when he penned the scene? We'll never know. The milky liquid in immature poppy pods has a soporific effect, which disappears as the pods and seeds ripen. Far from inducing sleep, mature poppy seeds, used in cakes, cookies, strudels, and breads, have been afternoon revivers for generations of prairie households. Immigrant women from Eastern Europe brought their love for the nutty flavor and crunchy texture of poppy seeds to the small towns and farms of the midwest. Even today, in Polish neighborhoods in Chicago, you will find huge bags of poppy seeds for sale in markets and fresh-baked pastries flecked with the tiny seeds in every bakery. In cakes and breads, poppy seeds are left whole, but for strudel or kolache fillings they need to be ground. Holland blue (actually blue-black in color) poppy seeds are the variety of choice. If you bake with poppy seeds often, they are less expensive when purchased in bulk from mail-order seed companies, health-food stores, or ethnic markets.

dough may be made ahead and refrigerated, covered, for up to 2 days.)

2. Preheat the oven to 350 degrees and lightly oil a baking sheet. Make the filling: Bring all of the filling ingredients to a boil in a saucepan. Reduce the heat and simmer, uncovered, for 5 minutes, stirring frequently, until the sugar and honey are well dissolved. Remove from the heat and set aside to cool slightly.

3. Roll out the dough on a floured board in a rectangle 1/3 inch thick. Spread the poppy seed filling on the dough and roll the rectangle from the long side as you would a jelly roll. Bake the roll for 40 to 45 minutes, or until lightly browned. Remove from the oven, let cool for 5 to 10 minutes, and slice while still warm into about 24 cookies.

CINNAMON STARS

Among German-American Christmas customs still very much alive in the midwest are these thin, crispy spice cookies meant to hang temptingly from the Christmas tree. Use a star-shaped cookie cutter about 2½ inches in diameter.

MAKES ABOUT 60 COOKIES

½ cup whole almonds, skins on
1⅔ cups cake flour
¾ teaspoon baking powder
2 tablespoons ground cinnamon
11 tablespoons unsalted butter,
　　chilled
¾ cup sugar
½ teaspoon grated lemon zest
1 egg, beaten with ¼ teaspoon salt

1. Grind the almonds in a food processor, spice grinder, or mortar and pestle until they are finely ground but are not yet a paste. Set aside.

2. Sift together the flour, baking powder, and cinnamon into a large bowl. With an electric mixer, cream together the butter and sugar in a separate bowl. Beat the ground almonds and the lemon zest into the butter and sugar, then beat in the egg. Blend in the flour mixture just until the dough holds together but still is grainy. Wrap the dough in plastic wrap and refrigerate for 2 hours or overnight.

3. Preheat the oven to 350 degrees. Let the dough come to room temperature for about ½ hour. Line 2 baking sheets with parchment paper and spray the paper with water. Roll out the dough on a lightly floured board into a square 12 to 13 inches on each side and between ⅛ and ¼ inch thick. Cut out about 30 cookies and place them on the baking sheets. (If you will be hanging the cookies on a tree, use a small round cutter to make a hole near a point on the star.)

4. Bake the first batch of cookies, opening the oven door every 5 minutes or so to release steam, for 18 to 20 minutes, or until they are golden brown. Meanwhile, gently pat together the leftover scraps of dough, wrap in plastic, and refrigerate for 30 minutes to firm up. Roll out, cut, and bake the second batch as you did the first.

DUTCH BUTTER-ALMOND COOKIES

The recipe for *schmeerbaaken* has been passed down in midwestern Dutch-American families for generations. The original version of this recipe calls for shelling the almonds, then blanching them to remove the skins, drying them in a slow oven, and chopping them to a fine paste with a small knife. Modern cooks may start with blanched almonds and use the food processor for an easier time of it. I like these cookies even better on the second or third day. Stored in an airtight container, they keep well for at least 1 week.

MAKES ABOUT 40 SMALL COOKIES

1 cup blanched almonds
1 cup sugar
½ pound (2 sticks) unsalted butter,
　　softened
1 large egg, beaten
2 to 2½ cups all-purpose flour

1. Preheat the oven to 300 degrees. Arrange the almonds on a baking sheet and lightly toast them in the oven for 15 to 20 minutes, or until they darken slightly. Remove the almonds from the oven and transfer them to a food processor. Increase the oven temperature to 400 degrees. Process the almonds with 1/2 cup of the sugar until the mixture resembles a fine paste.

2. With an electric mixer, cream together the remaining 1/2 cup of sugar with the butter and egg in a large bowl. Add the ground almonds and mix well. Add the flour, 1/2 cup at a time, until you have a stiff dough.

3. Lightly oil a baking sheet. For the traditional shape: Transfer the dough to a cookie press fitted with a star shape or a pastry bag fitted with the #4 star tube. Press or pipe the dough into figure 8 shapes about 3 inches long on the baking sheet. Alternatively, you can press, pipe, or cut the cookies into another shape you like. Bake the cookies for 8 to 10 minutes, or until the edges start to brown.

SUGAR HEARTS WITH ALMOND ICING

The heart of the home may be the kitchen, but the heart of the kitchen, for children at least, is the cookie jar. The oldest ones from Heartland kitchens were gray stoneware crocks, often bearing a flower design in blue. Then came glass canisters, pastel enamelware, and decorative tins. For your child's birthday treat to take to school, for your grandchildren who live too far away for your liking, or for a sweet treat to make when the mood strikes, this sugar cookie is a terrific choice.

MAKES ABOUT 48 COOKIES

FOR THE COOKIES:
  3 cups all-purpose flour
  1 teaspoon baking powder
  1/4 teaspoon salt
  1/2 pound (2 sticks) unsalted butter, softened
  1 1/2 cups granulated sugar
  2 eggs, beaten
  1 teaspoon almond extract

FOR THE ICING:
  4 tablespoons unsalted butter, softened
  1 pound confectioners' sugar, sifted
  3/4 teaspoon almond extract
  Milk, if necessary

1. Make the cookies: Sift together the flour, baking powder, and salt into a medium bowl. With an electric mixer, cream together the butter and sugar in a separate large bowl until the mixture is light and fluffy, then beat in the eggs and almond extract. Add the flour mixture, 1 cup at a time, and beat well after each addition. Wrap the dough in plastic wrap and refrigerate for at least 2 hours or overnight.

2. Preheat the oven to 350 degrees. Lightly oil a baking sheet. Roll out the dough on a lightly floured board to a ¼-inch thickness. Use a heart-shaped cookie cutter, or, if you like, another shape, to cut out the cookies. Transfer to the baking sheet, and bake for 7 to 8 minutes, or until golden. Remove from the oven and transfer to racks to cool.

3. Make the icing: Cream together the butter and sugar in a bowl or in a food processor. Blend in the almond extract. Add milk, if necessary for a piping or spreading consistency. When the cookies have cooled to room temperature, pipe or spread the icing onto the cookies.

VARIATION:

For a vanilla flavor rather than an almond one, substitute 3 teaspoons of vanilla extract for the almond extract in the cookie recipe and 1 tablespoon vanilla extract for the almond extract in the icing recipe.

ITALIAN FIG COOKIES

Also known as *cucchidatti*, these cookies can be habit-forming. Ask your Italian-American friends on The Hill in St. Louis or in Columbus Park in Kansas City, and they will tell you that these cookies are their favorites. Because they are time-consuming to make, they usually are prepared just once a year at home, for the St. Joseph Table or for Christmas. Bakeries, however, like the Missouri Baking Company on The Hill in St. Louis, make them regularly. The dough and filling may be made several days ahead and kept covered in the refrigerator.

MAKES ABOUT 72 COOKIES

FOR THE FILLING:
  1½ pounds dried figs
  ½ pound dried pitted dates
  1 pound dark raisins
  1 cup sugar
  10 ounces canned crushed
     pineapple
  8 ounces pecan pieces
  2 teaspoons fresh-grated nutmeg
  2 teaspoons ground cinnamon
  Grated zest of 1 orange
  ½ teaspoon fresh-ground black
     pepper
  3 tablespoons light corn syrup
  1 tablespoon whiskey, optional

FOR THE PASTRY:
  8 cups all-purpose flour
  3 level tablespoons baking powder
  1¼ cups sugar
  3 cups shortening
  5 eggs, beaten
  1 cup milk
  1½ tablespoons vanilla extract

1. Make the filling: Place the figs in a heat-proof bowl and pour in boiling water to cover. Let the figs steep for 5 minutes. Drain

the water, add the dates and raisins, and stir with a wooden spoon to combine evenly. Using a food grinder or a food processor, grind the figs, dates, and raisins together in batches and transfer the ground fruits to a large bowl. Add the sugar, crushed pineapple, pecans, nutmeg, cinnamon, orange zest, pepper, corn syrup, and, if you like, the whiskey. Work the filling with your hands until well blended. Cover the mixture with aluminum foil and let stand at room temperature overnight.

2. Make the pastry: Sift together the flour, baking powder, and sugar into a large bowl. Add the shortening and work the mixture with your hands until you have a crumbly dough that resembles small peas. Whisk together the eggs, milk, and vanilla in a separate bowl, and add this mixture to the flour mixture. Blend well with your hands and form the dough into a ball. Turn out the dough onto a floured board and knead, adding more flour if necessary, until the dough does not stick to your hands, about 5 minutes.

3. Preheat the oven to 400 degrees. Lightly oil 2 large baking sheets. Pinch off about 1 cup of dough and roll it out to an 8-by-3-inch rectangle that is about 1/4 inch thick. Spoon some of the filling down the center of the strip, leaving a 1-inch margin of dough on all sides. Bring the edges of the dough up and pinch them together with your fingers. Roll the strip gently into a tube shape, then cut it crosswise into 1-inch lengths. Place the cookies seam side down on a baking sheet. Continue with the remaining dough and fill-

ing. Bake the cookies for 20 to 25 minutes, or until they are just browned.

THUMBPRINT COOKIES

These cookies are a nice platform for showing off your homemade jellies or preserves. Stored in an airtight container, the cookies will keep for several weeks.

MAKES ABOUT 36 COOKIES

1/2 *pound (2 sticks) unsalted butter,*
  softened
1/2 *cup confectioners' sugar*
2 *cups all-purpose flour*
1/8 *teaspoon salt*
2 *teaspoons vanilla extract*
2 *egg whites, beaten*
1 1/2 *cups finely chopped pecans*
3/4 *cup strawberry, peach, or*
  apricot jelly or preserves

1. Preheat the oven to 350 degrees. With an electric mixer, cream together the butter and sugar in a medium bowl. Beat in the flour, salt, and vanilla until you have a stiff dough. Pinch off about 1 teaspoon of the dough and roll it into a ball. Repeat with the remaining dough.

2. Press a thumbprint in each ball of dough, dip the ball in the egg whites, and roll the ball in the chopped pecans. Put a teaspoon of jelly in the cookie's indentation and place it, jelly

side up, on an ungreased baking sheet. Repeat the process with the remaining dough balls. Bake the cookies for 15 to 17 minutes, or until they are golden brown.

PRAIRIE MOONS

In his short story "Buglesong," Wallace Stegner writes: "Through one half-open eye he had peered up from his pillow to see the moon skimming windily in a luminous sky; in his mind he had seen the prairie outside with its woolly grass and cactus white under the moon, and the wind, whining across that endless oceanic land, sang in the screens, and

sang him back to sleep." Here are some small, delicious white orbs to keep you in mind of a big prairie moon in a wide-open sky.

MAKES ABOUT 24 COOKIES

1 cup shelled pecans
1 cup sifted all-purpose flour
1/8 teaspoon salt
1 tablespoon sugar
1 teaspoon vanilla extract
1/4 pound (1 stick) unsalted butter
1 cup confectioners' sugar

1. Preheat the oven to 375 degrees. Lightly oil a baking sheet. Place the pecans in a food processor and grind the nuts fine. Add the

BOHEMIANS

Nineteenth-century immigrants from Bohemia, now part of the Czech Republic, brought their love of sweet-and-sour flavorings, dumplings of all kinds, dried fruits and mushrooms, and fruit-filled cakes and pastries with them to the midwest. On the prairie, wild duck or jackrabbit would be marinated in a vinegar and spice mixture, roasted in the oven, and served with a gravy thickened with sour cream. Dumplings made from flour, breadcrumbs, or potatoes would cook in simmering stews or soups. Dried fruits and dried mushrooms would be

plumped in liquid to be made into sweet or savory soups. Caraway seeds, poppy seeds, sage, and nutmeg were, and remain, favored seasonings in Bohemian and Czech cooking, and cold-weather vegetables like cabbage, carrots, potatoes, and parsnips play important roles.

Kolache, made of small balls of sweet yeast dough punched down in the middle and filled with homemade fruit butters or preserves, are the signature Bohemian baked good. The buttery little coffeecakes still come out fresh and hot from Nebraska, South Dakota, and Kansas kitchens.

flour, salt, and sugar, and process for a few seconds to combine. Add the vanilla and butter and process until the dough holds together.

2. Pinch off about 1 teaspoon of the dough, roll it into a ball, and transfer it to the baking sheet. Repeat with the remaining dough. Bake the cookies for 20 minutes, or until they are just browned. Remove from the oven and let cool slightly.

3. Pour the confectioners' sugar into a shallow bowl. While the cookies are still warm, dredge them in the sugar, then transfer them to racks to cool further.

BLUE RIBBON BROWNIES

These moist and dense fudge brownies are the brainchild of Teri Bavley of Prairie Village, Kansas, who brings them to neighborhood and church potlucks and, by popular request, brings them back the next year and the next.

MAKES 24 BROWNIES

1¼ cups cocoa powder
1¼ cups unbleached all-purpose flour
½ teaspoon salt
1 cup chopped nuts, such as pecans or walnuts, optional

3 cups sugar
¾ pound (3 sticks) unsalted butter, melted
7 large eggs
2 teaspoons vanilla extract

1. Preheat the oven to 350 degrees. Line a 9-by-13-inch baking pan with aluminum foil and lightly butter the foil. Stir together the cocoa, flour, salt, and, if you like, the nuts in a large bowl.

2. Stir the sugar into the butter in a separate bowl. Beat in the eggs until well blended. Stir in the vanilla. Add the butter-egg mixture to the dry ingredients and beat just until blended. Pour the batter into the prepared pan and bake the brownies for 40 to 45 minutes, or until a toothpick inserted in the center comes out almost clean. Remove the pan from the oven and let the brownies set for at least 10 minutes. Cut into squares, and serve.

NOTE: If brownies tend to burn on the edges in your oven, cover the perimeter of the brownies with strips of aluminum foil.

SOUR CREAM RAISIN BARS

The two essentials for a Minnesota potluck dinner are a *hot dish* and *bars*. Translated into rest-of-the-country English, that means a main-dish casserole and bar-shaped cookies. Like loaves and fishes, a hot dish and a pan of bars can be portioned according to how many people you need to serve. Pumpkin, raspberry, seven-layer, rhubarb, peanut butter, and pineapple are some of the bar cookies you will find at church dinners and like gatherings in the Gopher State. These rich and moist sour cream and raisin bars, however, are my favorites.

MAKES 12 LARGE OR 24 SMALL BAR COOKIES

2 cups dark or golden raisins
1¾ cups rolled oats
1¾ cups all-purpose flour
1 teaspoon baking soda
1 cup packed dark brown sugar
½ pound (2 sticks) unsalted butter,
    softened
3 egg yolks
1½ cups sour cream
1 cup granulated sugar
2½ tablespoons cornstarch
1 teaspoon vanilla extract

1. Preheat the oven to 350 degrees. Bring the raisins in water to cover to a boil in a small saucepan. Boil the raisins until they are plump, about 5 minutes, then drain them and set them aside.

2. Stir together the oats, flour, baking soda, brown sugar, and butter in a large bowl. Pat half of this crumb mixture into the bottom of a 9-by-13-inch baking pan. Bake the crust for 7 minutes, then remove from the oven. Meanwhile, whisk together the egg yolks, sour cream, granulated sugar, and cornstarch in a saucepan over medium heat. Continue whisking until the mixture thickens, about 10 minutes. Remove from the heat, and stir in the vanilla and the raisins.

3. Pour the filling over the partially baked crust. Sprinkle the remaining oats-brown sugar crumb mixture on top of the filling. Bake for 30 minutes, or until the top has browned. Let cool for 10 to 15 minutes, then cut into bars and serve.

TAPIOCA WITH HONEY-BAKED PEARS

There are two kinds of people: those who love tapioca and those who loathe it. I happen to love it. Large pearl tapioca, which had to be soaked overnight, became available in the midwest by the late nineteenth century, and big bowls of homemade tapioca pudding became fixtures of the farmstead table. I now make my tapioca in the microwave, where quick-cooking tapioca softens in minutes. This tapioca is light and fluffy, just right with fresh pears sweetened and baked with honey.

SERVES 4

FOR THE HONEY-BAKED PEARS:
    4 ripe pears, peeled, cored, and
        sliced
    ½ cup wildflower or other
        medium-colored honey

FOR THE TAPIOCA:
   3 tablespoons quick-cooking tapioca
   2 cups milk
   ½ cup sugar
   2 eggs, separated
   1 teaspoon vanilla extract

1. Bake the pears: Preheat the oven to 350 degrees. Lightly oil a glass baking dish and arrange the pear slices on the bottom; some overlap is fine. Drizzle the pears with the honey and cover the dish with aluminum foil. Bake for 30 minutes, or until the pears are softened and browned.

2. Meanwhile, make the tapioca: About 15 minutes before the pears are done, combine the tapioca, milk, and ¼ cup of the sugar in a microwaveable bowl, and microwave on high for 2 minutes, or until the mixture begins to boil. Beat the egg yolks in a separate small bowl. Remove the tapioca from the microwave and quickly (so as not to scramble the eggs) whisk 2 tablespoons of the hot tapioca mixture into the beaten egg yolks. Immediately whisk the egg yolk mixture back into the hot tapioca mixture and microwave on high for 2 minutes more, or until the tapioca boils again. Remove from the microwave, stir in the vanilla extract, and set the bowl in a larger bowl of ice water to cool and set slightly, about 5 minutes.

3. Beat the egg whites with the remaining ¼ cup of sugar until they form stiff peaks. Fold the egg whites into the tapioca. To serve, layer the pears and tapioca, parfait style, in parfait glasses or deep glass bowls. Or arrange the pear slices on plates and top with the tapioca. Serve the dish while the tapioca is still somewhat warm, and soon after you make it, or the tapioca will separate.

OLD-FASHIONED RICE PUDDING

In households of Scandinavian ancestry, rice pudding is often served on Christmas Eve or Christmas Day. Many families follow the tradition of placing an almond somewhere in the pudding; whoever finds the almond receives a special gift. This pudding is good plain or drizzled with a fruit syrup like Midsommersdag Elderberry Syrup (page 59).

SERVES 6

*1¼ cups uncooked short-grain
   white rice or Arborio rice*
8 cups whole milk
½ cup sugar
*1 vanilla bean or 1½ teaspoons
   vanilla extract*
1 cup heavy cream
1 whole almond, blanched

1. Bring the rice, milk, sugar, and vanilla bean to a boil in a large saucepan. (If you are using vanilla extract, add it after 30 minutes of cooking.) Reduce the heat and simmer very gently, uncovered, for 45 minutes, stirring every few minutes and removing the vanilla

bean (or adding the vanilla extract) after the first 30 minutes.

2. When the milk has been absorbed into the rice and the mixture is no longer runny, remove the pan from the heat. Cover, and set aside to cool to room temperature. Refrigerate, covered, if serving later, but let the pudding come to room temperature when ready to serve.

3. Just before serving, whip the cream until stiff peaks form. Fold the whipped cream into the rice mixture. Mound the pudding and hide the blanched almond in the middle. Transfer to dessert glasses or individual bowls, and serve.

Tea Room Prune Whip

First, think of prunes as more chic than you ever did. Call them "sun-dried plums," if that helps. Next, think retro, and imagine your prune whip being served in a 1940s-vintage tea room to ladies in hats and white gloves who have come downtown to shop. Now that tea rooms are making a comeback as department store eateries, can prune whip be far behind?

Serves 6

1½ *cups pitted prunes*
1 *teaspoon almond extract*

6 *egg whites*
½ *teaspoon salt*
½ *teaspoon cream of tartar*
¾ *cup sugar*
Sweetened whipped cream,
for garnish

1. Preheat the oven to 350 degrees. Lightly oil, or spray with cooking spray, a 9-by-13-inch baking pan. Bring the prunes and 2 cups of water to a boil in a saucepan. Reduce the heat and simmer, uncovered, for 15 minutes, or until the prunes are softened. Drain the water and mash the prunes. Stir in the almond extract.

2. Whisk the egg whites together with the salt and cream of tartar in a large bowl. Beat the egg whites until they form stiff peaks. Beat in the sugar, a little at a time, until the egg whites are glossy. Fold the prune mixture into the egg whites, then spread the mixture in the prepared baking pan. Carefully set the baking pan in a larger pan of water, transfer both containers to the oven, and bake for 30 minutes, or until the prune whip has browned and has begun to crack on the top. Remove from the oven and set aside for at least 10 minutes to set and cool. Cut into squares and serve warm or at room temperature. Top each portion with a dollop of whipped cream.

HONEY CUSTARDS WITH WARM SPICED BERRIES

Easy to make, fragrant with honey, and with a voluptuous texture, these custards make a great dessert for a summer lawn party. I make them with a wildflower honey produced by bees that have fed on prairie wildflowers, but any good medium to dark honey will do.

SERVES 6

2 cups milk
½ cup heavy cream
3 whole eggs plus 5 egg yolks, beaten together
⅛ teaspoon salt
⅓ cup plus ¼ cup wildflower or other medium- to dark-colored honey
3 cups fresh, preferably, or frozen blackberries, raspberries, or blueberries
1 teaspoon ground cinnamon
Juice of ½ lemon

1. Preheat the oven to 350 degrees. Whisk together the milk, cream, eggs, salt, and ⅓ cup of honey in a medium bowl. Pour the custard into 6 custard cups and place the cups in a deep-sided baking dish. Fill the baking dish with water to reach half way up the sides of the custard cups.

2. Bake the custards for 20 to 25 minutes, or until a knife inserted near the edge of a custard cup comes out clean. Remove the custards from the oven and from their water bath to cool. Refrigerate, covered, for at least 2 hours until ready to serve.

3. About 15 minutes before serving, put the berries, the remaining ¼ cup honey, and the cinnamon and lemon juice in a saucepan over medium heat. Cook, stirring occasionally, until the berries are warmed through and just beginning to release their juice, about 5 minutes. Remove from the heat. To serve, run a knife around the circumference of each custard cup and invert each custard onto a dessert plate. Top with the warm spiced berries, and serve.

OSTKAKA

This Old World cheese dessert from Varmland, Sweden, traveled along in the culinary repertoire of immigrants to Kansas and the Dakotas. In Lindsborg, Kansas, the dish is a main draw of the Midsommersdag festival in June, when girls in traditional Swedish pastel-colored dresses trimmed with lace serve up cups of *ostkaka* topped with lingonberry sauce.

SERVES 6 TO 8

4 cups Fresh Farmhouse Cheese (page 39) or 4 cups cottage cheese

3 eggs, lightly beaten
1 cup sugar
2 cups heavy cream
6 to 8 tablespoons lingonberry,
    chokecherry, or raspberry
    preserves or Red Currant
    Syrup (page 58)

1. If you are using cottage cheese, place the cheese in a cheesecloth-lined strainer over a bowl and let it drain for 30 minutes.

2. Preheat the oven to 350 degrees. Lightly butter a 2-quart baking dish. Stir together the cheese, eggs, sugar, and cream in a bowl. Pour the mixture into the baking dish. Set the baking dish on a tea towel in a larger pan containing water that reaches half way up the sides of the baking dish. Make sure that the tea towel is completely submerged, and transfer the 2 dishes to the oven.

3. Bake the *ostkaka* for 1½ hours, or until a knife inserted in the center comes out clean. Remove from the oven and spoon onto individual plates. Spoon a tablespoon of preserves or syrup over each portion, and serve hot. (Alternatively, the *ostkaka* may be refrigerated and served chilled.)

THE FRUITED PLAIN

"*Another source of pride was the apricots. The seed was brought from Russia, and the trees bore plentifully last year, and the Mennonites, taking them to Newton [Kansas] as a lunch, were agreeably surprised by an offer of $3 a bushel for them. Peter Schmidt showed all his arboreal treasures—apples, cherries, peaches, pears, all in bearing, where seven years ago the wind in passing found only the waving prairie grass.*"

—NOBLE L. PRENTIS,
From the Steppes to the Prairies

LEMON-SOUR CREAM MOUSSE

Scandinavian settlers brought to the midwest the tradition of making dishes with sweetened sour cream. The tradition remains alive today. As a light and airy finish to a heavy meal, this mousse is a nice choice for the holidays. In the summer, it is a cool treat that you can accompany with fresh strawberries or other fresh fruit.

SERVES 8

⅔ cup sugar
Grated zest and juice of 2 lemons
½ cup ice water
2 (¼-ounce) envelopes unflavored
    gelatin

6 egg whites
1/4 teaspoon salt
8 ounces cream cheese, softened
2 cups sour cream
Sprigs of fresh mint, for garnish,
   optional

1. Pour the sugar into a medium bowl. Using your fingers, work the lemon zest into the sugar. Pour the ice water into a separate small bowl and sprinkle the gelatin granules over the water. When the gelatin has soaked through, microwave on low for 1 minute, or transfer to a saucepan over medium-low heat for about 2 minutes, to heat the water and dissolve the gelatin. (Do not let the water boil; if you do, you must start over with new gelatin.)

2. Beat the egg whites with the salt in a large bowl until the whites are stiff but not dry. Add the lemon-sugar mixture, 1/3 at a time, and beat the whites into a glossy meringue. Beat in the gelatin mixture and the lemon juice until well blended. Cover and refrigerate until set, at least 10 minutes. Meanwhile, lightly oil a 2-quart mold or 8 1-cup individual molds.

3. Beat the cream cheese and sour cream together in a medium bowl until the mixture is light and fluffy. With a rubber spatula, fold the cream cheese mixture thoroughly into the meringue mixture. Pour the mousse into the prepared mold or molds. Cover with plastic wrap and refrigerate for at least 2 hours. Serve chilled, garnished with mint sprigs, if you like.

FRESH APRICOT MOOSS

Along with Turkey red winter wheat, which transformed the prairies into America's breadbasket, the Russian Mennonites also brought this fruit soup, which they call *mooss* (the pronunciation rhymes with "dose"). It is adaptable to almost any fruit, fresh or dried, and it remains the featured dessert at holiday gatherings. By now there are many versions (see the recipe that follows this one, for example, for a different fruit and a slightly different technique) from central Kansas through the wheat belt to Alberta, Saskatchewan, and Manitoba—the prairie provinces of Canada.

SERVES 4 TO 6

4 cups sliced pitted fresh apricots
1 vanilla bean
3 tablespoons all-purpose flour
3/4 cup sugar
1/2 cup heavy cream
2 cups milk

1. Put the apricots, vanilla bean, and 5 cups of water in a large saucepan over medium heat. Cook, uncovered, until the apricots are soft, about 10 minutes. Meanwhile, whisk the flour, sugar, and cream into a smooth paste in a small bowl.

2. Remove and discard (or reserve for another use) the vanilla bean. Stir the flour paste

into the apricots and continue cooking over medium heat until the mixture thickens somewhat, about 10 minutes. Stir in the milk. Remove from the heat and let cool slightly; alternatively, refrigerate, covered, for at least 2 hours to serve chilled. Ladle the mooss into glass bowls, and serve.

SOUR CHERRY MOOSS

Traditionally, cherry mooss (see the previous recipe for the origin of the term) was made with cherries that still had their pits. The pits imparted an almond flavor, but they also made the mooss difficult to eat. Here is an updated version that uses pitted cherries and almond extract instead. Modern-day Mennonite cooks add a little red food coloring as well. The mooss is handsome when it is served from a large glass bowl in the center of the table and ladled from there into individual glass bowls.

SERVES 8 TO 12

4 cups fresh or frozen pitted sour
*   cherries*
5 1/2 cups sugar
1/2 cup flour
1/2 teaspoon salt
3 cups milk
1/2 teaspoon almond extract
Several drops of red food coloring,
*   optional*

1. Put the cherries and 4 cups of the sugar in a large saucepan. Pour in 1 cup of water, bring to a boil, reduce the heat, and simmer, uncovered, until some of the cherry skins crack, about 10 minutes. Meanwhile, combine 1/2 cup of the sugar, the flour, and the salt in a medium bowl. Add the milk, and whisk until the mixture has a gravy-like consistency.

2. When the cherry skins have begun cracking, stir in the remaining 1 cup of the sugar. Increase the heat to medium-high and whisk in the flour-milk mixture. Whisk constantly until the mooss comes to a boil and the liquid coats the back of a spoon. Remove from the heat and whisk in the almond extract and, if you like, the food coloring. Transfer to a serving bowl and serve warm, or refrigerate, covered, to serve chilled.

PEACHES WITH PEACH LEAF CUSTARD SAUCE

A century ago, Heartland cooks used fresh peach leaves as flavorings for custards, sauces, and syrups. It is a custom that deserves a comeback. Get your unsprayed peach leaves from a neighbor's tree or order them ahead (yes, they probably will think you've gone around the bend) from an organic orchard or a farmers' market vendor. The sweet and delicate almond flavor these leaves impart is worth the effort of finding them. If you live in the midwest, use this recipe, if you like, as the occasion to try regional varieties of peaches like Red Haven, Glow Haven, Briscoe, or Summer Pearl.

SERVES 4

1 cup half-and-half
12 unsprayed peach leaves
5 egg yolks
3/4 cup sugar
Fresh lemon juice to taste, optional
4 ripe peaches, peeled and sliced

1. Bring the half-and-half and peach leaves just to a boil in a saucepan. Remove immediately from the heat and set aside to infuse for 30 minutes.

2. Whisk the egg yolks and sugar together in a medium bowl until well blended. Pour the half-and-half through a strainer into the egg yolk mixture. Whisk to blend. Pour the egg yolk mixture back into the saucepan and, over medium heat, whisk constantly until the custard coats the back of a spoon, about 5 minutes. (Do not boil or the custard will separate.) Taste the custard and stir in lemon juice, if you like. Remove the pan from the heat and let cool to room temperature. Put the peach slices in individual glass bowls or dishes, spoon the custard over the peaches, and serve.

SUMMERTIME FRESH FRUIT CUP

Simple, cool, refreshing, good for you, and very summery, this pretty fruit salad looks tempting and handsome in a glass bowl or glass cup. On really hot days, chill the bowls or cups beforehand.

SERVES 4

4 ripe peaches, peeled and sliced
1 cup fresh blueberries
1 cup fresh raspberries
1/2 cup Honeysuckle Syrup (page 61), Honey Syrup (page 61), or Peach Leaf Syrup (page 62)
Sprigs of fresh mint, for garnish, optional

1. Combine all of the ingredients except the mint sprigs in a bowl, and toss gently but thoroughly to coat the fruits with the syrup. Refrigerate, covered, for at least 1 hour.

2. Toss or stir once more and serve chilled, garnished with mint, if you like.

AUTUMN DRIED APPLE COMPOTE

Make this compote in the late fall and you will have a jump-start for your holiday entertaining. Take it out of the refrigerator, warm it up in a saucepan, and serve it as a dessert, accompanied by vanilla ice cream or Crinkle-Top Spice Cookies (page 365). Or, if you like, serve it in the morning with waffles or scones.

MAKES 1½ QUARTS COMPOTE

4½ cups dry white wine
Grated zest of ½ lemon
½ cup wildflower or other
    medium-colored honey
2 vanilla beans
2 cinnamon sticks
5 whole cloves
1 pound dried apples, sliced,
    or ½ pound each dried
    apples and dried apricots,
    sliced

1. Bring 2½ cups of water and all of the ingredients except the dried fruit to a boil in a large saucepan. Reduce the heat and simmer, uncovered, until the sugar is dissolved, 3 to 4 minutes. Add the dried apples and simmer, stirring occasionally, for 10 minutes more. Remove the pan from the heat and let the apples steep and cool for 15 minutes.

2. Remove and discard the vanilla beans and cinnamon sticks. Transfer the mixture to 3 1-pint jars or a lidded plastic tub. Cover the jar or tub. Refrigerated, the compote will keep for up to 3 weeks.

FESTIVE FRUITCAKES

Light, moist, and deeply flavorful without being too heavy, this fruitcake is made with a wealth of midwestern specialties. This is my children's grandmother's recipe, and she makes the cakes for a list that gets longer every year. (So she *knows* there's not just one that gets passed around.) When I receive my loaf, I wrap it well and carve off thin slices so that it lasts until February.

MAKES 6 SMALL OR 3 LARGE FRUITCAKES

4 cups all-purpose flour
1 pound white or golden raisins
2 pounds candied cherries
    (see Note)
2 cups chopped Preserved
    Watermelon Rind (page 63),
    or 2 cups candied pineapple
    (see Note)
2 pounds shelled hardshell or
    softshell pecans
1 pound (4 sticks) unsalted butter,
    softened

½ *pound light brown sugar*
12 *eggs, beaten*
1 *teaspoon baking powder*
10 *ounces elderberry jelly or*
  blackberry jelly
1 *teaspoon ground cloves*
2 *teaspoons ground cinnamon*
1 *teaspoon fresh-grated nutmeg*
Rum, almond liqueur, or French
  Valley Spiced Pear Cordial
  (page 112), for drizzling

1. Preheat the oven to 250 degrees. Line 3 large or 6 small loaf pans with greased parchment paper. Place 1 cup of the flour in a large mixing bowl, add the raisins, cherries, watermelon rind, and pecans, toss to coat well, and reserve.

2. With an electric mixer, cream together the butter and sugar in a large bowl. Add the eggs, about 2 or 3 at a time, and beat well after each addition. Add 1 more cup of the flour and the baking powder and mix well. Add the jelly and mix well again. Add 1 more cup of the flour and the cloves, cinnamon, and nutmeg, and mix well. Mix in the remaining 1 cup flour. Fold in the reserved fruit and nuts, about 1 cup at a time, discarding the extra flour, until all have been folded into the batter. The batter will be very lumpy.

3. Fill the prepared loaf pans ¾ full with the batter. For moistness, place a pan of water on the bottom rack of the oven. Place the loaf pans on the middle rack. Bake the small loaves for 2½ hours and the large loaves for 3 hours, checking occasionally to make sure there is water in the bottom pan. The fruit-cakes are done when the tops are browned, the cakes pull away from the sides of the pans, and a cake tester inserted in the center comes out clean.

4. Turn out the cakes onto racks to cool to room temperature. Sprinkle the cakes with rum, almond liqueur, or French Valley Spiced Pear Cordial to flavor them and keep them moist. Wrap the fruitcakes tight in aluminum foil and store them in airtight tins or zippered plastic bags.

NOTE: Candied cherries and pineapples are available during the holiday season in supermarkets. If you live near an Eastern European ethnic market you often can find glacéed cherries (and, occasionally, pineapple) that are especially good in a fruitcake.

HIDE THE FRUITCAKE

"*Baking begins in earnest weeks ahead. Waves of cookies, enough to feed an army, enough to render any army defenseless, including powerful rumballs and fruitcakes soaked with spirits (if the alcohol burns off in the baking, as they say, then why does Arlene hide them from her mother?).*"

—GARRISON KEILLOR,
Lake Wobegon Days

FLAKY PIE CRUST

Country cooks swear by a lard crust for flakiness. This recipe uses a mixture of lard and, for flavor, butter. If you prefer to avoid lard, use shortening instead.

MAKES CRUSTS FOR A 2-CRUST 9-INCH PIE OR 2 1-CRUST 9-INCH PIES

2 cups all-purpose flour
1/2 teaspoon salt
1/2 cup lard or shortening, chilled
2 tablespoons unsalted butter, chilled
6 tablespoons milk, chilled

1. Stir together the flour and salt in a mixing bowl. With a pastry blender or two knives, cut in the lard and butter until the mixture resembles coarse meal.

2. Using a fork, blend in the milk 1 tablespoon at a time. Pat down the dough with your hands and form it into a ball. Divide the dough in half, and wrap each half in plastic wrap. Refrigerate the dough for at least 30 minutes before using it in a recipe. Before rolling out the dough in a recipe, let it rest at room temperature for 15 minutes; this step prevents cracking.

VARIATION:

For recipes that call for a Prebaked Pie Crust, roll out 1/2 of the dough in this recipe and line a 9-inch pie pan. Prick the bottom and sides of the crust with a fork. Refrigerate for 30 minutes, then bake in a 350 degree oven for 10 to 12 minutes, until very lightly browned.

HOOSIER SUGAR CREAM PIE

If Indiana had a state pie, this would be it. It is on the menus of small-town cafés and urban cafeterias, and it is a favorite among home cooks. Not quite a custard pie, sugar cream pie is a cousin of southern chess pies and transparent pies. Originally the recipe came, via New England, to the nineteenth-century Shaker community in Pleasant Hill, Kentucky, and from there north and west into Ohio and Indiana. When I made the ultra-rich original recipe, I understood why some recipes need to evolve over time. Thankfully, Hoosier cooks have given it a lighter touch. Directions in the earliest recipes call for mixing the filling in the unbaked crust, then stirring it with the fingers as it baked. This contemporary version saves fingers from burning by combining the ingredients in a bowl and baking the filling without stirring.

MAKES 1 9-INCH PIE

1/2 recipe Flaky Pie Crust (preceding recipe) or other pastry for 1 9-inch pie crust
1 cup heavy cream
1 cup half-and-half
1 cup sugar

½ cup all-purpose flour
3 tablespoons unsalted butter, cut
   into dots
¼ teaspoon fresh-grated nutmeg

1. Preheat the oven to 425 degrees. Roll out the pie crust and place it in a 9-inch pie pan. Whisk together the cream, half-and-half, sugar, and flour in a medium bowl. Pour the filling into the pie shell. Dot with the butter and sprinkle with the nutmeg. Bake for 15 minutes.

2. Remove the pie from the oven and reduce the temperature to 350 degrees. Wrap the exposed edges of the crust with aluminum foil to prevent burning, and bake the pie for 45 minutes more, or until a knife inserted in the center comes out clean. Transfer the pie to a rack to cool and set for 10 minutes, and serve.

STE. GENEVIEVE ANGEL PIE

In the small city of Ste. Genevieve, which was originally a French Canadian outpost and now is popular with tourists and weekenders, along the Mississippi River in Missouri, this pie is a favorite at tea shops and bed-and-breakfasts, and during the annual *guignolée* on New Year's Eve and the Jour de Fête in August.

MAKES 1 9-INCH PIE

6 eggs, separated
1⅓ cups sugar
⅓ cup fresh lemon juice
1 prebaked Flaky Pie Crust (page
   384, see the Variation) or other
   prebaked 9-inch pie crust
¼ teaspoon cream of tartar

1. Preheat the oven to 300 degrees. Beat the egg yolks with 1 cup of the sugar for several minutes until light and lemon-colored. Mix in the lemon juice. Bring water to a simmer in the bottom pan of a double boiler and pour the egg yolk mixture into the top pan. Cook, stirring often, until the mixture thickens, about 5 minutes. Remove from the heat. Beat 3 of the egg whites until they hold stiff peaks and fold them into the hot yolk mixture. Pour this filling into the prebaked pie shell.

2. Beat the remaining 3 egg whites with the cream of tartar until they hold stiff peaks. Beat in the remaining ⅓ cup sugar until the whites are glossy. Spread the meringue over the pie shell and bake the pie until the meringue is browned, 18 to 20 minutes. Transfer to a rack to cool and set for 10 minutes, and serve.

The Art
of the Crust

Heartland cooks used to make homemade pies every week, developing a feel for the dough and a knack for rolling that resulted from years of practice. Few of us today make pies every week, or even several times a year, and so we do not develop the confidence that comes from long experience.

There are many pie crust recipes. Some tell you to cut in flour and chilled butter or lard by hand, while others say to beat the flour into hot water and vegetable oil or melted shortening. Pastry flour or cake flour makes a crumbly but tender crust. All-purpose flour makes a flaky crust when you use ample butter or lard. Recipes may call for one or the other or a combination of the two flour types. Sugar, sour cream, milk, or vinegar also might be added.

Whichever crust recipe you choose, veteran pie-makers have some rules of thumb that can make the novice feel more confident:

1. Make sure the fat (butter, shortening, or oil) combines well with the flour. If you are using butter or shortening with flour, the mixture should resemble coarse meal with no large lumps.

2. Use as little water as possible, and only enough to allow the crumbly fat-flour mixture to form a ball.

3. Let the dough rest before rolling it out. Cover the dough with plastic wrap and refrigerate it for up to several days before making your pie. However, let the dough come to just below room temperature before rolling it out, or the dough will break into pieces instead of rolling smoothly.

4. Roll out the dough with quick movements on a lightly floured flat surface with a lightly floured rolling pin. Roll from all angles to make sure the dough is an even thickness. For the bottom crust of a pie, roll out the dough in a circle 1½ inches larger in diameter than the outer rim of your pie pan. Carefully drape half of the dough circle over the rolling pin and lay the crust in the pie pan. Fit the dough loosely in the bottom of the pan so that you do not tear the crust. Then press gently on the bottom and up the sides to get a snug fit.

SHAKER LEMON PIE

Here is a pie for serious lemon-lovers. Puckery and rich, the filling is made with paper-thin slices of whole lemons. The simple yet ingenious idea is inspired by a nineteenth-century classic recipe from the North Union Shaker community in northern Ohio.

MAKES 1 9-INCH PIE

1 recipe Flaky Pie Crust (page 384)
    or other pastry for 2 9-inch
    pie crusts
2 large lemons, sliced as thin as
    possible and seeded, with any
    juice reserved
2 cups sugar
4 eggs, well beaten

1. Preheat the oven to 450 degrees. Roll out the pastry to make 2 crusts and place 1 of them in a 9-inch pie pan. Put the lemon slices and their juice into a large bowl and toss them gently but well with the sugar. Pour in the eggs and toss gently with a spatula to distribute evenly. Transfer the filling to the pie pan. Wet your fingertips with water and moisten the exposed edges of the crust. Cover with the top crust and crimp or flute the edges together. Cut several slits near the center of the pie to let steam escape.

2. Bake the pie for 15 minutes, reduce the heat to 375 degrees, and bake for 20 minutes more, or until a knife inserted near the edge of the pie comes out clean. Transfer to a rack to cool. The pie slices best when it is just faintly warm or is at room temperature.

LEMON-BUTTERMILK CUSTARD PIE

In the midwest, a small-town bakery or café, or a church supper, is known by the quality of its pies. When neighbors come to call, when business people need to talk over a deal, or when friends gather to gossip, pie and coffee are the official fare. The rich, tangy, homemade flavor of this pie wins it a blue ribbon any time of the year. For thrifty Heartland cooks, having a pie recipe that used up both yolks and whites was always a plus.

MAKES 1 9-INCH PIE

FOR THE FILLING:
    2 tablespoons all-purpose flour
    2 cups buttermilk
    4 tablespoons unsalted butter,
        melted
    1/4 cup sugar
    6 egg yolks, beaten
    Zest and juice of 1 lemon

1 prebaked Flaky Pie Crust (page
    384, see the Variation) or other
    prebaked 9-inch pie crust

FOR THE MERINGUE TOPPING:
- 6 egg whites
- 1/2 teaspoon cream of tartar
- 1 cup sugar
- 1 teaspoon vanilla extract

1. Preheat the oven to 325 degrees. Make the filling: Sift the flour into the buttermilk in a medium bowl and stir well with a wooden spoon until there are no lumps. Bring water to a simmer in the bottom pan of a double boiler and transfer the flour mixture to the top pan. Whisk in the butter and sugar. Gradually whisk in the egg yolks. Cook, whisking constantly, until the custard begins to thicken, about 10 minutes. Remove from the heat, whisk in the lemon zest and juice, and set aside to cool to room temperature.

2. When the filling has cooled, pour it into the prebaked pie shell. Bake the pie until the custard is just set, about 15 minutes. Remove from the oven, leaving the oven on, and transfer to a rack to cool.

3. Increase the oven temperature to 350 degrees. While the pie cools, make the meringue: Beat the egg whites with the cream of tartar in a bowl until stiff peaks form. Gradually beat in the sugar until the meringue appears glossy. Beat in the vanilla. Spread the meringue in a swirl pattern over the pie. Bake the pie for 10 minutes more, or until the meringue has cooked through and browned. Transfer the pie to a rack to cool for 10 minutes, and serve.

HICKORY NUT PIE

Hickory nut pies were common in midwestern cookbooks from the nineteenth century. In woodlands from Wisconsin down through Ohio, hickory nuts were there for the gathering. Because hickory nuts are as difficult to extract as pine nuts or black walnuts, they never became a grocery store staple. When people began to get their nuts from the grocery store rather than the wild, the popularity of the hickory nut faded as that of the pecan increased. Today, you can still gather hickory nuts in the fall or order them by mail-order (see Resources). Farmers' markets often have them, too.

MAKES 1 9-INCH PIE

- 1/2 recipe Flaky Pie Crust (page 384) or other pastry for 1 9-inch pie crust
- 2 tablespoons all-purpose flour
- 2 tablespoons sugar
- 3 eggs
- 1/3 cup milk
- 1 1/2 teaspoons vanilla extract
- 2 cups light corn syrup
- 1 tablespoon unsalted butter
- 1 cup chopped hickory nuts or chopped pecans
- 2 tablespoons graham cracker crumbs
- Whipped cream and additional chopped hickory nuts or chopped pecans, for garnish

1. Preheat the oven to 325 degrees. Roll out the pie crust and place it in a 9-inch pie pan. Stir together the flour and sugar in a medium bowl. Add the eggs, milk, and vanilla and beat the mixture until it is smooth. Bring the corn syrup and butter just to a boil in a saucepan, then remove from the heat and whisk the hot liquid into the egg mixture. Sprinkle the nuts and cracker crumbs over the bottom of the pie crust and pour the filling over them.

2. Bake the pie for 45 minutes, or until the filling has just set. Transfer the pie to a rack to cool to room temperature, and serve, garnished with whipped cream and additional nuts.

SUGAR PUMPKIN PIE

When small sugar pumpkins come on the market around Halloween, snap up a few to save in a cool cellar or in the refrigerator for Thanksgiving pies. Made from fresh pumpkin, the traditional Thanksgiving pie has a lighter and fresher flavor that may convert some who think they do not like pumpkin pie.

MAKES 1 9-INCH PIE

1 medium (about 3 pounds) sugar
    pumpkin, preferably, or 3 cups
    canned pumpkin puree
½ recipe Flaky Pie Crust (page
384) or other pastry for
    1 9-inch pie crust
4 eggs, lightly beaten
¾ cup wildflower or other
    medium-colored honey
1 cup half-and-half or evaporated
    milk
½ teaspoon fresh-grated nutmeg
½ teaspoon ground cinnamon
1 teaspoon salt

1. If you are using fresh pumpkin, cut the pumpkin into large chunks and remove and discard the seeds. Place the chunks, a few at a time, cut side down in a dish and microwave on high for 5 to 8 minutes, or until the pumpkin flesh is cooked through and softened. Alternatively, place the pumpkin cut side down on a cookie sheet and bake at 350 degrees for 45 minutes, or until softened. Scoop the pumpkin flesh from the skin into the bowl of a food processor and puree until smooth.

2. Preheat the oven to 375 degrees. Roll out the pie crust and place it in a 9-inch pie pan. Measure 3 cups of pumpkin puree and place the puree in a mixing bowl. Beat in the eggs, honey, half-and-half, nutmeg, cinnamon, and salt.

3. Pour or spoon the filling over the crust. Place the pie pan on a cookie sheet in the middle of the oven, and bake the pie for 1 hour, or until the filling is firm and is glossy on top. Transfer to a rack to cool to room temperature, and serve.

SOUR CHERRY PIE

The lake effect does wonders for fruit orchards on the bluff country surrounding Lake Michigan. In late May, the froth of pink blossoms on cherry trees in Michigan and Wisconsin forecast bumper crops of sour cherries later in July. If you are lucky enough to have a cherry tree in your yard or garden, take a tip from a veteran pie-maker: Remove the cherry pits with a hairpin to help the cherries keep their shape. "Officially," you can freeze a well-wrapped unbaked fruit pie for up to 4 months, but I have frozen them for a year and then baked them with no discernible loss in taste. It's all in how well they're wrapped.

MAKES 1 9-INCH PIE

1 recipe Flaky Pie Crust (page 384)
    or other pastry for 2 9-inch
    pie crusts
1 cup plus 1 teaspoon sugar
3 tablespoons instant tapioca
1 tablespoon lemon juice
1/2 teaspoon almond extract
4 cups sour cherries, pitted
1 tablespoon unsalted butter, cut
    into dots
2 tablespoons milk or light cream

1. Preheat the oven to 425 degrees. Roll out the pastry to make 2 crusts and place 1 of them in a 9-inch pie pan.

2. Stir together the 1 cup sugar and the tapioca, lemon juice, and almond extract in a large bowl. Add the sour cherries and toss gently to coat the fruit. Spoon the mixture into the pie pan and dot the top with the butter. Wet your fingertips with water and moisten the exposed edges of the crust. Cover with the top crust and crimp or flute the edges together. Cut several steam vents in the top crust (see Note). Brush the top crust with the milk and sprinkle with the 1 teaspoon sugar.

3. Bake the pie for 15 minutes, reduce the heat to 350 degrees, and bake for 45 to 55 minutes more, or until the cherries are tender, the filling has thickened, and the crust is golden brown. Transfer to a rack to cool, and serve.

NOTE: The pie may be frozen, wrapped in wax paper or aluminum foil and placed in a zippered plastic storage bag, at this point if you like. Bake the frozen pie in a 450 degree oven for 15 minutes, reduce the heat to 375 degrees, and bake for about 60 minutes more, or until the filling has thickened and the crust is golden brown.

SOUR CHERRIES

The climate and soil conditions around the Great Lakes, especially along the shores of Lake Michigan in eastern Wisconsin and western Michigan, are ideal for growing Montmorency cherries, the most common variety of what are called tart cherries or sour cherries. Michigan, particularly Oceana and Leelanau Counties, accounts for more than three-quarters of the U.S. sour cherry crop. Wisconsin, especially Door County, produces another 5 percent. Because sour cherries are very perishable and can lose their vibrant red color very quickly, they are rarely sold fresh. Unless you have access to sour cherry trees, you probably will have to buy them frozen or canned. When you do find fresh ones, use them soon before their color and flavor fade.

JUNEBERRY OR BLACK RASPBERRY PIE

In the Dakotas and in Canada's prairie provinces, juneberries ripen in the month for which they are named. Home cooks pick the berries and then make pies to eat or freeze. In Louise Erdrich's novel *The Bingo Palace*, pow-wow dancer Shawnee Ray surveys the potluck dinner table and finds "corn soup, fry bread, juneberry pie, bangs [small flatbreads] with jelly. Tripe soup, boiled meat, plates of sliced cantaloupes and watermelon." You will enjoy this luscious pie even without all those accompaniments, and you may substitute black raspberries if you have no supply of juneberries.

MAKES 1 9-INCH PIE

1 recipe Flaky Pie Crust (page 384) or other pastry for 2 9-inch pie crusts
2 cups juneberries or black raspberries
¾ cup sugar
1 tablespoon instant tapioca
Pinch of salt
2 tablespoons fresh lemon juice

1. Preheat the oven to 425 degrees. Roll out the pastry to make 2 crusts and place 1 of them in a 9-inch pie pan. Gently but thoroughly toss together the juneberries, sugar, tapioca, salt, and lemon juice in a medium bowl. Spoon or pour the mixture into the pie pan. Wet your fingertips with water and moisten the exposed edges of the crust.

PRAIRIE PIES

Cafés, diners, and restaurants across the broad expanse of the Heartland pride themselves on homemade pies. Is it really homemade if it is sold in a restaurant? In fact, many small-town eateries hire a local housewife to come in for a few hours in the morning to bake a dozen or so pies. Great pie recipes, jealously and secretively guarded, are passed down in families. My grandmother was known for her creamy and rich butterscotch pie. She passed along her pie-making genes to my mother, who won a blue ribbon in an Ohio apple pie contest.

In the midwest, pie is a comforting fact of life. A piece of pie with a cup of coffee is an excuse for visiting with neighbors, taking a break during a long trip, or introducing yourself to a new acquaintance. A pie in the freezer is an insurance policy against unexpected guests or a kitchen disaster. Now specialty pie bakeries like the Broad Ripple Pie Company in Indianapolis and Tippin's in Kansas City offer a sense of security for women who feel they should have a pie on hand but may not have had the time to make one.

Nowadays people take home pie safes from antique stores and flea markets and seem to put just about anything in them except pies. In homesteading days, the pie safe, a wooden cabinet with punched tin panels that let air in and kept insects out, was a fixture in kitchens or on back porches—and it really was used for pies. New immigrant farm families quickly learned how to make an American-style pie, with a short, flaky pastry that enclosed a sweetened cooked filling. The traditional fillings were made from the bounty of the seasons, such as: rhubarb in the spring; blackberry, mulberry, sour cherry, gooseberry, and blueberry in early summer; peach in late summer; and apple, pecan, and pumpkin in the fall. One-crust pies topped with meringue and with custard or custard-like fillings of lemon chiffon, chocolate cream, or coconut cream have long been popular as well.

Cover with the top crust and crimp or flute the edges together. Cut several steam vents in the top crust.

2. Bake the pie for 50 minutes, or until the crust is golden brown and the filling is bubbling. Transfer to a rack to cool, and serve.

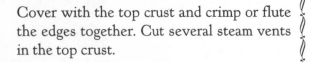

County Fair Caramel Apple Tartlets

All the autumn delights of the first caramel apple reconfigure in this homey dessert. I use Golden Delicious apples for their sweet flavor and soft texture. You will have about 2½ cups of caramel sauce. If your guests do not use it all on their tartlets, keep the extra (it may be served warm, at room temperature, or chilled) to serve over ice cream, baked pears, or bread pudding.

Serves 4

FOR THE CARAMEL SAUCE:
    1 cup sugar
    1 teaspoon vanilla extract
    1 cup heavy cream or evaporated
        lowfat or skim milk

FOR THE TARTLETS:
    ½ package frozen puff pastry,
        thawed
    8 medium to large Golden
        Delicious apples, peeled, cored,
        and sliced very thin
    4 teaspoons sugar
    2 tablespoons unsalted butter, cut
        into dots

1. Preheat the oven to 325 degrees. While the oven heats, make the caramel sauce: Combine the sugar and vanilla with ¾ cup water in a heavy-bottomed saucepan over low heat. Cook, stirring often, until the sugar dissolves, 3 to 4 minutes. Increase the heat to medium-high and bring the mixture to a boil. Cook at a gentle boil, without stirring, until the mixture begins to turn golden, about 20 minutes. When it reaches a golden brown, remove from the heat immediately so the caramel will not darken and turn bitter. With heavy-duty oven mitts on each hand, pour in the cream or evaporated milk and whisk to blend. (The hot caramel may splatter a little as you do this.)

2. Make the tartlets: Roll out the pastry on a lightly floured board and cut 4 pastry circles 6 inches in diameter each. Transfer the pastry circles to a baking sheet. Arrange the apple slices in an overlapping pattern on each pastry circle. Sprinkle each tartlet with a teaspoon of sugar and dot the tartlets with butter. Bake for 10 to 15 minutes or until the pastry is browned and cooked through.

3. Remove the tartlets from the oven and transfer them to individual plates. Drizzle them with caramel sauce, and serve, passing the extra sauce in a boat or bowl at the table.

German Cheese Tart

In midwestern households of the nineteenth century and into the twentieth century, essential ingredients for most recipes were made at home. Only the ingredients you could not make yourself were bought at the store. Recipes like this one evolved to make use of what you had on hand. Although this tart tastes wonderful with packaged zwieback and cottage cheese from the grocery store, it is even better with homemade toasted zwieback (page 345) and Fresh Farmhouse Cheese (page 39). Serve with fresh fruit or a fruit syrup, if you like.

MAKES 1 9-INCH TART

FOR THE CRUST:
   6 Wheat Country Zwieback (page 345), sliced and toasted, or 6 ounces packaged zwieback
   1 cup sugar
   1 teaspoon ground cinnamon
   1/4 pound (1 stick) unsalted butter, melted

FOR THE FILLING:
   5 cups Fresh Farmhouse Cheese (page 39) or 5 cups small-curd cottage cheese
   1 cup sugar
   4 eggs
   3/4 cup heavy cream
   1 teaspoon vanilla extract
   1/4 teaspoon salt
   1/4 cup all-purpose flour

1. Lightly butter a 9-inch springform pan. Make fine crumbs of the zwieback by processing in a food processor (or by placing the zwieback between sheets of wax paper and rolling with a rolling pin). Add the sugar, cinnamon, and butter to the food processor (or to a bowl to which you have added the crumbs). Process or stir until you have a crumbly mixture that resembles a cheesecake

MERINGUE MYSTERIES

Meringue pies are home-cooking favorites, but making a perfect meringue gives some cooks fits. For a while, I was one of them. Either my meringue "wept"–developed small beads of liquid that browned as the meringue baked–or it wanted to slide off the filling. Food scientist Shirley Corriher came to my rescue. I tried her technique of heating a mixture of 1 tablespoon cornstarch with 1/3 cup water in the microwave until it formed a gel. I then mixed this in with the egg whites to make the meringue, and this produced a more stable meringue. She also suggested sprinkling fine cake crumbs on a hot filling before spreading the meringue over the filling and baking it. I did this too, with perfect results. You want to spread the meringue on hot filling, not a cold or room temperature filling, so that the meringue cooks evenly on top and bottom.

crust. Set aside ¾ cup of the mixture, and pat the remainder of it into the bottom and sides of the springform pan.

2. Preheat the oven to 375 degrees. Make the filling: Put all of the filling ingredients in the bowl of a food processor and blend until smooth; or pass the farmhouse cheese or cottage cheese through a food mill or, using the back of a spoon, push it through a sieve, then combine it with the remaining filling ingredients in a bowl. Pour the filling slowly over the crust in the springform pan. Sprinkle the reserved ¾ cup of the crumb mixture on top.

3. Bake the tart for at least 1 hour, or until the filling has set (depending on the kind of cottage cheese you use, the filling can take up to 2 hours to set) and a knife inserted into the center of the tart comes out clean. Remove from the oven to cool slightly, and serve.

SUMMERTIME DEEP DISH PEACH COBBLER

Deep dish cobblers, especially popular along the southern edge of the midwest, come in all shapes and sizes. Some have just a bottom crust and others, like this one, have a top crust as well. Midwestern peach crops are notoriously fickle, subject to failure due to late frost. As we do today, early settlers who had planted orchards happily celebrated the summer of a "good peach year."

SERVES 8 TO 12

FOR THE CRUST:
   4 cups unbleached all-purpose flour
   ½ pound (2 sticks) butter, chilled, cut into small pieces
   1 cup shortening, chilled
   ½ teaspoon salt
   7 tablespoons ice water

FOR THE FILLING:
   10 cups peeled, pitted, and sliced fresh peaches
   3 tablespoons fresh lemon juice
   1 cup sugar
   1 teaspoon ground cinnamon
   ¼ teaspoon fresh-grated nutmeg
   ¼ cup unbleached all-purpose flour

1. Prepare the crust: Place the flour, butter, shortening, and salt in a large bowl. Using a pastry blender or two knives, cut the butter and shortening into the flour until the mixture resembles coarse meal. Add the ice water, 1 tablespoon at a time, stirring it in with a fork. Pat the dough into a ball, wrap it in plastic wrap, and refrigerate it for at least 1 hour.

2. Preheat the oven to 375 degrees. When the dough has chilled, divide it in half. Wrap 1 half in plastic wrap and return it to the refrigerator. Roll out the other half on a floured board and fit it into the bottom and sides of a 9-by-13-inch baking pan.

3. Prepare the filling: Very gently toss the peaches in the lemon juice in a large bowl. Add the sugar, cinnamon, nutmeg, and flour, and toss again with a spatula or wooden spoon to blend. Spoon the filling on top of the bottom crust. Roll out the remaining pastry on a floured board. Wet your fingertips with water and moisten the exposed edges of the bottom crust. Place the top crust over the peach filling and crimp or flute the edges together. Cut several steam vents in the top crust.

4. Bake the cobbler for 1¼ to 1½ hours, or until the crust is golden brown and the filling is bubbling. Transfer to a rack to cool, and serve.

LEMON-ZESTED MULBERRY AND RHUBARB CRISP

Mulberries originally were brought to the prairie by European immigrants who wanted to try raising silkworms. The mulberry is a large bush (or a small tree) that has leaves in three different shapes. Mulberry fruits ripen in the midwest from mid- to late-June. They are very perishable, which is why you do not see them at farmers' markets or in grocery stores. This tasty crisp offers a good reason to gather them yourself. If they are hard for you to come by, use blackberries instead.

SERVES 6 TO 8

2 cups fresh mulberries or fresh blackberries
4 cups 1-inch slices fresh rhubarb
1 tablespoon instant tapioca
Juice and grated zest of 1 lemon
2 cups sugar
1 cup all-purpose flour
½ cup unsalted butter, softened

1. Preheat the oven to 375 degrees. Lightly butter a large baking dish. Combine the berries, rhubarb, tapioca, lemon juice, and 1 cup of the sugar in a large bowl. Stir gently to blend well.

2. Transfer the fruit mixture to the baking dish. Combine the remaining 1 cup of sugar, the flour, and the lemon zest in a small bowl. Using your fingers, rub the butter into the flour mixture to form large crumbs. Sprinkle the large crumbs on top of the fruit and bake for 35 minutes, or until the top is browned and crispy. Serve hot.

SCHAUM TORTES WITH STRAWBERRY CREAM

One of the favored desserts in Milwaukee, with its large community of German-Americans, is the Schaum torte, a large basket or shell of crisp meringue enclosing a whipped cream filling with strawberries or other fresh fruit.

SERVES 8

FOR THE MERINGUE "TORTES":
    4 egg whites
    4 cups sifted confectioners' sugar
    1 teaspoon vanilla extract

FOR THE FILLING:
    2 pints small to medium fresh
        strawberries
    Juice of 1/2 lemon
    1/2 cup granulated sugar, or more
        to taste
    1 cup heavy cream

1. Preheat the oven to 250 degrees. Line a baking sheet with parchment paper. Bring water to a simmer in the bottom pan of a double boiler, add the egg whites and confectioners' sugar to the top pan, and cook, whisking constantly, until the mixture is very thick and will hold its shape, about 10 minutes. Whisk in the vanilla, remove from the heat, and set aside until cool enough to handle. Spoon the mixture, in batches if necessary, into a pastry bag fitted with a decorative tube (or form a rectangle of waxed paper into a funnel shape and snip off the pointed end to make a pastry tube).

2. Pipe onto the parchment-lined baking sheet 8 meringue circles each about 4 inches in diameter. Pipe more meringue into the center of each circle to form the bottom of the basket. In a circular motion, pipe more meringue around the perimeter of each basket to make the sides of the basket. Bake for 45 minutes to 1 hour, or until the meringues are set and crisp on the outside. Remove from the oven and set aside to cool to room temperature. (The meringues may be made several days ahead and kept in an airtight tin.)

3. Make the filling: Reserve 8 perfect strawberries for garnish. Mash the remaining strawberries with a potato masher in a large bowl. Stir in the lemon juice and then the sugar. Taste, and add more sugar if you like. Beat the cream until it holds soft peaks. Fold the whipped cream into the strawberry mixture. Place the meringues on individual plates, spoon the strawberry mixture into the baskets, garnish each serving with a fresh strawberry, and serve.

PEAR AND ALMOND UPSIDE-DOWN CAKE

Beginning in the 1920s or so, pineapple producers and canners developed and publicized in women's magazines a wealth of pineapple recipes, for gelatin salads and upside-down cakes, for example. Many of our mothers and grandmothers made upside-down cakes part of their kitchen repertoire, as many of us remember from Sunday dinners in the past. This recipe is my update, which weds the traditional idea to something like a *tarte tatin*, the French upside down tart made with apples or pears.

SERVES 6 TO 8

½ pound (2 sticks) unsalted butter
½ cup plus ⅔ cup sugar
½ cup unblanched almonds
1 cup self-rising flour
2 eggs
1 teaspoon almond extract
4 firm but not underripe pears,
    peeled, cored, and sliced
Juice of 1 lemon
Whipped cream, for garnish,
    optional

1. In a cast-iron skillet or other ovenproof skillet, melt 1 stick of the butter and stir in the ½ cup sugar. Cook, stirring occasionally, over medium-low heat for 25 to 30 minutes, until the mixture takes on a caramel color and has thickened somewhat. As the mixture cooks, preheat the oven to 375 degrees and make the filling: Put the almonds and the ⅔ cup sugar in a food processor and grind to a fine consistency. Add the flour and process to blend. Add the eggs and almond extract and blend again to make a smooth batter.

2. When the butter-sugar mixture has caramelized, place the pear slices in a circular pattern on top of it. Drizzle the pears with the lemon juice. Pour the batter over the pears and put the skillet in the oven to bake for 45 minutes, or until the top of the cake is browned and the cake has risen. Reduce the heat to 350 degrees and bake for 10 to 15

minutes more, or until a knife inserted in the center comes out clean.

3. Remove from the oven and run a knife around the edges of the skillet. Set the cake aside to cool for 10 minutes. Place a heatproof serving plate over the top of the skillet, carefully invert the cake onto the plate, and serve, with whipped cream if you like.

ANGEL FOOD CAKE WITH HONEYED BERRIES

If you want dramatic proof that homemade is better, taste this cake alongside one you buy in a grocery store or one made from a mix. If berries are not in season, serve the cake unadorned or topped with an icing of your choice.

SERVES 8

8 medium egg whites
¼ teaspoon cream of tartar
¼ teaspoon salt
1 cup sugar
1 teaspoon vanilla extract
¾ cup cake flour
3 cups mixed fresh berries, such as
    strawberries, blueberries, and
    raspberries
¾ cup Honey Syrup (page 61) or
    Honeysuckle Syrup (page 61)

RASPBERRIES

Of all the berries prized by Heartland gardeners and gourmets alike, the raspberry is queen. The tiny ruby berries must be carefully pried from thick, thorny tangles that always try to escape the most carefully constructed arbor, frame, or fence. Most raspberries ripen in late June and early July. Other varieties, especially golden raspberries, offer up their harvest in September. Because the berries are very perishable, they must be used quickly or frozen.

Raspberry varieties that do well in the extremes of climate in the Heartland are Boyne and Killarney, which provide red summer raspberries; Royalty and Estate, for summer black raspberries; Honey Queen, which yields yellow summer raspberries; Autumn Bliss, Heritage, and Red Wing, which bear autumn red raspberries; and Golden Harvest, for yellow raspberries that ripen in the fall. Wild red raspberries do well in spring, but they wilt in the heat of summer and must be watered very often if you bring them into the garden. At U-pick berry farms such as Marshall's Great River Vineyard in Lake City, Minnesota, nongardening raspberry lovers can pick their fill from early July through early October.

1. Preheat the oven to 350 degrees. Have ready an ungreased 10-inch angel food cake pan. Beat the egg whites with the cream of tartar and the salt in a large bowl until soft peaks form. Add the sugar, 1/4 cup at a time, beating constantly. When stiff, glossy peaks form, beat in the vanilla. Gently fold in the flour, 1/8 cup at a time. Spoon the batter into the cake pan.

2. Bake the cake for 20 minutes, or until a toothpick inserted in the center comes out clean. While the cake bakes, gently toss together the berries and syrup in a bowl. Invert the cake onto a serving plate and let cool to room temperature. Slice the cake and serve, spooning the berries onto the slices.

VARIATION:

In hot weather, prepare the berries at least 1 hour ahead and refrigerate them, covered, until ready to serve.

BLACK WALNUT POUND CAKE

You find a lot of recipes around the midwest that marry black walnuts and apples. Bess Truman, for example, celebrated the union with a pudding recipe that circulated during her husband's presidency. Here is a simple walnut-flavored pound cake that you serve with sautéed apples.

SERVES 8

*1/2 pound (2 sticks) unsalted butter,
    softened*
2 cups sugar
2 cups sifted all-purpose flour
1/4 teaspoon salt
1 teaspoon grated lemon zest
5 large eggs
*1 cup black walnut pieces,
    preferably, or walnut pieces*
2 medium apples
*Whipped cream, for garnish,
    optional*

1. Preheat the oven to 350 degrees. Lightly oil and flour a 9-inch springform pan or a 10-inch Bundt pan. Cream together the butter and sugar until smooth and fluffy. Beat in the flour, salt, and lemon zest. Beat in the eggs until the batter is a very light yellow. Fold in the walnuts and spoon the batter into the prepared pan.

2. Bake the cake for 1 to 1¼ hours, or until a knife inserted in the center comes out clean. Check carefully during the last few minutes to avoid overbaking. Set the cake on a rack to cool for 10 minutes. Meanwhile, peel, quarter, core, and slice the apples, and sauté them, stirring occasionally, in a little butter over medium-low heat for 5 minutes. Slice the cake, top the slices with the apples, and serve, garnished with whipped cream, if you like.

LEMON VERBENA POUND CAKE WITH LEMONADE GLAZE

This is an old-fashioned cake, pretty to look at and very fragrant, that you might serve for tea or take to a picnic.

SERVES 10 TO 12

*1/2 pound (2 sticks) unsalted butter,
    softened*
3 cups sugar
6 eggs, at room temperature
3 cups all-purpose flour
1/4 teaspoon salt
1 cup sour cream
2 teaspoons grated lemon zest
1 teaspoon vanilla extract

15 fresh lemon verbena leaves,
  lemon balm leaves, or lemon
  geranium leaves, rinsed and
  dried
½ cup fresh lemon juice
1 cup sugar, Honeysuckle Syrup
  (page 61), or Honey Syrup
  (page 61)
Additional lemon verbena, lemon
  balm, or lemon geranium
  leaves, for garnish, optional

1. Preheat the oven to 350 degrees. Lightly butter and flour a 10-inch Bundt pan, tube pan, or angel food cake pan. With an electric mixer, cream together the butter and sugar in a large bowl. Beat in the eggs, 1 at a time, beating well after each addition. Beat in the flour, 1 cup at a time, and then the salt and the sour cream. Finally, beat in the lemon zest and vanilla.

2. Place the 15 lemon verbena leaves in a decorative pattern at the bottom of the cake pan. Slowly pour in the batter, trying not to disturb the leaf pattern. Bake the cake for 1¼ hours or until a wooden toothpick inserted in the middle comes out clean. Invert the cake onto a rack to cool for 10 minutes.

3. As the cake cools, bring the lemon juice and the sugar or syrup to a boil in a saucepan. Remove from the heat and stir. Transfer the cake to a serving plate or cake stand. Stir the glaze again and brush it over the warm cake. Let the glaze cool and set for 5 to 10 minutes, slice, and serve, garnishing the slices with additional lemon verbena leaves, if you like.

FRESH BLACKBERRY CAKE ROLL

In the summers of my childhood, blackberry picking required preparation. First there were the long pants to protect us from chiggers and the powdered sulfur in the shoes to ward them off. Then there was a cool drink to pack, so that we would not expire from thirst on the way home—even though the blackberry thickets were in the woods just across the street from our house. To this day I walk and drive to blackberry patches and pick my fill whenever I get a chance. The fresh taste and pleasing color of this dessert make the effort worthwhile.

SERVES 6 TO 8

FOR THE CAKE ROLL:
  4 cups fresh blackberries,
    preferably, or 4 cups
    frozen and thawed
    blackberries
  ½ cup confectioners' sugar, plus
    more for dusting
  2 large eggs, beaten
  ¼ cup granulated sugar
  ½ cup all-purpose flour
  Fresh mint leaves, for garnish,
    optional
  Whipped cream, for garnish,
    optional

FOR THE FILLING:
    1 cup heavy cream
    ¼ cup confectioners' sugar
    1 cup fresh blackberries,
        preferably, or 1 cup frozen
        and thawed blackberries

1. Preheat the oven to 350 degrees. Line a 15-by-10-inch jelly roll pan with aluminum foil and oil or butter the foil well. Puree the 4 cups blackberries and ½ cup confectioners' sugar in a food processor. To remove the seeds, press the mixture through a fine-meshed sieve into a bowl.

2. Rinse out the food processor and put the eggs and granulated sugar in the bowl. Process until the mixture turns a light yellow and increases in volume, 3 to 4 minutes. (This step insures a lighter, higher cake.) Fold in the blackberry puree and the flour. Pour the batter into the prepared pan and bake for 20 to 25 minutes, or until the top is browned. Remove the pan from the oven and set aside to cool to room temperature.

3. Meanwhile, prepare the filling: Beat the cream in a medium bowl until soft peaks form. Beat in the ¼ cup confectioners' sugar, a tablespoon at a time, until the mixture holds stiff peaks.

4. When the cake has cooled, invert the cake onto a tea towel well dusted with confectioners' sugar. Spread the cream filling over the cake, leaving a border of 1 inch on all sides. Arrange the 1 cup of berries on the cream filling. Starting with a shorter end, roll the cake with the aid of the tea towel (use the towel for gripping but do not roll it in with the cake). Make the first turn firmly, then roll more gently. Wrap the roll in plastic wrap and refrigerate for at least 1 hour until ready to serve. To serve, remove the plastic wrap from the roll and slice. If you like, garnish the slices with mint leaves and whipped cream.

PERSIMMON CAKE ROLL

This version of the classic jelly roll is mellow and spicy, a perfect dessert for an autumn or Thanksgiving meal. Native persimmons ripen in the early fall, and the pulp must be strained because of all the seeds in the fruit. If you cannot get native persimmons in your area, you can find persimmon pulp in some specialty stores or from mail-order retailers. Although the flavor will be different, of course, canned pumpkin puree works in this recipe as well.

SERVES 6 TO 8

FOR THE CAKE ROLL:
    ¾ cup cake flour
    1 teaspoon baking powder
    2 teaspoons ground cinnamon
    1 teaspoon ground dried ginger
    ½ teaspoon fresh-grated nutmeg
    ½ teaspoon salt
    3 eggs
    1 cup granulated sugar

NATIVE PERSIMMONS

The American persimmon, Diospyros virginiana, which grows in the wild across the southern half of the Heartland and in patches to the north, is a small orange fruit that ripens in the early autumn. When it falls from the tree, it's ready to eat. Unripe persimmons have a bitter, puckery flavor. Ripe ones have a mild flavor like a slightly sweetened squash or pumpkin. (They are often cooked with the same spices as squashes.) During the annual Persimmon Festival in Mitchell, Indiana, you can sample persimmon puddings, cakes, cookies, waffles, ice cream, and more. If you have access to persimmon trees, you can harvest and prepare your own persimmon pulp to cook with

or to freeze for the coming year. You also can buy both canned and frozen persimmon pulp.

Once you have gathered your ripe fruits, you will need to process them within a day, because they will spoil quickly. Rinse the persimmons in cold water to remove any dirt. Pat them dry. Use a paring knife to cut away the small black stem. Put the persimmons, in batches if necessary, in a conical sieve and sieve the pulp into a bowl. This will remove the skins and the tiny black seeds and leave you with the orange pulp. Persimmon recipes commonly require 1 to 2 cups of pulp, so these are good quantities to transfer to freezer containers and freeze.

2/3 cup strained fresh persimmon
   pulp or canned persimmon
   pulp, preferably, or 2/3 cup
   canned pumpkin puree
1 teaspoon fresh lemon juice
Confectioners' sugar, for dusting

FOR THE FILLING:
   1 cup confectioners' sugar, plus
      more for dusting
   6 ounces cream cheese, softened
   4 tablespoons unsalted butter,
      softened
   1/2 teaspoon vanilla extract

1. Preheat the oven to 375 degrees. Line a 15-by-10-inch jelly roll pan with wax paper. Sift together the flour, baking powder, cinnamon, ginger, nutmeg, and salt into a bowl.

2. With an electric mixer, beat the eggs and sugar together in a large bowl for 5 minutes, or until the mixture is pale yellow. Stir in the persimmon pulp and lemon juice. Fold in the flour mixture. Pour the batter into the prepared pan and bake for 15 minutes, or until the cake has risen and browned. Remove from the oven and set aside for 5 minutes to cool slightly.

3. Invert the cake onto a tea towel well dusted with confectioners' sugar. Carefully remove the wax paper and trim off any uneven edges or browned spots on the cake with a sharp knife. Starting with a shorter end, roll the cake with the aid of the tea towel (use the towel for gripping but do not roll it in with the cake). Set the cake aside to cool further.

4. Meanwhile, cream together the filling ingredients in a bowl. Unroll the cake roll and spread the filling over the cake. Roll up the cake again, dust with confectioners' sugar, slice, and serve.

COFFEE AND WALNUT WEDDING TORTE

At the former Molnar Bakery in Wyandotte, Michigan, at the southern edge of Detroit, a multilayered walnut torte was the favored wedding cake in the surrounding Hungarian-American community. Michelle Molnar Churches, to whom I am indebted for this recipe, remembers helping her grandmother, Julia Molnar, make these cakes in the small bakery at the front of the family's farm. Michelle's father delivered the wedding cakes on weekends, when he was off-duty at the fire department. I have adapted the Molnars' recipe for a smaller two-layer cake.

MAKES 1 9-INCH CAKE

FOR THE CAKE:
  6 eggs, separated
  1 cup sugar
  1 cup chopped walnuts, toasted
  1 cup fine breadcrumbs
  1 teaspoon baking powder

FOR THE FILLING:
  6 tablespoons flour
  2/3 cup sugar
  1/4 teaspoon salt
  2 cups milk
  2 eggs, beaten
  3 tablespoons strong black coffee
  1 tablespoon unsalted butter

1. Preheat the oven to 350 degrees. Lightly oil a 9-inch round cake pan. Beat the egg yolks with the sugar in a medium bowl until the mixture is pale yellow. Gradually beat in the walnuts, breadcrumbs, and baking powder. Beat the egg whites in a separate bowl until they hold stiff peaks, then fold them into the batter. Pour the batter into the cake pan and bake for 25 to 30 minutes, until the cake has risen and is lightly browned.

2. Transfer the cake to a rack to cool for at least 15 minutes. Meanwhile, make the filling: In the top of a double boiler over simmering water, briefly stir together the flour, sugar, and salt. Whisk in the milk and eggs. Cook, whisking constantly, until the custard thickens, about 10 minutes. Remove from the heat and whisk in the coffee and butter. Set aside to cool to room temperature.

3. Using a long and sharp serrated knife, carefully cut the cake in half horizontally. Spread the filling over the cut half of the bottom layer and place the top layer cut side down over the filling. Slice and serve.

BLITZ TORTE

This cake brings back wonderful memories of my birthdays as I was growing up. Part of the delight is remembrance, but another part is the magical chemistry in the way all the elements of this confection work together. Although it never lasted that long when I was a child, I now find that the cake tastes even better the second day.

SERVES 8 TO 10

FOR THE CAKE:
1 cup sifted cake flour
1 teaspoon baking powder
1/8 teaspoon salt
1/2 cup shortening or unsalted butter
1/2 cup plus 3/4 cup sugar
4 eggs, separated
1 teaspoon vanilla extract
3 tablespoons milk

FOR THE TOPPING:
1/2 cup chopped pecans
1 tablespoon sugar
1/2 teaspoon ground cinnamon

FOR THE FILLING:
6 tablespoons all-purpose flour
2/3 cup sugar
1/4 teaspoon salt
2 cups milk
2 eggs, beaten
1 teaspoon vanilla extract
1 tablespoon unsalted butter

1. Preheat the oven to 350 degrees. Lightly butter 2 9-inch round cake pans. Make the cake: Sift together the cake flour, baking powder, and salt in a bowl; set aside. Cream the shortening with the 1/2 cup sugar in a separate large bowl. Add the 4 egg yolks and beat for several minutes until the mixture is pale yellow. Beat in the vanilla extract and milk, then beat in the flour mixture. Spread the batter in the 2 cake pans and set aside.

2. Beat the 4 egg whites in a third bowl until they form stiff peaks. Add the remaining 3/4 cup sugar gradually and beat until the meringue is glossy. Spread this meringue over the cake batter in the pans. Combine the topping ingredients and sprinkle this mixture over the meringue. Bake for 30 minutes, or until a knife inserted in the center comes out clean. Remove from the oven and set aside to cool.

3. While the 2 cake layers are cooling, make the filling: In the top of a double boiler over simmering water, briefly stir together the flour, sugar, and salt. Whisk in the milk and eggs and cook, whisking constantly, until the custard thickens, about 10 minutes. Whisk

in the vanilla and butter and remove from the heat. Let cool slightly.

4. To assemble the cake: Loosen the sides of the cakes with a knife and gently invert the cakes onto a wire rack. Place 1 of the cakes, now the bottom layer, on a cake plate. Spread the filling on top of this layer, and place the second cake, meringue side up, on top. Slice and serve.

Black Walnut Applesauce Cake

If you have a friend who gathers black walnuts, offer to make this classic spice cake in exchange for some of the bounty. (Don't forget to make a cake for your own family, too.) Or, in the fall, put up some homemade applesauce, trade a batch of that for the nuts, and each of you can make your own cake.

SERVES 10 TO 12

FOR THE CAKE:
    1/2 cup shortening
    2 cups sugar
    1 egg, beaten
    2 cups chunky or smooth
        homemade or store-bought
        applesauce
    2 1/2 cups all-purpose flour
    1/2 teaspoon ground cinnamon

1/2 teaspoon ground cloves
1/2 teaspoon ground allspice
1 cup finely chopped black
    walnuts, walnuts, or pecans
2 teaspoons baking soda
1/2 cup boiling water

FOR THE FROSTING:
    8 ounces cream cheese, softened
    1/4 pound (1 stick) unsalted butter,
        softened
    2 cups confectioners' sugar
    1 teaspoon vanilla extract

1. Preheat the oven to 350 degrees. Lightly grease and flour 2 8-inch round cake pans. With an electric mixer, cream together the shortening and sugar in a large bowl. Mix in the egg and applesauce. Add the flour, spices, and nuts and mix well. Stir the baking soda into the boiling water and blend the mixture into the batter. Pour the batter into the cake pans.

2. Bake the cakes for 35 minutes, or until a knife inserted in the center comes out clean. Transfer the cakes to racks to cool slightly.

3. Meanwhile, make the frosting: Cream together the cheese and butter in a medium bowl until smooth. Add the sugar and vanilla and beat well.

4. Remove the cakes from the pans. Spread 1/3 of the frosting on the surface of 1 cake and top with the second cake. Frost the sides and top of the entire assembled cake with the remaining frosting, and serve.

OLD-FASHIONED CHOCOLATE CAKE WITH BOILED FROSTING

Perched high on a glass cake pedestal, this glossy white cake will have everyone at your table anticipating dessert. Its fresh and mellow flavor will forever banish any thoughts you might have about making another cake from a box. The "boiled frosting" that our mothers and grandmothers made is actually an Italian meringue made with hot syrup. Besides being low in fat, this delicious frosting is easy to work with—you can loop, swirl, wave, or curl the confection over the cake to your heart's content.

SERVES 10 TO 12

FOR THE CAKE:

3 cups sifted all-purpose flour
2 heaping teaspoons baking soda
1 scant teaspoon salt
2 teaspoons ground cinnamon
1/2 teaspoon fresh-grated nutmeg
1 cup shortening
2 cups sugar
2 eggs
2 teaspoons vanilla extract
2 cups buttermilk
1 cup very hot French roast coffee
    or espresso or 1 cup boiling
    water
3/4 cup cocoa powder

FOR THE BOILED FROSTING:

2 cups sugar
1 tablespoon corn syrup
1/4 teaspoon salt
2 egg whites, beaten until stiff
    peaks form, in a medium
    heatproof bowl
1 teaspoon vanilla
1 cup flaked sweetened coconut

1. Preheat the oven to 300 degrees. Lightly grease and flour 3 9-inch round cake pans. Sift together the flour, baking soda, salt, cinnamon, and nutmeg 3 separate times into a medium bowl. Cream together the shortening, sugar, eggs, and vanilla in a separate large bowl until the mixture is light and fluffy. In a third small bowl, stir together the buttermilk, coffee (if you want some coffee flavor in the cake) or boiling water, and cocoa. With an electric mixer, mix the dry ingredients and the buttermilk mixture alternately into the shortening mixture until you have a smooth batter.

2. Pour the batter into the 3 cake pans and bake for 30 to 35 minutes, or until a toothpick inserted in the center comes out clean. When the cakes are done, invert them onto wire racks to cool to room temperature.

3. While the cake layers are baking, make the boiled frosting: Put the sugar, corn syrup, salt, and 3/4 cup water in a saucepan over low heat. Cook, stirring frequently, until the sugar dissolves, 3 to 4 minutes. Cover the saucepan and continue cooking for 2 to 3 minutes to dissolve the sugar crystals on the side of the

pan. Increase the heat to medium and cook, uncovered, until the mixture reaches the soft ball stage, 240 degrees on a candy thermometer (or when a drop of the mixture makes a soft ball when dropped into a glass of cold water). Gradually pour this hot syrup into the beaten egg whites, beating constantly until the frosting is very white and fluffy. Beat in the vanilla and continue beating until the frosting is of spreadable consistency.

4. Place one of the cakes, now the bottom layer, on a cake plate. Frost the top with about 1/2 cup frosting. Place the second layer on top, and frost with another 1/2 cup of frosting. Place the final layer on top, and use the remaining frosting to frost the top and sides of the assembled cake. Sprinkle the top and sides with the flaked coconut, and serve.

WISCONSIN CRANBERRY ICE

Unless you are from the Badger State, and perhaps even then, you may be surprised to learn that Wisconsin recently surpassed Massachusetts as the largest producer of cranberries. Here is a simple recipe named to honor the ascension. The tart late-season fruit comes fresh into the market just as other berries are dwindling. This is an invigorating granita to serve during the holiday season, whether as a midmeal palate-cleanser or as a dessert accompanied, if you like, by homemade cookies.

MAKES ABOUT 1 QUART GRANITA

4 cups cranberry juice cocktail
1 cup orange juice
Juice of 1 lemon
1/2 cup sugar

1. Bring the 3 juices and the sugar to a boil in a large saucepan, stirring to dissolve the sugar. Remove from the heat and set aside to cool to room temperature.

2. Pour the mixture into an ice cream maker and freeze according to the manufacturer's directions. Spoon into chilled small glasses, and serve.

BLACKBERRY ICE CREAM

Dark purple and luscious, this frozen confection is a sublime treat, especially if you serve it with a crisp butter cookie.

MAKES ABOUT 1 QUART ICE CREAM

4 cups fresh blackberries or
unsweetened frozen and
thawed blackberries
Juice of 1/2 lemon
About 2 cups sugar
2 1/2 cups heavy cream
Additional blackberries, for
garnish
Fresh mint leaves, for garnish

1. Line a strainer with two layers of dampened cheesecloth and place the strainer over a large bowl. Combine the blackberries, lemon juice, and 1 cup water in a saucepan and slowly bring to a boil, partially covered, over medium heat. Reduce the heat and simmer gently, uncovered, until the berries have softened, about 10 minutes.

2. Pour the blackberry mixture into the cheesecloth-lined strainer. Let the berries drain their juice into the bowl for 30 minutes. Gently squeeze the berries to extract more juice.

3. Measure the berry juice into a saucepan; you should have about 2 cups juice. Add 1 cup sugar for each cup juice. Cook over medium-low heat, swirling the pan occasionally, until the sugar dissolves, 4 to 5 minutes. Increase the heat and bring to a boil. Boil the syrup for 2 minutes. Remove from the heat, cover, and set aside to cool to room temperature. Mix 2½ cups syrup with the cream (you may have some syrup left over). Refrigerate the syrup-cream mixture, covered, for at least 2 hours.

4. Pour the mixture into an ice cream maker and freeze according to the manufacturer's instructions. The ice cream will be on the soft side. Garnish with fresh berries and mint leaves, and serve.

GOOSEBERRY ICE CREAM

Old-fashioned Pixwell gooseberries thrive in the humid heat of midwestern summers. After a visit to a U-Pick farm or your own garden on a hot June day, turn your treasure into this pale green elixir. I serve this ice cream with delicate sugar cookies.

MAKES ABOUT 1 QUART
ICE CREAM

1 pound gooseberries, trimmed of
top stems and bottom "tails"
²/3 cup sugar
1 vanilla bean
Juice of ½ lemon
1 cup heavy cream

1. Place the gooseberries in a saucepan with the sugar, vanilla bean, and enough water to reach half way up the fruit. Bring to a boil, reduce the heat, and simmer gently, covered, stirring occasionally, until the gooseberries are quite soft, about 15 minutes. Remove from the heat, stir in the lemon juice, and set aside to cool to room temperature.

2. Whip the cream until soft peaks form. Remove the vanilla bean from the gooseberries, and fold the cream into the berry mixture. Spoon the mixture into an ice cream maker and freeze according to the manufacturer's directions.

WILD RASPBERRY ICE CREAM

MAKES 1 GENEROUS QUART
ICE CREAM

My wild raspberries resist their lattice "cage" on the side of my house. During the spring and summer, there is always a wild, thorny branch that escapes and tries to run off somewhere else. I know they would rather be in the north woods than on the tame Kansas prairie, but you bloom where you're planted. The first decent harvest I got I transformed into this ice cream. Compared to other fruit, wild raspberries are intensely flavorful and very tart, so to make this ice cream you need less fruit and more sugar.

1 pint fresh wild raspberries, preferably, or fresh or frozen and thawed cultivated raspberries
1½ cups sugar
Juice of ½ lemon
2 large eggs
2 cups heavy cream
1 cup milk

1. Toss together the raspberries, ¾ cup of the sugar, and the lemon juice in a bowl. Cover and refrigerate for 2 hours, stirring every 30 minutes.

SWEET AND SOCIAL

If you live in Los Angeles or New York, you may not think that ice cream socials still take place. You might even believe they never did. But in communities across the Heartland, the events, sponsored by churches, schools, or community organizations, are very much alive. The annual ones are eagerly anticipated, and the best ones feature homemade ice cream. Vanilla is still the favorite flavor, but strawberry and peach run close behind.

At festivals honoring locally grown specialties, ice cream made with the celebrated produce is a must. Travel around the midwest in the summer and fall and you can sample pumpkin ice cream in Circleville, Ohio; persimmon ice cream in Brown County, Indiana; sour cherry ice cream in Traverse City, Michigan; cranberry ice cream in Warrens, Wisconsin; honey ice cream in Hamilton, Ohio; highbush blueberry ice cream in Montrose, Michigan; and raspberry ice cream in Hopkins, Minnesota.

Because homemade ice cream lacks the preservatives and emulsifiers that keep the texture soft even after being frozen hard, it is best when eaten soon after it is made. But that's the whole point, isn't it?

2. Whisk the eggs in a mixing bowl until light and fluffy, 1 to 2 minutes. Whisk in the remaining ¾ cup sugar, ¼ cup at a time. Continue whisking until well blended, about 1 minute more. Pour in the cream and milk and whisk to blend. Pour the mixture into a saucepan and cook over medium heat, whisking constantly, until it thickens to a custard, about 10 minutes. Remove from the heat and let cool to room temperature.

3. Drain the juice from the raspberries into the cream mixture and stir to blend. Mash the raspberries to a puree by hand or in a food processor and stir the puree into the cream mixture. Transfer the mixture to an ice cream maker and freeze according to the manufacturer's instructions.

FRESH PEACH AND PEACH LEAF ICE CREAM

The pride of small-town ice cream socials, fresh peach ice cream is a once-a-year treat, best made when peaches are ripe, juicy, and sugary and when the temperature is hot enough to appreciate the frozen confection. The almond-like flavor of peach leaves steeped in the milk and cream makes this extra special.

MAKES ABOUT 2 QUARTS ICE CREAM

½ cup half-and-half or light cream
¾ cup milk
24 unsprayed peach leaves
   (see Note)
¾ cup sugar
2 egg yolks, beaten
4 large or 8 small ripe peaches
Juice of 1 lemon
⅛ teaspoon salt
1 cup heavy cream

1. Combine the half-and-half, milk, and peach leaves in the top pan of a double boiler over vigorously simmering water and bring to a boil. Remove from the heat immediately. Cover the mixture and let it infuse for 20 minutes. Remove and discard the peach leaves.

2. Whisk together ½ cup of the sugar with the egg yolks in a small bowl. Whisk this mixture into the warm milk mixture. Return to the top pan of a double boiler over simmering water and cook, whisking constantly, until the mixture has thickened to a custard that will coat the back of a spoon. Remove the custard from the heat and set aside.

3. Peel and pit 3 of the large peaches (or 6 of the small ones) and puree them in a blender or food processor. Fold the peach puree into the custard. Add the lemon juice and salt and stir to blend. Cover and refrigerate until the custard is well chilled, about 2 hours.

4. Peel, pit, and finely chop the remaining peach (or peaches), toss in a bowl with the remaining ¼ cup sugar, and reserve. Stir together the chilled custard and the heavy

cream. Transfer the mixture to an ice cream maker and freeze according to the manufacturer's instructions. After the ice cream is just solid but not entirely stiffened (about 2 minutes before it is done in most ice cream makers), add the reserved peaches, and continue freezing until the ice cream is ready.

NOTE: If you cannot find peach leaves, substitute 1 teaspoon almond extract.

LEMONY RHUBARB CRUMBLE ICE CREAM

For Easter dinner, I like to work in the spring colors of pale green and pink. Steamed asparagus usually takes care of the pale green, and this ice cream dish, which I created this past Easter, now takes care of the pale pink.

MAKES 1 GENEROUS QUART ICE CREAM

1/4 cup all-purpose flour
1 teaspoon lemon zest
1 1/2 cups sugar
2 tablespoons unsalted butter,
    softened
1 pound rhubarb, cut into 1/2-inch
    pieces
1 tablespoon fresh lemon juice
2 cups heavy cream

1. Make the crumble: Preheat the oven to 350 degrees. Combine the flour, lemon zest, and 1/4 cup of the sugar in a small bowl. Using your fingers, rub the butter into the flour mixture to form large crumbs. Sprinkle these large crumbs in a baking dish and bake for 7 to 10 minutes, or until the crumbs begin to brown. Remove from the oven and set aside to cool, but keep the oven on.

2. Place the rhubarb in a large, shallow baking dish. Sprinkle with the remaining 1 1/4 cups sugar and the lemon juice. Bake on a lower shelf in the oven for 25 to 30 minutes, or until the rhubarb is tender when pierced with a knife. Remove from the oven and let cool to room temperature. Transfer the rhubarb to a food processor and puree until smooth.

3. Using your hands, break up the cooled crumble to small pea-sized pieces. Set aside. Stir the cream into the rhubarb puree and pour this mixture into an ice cream maker. Begin the freezing process, and when the mixture has the consistency of softly whipped cream, sprinkle in the crumble pieces, working quickly. Finish freezing the ice cream according to the manufacturer's directions.

Family Reunion Vanilla Pudding Ice Cream

This is a great ice cream for a crowd, especially one that includes children who balk at unusual flavors. (And all children love the word *pudding*.) The recipe requires a 6-quart ice cream maker.

Makes 1 generous gallon ice cream

1/4 cup all-purpose flour
4 cups sugar
7 eggs, beaten
1 teaspoon salt
2 cups milk
3 tablespoons vanilla extract
1 quart half-and-half
Additional milk, for the ice cream
    maker

1. Make a pudding: Stir together the flour and sugar in a large bowl. Whisk in the eggs. Whisk in the salt and milk, and continue whisking until the mixture is smooth. Transfer to a large saucepan and cook over medium heat, whisking constantly, until the mixture comes to a boil and thickens. Remove from the heat and stir in the vanilla. Cover the pudding and refrigerate it for at least 2 hours.

2. Whisk the half-and-half into the pudding. Transfer to the ice cream maker, and add

milk to fill 2/3 full (or, depending on the model, to the fill line). Freeze according to the manufacturer's instructions. Serve, if you like, with Decadent Hot Fudge Sauce, the recipe that follows.

Decadent Hot Fudge Sauce

Are you tired of the cardboardy taste of bottled fudge sauces? Homemade versions are easy to make and taste a whole lot better. Serve in a sundae with vanilla ice cream, such as Family Reunion Vanilla Pudding Ice Cream (the preceding recipe).

Makes 2 cups sauce

1/2 cup corn syrup
2/3 cup sugar
1/2 cup cocoa powder
3/4 cup heavy cream
2 tablespoons instant espresso
    powder or instant coffee
    powder
2 tablespoons unsalted butter
1 teaspoon vanilla extract

1. Bring the corn syrup, sugar, cocoa, cream, and espresso powder to a boil in a saucepan. Boil gently, stirring often, for 4 to 5 minutes.

2. Remove from the heat, add the butter and vanilla, and stir until smooth, 1 to 2 minutes

more. Serve warm, at room temperature, or chilled. The sauce keeps indefinitely in a lidded jar in the refrigerator.

MOCHA ICE CREAM SANDWICHES

I have adapted this recipe from a creation by Karen Hornung, a cooking instructor in Chicago. Karen adds hazelnut liqueur to the softened ice cream, but I have left it out. Either way you make this cool dessert, it's addictive.

MAKES 12 ICE CREAM SANDWICHES

1/4 pound (1 stick) unsalted butter, softened
5 tablespoons sugar, plus more for dusting
1 teaspoon vanilla extract

1 cup all-purpose flour
5 tablespoons cocoa powder
1/4 teaspoon salt
1 quart good-quality coffee ice cream, slightly softened
1 1/2 cups Decadent Hot Fudge Sauce (page 413), warmed

1. With an electric mixer, cream the butter in a mixing bowl until light and fluffy. Add the sugar and vanilla and mix well. Sift together the flour, cocoa powder, and salt into the bowl, and mix until you have smooth dough. Wrap the dough in plastic wrap and refrigerate for at least 15 minutes.

2. Preheat the oven to 275 degrees. Lightly oil a baking sheet. On a lightly sugared work surface, roll out the dough to a circle 3/8 inch thick. Cut out 24 cookies with a 2 1/2-inch round cookie cutter. Transfer the cookies to the baking sheet. Prick the dough all over with a fork. Bake the cookies for 40 to 45 minutes, or until they are firm to the touch. Remove the cookies from the oven, let them rest for 5 minutes on the baking sheet, then transfer them to racks to cool. (The cookies may be made ahead to this point and stored in an airtight container for up to 1 week.)

3. Line a 15-by-10-inch jelly roll pan with aluminum foil. Work the softened ice cream in a bowl with a large spoon until it is soft and spreadable but not melted. Spread the softened ice cream in half of the jelly roll pan to form a 7 1/2-by-10-inch rectangle. Roll up the foil on the empty end of the pan to form a "wall" so the ice cream will not spread.

Freeze, uncovered, for 1 to 2 hours, or until solid. When the ice cream has frozen solid, cover the top with plastic wrap.

4. To assemble the cookies, remove the ice cream from the freezer. Remove the plastic wrap. Carefully lift up the ice cream block and peel away the foil. Using the same 2½-inch cookie cutter, dip the cutter in warm water and cut 12 circles of ice cream from the block. Place each circle of ice cream between two cookies and serve the ice cream sandwiches on plates, surrounded by a pool of fudge sauce.

Resources

AMERICAN SPOON FOODS, INC.
411 East Lake Street
Petoskey, Michigan 49770
800-222-5886

Dried fruits, jams and jellies, hickory nuts and black walnuts, persimmon pulp, smoked white-fish, morels, and other midwestern products. Catalog for mail-order, and some retail stores.

AMERICAN WOOD PRODUCTS
9540 Riggs
Overland Park, Kansas 66212
800-223-9046

Aromatic woods for smoke-cooking, including alder, apple, cherry, grape, hickory, mesquite, oak, peach, pecan, and sassafras, in logs, slabs, chunks, and chips. Price list; mail-order.

APPLESOURCE
Route 1
Chapin, Illinois 62628
800-588-3854
www.applesource.com

Heirloom and modern varieties of midwestern apples. Catalog; mail-order.

AVRIL AND SON
33 East Court Street
Cincinnati, Ohio 45202
513-241-2433

Goetta (see page 34), cottage ham, city chicken (see page 217), and handcrafted deli meats.

EARTHY DELIGHTS
4180 Keller, Suite B
Holt, Michigan 48842
800-367-4709
www.earthy.com

Morels, dried tart cherries, wheatberries, wild leeks, and farmstead goat cheeses. Catalog; mail-order.

GRAMMA BEP'S GOURMET FOODS
675 Cheadle Street West
Swift Current, Saskatchewan
Canada S9H OC1
306-773-7224
www.t2.net/beps

Canadian prairie jams, jellies, syrups, and sauces made from native highbush cranberries, chokecherries, and Saskatoon berries. Catalog; mail-order.

GREEN RIVER TROUT FARM
Route 1, Box 267
Mancelona, Michigan 49659
616-584-2654

Fresh and hickory-smoked trout, along with venison, buffalo, pheasant, and quail. Also morels and Michigan leeks. Catalog; mail-order.

HAMMONDS PANTRY
414 North Street
Stockton, Missouri 65785
800-872-6879

Midwestern black walnuts, pecans, and hickory nuts. Catalog; mail-order.

INDIAN HAND GIFTS
Colleen's Gardens
P.O. Box 68
Marvin, South Dakota 57251
605-398-6923
www.indiangifts.com

Traditional Native American *waskuya* (sun- and wind-dried sweet corn), plus hand-harvested wild rice and prairie herbs. Information packet; mail-order.

KING ARTHUR FLOUR
P.O. Box 876
Norwich, Vermont 05055
800-827-6838
www.kingarthurflour.com

Wide variety of flours, including organic bread flours like Golden Buffalo from Heartland Mill in Marienthal, Kansas. Catalog; mail-order.

MAYTAG DAIRY FARMS
P.O. Box 806
Newton, Iowa 50208
800-247-2458

America's premier blue cheese, made from sweet, fresh Holstein milk. Catalog; mail-order.

NUESKE HILLCREST FARM MEATS
Rural Route 2
Wittenberg, Wisconsin 54499
715-253-2226

Apple-smoked bacon, sausages, ham, duck, pheasant, turkey, chicken, and pork chops. Catalog; mail-order.

PENZEYS SPICES
P.O. Box 933
Muskego, Wisconsin 53150
414-679-7207
www.penzeys.com

Common and hard-to-find seasonings, including China Cassia cinnamon and Holland blue poppy seeds. Catalog; mail-order.

THE SECRET GARDEN
P.O. Box 544
Park Rapids, Minnesota 56470
800-950-4409
www.secretgardengourmet.com
Unusual prairie products such as natural wild rice

(and wild rice pancake mix), wild bergamot and giant hyssop teas, wild fruit syrups, and clover-basswood blossom honey. Catalog; mail-order.

SEED SAVERS EXCHANGE
3076 North Winn Road
Decorah, Iowa 52101

Nonprofit group that grows over two thousand varieties of heirloom vegetables and fruits on its farm. To buy seeds from the Exchange, you must become a member. Anyone, however, may visit the farm, open from June through September, or purchase the Exchange's yearbooks, which are full of information on heirloom produce.

SEEDS BLUM
HC 33 Idaho City Stage
Boise, Idaho 83706
800-742-1423
www.seedsblum.com

Heirloom and hard-to-find seeds for gardeners interested in native food plants of the prairie and Great Plains. Catalog; mail-order.

THE SMOKE HOUSE MARKET
16806 Chesterfield Airport Road
Chesterfield, Missouri 63005
314-532-3314

Farmstead cheeses, cottage hams, smoked meats, fresh pastas, condiments, oils, and vinegars. Brochure; mail-order.

STAFFORD COUNTY FLOUR MILLS COMPANY
P.O. Box 7
Hudson, Kansas 67545
316-458-4121
www.flour.com

Makers of Hudson Cream Flour, a well-respected all-purpose flour, and sellers of that and other flours, including ones from Prairie Flour Mills in Manitoba's Red River Valley. Catalog; mail-order.

SELECT BIBLIOGRAPHY

PERSONAL NARRATIVES

Andrews, Clarence A., editor. *Growing Up in the Midwest.* Iowa City: University of Iowa Press, 1981.

Ebbutt, Percy G. *Emigrant Life in Kansas, 1886.* Reprint, North Stratford, New Hampshire: Arno Press, 1975.

Hirschfelder, Arlene, editor. *Native Heritage: Personal Accounts by American Indians, 1790 to the Present.* New York: Macmillan, 1995.

Lewis, Meriwether. *The Explorations of Lewis and Clark, volumes 1 and 2, 1814.* Reprint, Ann Arbor: March of America Series, 1966.

Moon, William Least-Heat. *PrairyErth: A Deep Map.* Boston: Houghton Mifflin Company, 1991.

Nelson, Lynn H. *The Root Cellar.* Lawrence: Kansas Collection Articles at the University of Kansas, at: http://www.ukans.edu/carrie/kan-coll/articles/nelson/cellar.htm

Sneve, Virginia Driving Hawk. *Completing the Circle.* Lincoln: University of Nebraska Press, 1995.

Wilson, Gilbert, editor. *Buffalo Bird Woman's Garden: Agriculture of the Hidatsa Indians, 1917.* Reprint, St. Paul, Minnesota: Minnesota Historical Society Press, 1987.

Young, Carrie. *Nothing to Do But Stay: My Pioneer Mother.* Iowa City: University of Iowa Press, 1991.

REFERENCE WORKS

Corriher, Shirley. *Cookwise: The Hows and Whys of Successful Cooking.* New York: William Morrow, 1997.

Farb, Peter, and George Armelagos. *Consuming Passions: The Anthropology of Eating.* Boston: Houghton Mifflin, 1980.

Jones, Evan. *American Food: The Gastronomic Story, second edition.* New York, Vintage Books, 1981.

Kindscher, Kelly. *Edible Wild Plants of the Prairie.* Lawrence: University Press of Kansas, 1987.

McGee, Harold. *The Curious Cook: More Kitchen Science and Lore.* New York: Macmillan, 1990.

McGee, Harold. *On Food and Cooking: The Science and Lore of the Kitchen.* New York: Scribner, 1984.

Welsch, Roger L., and Linda K. Welsch. *Cather's Kitchens: Foodways in Literature and Life.* Lincoln: University of Nebraska Press, 1987.

COOKBOOKS

American Daughters of Columbus. *American Daughters of Columbus Cook Book, fourth edition.* Kansas City: Cookbook Publishers, Inc., 1997.

Baird, Elizabeth. *Classic Canadian Cooking: Menus for the Seasons.* Toronto: James Lorimer and Company, 1995.

Bethany College Auxiliary. *Measure for Pleasure.* Lindsborg, Kansas, 1991.

Buckeye Cookery and Practical Housekeeping, 1877. Reprint, Minneapolis: Steck-Warleck Company, 1970.

Episcopal Church Women of the St. James Episcopal Church. *Our Daily Bread.* Enemy Swim Lake, Waubay, South Dakota, 1991.

German Village Society. *German Village Cook Book.* Columbus, Ohio, 1968.

Gregory, Jim, with Lois Rosenthal. *The Chef Gregory Cookbook*. Cincinnati: F & W Publishing, 1972.

Griffith, Linda, and Fred Griffith. *The Best of the Midwest*. New York: Viking, 1990.

Hoffman, Emmet Joseph, editor. *Deutsch-Böhmische Küche*. Waseca, Minnesota: Walter's Cookbooks, 1991.

Hoiness, Merlin, compiler. *Amish Recipes and Household Hints: Handwritten by Amish Families of Southeast Minnesota*. Harmony, Minnesota: Big Woods Graphics, 1993.

Johnson, L.W., editor. *The Wild Game Cookbook*. White Plains, New York: The Benjamin Company, 1977.

Kander, Mrs. Simon, and Mrs. Henry Schoenfeld, compilers. *The Settlement Cookbook: The Way to a Man's Heart,* Milwaukee, 1903. Reprint, Bedford, Massachusetts: Applewood Books, 1996.

Langlois, Stephen, with Margaret Guthrie. *Prairie: Cuisine from the Heartland*. Chicago: Contemporary Books, 1990.

Lindsborg [Kansas] Swedish Folk Dancers. *Swedish Folk Dancers' Cookbook: A Collection of Sweets and Breads*. Pipestone, Minnesota: Nicollet Cookbooks, 1979.

Midwestern Home Cookery: A cookbook comprising the Presbyterian Cookbook, compiled by the Ladies of the First Presbyterian Church, Dayton, Ohio, 1875, and the Capital City Cookbook, compiled by the Woman's Guild of Grace Church, Madison, Wisconsin, 1906. Introduction and suggested recipes by Louis Szathmary. New York: Promontory Press, 1973.

Miller, Amy Bess, and Persis Wellington Fuller, editors. *The Best of Shaker Cooking*. New York: Macmillan, 1970.

Powers, Jo Marie, and Anita Stewart, editors. *Northern Bounty: A Celebration of Canadian Cuisine*. Mississauga, Ontario: Random House of Canada, 1995.

Ray, Christopher. *The Wild Menu*. Minocqua, Wisconsin: Willow Creek Press, 1995.

St. Ambrose Parish. *"On the Hill" Cookbook*. St. Louis, 1990.

St. George Council of Catholic Women. *What's Cooking in St. George, Minnesota?* Audubon, Iowa: Jumbo Jack's Cookbooks, 1996.

Schumacher, John. *Wild Game Cooking Made Easy*. Minnetonka, Minnesota: North American Hunting Club, 1997.

Sykora, Lester, and John A. Kuba. *Our Favorite 106 Czech Pastry Recipes Cookbook*. Cedar Rapids, Iowa: Sykora Bakery, no date.

Unruh, Ruth, and Jan Schmidt, compilers. *From Pluma Moos to Pie, revised edition*. Goessel, Kansas: Mennonite Heritage Museum, 1991.

Voth, Norma Jost. *Mennonite Foods and Folkways from South Russia, volumes 1 and 2*. Intercourse, Pennsylvania: Good Books, 1994.

Wesleyan Service Guild of the Methodist Church. *Brown County Cookery, third edition*. Nashville, Indiana, 1961.

INDEX

INDEX

Index

INDEX

INDEX

INDEX

INDEX

INDEX